# What the Raven Said

# What the Raven Said

Jane Galer · Medea Isphording Bern

## Poiêsis Press

Mendocino · Manasota Key

Poiêsis Press
An imprint of Poiêsis Publishing Group
Mendocino, California

Library of Congress Control Number: 2023900869

Names: Bern, Medea Isphording, author; Galer, Jane, author.
Title: *What the Raven Said* / Jane Galer, Medea Isphording Bern, authors.
Description: Mendocino, Poiêsis Press, [2023]
Identifiers: LCCN: 2023900869,
        ISBN: 978-0-9981323-7-2 (Hardcover),
        ISBN: 978-0-9981323-8-9 (Softcover)
Subjects: LCSH: Human-animal relationships.

        ISBN: 978-0-9981323-2-7 (Ebook)

Produced by Diane Reynolds

Poem credits: *Brown Pelican, Heart Dance* © Jane Galer, *Outskirts: Collected Poems,* 2016. *Open Windows, Blow, Seven Ravens Omen* © Jane Galer, *Forward & In the Dark,* 2021

Cover image: *The Offering* by Kim Englishbee, © 2022 Kim Englishbee. With many thanks to Kim for her generosity.

*For the finned, the furred, and the feathered*

# Preface

*What the Raven Said* is an unlikely and entirely evolutionary product of a friendship between two writers who know one another well but who have never actually met.

We made one another's acquaintance as classmates in a semester-long online writing program. If you have ever taken an online writing class of any length, you know that an intimacy born of sharing both personal stories and the vulnerability inherent in sharing 'shitty first drafts' can create bonds that transcend physical distances. At the time of this class, Jane was nearing the end of treatment for breast cancer. Medea had recently received her breast cancer diagnosis. We initially bonded over the fear that a cancer diagnosis brings to one's self, to our family and to our friends. Our workshop assignments revealed that we both love our domestic pets, our quirky Scorpio husbands, our smart, sensitive sons, and the sense of limitlessness that comes from spending time on the water.

After the seminar ended, our emails continued. Jane offered her shamanic power as an extra layer of protection during Medea's bilateral mastectomy. We both tried and failed to arrange an in-person meeting during Jane's annual visits to Stanford until Jane finally decided that the anticipatory anxiety was worse than any diagnosis a mammogram might reveal.

Our emails over the past twelve or so years spanned myriad subjects, from the latest activities of her grandson to my sons' progression through high school, college and the dizzying world of adulthood. We mourned the loss of beloved dogs and cats. We celebrated birthdays, anniversaries and equinoxes. We marvel at our utter incompatibility when it comes to climate. It has never mattered to either of us that we've never met; our friendship thrives just the same.

One recurring theme of our emails has been nudging each other to complete different writing projects that for one reason or another had stalled. We relish the role we play as one another's champions; it is responsible for four books between us. This book marks number five.

During a particularly robust round of correspondence in June of 2021, we realized that our letters had taken on a more serious tone. Because of the forced isolation from not only the pandemic but various natural disasters that often trapped us indoors, our letters took on a quality of greater introspection, of deeper questioning about things we may have taken for granted. We were seeing things—the habits of the ravens, the cycles of the plum trees, the ravages to ecosystems near and far—in our immediate surroundings and beyond with different, more discerning eyes. Ours felt like a more complex correspondence, like our individual consciousness was shifting, word by word.

"Do you think these letters could become a book?" Jane asked in a letter on the 25th of July. Without hesitation, Medea replied, "Yes, I think they can!"

Originally, we intended to write as close to daily as possible through the end of 2021. As the sun set on 2021, our instincts told us that our work was not yet done; stories remained to be told about our wild friends and the threats they face from foes apparent and invisible. Events domestic and international colored our perspectives and demanded a place on the page. Personal triumphs and woes ebb and flow like the tides that govern our lives, ever-present and certain.

*What the Raven Said* represents a year of shared ideas, observations, and ideals between two friends who have yet to see one another's faces. We don't always agree, but we listen, respectfully, without judgment. We look for the beauty in the smallest detail. We stand in awe of the flora, fauna, and even slime that share this space with us. We invite you to do the same.

—MIB and JG.

*Monday, July 26, 2021 Fog, 55 degrees, northern California coast*

Dear Medea,

This morning the little herd of seven deer appeared out of the woods in a line stopping only now and then as the matriarch led them purposefully along the edge of the brush, not exactly protected but at least with a chance of dispersing safely. They didn't pause in the yard, there being few dandelions left, and the grass dry and brown without nutrients. The twin fawns stayed carefully together, side by side comparing steps now and then to be sure of each other and keep pace in the middle of the group. The youngest juvenile, the "runt" fawn from last year who survived an infection of some sort in her lungs, brought up the rear but seemed to be encouraged by the largest of the group, maybe her twin all grown big and strong. They crossed the yard and disappeared into the trees, surely headed for the creek and a drink.

I wonder how much water is there for them. As we clear and "hardscape" to protect our houses from wildfire, we are exposing small wetlands to drying conditions, diminishing the available water for thirsty animals. Every step in one direction ricochets consequences down a line of living things enhancing our obligation of care. Sometime soon I will walk to the creek and check on whether there is water or not. Downstream a landowner is pirating the run for his elaborate garden. Another step away from grace.

I have this image in my head, I wish I could draw, of me or us or Gaia.... opening her great embroidered and quilted billowing robe and cascading it gently over all creatures. For now,

with Love,
Jane

*26 July 2021 68 degrees, blustery, gray—a NorCal summer's day*

Dear Jane,

It's nearly 5pm. The men from the tree company are packing up after a day of destruction on the property across the street. So far, the palm stub, shorn of its fronds, remains (mostly) intact, erect, proud. I know it is not my tree. Nor does it "belong" to the owners of the property; they are mere stewards. The unscathed palm in the left lot corner still can wave its arms in the air like a graceful ballet dancer. I can't help but imagine that its decapitated twin on the right would bellow at the men with the chain saws if it could. The indignity it must feel. It's hard to say what the property owners will do now—will they wait for the cloak of an inky night and poison the tree's roots? Did we simply catch their agents in the midst of this treacherous act, leaving them trapped with one and three-quarters trees on an acre of land they have otherwise denuded?

The birds that plucked insects from the crooks and crevices at the base of the fronds have flown across to my bird feeders. I watch the Black-Capped Chickadees stand in line on the branches of the Japanese plum near the suet feeder. They mostly wait their turn. Then, one hungry bird loses its temper and *skeetskeetskeetes* at the guy who was grazing too long at the trough. A fluff of feathers as bird tumbles over bird, then calm returns as quickly as the kerfuffle started.

Offering these birds an easy option to the loss of the food source is both kind and selfish. They are not "my" birds, yet having fed them and watched their tree lose its head, I feel an obligation to keep the feeders full. After reporting the palm boors to the proper authorities, I sense an equal obligation to safeguard the trees from further insult. So, imagine this: I could haul the rocking chair my grandparents gave to me when I was a baby down to the corner. Maybe take a book, too; how about *The Overstory* by Richard Powers? Nestle a .22 (not that I actually own one) under my ample Outside Lands souvenir blanket. Pour a tumbler of tequila. If a squad arrives to take out the palms, I'll be waiting.

Gaia's soldier, reporting for duty.

Love,
Medea


*July 27, 2021 Some high clouds. 66 degrees. Clear air, because now that's a thing*

Dear Medea,
About ownership, I think about that a lot when I feed the raven family. How dependent are they on me? Have I ruined an entire generation of its natural order? What do the birds themselves think: do they wonder if they have instructed me in their ways? Am I their protector or their project? Is our relationship structural or symbiotic?

The ravens, the young ones, seem to be dispersing from the nest (which is in a secret location they carefully conceal by flying deviating patterns of return), to a variety of tall pine and fir along the creek line and within view of the house, or I should say, me. It's clear they watch my every move, taking turns on watch and often flying around the house to get my attention. If it weren't me they were watching, what would they be doing? Looking for nests to rob, eggs to filch, chicks to kill. My neighbor Jane says once she collected a bucket of eggs from the hen house and then set the bucket in the bushes while she walked out to the mailboxes. When she returned every egg was gone. We are all watched all the time. I belong, I hope, to the ravens.

Love,
Jane


*28 July 2021 Filmy, high clouds, humid, still. 66 degrees going up to 79. Air quality: Good*

Dear Jane,
The birds spend all day foraging for food. If they forage, urging their purpose-shaped beaks underneath bark and branch, they find nourishment. If they cheat and fly right for the suet ball, will they use that spare time to play or sleep or mate? I did see two Mourning Doves "kissing" on the front patio yesterday. This pair returned after two months away; they snuggle on the peak of the roof, *coocoocooing* as they promenade along the garden paths, their tiny heads in a staccato swivel, watching. They (or a pair very similar to them) have blessed our house for probably ten years now; I installed the feeders in February. Do they just feel safe here, with me? Does that improve their quality of life as we know it does ours? I don't think we will impact millennia of instinct by feeding the birds. If we instill trust, bird for human, as long as we control these areas, the birds remain safe.

This morning, my sister, South Florida's version of Dr. Doolittle, described a moment of magic she experienced with six Cattle Egrets at an open field where she feeds feral cats. Today, she extended a bit of bread between her outstretched fingers. First, one wispy white body approached, extending its bill toward her offering. It took the piece, cautiously. Then a second approached, and within minutes, she had half a dozen egrets eating from her hand. Perhaps they intuited that today is her birthday.

Yesterday, it was my turn to play executioner. Eric from the mosquito abatement office arrived dressed head-to-toe in a beekeeper's costume, dust delivery device in hand to extinguish the yellow jackets nesting in my back yard. An hour later, Douglas the ant annihilator returned for a third pass at the Argentine colonies that have migrated from the planted beds in the front yard to an inconvenient location beneath the kitchen. I could make the case that yellow jackets are just plain aggressive, party-pooper pests with no redeeming natural qualities, unless you consider feasting on the dead insects and small mammals that had the misfortune to perish in the gopher tunnels redeeming. These ants present a trickier justification for extermination. They don't bite or sting. Still, a pantry, countertop and stove squirming with tiny black intruders ignites an atavistic revulsion in my gut for sharing space with bugs.

Yellow jackets and ants lack a PETA equivalent protector organization. No one expresses outrage when I mention these executions. In fact, the guests at our barbecue on Friday will not have to monitor their chicken burgers to avoid biting into a "meat bee." But I can't help feeling a sense of colonial overreach. We obviously don't have treaties with the flora and fauna over which we have built our homes. Yet, as stewards of this land, ethics demand we treat all living things with dignity and respect. I've seen a yellow jacket sting a nuthatch at the suet feeder. In my mind's hierarchy, bird beats bug. In my neighbor's hierarchy, people beat birds and trees. In the mind of the developer seeking to construct mega-mansions on a fire-prone slope near my house, which is currently home to California Quail, hawks, deer, oaks, and wild onions, his freedom trumps every living thing.

Love,
Medea

*July 30, 2021 Fog, blessed fog. 59 degrees. Air quality good.*

Dear Medea,
I'm very fond of Mourning Doves. Only lately have we had them close by. Lately as in the past couple of years. Perhaps this means something else moved on, owls? The doves are flagrant in their affection for discussion and um, other things. A friend of ours once said in disgust, "All they do is fuck." I suppose that's all any living thing would do, given the chance. I think of them as more loving and gentle than sexual though. Speaking of sex, the ravens are, I think, moving into the season where they speak the language of love, that throaty, bobbly noise no human can reproduce. I think that means they are pairing up, and having never heard of hemophilia or Methodist cousins does that mean sisters and brothers are conveniently fair game? It might explain their pairing for life.

Last evening the resident herd of seven White Tail Deer returned to graze the grass over the septic leach field. A meager strip of 3X30 lush grass that must be rich in nutrients. It leads them close to the house, but they don't mind. Still wary because of the watchful Border Collie, Tweed, but we think they find us benign and often bed down up close to the house overnight. There are so many deer in Northern California. They say if you have deer, you have mountain lions, and we do. Here's the problem, and it's not the mountain lions: vineyards are wiring up the wilderness, sucking the rivers dry, and fencing off not just great swaths of land, but *all* of the land, over hills and into swales. The Russian River headwaters are diverted, excavated, and warming beyond the ability of life to remain in symbiosis. Once I saw a mountain lion walking between lines of staked up grape vines, I was on Highway 101! As vineyards suck the water from under and around us, they also push the wildlife to their extreme limits. I can't justify building my own house on old ranch land, but at least I am careful of the remaining habitat I own and hopefully offering the deer and the bears and the mountain lions a safe place to roam.

I read the other day that it takes 600 gallons of water to make a bottle of wine. Can that be true? Does it count that I drink French wine and they have rain all the time in France?

Love,
Jane

P.S. This just in, the good news and the bad, there are nine turkeys in the yard, foraging the same septic field strip of grass—that's the bad news. Turkeys are messy birds. The good news is that I think they eat deer poop and we have plenty of that. How's that for natural balance? At least the turkeys mosey on and haven't decided to roost here. There is one old Tom, two adult females and six children. Even turkeys care greatly about their young, ever vigilant. Hard to imagine something that looks like that can be the focus of millions of appetites once a year.

*30 July 2021. 4pm Sunny! Warm! Perfect! 78 degrees, dropping to 61 as Dylan's farewell party whips into full swing. Thank heaven for patio heaters.*

Dear Jane,
People tell me that Mourning Doves are birds of very little brain. I'm not sure what that actually means—compared to what? They do build nests in inopportune spots, but if this bird has managed to repopulate across this and countless other countries, to find food, to coax people into mimicking their cooing, and delight writers who write about them, who's to question their mental capacity?

This morning, a tiny lizard scampered half way up my screen door. The lizard life perks up this time of year with the heat. Most of the lizards in the yard are taupe with black geometry along their spines. In my Florida hometown, Venice, our yard teemed with spring green lizards, dark bronze lizards, lizards similar in hue to those we have here. My first vivid lizard memory involves a swing set in my Dad's best friend, Don's, Puerto Rican back yard. We kids, my sister and me and Don's five, were taking a break from competitive swinging (who can fly highest? Who can jump from the swing at the top of the arc and land without breaking a leg?) when a lizard jumped onto my shoulder then clamped its jaw onto my earlobe. This dancing earring that elicited a shriek (mine) heard `round the neighborhood. It's taken a few decades to tamp down that memory and just marvel at their speed and designs. My indoor cat, Odin, knew he should attack this tiny lizard. His body tensed and his tail twitched as he sat at attention, thinking about his next move. Since the screen door is new, and Odin's claws sharp, I gently nudged the potential morsel off the screen and onto a potted bougainvillea.

I heard a cacophonous, unfamiliar bird call while walking along the shore in Half Moon Bay on Wednesday. Louder than a *cawcawcaw*, it also let loose a throaty growl that sounded like the bird was grinding pebbles in its craw. Scanning the tree above my head, I was surprised to see a raven—an insanely huge raven, but a raven still—wailing its heart out. Could this be its mating call?

Love,
Medea

*Not really July anymore. Sun*

Dear Medea,
Your evocative bird sounds remind me of my crazy Uncle Jim. He wrote an entire short story in bird language. He also spoke to trees and took himself off to the forest near the Illinois River and built a cabin where he spent most of his time drinking whiskey and writing. I recognize The Hermit in myself as in him. I'm sure he could recite *The Lake Isle of Innisfree* by heart. "And live alone in the bee loud glade." Well, maybe not meat bees. They are a horror! Especially for small children with peanut butter and jelly sandwiches. We sometimes have nests of mud wasps. The fix is cat food: put an open can of cat food, fish preferred, near the opening of the nest. Overnight skunks will come and feed on the cat food and finish off their fine dining with a dessert of wasps which they love almost as much as cat food.

The single fawn and her mother come by once a day. I am sad that they haven't rejoined the herd yet. Or will they never? So much I don't know. I Googled books on deer behavior and they were all about how to trick, trap, and shoot them. It makes me sick to my stomach. I want very much for those NRA people to die by their own means. With an elephant tail wrapped tight around their necks.

Love,
Jane

P.S. Have you tried feeding the ravens cat kibble? I hear they love it.

*Extra from the coast on a sunny Sunday*

Good Morning,

You asked about the news piece chasing round the globe about the nearby town of Mendocino running out of water. The village of Mendocino runs out of water every year, so that part of it is not shocking. That news piece has sure had a run in a number of venues—I guess everyone loves to read about other people's bad luck. Is it necessary to measure our own worth by the lack in others? I despair.

Buying water is a regular occurrence for the village and for many people in the area. However, usually it's not as expensive or difficult to access water to buy and have trucked in. Because everyone seems to have decided to head for the coast, the tourist burden is higher than ever. The locals know to conserve water. The tourists figure they don't have to. Tourism should be capped or banned entirely until the drought ends but I'm not in charge of the village.

As for us, like most people here we are on our own well with a 4k gallon storage tank. So far it is producing normally. But that said, we have in the past had it slow down, and once, when Chris and a long-haired girlfriend lived here, we ran out of water and did have to buy it. The price of a truck of water was $350. Now it's at least double and people can't access it because the inns are taking it all. Water wars are here. The water for the village here, comes from a solidly producing vein in Greenwood creek. They have plenty of town water and also sell water but some of us are starting to think they shouldn't be selling water to anyone out of our zip code. I guess I should have volunteered for the local Water District Board when I had a chance!

Besides a deep well, we also have a shallow well and a large storage tank under pressure. This water is not currently potable, but it could be. I use a little for watering my herbs, but mostly it is stored water for firefighting. There are three other small wetland areas that could be developed but we don't need to, and the wildlife need to have water as well. Also, being in the coastal zone, that wouldn't be legal and we're not renegades. At least not yet. We are watching our water use habits and do our best to not waste it. Gray water and such go through the septic system and back to the ground, creating a nice green patch for the rabbits and the deer.

Water is a funny thing. The village of Mendocino doesn't have any, but people on the east side of the highway have plenty. We have enough for us (meaning a household of two) but our neighbor to the west drilled 100 test pits to look for more water than he had and never found any. To the north of us across the street on the ridge of the Navarro River canyon there is plenty of water. I have been thinking I should spend some time dowsing our ten acres and see what else I find. If I found water now, in this drought season, that would be impressive. Dowsing is another shaman skill. Once when Gene was looking for the second septic tank I used my pendulum to find it. He kept insisting it was farther from the house and I kept saying no, it's right here, as the pendulum whirled away. I was right. Maybe I should put up a sign. Dowser for Hire. You know how I learned to dowse? Two middle aged British nerds at Stonehenge taught us. What a gas!

Back in 1990 when I was at Sac State getting my masters, I did a year in Public History and interned searching records etc. for modern ongoing applications in the county. At one point I was in the county records down in Jackson along Hwy 49. I suddenly realized that all of the rivers had land grants claimed along them back in the late 19th c. Not much land, just enough to cover the rivers and their banks, claims posted by PG&E. They were, then, claiming the water course for dams and for fresh water. The old claims were, when I saw them, 100 yrs. old. Even then, water was the real gold.

Love,
Jane

*1 August 2021 Sitting in the kitchen, watching the wild wind push the smoke eastward. 78 degrees.*

Dear Jane,

Your Uncle Jim wrote an entire book in bird language? Did he choose a particular bird's call or did he make the whole thing up? Did you read it in its original form? Bruce told me that he fully expects me to be fluent in bird by this time next year.

The eternal water wars should be cause for legislators to act. Do they act in the public's interest any longer? The patchwork of water you and your neighbors cobble together impresses me. Undeveloped wetland is as valuable as silicon chips, nearly as hard to come by these days. And yet, water angels pick up the government's slack. There is a man in Alviso, at the triangle tip of the Bay, who spends his days trying to convince local and state decision-makers to restore the wetlands there to the soggy glory of the turn of the last century. Between fill and Facebook, the over-development eradicated habitat for most of the indigenous shorebirds. He is making progress, and at least the red-legged stilts and some egrets are tiptoeing back.

Those Mendocino tourists must be forced to conserve, or not be invited back. Dylan told me this morning that the latest land boom is mosquito-infested/snow-covered Minnesota. Minnesota! The Land of a Thousand Lakes, but for how long? When fear motivates folks to consider moving to the semi-frozen heart of North America to escape rising sea levels, it's time to ditch the car for a bicycle.

Tinker obviously sees you as a friend, and ally, a kind person who offers treats. That she watches over you as you wander the forest speaks both to your goodness and to hers. You treat your adopted home with the respect that the deer and the turkeys and Tinker understand. We enchant ourselves by noticing the rustling of falling leaves, a rainbow smudge of sunlight on a wall, the rushing and retreat of a single wave over shards of shell and grains of sand, the spicy scent of jasmine or the nauseating smell of decay.

Love,
Medea

*2 August 2021 72 degrees, scattered wisps of cloud, NW winds 11mph*

Dear Jane,

So, 600 gallons of water go in to creating a single bottle of wine? Is that 100% true? As earth stewards and oenophiles what are we to do with that information? Pretend we didn't hear it and become part of the problem ourselves?

Philosophy butts right up against pragmatism with these water wars. What right does a landowner have to tap the public's water source to grow his grapes? Who decides which land use is "best?" Certainly not PG&E. In a climate such as ours, where drought is the norm rather than the exception, why are any water-intensive crops cultivated? Almonds? Rice? Does this make any sense from a policy standpoint, much less from a common sense POV? Like you, I take pains to plant only those trees and shrubs and succulents that drink very little. They look happy. We do our part on our plots. Still, we do love wine and almonds.

The owner of part of the canyon at the end of our cul de sac has storm fenced some ten acres, effectively cutting off the deer and bobcats, coyotes and mountain lions from the creek that runs through the land and ultimately joins San Mateo Creek, which flows into the Bay. Since he built his wall, we have coyotes that promenade, single file, or two by two, up and down our road and through our neighborhood at all hours, searching for water. Before we pruned back a good bit of our foliage, I noticed a matted-down oval of grasses, about four feet long and two feet wide. Just the right size for a sleepy coyote. I suppose I should be disturbed, frightened, perhaps, but what I feel is humility tinged with honor. And a righteous bit of indignation toward he who built the wall.

The commentator on KCBS referred to "August" as *"Fogust"* this morning. For thirty-three years I've shivered through Northern California's summer gloom; this is the first I've heard of *Fogust*. August's misty welcome mat has driven generations of sun-worshippers inland, where they stay put until after Labor Day. *Fogust*. There is a right word for everything if you listen long enough.

Speaking of listening, the raucous ravens gave me an earful yesterday. Perhaps a family of three, or three teenaged toughs, or just three random ravens—I don't know their genealogy—but they speak with a single mind. The issue? They apparently like the suet cake I've been offering. Originally, I placed the feeders to benefit cute, petit passerines. Occasionally, as many as six or eight of the tiny birds cluster around the cage together and feed. Even eight birds each weighing two ounces require two or three days to consume a pound of suet and seed. In the last week, the squares were disappearing in under 24 hours. Ravens being ravens, (and *ravenous*, from the Old English ravinous, meaning "extremely greedy") I suspect that they learned to release the two hooks that secure the food square inside the cage and liberate it for their own consumption. So, I zip tied it shut. For the benefit of all local avian life.

The threesome swooped above my head as I reloaded the feeder.

"*Rrrock! Rrrock!*" "Thank you!", I imagined them saying. But then, they flew past the fuchsia tree, over the juniper and onto the peaks of a small stand of tall pines. The wind tossed the boughs from side to side yet the ravens held tight. How they manage to hold on, at the apex of this spindly tree, with wind blowing seventeen knots is another of nature's marvels. Anyway, they began to talk amongst themselves.

"*Haw haw haw*, tell her to take the damned lock off the feeder."

"*Quork*, no you tell her!"

"*Haw haw*, she's right there! What are you, chicken?"

"*Quirk, quirk*, who are you calling 'chicken'?"

*Rattling, quacking* and *haw haw hawing*, they debated next steps until it became clear no one would ask me to remove the offending tie. The three of them lifted off into the sky, flying around each other in wide circles, then crossing each other, like a sleek, airborne triple helix.

The chickadees, between suet nibbles, just snickered, *chickadeedeedee*. I guess even birds have a right word for everything.

Love,
Medea

*4 August 2021 66 degrees, sunny with fog threatening. Toasty in the front yard, breezy and cooler in the back.*

Dear Jane,

The ravens taunt me. The new feeder that is large enough to accommodate a football-sized bird family of three hangs on the cherry tree, not far from the square feeder. Nearby, a four-pound cylinder of "hot and spicy seeds" sits in the center of a half-moon metal flower pot. "The ravens will love this," the lady at Birder's Garden told me. But alas. My rabble of ravens visited this afternoon, *croaked* and *hawed*, and snubbed the hot and spicy seeds.

The hungry chickadees remind me of those cruise ship guests who go back to the salad and pizza bars for seconds and thirds and fourths. I hope I'm not contributing to an obesity epidemic amongst these birds. Before dawn's first light, they *chick-a-dee* between pecks of seed. The nuthatches chime in with their *whi-whi-whi*. The chickadees will circle back a few more times this evening before they turn in for the night. I was listening this evening while watering the birdbath and heard an unfamiliar *peek*, and tiptoed across the chocolate mulch carpet, around the shaving brush palm to see who had come to dinner.

A Hairy Woodpecker! It caught me gawking and ducked into the pine. I stood still and waited. It returned, not to the hot and spicy cylinder, but to the (new) berry and nut square. Hairy is almost too long for this feeder, but he shows no trepidation about overwhelming the feeder the way the ravens do. His orange-red triangle of a mohawk is nearly imperceptible in the late-afternoon sun, but his snowy breast with its bold black spots glow. The backyard hosts a living, breathing art installation.

Love,
Medea


*August 7, 2021 Sun, 70 degrees, moderate air quality 50*

Dear Medea,
I'm torn between running the AC to keep from breathing any bad air or saving the planet and losing my breath. I'll think about it over a glass of wine. I was at the kitchen window the other day when Tinker, the smallest raven, was pecking at something on the ground. At first, I thought it was an egg, but Tinker picked it up and threw it down to break it and when that failed, she (only guessing) pecked at it and kicked it. Suddenly I realized it was a faded old Kong rubber toy from some time when we had puppies here! I ran out the door and retrieved the hard rubber toy for the trash. I replaced it by hiding half dozen not so fresh eggs. Tinker and her siblings were delighted.

A few days ago, Tweed and I walked through the woods to the road where our mailbox is. Three of the ravens came with us, flying from tree to tree just above my head, clearly unsure of how able I might be in my forest skills. They have discovered where I sleep at night and wait patiently in the morning for me to come down. I think they are so protective of me that if I ran into a creature I needed to avoid, they would do their best to help me. As I write this, Tinker has landed on the madrone tree only ten feet from my chair. I don't think birds generally love madrone, perhaps because the bark is so oily it's rather sticky? But she will sit and wait for me to move, hoping I'm moving in the direction of the kitchen.

I read in the paper that a firefighter spotted a large gathering of deer clustered on green grass with a sprinkler going in the middle of the Dixie Fire. I am so sad about the loss, most particularly the wildlife that doesn't survive. The prevalence of media coverage makes it impossible to say, "I can't imagine."

Love,
Jane

P.S. I love your coyote nest. I would feel humble as well. But it's good that you keep your cats inside. In our wood there are a few places where deer bed down, and once, a few years ago I found a spot where a mountain lion had spent time, scratching on a tree trunk, eating something—maybe a stolen chicken—and sleeping, matting down a good-sized bit of grass under the water willow.

*7 August 2021 A steamy Saturday, 80 degrees, high clouds with a hint of smoke*

Dear Jane,

Spreading cocoa mulch (again, maybe finally, at least for this season) all of the garden delights and perils rush up to meet me. Despite the executioner's visits, yellow jackets still buzz about, looking for meat or the essence of meat. They are in thrall around the flowering seed clusters of the bush palmettos. They argue with the finches over nectar from the flowering crimson brushes of the Callistemon. I posited to Bruce that the reason the ants refuse to leave is our fault; a weekly dusting of tasty chocolate hulls is an ant's sweet dream come true.

I watch the slow change in hue of all of my tomatoes, tiny globes of Early Girls, pendulous barrels of San Marzanos, spheres of Beefsteaks as they ripen from pale sage to forest green to salmon and finally fully florid and ready to pluck and eat, warm from the sun, or slice into thick, meaty tranches and pair with a lush, creamy burrata.

This garden being what it is (a botanical nature preserve) the animal sightings extend beyond the avian. I've mentioned the brown Cottontail bunnies. The thick-tailed rats. The evidence of coyotes. Monarch Butterflies. Gophers. And since life is a complement to death, these creatures both live and die in the garden. In the past month, we've witnessed the remains of two drowned rats, a half-desiccated field mouse, bunny fur, baby bird body parts. I say a little prayer, "I honor your life and thank you for your contribution to this garden's web."

Then, yesterday, this:

Curled up in a bed of mulch underneath a tea tree, a gray pelt of fur surprised me as I was brushing smooth the last bag of mulch. It had a little piggy snout, small beads of eyes, and tiny claw hands that seemed to be grasping for some invisible reprieve. At first, I feared that we'd killed it with the cocoa mulch, as it's toxic to dogs (but not cats), but Bruce thinks it was dropped by a raptor, probably a hawk, and had its wee neck broken upon impact. Still, before I buried and blessed Mole, I imagined it wearing petite spectacles and a cozy jumper, perhaps conversing with a passing dragonfly. *The Wind in the Willows,* come to life.

Love,
Medea


*August ɪɪ 9, 2021 Monday, of that I am sure. Fog, blessed fog 58 degrees.*

Dear Medea,
After a few days of sun, I'm happy back in dense fog. Today it matches my brain.

I'm so glad you honor the poor dead creatures. For years now I've had a mantra and some unwinding gestures that I perform, usually when driving past road kill, but really whenever necessary. I also do it on planes, unhooking everyone onboard from the earth so that we can fly safely.

Today Tinker was outside, perhaps not too patiently, picking up tiny stones and then putting them down again when they don't turn out to be dog food. In my defense, I feed them grain free protein. They are one lucky gang. That reminds me, I have a new word for a group of ravens, a "reciprocal." I love and feed them, they love and protect me. I haven't seen a single snake since they arrived.

The calm this morning was disturbed early by the sounds of several chain saws. I wonder why it's not possible to build a chain saw that actually keeps running without being revved all the time? Anyway, it is a crew under the broad direction of PG&E clearing under and near the power lines—which are the big main lines in our case—and they run along the lane and border our property from, of all people, Kris Kristofferson's, next door. He is an absentee landlord and the ranch is really cow pasture. I would be happy if there were more cows. I love cows and wish I had lived a life where I had my own. My mother's family had a couple of cows during the Depression. They sold one to pay her tuition to Northwestern. This is only a really odd story because my mother looked like Elizabeth Taylor and would never have been taken for someone who knew a thing about cows. Anyway, back to the brush clearing. Without Gene here to run interference I was forced to state our demands myself. They may cut as they wish but only if they remove everything. They will be back tomorrow after consulting with the boss. This is an ongoing war we have with the brush/tree cutting contractors. They make messes and I make them clean up. Otherwise, it's just another kind of fire hazard. All of the wildlife have decamped to the invisible parts of the woods. I don't blame them. At least there aren't any nestlings in danger this time of year.

I have limited experience about cocoa mulch but am alarmed to hear it's toxic to dogs. It is odd that some things are to dogs, some to cats, and

14

almost never to both at once. But I would worry about wildlife. Of course, the manufacturer doesn't need to care about wild animals. Only pets. Your cats don't go outside, is that right? That may be best, what with coyotes.

Love,
Jane


*August H 9, 2021 again*

Dear Medea,
I'm worried if we fret and delve too deeply into all this destruction that we will damage our own hearts. We need to find gods and goddesses to place in charge. Maybe you have some suggestions for names and job descriptions?

I really hate hearing that people are flocking to MN and WI and buying everything up. That was my last bolt hole idea! Damn them! On the other hand, the non-believers being the other party means at least the crowd will be like-minded Democrats. Did you know there are lakes in Wisconsin designated "slow" lakes with a 5-mph maximum speed limit? That's my kind of place. Sigh. I would love to live in Wisconsin all year round. A nice warm cabin, fully stocked, we could sit in the window and watch snow fall. As a Floridian, do you know how quiet the world is in snow? I miss that. I miss it the way you miss hot sand, I guess.

My Uncle Jim's story is in accurate bird song dialog as far as I know (not being good with bird songs except the owls, ravens, and thrushes. Thrush? As I recall it's only a couple of pages long, and may well be illustrated by my aunt Enid.

I'm going to have a nap and think about new gods/goddesses who could do something important, not on our behalf, but for Earth.

Love,
Jane


*9 August 2021 Summer sun, summer breeze, 75 degrees*

Dear Jane,
You live only a few hours from here, but it's already Wednesday there! I love how Covid has changed our relationships with time. Calendars and clocks cannot compete with the rhythms that our bodies feel. It's Wednesday at your house, and most definitely Monday here. Or maybe it's a Tuesday in January. Does it really matter?

Driving up to San Francisco this morning, I noticed rivers of wildflowers along the freeway. Most were yellow, perhaps buttercups? California's native poppies. Mexican daisies. And the pink lilies with huge heads that stand atop impossibly narrow stems, aptly named "naked ladies." We've had no rain in months; what are they drinking?

You would have loved my jaunt across the Bay this morning. The fog roared in from the Pacific, snarly and insistent. It curled around my bones as I stood at dear old Windsong's helm as the tow boat delivered her to the marina for service. Honking geese flew overhead. A pair of Great Blue Herons and another of Snowy Egrets were on patrol at the SF harbor. No reciprocals of ravens, but plenty of cormorants, seagulls and swifts. Shorebirds may be drab, but I think it requires extrasensory perception to notice their uniqueness. Still, I would welcome a few flamboyances of flamingoes to liven up our watery neighborhood.

The Bay churned only slightly during the crossing. Windsong and the towboat were the only vessels between SF and Sausalito except for the ferry. If we exceeded five knots, I'd be surprised. Slow boats, slow pulse. The whisper of the wind in the sails is like the silence of your snowy lake. Kayaking brings that same soothing oneness with the elements.

I'm not surprised that you untether everyone from their seatbelts when you fly. My untethering equivalent is to say a blessing for the captain, crew, fellow passengers that we arrive safely at our final destination—well, that was the prayer, until the "Final Destination" movie franchise hit theaters. Now, I simply suggest that we all would appreciate it if the plane doesn't fall out of the sky before we reach the next airport.

What gods do we need now, you ask? I can think of a few:

The god "Enough." Enough's superpower is to paralyze our keyboards before we can hit "add to cart."

The goddess "Spark." Spark's superpower is to stimulate our minds and tickle our fancies to satiety with butterflies and sunsets.

The god "Rustle." Rustle is charged with giving us the power to notice when fronds wave, fish jump, bird wings flap, children laugh. And the grace to hear the poetry in silence.

The goddess "Pique." Pique visits the unvaccinated while they sleep.

What do you think?

Love,
Medea

*August 10, 2021 I looked it up, it's Tuesday. Still, as in completely quiet, fog making the forest have that towering cathedral look, but sun is coming fast*

Dear Medea,

Did your time on the water give you the relief that it often does me? Nothing will rest the inner body as well as the outer structure as thoroughly as water, though it would help not to have to dodge ferry traffic. I'm just a prairie girl looking for a little quiet lake. I'll leave the big stuff to others.

Pink Ladies! I don't think they are native plants. Like the Calla lilies along Highway 1, I think they came with midwestern Swedes and settling folks from the east. I read somewhere recently that the California poppy isn't protected after all. It's legal to pick it. Someone started that rumor about leaving them be back in the 60s. Bless them. Wild flowers have their own protective system. It seems like they don't "pick" well, they just sort of slump over and give up. So, we should leave them be. Rather than tell humans the plants have wisely chosen to show us by best practices instead. Yesterday driving north from the village on One I came up the grade slowly noticing the lovely pale pink puffs of flowers covering the rock wall. I don't know what they are but I wanted them to be Sea Thrift. I'll look it up and report back.

I've written about the cormorants and herons in my poems, for some reason especially during the cancer years. Maybe that was when my focus changed, sharpened. (Is that what cancer patients mean by it changed them?) For a pelagic bird species, they both spend an inordinate amount of time on snags in the river—herons and cormorants, not cancer patients. Herons seem so adaptable, they are a sacred bird in the shamanic world because they so often stand in still water, watching, and are thus straddling the three worlds—upper, middle, and lower—gathering wisdom. Lots of mornings I feel like a cormorant on a snag "feeling greasy and stuck, clock ticking, the tide rising…wings not dry enough to fly." (Waiting on a Snag, *The Spirit Birds*).

I think of your goddesses, I love Pique the best. Excellent pantheon.

Love,
Jane


*10 August 2021 Hot. 85 delightful degrees.*

Dear Jane,

You will appreciate that the cormorant floating around the harbor yesterday held a flapping silver fish in its beak. It looked not stuck, but triumphant.

The idea of a loon on vacation reminds me of my parents, sometimes of myself. The Arctic Loon is technically a "snowbird", and you know human snowbirds raise my ire. But the Arctic Loon, like the grosbeaks that are visiting me now but will soon head back north, move in harmony with their vacation homes. I've never heard a grosbeak squawk that the food here can't compare to the food at home.

The herons offer hours of entertainment when I see them at the beach. It's not a surprise to learn that they are sacred in shamanic tradition. As tall and imposing as a heron can be, some reaching four feet in height, it's the play between their bodies and the shadows they cast while hunting that entrances me, straddling three worlds and creating another, ephemeral space.

We share that restorative water feeling. I once met Wallace J. Nichols, PhD, author of *The Blue Mind*, at a talk in San Francisco. He stood at the podium, though you'd be forgiven if you sensed that he was levitating. His thesis is that being near the water, any water, soothes the ruffled mind, and that simply sitting in proximity to the ocean, lake, even a fountain can bring calm if we allow it. (How much grief we cause ourselves by resisting!) At the end of his presentation, he gave everyone a blue marble, symbolizing our blue world. We were asked to give the marble to someone as a reminder to get in touch with our inner "merperson" and instruct that person to do the same. I wonder who has that marble now?

The floppy wildflower should deter us from plucking flowers from the ground. But there is no more heartwarming treasure than a tiny fistful of billowy white "dandy roses" picked especially for Mama by her little boy. My garden offers lots of flowers to cut and enjoy indoors. My favorite is a Hawaiian Ginger with a sweet, spicy, almost plumeria-like fragrance. It sort of resembles an exploding firework: a foot-tall column of vertically-oriented lemon-yellow petals holding orange-red pistils out for your nose to breathe in. It is possible to vacation without leaving home.

Did you know that the Egyptians revered flamingos as incarnations of Ra, the Sun God? A coral-colored bird that is the sun in disguise. No wonder I'm smitten.

Love,
Medea


*August 11, 2021 Fog and cool. You would say cold. We are so incompatible.*

Dear Medea,
I sometimes rock myself to sleep with the imagined sensation of waves lapping against and gently rocking a small boat. There is a place in Wisconsin called Spread Eagle where my father's father lived in a grand log cabin built by a Finn

carpenter in a Depression era winter, sledding logs across the frozen lake to the peninsula. There was a dock there and clear water washing over a stony shoreline. The only thing more calming than imagining that sound is to add the call of the loon, often heard in evening and morning, and put myself in a kayak, drifting, paddle still. Sadly, these days those waters are clogged with your same snowbirds in their summer form racing jet skis and partying long into the night. I'm related to a few of them, though I'm sure none of my kin would ever complain about food or service.

Yesterday in the afternoon I noticed my ravens were gone. Not one was watching. Even when I went outside with some irresistible chicken there wasn't a sound, a caw, a warble, no alarm went out to bring them flapping. It was eerie and because I believe wholly in the energy of our connection, it was a sign. I fretted. I walked around the house. I filled the feeder dish. I looked in and through the trees. I called. Nothing. Gene came home and I told him the ravens were gone. The phone rang, it was his doctor with bad news, a bit of melanoma.

The ravens returned. Message delivered. I was ready for it. Their job was done.

Love,
Jane


*11 August, 2021 Watching my Japanese Maple welcome scores of tiny birds. 82 degrees, and it's 6pm. Ahhhh....*

My dear friend, Jane,
The ravens did their job. Handling the message requires deep confidence in and comfort with the natural order of things. We learned how to do so with grace and acceptance when our ravens delivered our respective cancer messages over a decade ago.

Gene will too.

Of all of the experiences one might encounter in a lifetime, dragging logs across a frozen lake during a Depression-era winter would not make my top ten. And, yet, your grandfather's Finnish builder did that. He dragged those logs across that ice. His hands must have looked like ragged beets. Think about his craggy, stubbled face, his pale hair under (we hope) some kind of cap, his ice blue eyes intent on his destination. The winter's sky an indecipherable white, reaching to the edges of the frozen lake. How did he navigate with snow pelting his face? Could he imagine the gift he gave to you? Did he consider who might live there after his demise, or was he one of those introspective craftspeople, thinking only of the fires he'd build and the wife he'd bed in front in the hearth he'd set?

Remind me to tell you what Bruce's surfer friend said about feeding wild birds. Spoiler alert: he would turn you in to the purists for feeding kibble to the ravens, and me for offering a short-cut to my passerines. I get it. And I am sitting here, the sun bright and warm and probably adding another five years to my "presbyotic" skin, watching a Japanese Maple offer footing (toeing?) to at least twenty nuthatches and chickadees. It's like a living Christmas tree with animated ornaments. Despite the feeders, the birds forage for insects in the bark. They flit into neighbors' trees for a varied next course. It's a progressive dinner for birds.

If you offer a living thing something for free, if you remove its *raison de travailler*, and yet it continues to work for extra supper, are you a crippling enabler or a thoughtful facilitator? If we keep asking this question, will the birds ultimately offer an answer?

I need Uncle Jim. The ravens, the nuthatches, the Hairy Woodpecker, even the hummingbirds are expressing opinions.

Love,
Medea

P.S. We are only climatologically incompatible. In the ether, we are blood sisters.

*August 12, 2021 High overcast, mild mid-60s*

Dear Medea,
I miss my Uncle Jim. I think I'm like him in many ways. He was a true creature of the woods, though, more so than me. Probably more so than Thoreau who took his dirty linen back to his mother for washing. My uncle was subjected to electroshock therapy when he fell apart after returning from Europe after WW II. Tall, handsome, and wild eyed. He was independent and brilliant. He drank heavily and became a scholar of late Roman history. No idea why. Or maybe I do, escaping by finding a subject no one else gives a damn about? Uh huh. I get that.

So, back to Thoreau, I heard Walden Pond has such a high concentration of human urine now that one really should avoid swimming in it. That sort of sums it up, doesn't it? Did you know there's a registry online of the mercury content of all the lakes in the North Woods (we like to capitalize it because the fairies live there). You can look up the lake you want to fish and figure out whether to eat what you catch or toss it back. We have gone far far past the point of ignoring the reality of human desecration. The real question now is whether there is any future for our sons?

Bruce's surfer friend and I will have to disagree. Not having a personal relationship with the wild is exactly what made man think he could kill for sport, trap animals that smell bad, get in the way, or are just too damn ugly. Ravens in particular are scavengers. If I didn't treat them to goodies that are healthy for them, they'd raid the neighbor's BBQ fire for charred pork chops. Where would he draw the line? Aside from food, if he surfed up on shore next to a stranded whale, would he join the group trying to heave her off? Or keep walking so as to let nature take its course? You don't have to ask him; I don't want to start a fight.

Love,
Jane


*12 August 2021 It's clear, bright, warm. The blackberries are popping purple here. Reading* The Sound of the Sea: Seashells and the Fate of the Ocean *by Cynthia Barnett*

Dear Jane,
This letter must be brief as I'm shortly driving to the Delta. I will make notes for a long letter upon my return. The herons that live on the Island where I'll spend the night utter the most guttural squawks you've heard. Piercing, like the ravens.

Speaking of ravens, I dashed outside to grab some of the aforementioned blackberries, a couple of lemons and a tomato to pack for the drive. As I walked out the sliding screen door, the three ravens began chortling for or chiding me; I'm not sure which, though the square feeder is empty, again, so I believe it might be a gentle reminder to refill before I leave. I saw a photo this morning taken by a woman who had ministered to an injured crow. The crow gifted her a screw, a button, three pearls.

Like you, I think that surfer might contemplate interconnectedness a bit more carefully. And also like you, I chuckle to think of Thoreau taking his washing home to Mama.

Oh, and after a brilliant blue sky yesterday, the smoke rolled in from the Dixie fire and all afternoon the light looked like the light during a solar eclipse. That lasted until evening, when the sunset exploded like a study in crimson and orange. Pollution is no gift, but it sure produces kaleidoscopic sunsets.

Love,
Medea

*Friday the 13th, August 2021 An orange demanding sunrise through a dark blue cloud. Reading* The Radiant Lives of Animals *by Linda Hogan.*

Dear Medea,

The light is that yellow tinge slant that indicates a shift. The weather report still shows the wind direction as onshore, but only barely. The cloud to the east was eerie as it plumed from the horizon to the sky and the sun was diminished in its rise. We wondered if it was smoke, and I still couldn't swear it wasn't but there are clouds on the radar so perhaps panic is premature.

Yesterday the front page of the SF Chronicle encouraged everyone to take a break and come to Mendocino. What is wrong with people? First, they put us on the front page with our water woes and not a few days later they are listing hotels and campgrounds and encouraging SF to empty out for the weekend and head north. No! I broke my own rule about not making comments on newspaper stories. Stienstra should know better, he's been around long enough. I don't understand the editorial logic at work in the San Francisco paper. Maybe the new editor's New York way of behaving?

Linda Hogan is a Native American poet and essayist with such a gentle and delicate touch. One of those writers you want to slow way down to read, or to put another way, she makes me realize I read too fast, and reminds me to stay in the present, the future will be with us soon enough. Her writing is like a gospel of native nature. She says: "In our human place, we are only one of earth's beings, surrounded by other intelligences we seek to understand."

I think I've figured out that the male ravens have a bit of a hooded cap while the females do not. I could look this up someplace but I decided that, like explorers before us, sometimes observation and intuition are better teachers. One of the females is recognizable by her very fluffy appearance. She's got something different in her feather growth, let's hope it's not bugs. It is lovely to see how they groom and preen and are affectionate. Especially the mated pair who parent the five juveniles. Focusing on them gives me a little peace.

This day has begun with some sadness and with trepidation. Superstition doesn't improve the way the day will or won't flow. When the worry over the future collides with the regret of the past, what is the way out for the present moment? Only, perhaps, to bear witness. Or, not to take myself so seriously, to witness a bear. I'd love that.

Love,
Jane

*August 15, 2021. Sunday—just to be clear. Warm, sun, orange cast to the light means high smoke.*

Dear Medea,

Last fall our Navarro River was declared toxic during the fall until the winter ocean chewed away at the sand bar and opened the waterway. The beach is managed by California State Parks system who are adamant about letting nature take its course but have no power to stop vineyards inland from sucking the river dry. In the "old days" some locals would sneak down during the night with a tractor and bulldoze the sand open so that the salmon could run more easily and the water wouldn't become stagnant. There is debate, of course, about the wisdom on both sides. Without the draining of the river by vineyards inland and, it must also be said, pot growers who sneak down to the river at night with water trucks and load up to water their hidden grows in the forest, perhaps the river health would regulate itself drought or no. It's every man for himself, and I say "man" with the opinion that women wouldn't do such a thing. I hope. The river water temperature encourages the algae growth and discourages the salmonid population. There are no winners. Even the grape growers must realize there is a finite and very real death coming to their adventures in wine making?

In the avian world here, Tinker remains our loyal companion while the rest of the juveniles are scattering farther afield. Some days they come, and some days they don't. Tinker is getting fatter and friendlier as a result. Today he played ball with Tweed and me, flying low above Tweed as he ran for the ball, back and forth. Tinker's family hasn't abandoned him, at least one parent shows up once a day, and they are all quite active in the dawn hours, squawking and swooping through the forest.

As to gifts, as long as we've had dogs here, we've had ravens who wanted to play tag. Often the ravens would fly around the house at window level until the dog would ask to go outside where they would case around the house, first one way and then the other. One of our dogs lost his tags off his collar in the woods. We looked everywhere. A few days later we found them prominently placed in the driveway. When I first started feeding this current family, they brought gifts and left them by the back door on the brick walkway: a dead vole, an eaten pork chop bone (not ours), two eaten corn cobs (also not ours), and several raven feathers. The food was proof that the ravens weren't dependent entirely on me and were ranging at least as far as the neighbors ten acres away across the street who often BBQ and toss their remains for the critters.

In general, it's clear that humans and their shit are exactly the problem. It's certainly the reason I quit backpacking/camping. We think it's bad here, have you been to India? Without resources, it seems to me that we who can afford to dump our bilge properly must do extra duty, compensate for, escalate, and finance those without even basic resources elsewhere. Code Red indeed. The report this week on Climate Disaster is terrifying. What world will our sons endure?

Love,
Jane

P.S. After I closed there was a bit of crashing and banging around outside. I looked out the front door and Tinker was on the porch. I think he'd been trying to open the bright blue shiny delivery box. We exchanged looks of impossibility.

*15 August 2021 A muggy 75 degrees. The sky is the color of milk, and at 3pm the light looks more dawn-like.*

Dear Jane,
I missed writing to you yesterday as I was focused on absorbing as much Island vibe as my body and soul could carry back home. This island, off the San Joaquin River just north of Stockton, was acquired in the 1950s by a group of mariners who sought a reprieve from their chilly hometown San Francisco summers. While SF shivers under a cold blanket of fog, the Delta's daytime summer temperatures typically hover around the mid-90s. Spending long, lazy summer days here taught my kids how to slow down. How to read the tides and currents. How to create a tribe, even if that tribe lasts only a single summer. Talking to parents of kindergarteners and elementary school students, it's reassuring for the future of humanity to note that despite intense societal pressure, this generation of parents also understands the value in unplugging. The Island operates as a very small town. It's not uncommon for an adult to discover a kid trying to smoke in the bathroom or a hormonal teen couple having forbidden sex in the shower. Parents are informed. Consequences ensue. You learn early that no one is invisible.

The corollary is that most adults have eyes and ears on all sides of our heads. We watch over other people's children silently, intently. We also speak with other's children to learn about their lives and interests. Yesterday, I spent some time with a seven-year-old son of a friend whose initial single-word-reply reticence slowly gave way to a full sentence, then to an entire story about his friend Dylan, whose father is the principal of the school but whose Covid mask is too big so it falls below his nose. Next summer, this boy will be eight, and in ten years he'll be a high school graduate. And I have a front row seat to marvel and cheer as his life unfolds.

The Island's forty-plus acres is contained inside a berm, which is surrounded by the aforementioned lagoon, which is in turn circled by tule, scrub oak and eucalyptus trees. Birds and otters love it. I woke up with the sun yesterday and hit the walking path that wreathes the perimeter. The only sounds at that hour are birdsongs. The Eurasian Collard Doves must have been in convention. They not only *coo-coo-cooed*, but *anhh-anhh-anhhed*, swooping and diving and demanding attention. I noticed a shy Downy Woodpecker skirting the trimmed trunk of a Mexican Fan Palm, looking for breakfast. Wren-tits, House Finches, and Western Kingbirds *chipped* and *tweeted*, sometimes sounding like the old dial-up sounds we would hear in the early days of the internet. In the eaves of the Lighthouse was a mama Red Robin and her three chicks. It seems late in the year for nests and chicks, but there they were. I'd gone out in search of my beloved herons, especially the Night Herons who frequent the foliage on the other side of the lagoon, but they have decamped to a different island.

My mom, in the weary voice of an octogenarian living in an increasingly unfamiliar world, told me this morning that she is afraid. "I don't understand Afghanistan. The news shows are more interested in Britney Spears. I don't like the way the world is moving," she said.

Mom grew up in a materially modest, emotionally rich household. She lived through the end of the depression, WWII, the Korean and Vietnamese wars, the Cuban Missile Crisis (which was unfolding ninety miles south of our house), AIDS, 9/11, cancer, and the deaths of her parents and her younger brother. Her hide is thick. This present moment, the moment we cleave to in its shimmering now-ness... must not be her undoing.

She would find her breath, I believe, were she to go into the woods and witness a bear.

Love,
Medea


*17 August 2021 64 degrees, white sky here at home. Windspeed is expected to accelerate from 10 mph now to 25 by 2pm*

Dear Jane,

We have another tree executioner in the neighborhood. Have none of these homeowners read *The Hidden Life of Trees*? I might have to start distributing copies. This pine is one we have loved for three decades. It's gnarled and twin-trunked, with a candelabra of ancillary branches that reach(ed) twenty-five feet into the sky. The man who owned the house, Chuck, babied that tree. He printed a sign warning of falling cones for the unobservant who might park underneath. Half of the branches are gone now. The tree looks naked and ashamed. When we walked past last evening, I walked over and gave it a kiss—followed by a middle-finger salute to the new owner's security camera.

Barry Lopez said in his ultimate book, *Horizon*, "As time grows short, the necessity to listen attentively to foundational stories other than our own becomes imperative." Are you listening, tree killers?

Love,
Medea


*August 18, 2021 Wednesday Orange light, 69 degrees inside and outside, light breeze from the north*

Dear Medea,
Surely we all need bears. Perhaps there's a way to adopt the scorched cub that was recently found near the fire in the Sierra. I'm afraid to check whether it survived. It may be a sign of the times in the same way that your mother is finding this latest human catastrophe hardest to manage, but I'm finding it more and more difficult to accept the destruction of wild life–whether by human action or random cycles of life. Somehow, this broken heart I have continues to peel and crack. Nowhere to run, nowhere to hide…as the lyrics go.

In local news, Tinker has been active the last few days often visiting on his own and reaping the benefits of solo trips to the feeder. He also has discovered the garden chairs, BBQ, and the porch and at one point was clambering at the garden window to get my attention. I may have gone too far. I am glad to see that at least once a day he comes with one or both of the parents still. Like the teenager forced to dine out with the family, there is some disagreement but in the end everyone eats well. There have been three new deer. I think they are males coming together to discuss who's in charge of the ladies this year. The biggest one, obviously, knows it's his job to lose. Yesterday all three came charging down the path in a not so friendly game of tag. Tweed seems to know they are out of his league and is content to watch from the window of the living room.

Love,
Jane


*August 18, 2021 still Wednesday Still orange vague light, but the winds of yesterday are gone*

Dear Medea,
The threat of fire invades every part of our lives now, including at 4 am when an evacuation alarm like the claxon of a Nazi police car brought me upright in

bed. It took a moment, but soon became clear the order was for Willits which is at least 30 miles away. Drifted smoke, though, had seeped into my bedroom enough that I got up to close windows and open shades in hopes that if I couldn't hear danger, perhaps I would be able to see it. Reading about the fire east of Placerville where I used to live which grew to 50k acres in 24 hours and is too big and too fast for CalFire to make a map, much less fight the fire. This is our future, the one we have created. Is this any way to live? Your mother has a point. And yet, it could be so much worse, maybe not for Britney Spears, but right now, for so many people, hell is not of their own making and there is much to be done before we can walk away into the woods to search for our bears.

Have you introduced yourself to your tree-killing neighbor or are you content to flip him off when the opportunity arises? I'm sad for your tree. I'm trying desperately to keep my thirsty hawthorn alive. It's my "clouty" tree, a Celtic tradition of hanging strips of cloth on the branches along with a wish or a prayer. I have invested a lot of superstition in my tree, losing it now would only add to the jagged crack in my heart.

Love,
Jane


*18 August 2021 Warm, thick air with a sky that now looks more like pale hot chocolate than a tall, cold glass of skim milk.*

Dear Jane,
The heritage pine tree is now completely down. Destroyed. Yesterday afternoon, the hackers severed the rest of its limbs. They left one tiny sprout with a shock of spindly needles at the top; it looked like Alfalfa from The Little Rascals. Today, the pros arrived to finish the job. This swarm of executioners rode, high style, in a clean, new, white logoed truck; the wet work guys skulked in in a rusty, dirty unbadged pickup.

The proud tree proved a formidable foe. Five muscled and tanned wranglers vs one wooden old dude. The battle raged for nearly seven hours. Bits of bark flew across the street and atop the roof. Sawdust everywhere. The neighbors will be sweeping their driveways for weeks. Remnants of a sentry that watched over the neighborhood since long before most of their parents were born. A cross-section of the trunk sits vertically on the curb. It is nearly as tall as one of the pros who chipped away it before giving up, probably leaving it for tomorrow's clean-up crew.

The new owners, who will be renting the place out and whom I thus will likely never meet, have opened a vista into the across-the-street neighbor's kitchen window. Chuck lived with that tree for forty-three years, since the home and the neighborhood were new. Birds and squirrels kept it company before Chuck. I wonder what karma has in store for the new owners?

In a reassuring twist, the decapitated Canary Island Palm across the street has declared its intention to *live*. New fronds that merely suggested survival on Monday now extend about eighteen inches from the apex of the trunk like a defiant promise.

Love,
Medea


*August 20, 2021 Friday Waxing moon. Fog and 64 degrees.*

Dear Medea,
We may be the only slice of northern California with decent air. The app on my phone shows this narrow spit from Pt. Arena to the Oregon border, oddly surrounded by yellow, an apt color choice for moderately unhealthy. There is so much brown in our world, brown crackly grass, brown spots of desperation on the trees, premature fall fade on the Japanese maples. I find myself spending too much time staring at weather apps and fire maps, as if the quantity of my viewing time might create a shift, might ameliorate some of the disaster staring back at me. The fog makes everything, inside and out, look like it would to have lightly yellow-tinted glasses on.

In pulling apart the various pressures and stresses in order to allow for healthy attitudes in the first place I'm sort of appalled at the state of our world all over again, right? Will we look back on this and find ourselves in some kind of PTSD over what we've been muscling through as best we can? I have this awareness of a flatness to the energy—there's nothing out there that can give way to make room for shift. We are all metaphorically stuck in the hallway. Which door is even going to open, never mind be a positive change? I feel a bit like Winnie the Pooh and his circular tautological logic. Or maybe I wish I had a big stuffed animal to clutch while I hide in my bedroom? At least I have Tweed, even better than a stuffed animal, he is happy to snuggle. I worry about the piling on of one disaster after another, even as observers, we can't come away unchanged. The anger roused by rampant stupidity over climate change, over threats to our fundamental rights and the rights of all creatures, can we sustain that anger in order to use it to create a shift? It's hard to use anger that way. Anger is the sword of the ignorant, intellect is the cup in which answers to problems are shared.

Something is shifting in the natural world here. Perhaps a normal preamble to the end of summer: the scarcity of food and water. The deer must be spending more time deeper in the woods where there still is something green and at least damp. I was wondering if I should move the horse trough to the edge of the wood (and near a spigot) and fill it. I don't usually have water in containers that aren't regularly emptied because of mosquitos. But I worry that the wetlands are drying up. I will walk to the creek and see whether it is giving the wild ones water. As to other food for bigger creatures, the blackberries are drying faster than they ripen but some of them are making it through if the contents of the bird's droppings are any judge. It is the time of year we might see a bear, or at least the scat filled with berries. Speaking of birds, the little cheeky Gray Jays have discovered where the ravens get their treats. They don't seem very intimidated by their bigger brothers. The Gray Jay is so friendly and sweet, unlike the harping of the Steller's Blue Jay who has been at it every morning early lately, rousing everyone out of bed like a drill Sgt. at boot camp.

I'm sorry for the death of your ancient tree. It seems such a random violence. As if the physics of the universe just didn't get it right at the edges. Is it possible to collect pine cones and get them to seed? I speak from complete ignorance.

Love,
Jane


*Saturday, August 21, 2021 Barreling down on a full moon, light fog, overcast, cool 64 degrees*

Dear Medea,
What joy this morning to look out the window and see all eleven quail alive and well! I hope they were doing their part to curb the earwig population which seems to have boomed. I do worry about the quail and their vulnerability to the ravens, but I have seen them almost side by side without incident so perhaps ravens haven't watched *Babette's Feast*? This morning the quail were busy pecking away at the ground in front of them, a lone deer grazing, and two ravens not too far off who might have been on watch for me or were just minding their own business, which I guess would also include watching for me. Ma and Pa raven and two juveniles came for breakfast. To me this indicates that all is well. The juveniles are almost indistinguishable from the parents now, even Tinker has grown to full and healthy size, no longer the runt.

After mentioning the horse trough yesterday, I read an article about airlifting water to drought ridden hinterlands. The photo showed bears drinking. So, today's chore will be to find the trough and get it filled. There's a nice spot for it right by a spigot at the edge of the wood.

Yesterday, the sounds of chain saws made everything jittery. The ravens stayed hidden and quiet until the last tree fell and the last man drove away. Today's return to normal confirms they are wary and disturbed by the destruction and noise. It is as if PG&E is mandating noise instead of logic. Look, see us doing all this man work! They cut the trees and leave a bare twenty-foot scar. Until we complained they left slash piles. How is that not a bigger threat of fire than doing nothing at all? I'm the witch who called them back and made them take away what they destroyed. Every year they try to pretend they don't know their own job. Every year my witch's hat has to get taller and pointier. Shrug. Sometimes the crone is exactly what we need.

Love,
Jane


*Sunday, August 22, 2021 Overcast, light fog, cool temps*

Dear Medea,
As I write this there are two deer not ten feet from my window. When I sat down and saw them, they were both sitting under a water willow bush, and stared hard at me for a while to be sure I wasn't a threat. Now they are grazing so close that I can see the ruffles of their coats where they twitch and scratch at their itchy skin. I'm wishing Gene had put the horse trough here by the house where I wanted him to rather than where he did put it which is in a spot I don't think they will ever see, or smell, or whatever sense is required to notice a source of water. Tomorrow I'll make him move the trough. This morning I have seen all 9 members of the deer herd and am eased in my own stress about global affairs by seeing them. The same is true of the ravens who have been very vocal and social this morning. It's Sunday, surely the complete quiet and absence of chain saws and trucks ravaging the grade along the canyon gives the birds and the deer a signal they can come out of hiding.

As we return to a state of covid fear and find ourselves vulnerable again, finding ways to distract and ease the stress is so important. It's a matter now of just not thinking at all. Problem solving is an unsolvable puzzle. The fire in the Sierra so close to where we lived for many years is incomprehensible in scope. As I return my focus to the two deer now nibbling their way across the dry grass searching for something, anything, just giving them all of my energy and attention helps. I urge them along, down toward the narrowing streambed, always to safety. Always to safety.

Love,
Jane


*August 24, 2021 Overcast, the faintest of mists in the air. 59 degrees.*

Dear Medea,
I know you are focused inward the past few days, healing from surgery. I hope it is also a time of immersing yourself in the moment without the distraction of everything that tries to disrupt our experience of joy when it comes. Maybe that's what I cherish most about our letters–the requirement to just "be", to bring the lens to the small and immediate things, the good things more than the bad surely. These are the tools of healing. The imprints left by the birdsong in the wee hours of the morning, or the cat knowing when to curl up so that you are forced to stay as you are. For now, let the universe come to you in small things.

Tinker reciprocated the gift of raw eggs with leaving a marrow bone, long baked dry, in the middle of the driveway where I would find it first thing. When the various dogs were puppies, they were given a marrow bone by the breeder. We would let them have it for a brief time but knowing our vet did not approve of bones at all, we would allow the bones to disappear outside. This bone must have been at least nine years in the dirt outside, perhaps in a gopher hole. It makes me sad to think of the sweet dogs we have lost.

I'm happy to report that Gene has agreed about moving the trough to a better location. General advice (meaning Google) dictates it would be better to find and expand a wetland because the deer prefer standing water at ground level, but the trough will have to do. We know from past experience that animals do come to the trough when it has water in it, we even found mountain lion tracks one year. To prevent small critters from drowning I found a few bricks to make "stairs."

The last three days we have seen a return of the red-tail hawk to his/her perch on the pine tree overlooking the front yard. The yard is pocked with gopher holes, so we are happy to see the hawk and wish him good hunting. He always comes at five o'clock. Just as the others have their schedule to keep—the ravens at breakfast and dinner, I suppose because they see me in the kitchen, the deer make a counterclockwise circuit around the wood, surely directly out of their beds and in search of water and tender shoots, there are so few of those now, they move close to the house early and late so as to avoid the dog. Tweed's knowledge of and reaction to them is half-hearted at best these days. They both seem to know he's no danger to them. What I have missed this year is the constancy of the Hermit Thrush who starts in spring with the first measure of song, an upward trill of hope. By midsummer eve the thrush has peaked the top note and descended. We heard the early enthusiasms but it seemed to me that the tensions of high summer have made the birds silent. Perhaps it's just me. Not that I am silent, but there is an inner stress that is unmanageable and a damper on any optimism, and it is surely optimism that is the chorus of the thrush.

Love,
Jane

*Evening at home, the 24th of August. A plane's engines muffled through the lingering smoke, though I can see some sun. It's breezy and cool and felt more like fall than summer as I just stepped out to pick a few apples for dinner. 65 degrees.*

Dear Jane,
Tomorrow, I will sit with your letters of the past few days, diligent as you are while I lazed about. Well, not exactly "lazed," more like "extended healing required" after last Thursday's surgery. Thank you for carrying the load while my chest wounds closed and my equilibrium reset.

Once again while in the hospital I marveled at the egregious quantity of medical waste. During my three-day December hospital stay, the nurse told me not to worry about it because "we are going to blast it all into space." On Thursday, the (wiser, more in-touch) nurse agreed with me and still questions what the alternative might be. Shall we reuse needles and drapes? No. Does every gown have to be made of disposable paper? Is washing a gown a waste of water? What happens to the gray water from hospitals? The nurse handed me a (disposable) toothbrush, gum swab and oral antiseptic liquid pre-op for disinfecting of my mouth, tongue and gums. I am not having oral surgery. No matter. I brushed and swabbed and swished and all of the plastic went into the garbage can.

If all the items we discard were deposited on top of our beds, would we feel moved to use less?

You are right that the world is in an execrable state. Events pile upon traumas and bury us under floods and ashes. But here's a thought. What if instead of despair, we choose decency? What if, rather than rail against whichever useless politician is behaving the most outrageously on a given day, we instead decide to make eye contact with the mail carrier and thank her, by name, for bringing us our catalogues and bills? How about taking the time to see the people we (unintentionally, I know) sometimes look through?

We're all moving too fast, chasing things that, in the end, don't matter one whit. What matters to you, Jane? What matters to Gene and Tweed and Tinker and the covey of quail?

Meaning. Hope. Connection. These matter to me. I've read that a person's idea of what or who God is tells one more about the person than it does about the deity. Some force precipitated the Big Bang. Was it divine intervention? Is it a different belief structure to know that God keeps His eye on us all, as opposed to sensing that the Universe acts as our caretaker and guide?

Miracles abound: in the baby lizards that seem to skitter across every inch of pavement just ahead of my bare feet; in the plaintive eyes of my needy cat, Odin, who thinks he's my boyfriend and who scratches Bruce if Bruce tries to hold my hand while Odin rests in my lap; in the reliable spectacle and magnificent fanfare of sunrise and sunset. I rest my faith in these things, which I suppose makes me either an infidel or a zealot, depending on your creed.

We're too far away from nature, Jane. That distance is like a black hole, sucking the life out of us from without and from within.

Love,
Medea


*August 25, 2021. There is warmth in the air and a sun peeking through high overcast 65°F*

Dear Medea,
Your hospital stay sounds awful. Or, at least starkly out of tune with your own way of being. I wish, fervently, for your speedy healing.

When I was in college fifty-five years ago studying for my philosophy degree I would have said I was an atheist, a phenomenologist, or sometimes an existentialist but not in the way of Sartre, or Camus, poor bloke. I studied Heidegger's ideas about Being, and Kierkegaard's dependence on God (which by the way apparently were sufficient to justify his completely bizarre treatment of the woman who loved him). Our old highly quotable George Santayana comforted me as he was clearly profoundly baffled by the way humans behaved. From the strictures of textual philosophy, I found spiritualist practices spoke to a deeper, older part of my soul. Awakened my witch. My shaman aspirations came much later but fitting in with the evolution of an ontology that sees Being as the core of the universe, we as a part of the whole, and tasked with evolving out of this terrible state we have been languishing in since before recorded time. Perhaps we are a virus the universe is trying, has been trying, to shake off for many, many years. God is a word I find hard to use except as an expletive. But as a source, a beginning, a returning, a fullness, yes. I'd like a better noun.

That's the purer side of the discussion. We can leave the politics of religion to another time, though certainly, the fix we are in as Earth has everything to do with the politics of religion. I suppose we will have to address it eventually.

I'm just happy to know that Bruce occasionally battles with Odin to hold your hand.

Love,
Jane


*25 August 2021 72 and sunny, fair blue skies. Reading* A Land Remembered *by Patrick D. Smith.*

Dear Jane,

You could write a calendar with your critter sightings. Or a day log. Is it me or are my birds more unruly, less predictable than yours? No, it is probably that in beginning to notice the birds, I'm noticing scattershot antics; over time, that learning curve should flatten and these birds will behave more like yours. Though just a second ago, the Anna's Hummingbird that loves to poke its forked tongue into the fuchsia just outside the screen door helicoptered in, buzzing like a distant outboard motor. It's hard to believe that these terminal blooms continue to hold nectar, but the hummers just keep on coming. Their only routine, as far as I can tell, is to chase one another like fighter pilots every evening.

It's just after five now, and a reciprocal of punctual ravens is winging around the tops of the pines.

A black squirrel just leaped from the roof onto the Japanese Maple and it's stuffing its cheeks with seed pods. The maple began to issue these seeds last year—or maybe this was the first time that I noticed. They float at the ends of the leaves, and look like rose-colored dragonfly wings. Last year, the chickadees devoured them, but since they now have a feeder on this tree, the squirrel takes seed advantage. When I moved to this area thirty-three years ago, I'd never seen a black squirrel, only gray and occasionally red. Now, they're everywhere.

The book that I am reading is a fictional history of early Florida, back when mosquitos hatched into clouds so dense they could stuff a cow's mouth, ears and nostrils, and sting with such ferocity that said cow would die. It follows generations of the MacIvey family, beginning in the mid 1860s and ending in 1968. The non-fictional descriptions of what Florida once was, the profuse bird life, the Pay-Hay-Okee, or River of Grass as the Everglades was known, weaving across the southern third of the state in her silvery regalia, the cypress trees reaching a hundred feet into the air—all of it brings me to tears. The last wild Carolina Parakeet was killed in Okeechobee County in 1904, when its population had dwindled to almost nothing. The sweet-faced, yellow-headed green-bodied birds were squeezed from their forest homes as that land was wrangled into the service of agriculture. Too many others were shot as pests or as adornments for ladies' hats. It makes me ashamed to be bipedal.

Love,
Medea

P.S. The pine cones from Chuck's tree were swept up with the rest of the sawdust. Its majesty, like the Carolina Parakeet, lives in our memory now.

*August 26, 2021 Sunshine and warm. Blue sky and not a hint of smoke. Reading* Native *by Patrick Laurie.*

Dear Medea,
I didn't know that about black squirrels. They are sort of sinister looking, aren't they? They abound around Palo Alto. What I remember about them is how they take advantage of the power lines and power poles, and one notices the mess of jangled wires everywhere. Shameful in a community of such wealth! PG&E should have put these lines underground long, long ago. Squirrels on a fence line reminds me of my grandfather's log cabin (again). They tied twine between the Adirondack chairs and fixed peanuts to the twine. During cocktail hour (which, incidentally, started earlier and earlier and went longer and longer as they grew older), anyway, during cocktail hour the chipmunks would scamper up and perform acrobatics to reach the nuts, becoming so tame they would climb in the lap of anyone sitting still enough.

This morning Tinker the Raven was just outside the back door while I made my tea. I went out to water my herb garden and we had a very long conversation about something. He seems to be learning to make those amazing guttural clucking sounds–I don't think there are words to describe that noise they make. Is it romance? He's got a lot to tell me lately. I hope I don't disappoint him.

I finally finished *Waterlog*, a chronicle of swimming up and down Britain's pools, ponds, waterways and oceans. As a swimmer I loved it. Beneath the descriptions of the joys of swimming, is a sad tale of the state of our natural water courses. Now I'm reading *Native*, a memoir of crofting in the borders, the part of Scotland hard up against England. Patrick Laurie has ancestral title to the lands and his experience. He is raising Galloway cattle, named for his part of the Border counties. We find men there determined to breed some pure color, in this case black, determined to control, eradicate, and fix as human engineered even the color of the hides of these cows. Why? Why must we do that to every living thing? Why do we need hybrid roses in colors mother nature wouldn't recognize? Why do we need to inbreed dogs until they can't breathe through their noses? What difference does it make if a cow has a white stripe down her back or, god forbid, she's not black at all but a beautiful roan? Do we humans have nothing else to do with our tiny minds and big mouths full of adamancy and ego? To his credit, this farmer, Patrick Laurie, scorns the colorblindness of his fellow farmers and has found joy in the diversity of black and white. And sometimes brown.

Your book about Florida sounds interesting. I don't know anything about the history of the area between the Native Americans and Colonial Spanish and Marjorie Kinnan Rawlings–a good 200 years of settlement. The Seminole indigenous people have an interesting wealth of culture and history.

Not to ignore the elephant in the room, and what a funny thing *that* would be, but our covid home tests arrived, and our certified approved N95 masks, so I guess now we wait and see where we are in a month after the completely unvaccinated kids have sufficiently mingled. Who is in charge here?

Love,
Jane

P.S. Just read a BBC article about patterning a new sewage system after cow's three stomachs. Finally, cows get some credit.

*26 August 2021 Sunny hazy and warm here, 79 degrees, a whisper of breeze in the willow behind me. The palms are rustling; the sound of home*

Dear Jane,
Who IS in charge, anywhere?! Crossing fingers that your tests come back negative. The double-dose vaccine holds only 66% efficacy, they are saying now, against Delta. As obnoxious as I find those N95s, they do work. As obnoxious as I find Rand Paul, he is correct that cloth masks are useless. Would the rest of the country just get themselves jabbed already?

Your books sound like they could share a shelf with *A Land Remembered*, which I finished reading about an hour ago and I'm still weeping. I've read countless non-fiction accounts of the land booms and busts, the horrific hurricane that destroyed the lower east coast in 1926, the carnival atmosphere surrounding Miami land sales before and after that time. Greedy and short-sighted, the rape of Florida I fear will continue until the sea swallows her whole again.

When I was a kid and we'd drive from Venice to Sarasota and see yet another bulldozed palmetto grove I vowed to my parents that, when I was older and rich, I'd buy up every last lot of vacant land and leave it be. I miscalculated how much it takes to be rich enough to buy up vast tracts of land and pay the taxes and maintenance on those; thank goodness for land trusts.

It's so (not for me but for the rest of the local living world!) hot here today that the birds and squirrels are resting in the shade. I've heard only a single *chikadeedee* from a single chickadee since early this morning.

Your grandfather continues to entertain me. Who would think of stringing nuts between chairs to provide happy hour cheer? My dad might—he takes peanuts to the wide median on Venice Ave that is lined with decades-old Live Oaks where the squirrels frolic. They crawl up in his lap to take their prize, to his profound delight. My dad is adorable, as was your grandpa.

What's wrong with the existing cows? Those cattle breeders bent on single-hued bovines miss the point of reveling in what nature has already given. It's as meddlesome as trying to straighten a river or hold back the sea.

Love,
Medea

P.S. Bruce thinks he'd like to own a shotgun. Maybe he's thinking ahead to a time when I'll have to saddle up the rocking chair in service to those palms across the street.

*August 27, 2021 Moderate air quality, light smoke, sunshine and warmish 78 degrees*

Dear Medea,
How did we get so lucky as to find each other? We might consider dressing up in our granny dresses and boots for the cover of this book we seem to be writing. I have my lever action .22—Annie Oakley's preferred weapon. Should have kept that granny dress from the 70s—oh how I loved that. Back in the early 70s we went camping down in Big Sur and I saw a hippie chick in a granny dress heading for the loo. I looked at myself in sensible shorts and T-shirt and knew a pang of recognition and jealousy I will never forget. Why couldn't I actually live the beautiful life that framed my imagination? Why? "Oh, now" as the Irish would say in a terminal interrogatory pause.

It's very hard for me to resist wishing terrible fates to all those worse than useless people who have and continue to spoil the universe. I don't have the Buddhist ability to smile with some inner knowledge that they will learn in their own time. As shaman we are taught that ill will is sorcery. But just this once would it be ok? I want in the core of my being to wave my magic wand and strike a whole bunch of people clean off the earth. But maybe I don't have to, since it appears covid is going to do that. The politicization of the pandemic is not to be dismissed as "business as usual." It is getting all of us killed.

Love,
Jane


*27 August 2021 88 degrees at 6:30. Usually I'd welcome the warm, but the smoke is holding the heat inside the atmosphere above. I can't see the sky.*

Dear Jane,
I'm sitting on my front porch, sipping air through my N95. We can't go outdoors without one here today—the particulate matter has reached the red level. When I last checked, the count totaled 187ppm. Usually, I'd just be so pleased to be sitting outside, in shorts and a t-shirt, in the evening, in Fogust.

But this is what I've witnessed today:

The little birds don't sing, call, chirp. Are they smart enough to keep their beaks shut or are they fearful of breathing this heavily laden air? The juncos just hop on the ground, not even bothering to try and send a warning signal.

The little birds don't visit the feeders. Are they concerned that the food is now tainted with the fried feathers of their brethren, pushed downwind from the north? Or maybe the heat is affecting their appetites the way it does mine and they can't face the thought of having to actually metabolize food. Way too much work.

The ravens are in hiding. I've seen four today, two soaring, two strolling in a neighbor's yard. On a typical day, I'd see closer to thirty. They would spend half the time in flight and half the time walking around and discussing the fate of the universe. When even the ravens are fermished, you know something is seriously wrong.

And on to your question: How DID we find each other? Shall we credit Scott? Stanford? Cancer? Nope. I think there is a quantum thread that extends from my front porch to your field. We met along that filament—gosh, is it twelve years ago now? You and me, Annie Oakley and whoever Annie Oakley's seaside counterpart might have been: maybe Marjorie Kinnan Rawlings? (Though I'd rather assume Marjory Stoneman Douglas' persona—badass lived to 108 and still worked herself silly saving the Everglades.) Our thoughts, concerns, fears all align.

For two people who have never actually seen one another face to face, we share more than many who've lived side-by-side their entire lives.

It's now 7 pm. The native grasses nod in the welcome evening breeze. The tiny birds begin to chatter.

Love,
Medea


*August 28, 2021 Sun, moderate AQ, On Shore non-breeze meaning: dead still. Earthquake weather. Warm. Warm for here anyway. Too warm for me.*

Dear Medea,
People ask me about how it is I have friendships for so long and from so far away. I credit learning the craft of letter writing to my teen years in Iran and Lebanon. Particularly boarding school in Beirut. No phones, no way to even call home. Every emergency, every delight, every basic need, every bit of wishful thinking happened on paper. To keep friends meant writing letters. Many of my fellow teens came and went in two-year shifts. It was unusual to stay for second and third rounds in those jobs and those conditions. I was a miserable child, pen and paper were my solace. Every day the mail would be sorted by the school bursar. Every day I would stand back staring hard at my slot, hoping for mail. I probably got an average amount, so I wasn't always disappointed. My friends wrote back. My parents wrote diligently, consoling and extolling and cajoling and for three years of bs (boarding school and the pun is not lost) begging me to be happy so that they could get on with their thrilling lives. I know how to keep friends even without in person time, though I do hope someday we will have a glass of wine together face to face. I think you are right, though, there is a line of the energetic kind that binds us. Whatever circumstances came together to bring us to this point, oh my, they could so easily not have happened. Sometimes Fate is magic.

Except for the rattling blue jays, always the neighbors who argue right through the day, the birds here have grown scarce as well. I don't think they are gearing up for something to come, but perhaps they are in that space between courtship and nest building? Tinker has continued to perch on the garage roof morning and evening, more often than not alone, but sometimes with the companion I think might be his mother. The flock of turkeys is growing bigger by the minute and convincing me I might never want to eat turkey again but I am grateful they are so good at eating earwigs. It has been the season of the earwig; the farmers have complained. Because of water resources, our local farm stand reports they will probably close after Labor Day, a good two months before a normal year closure. Yesterday I planted some butter lettuce seeds, but I don't have much confidence in my ability to nurture seeds outdoors.

The reports of the enormous fires seem surreal. To protect myself, I've tried not to think of the animals, dead or displaced and not just by fire, I'm haunted by the abandoned dogs in Afghanistan. All of this is becoming too large to absorb, too difficult to accommodate into a regular day. Every day is crisis day. It is unsustainable.

Love,
Jane


*28 August 2021 88 degrees outside. Indoors, it might be 90. Air quality improved from 186ppm most of the day to a barely non-lethal 105 now. Unsustainable, indeed.*

Dear Jane,
This is why we love our letters. The anticipation of walking to the mailbox, inserting a key, extracting the envelopes, or awaiting disbursement from the bursar defined our connection back then. When I was little, my folks lived several states away from their own. On Sundays, my mom would titter as 5pm approached, since that meant she could share a few precious, spoken words through the beige, wall-mounted phone with her Mama and Daddy. They worked on the lines in the Cone mills in North Carolina at the time. Work so hard it bent my Poppa's spine into the shape of a cane; Nana eventually escaped the mill and earned her cosmetology license. Still, both jobs found them on their feet all day, every day. Making time to write a letter, go to the post office, buy a stamp and then mail it took effort for two bone-tired folks in their mid-40s. Forty was considered middle aged back then. Imagine that.

Love,
Medea


*August 29, 2021 Sunday even though I have twice mistaken it for Friday. Mild with dense fog*

Dear Medea,
I should have known it was Sunday because it was quiet. The plague of motorcycles, logging trucks, and mega-Camper vans took the morning off leaving the only sound that of the ocean. I have noticed that the key the ocean plays most often is A, or sometimes B-flat. There is a new installation for ocean monitoring just north at Albion River, it looks like a 60s space capsule, you

expect to see a disoriented astronaut climb out at any moment. The fog horn at Albion can be controlled by cell phone. Local youths sometimes call up and start it in the middle of the night just to annoy tourists at the inn on the cove peak. There are times when the fog horn is quite audible here and that always augers sunshine. This evening though, the fog was different than usual. Normal ocean fog comes in swirling and dipping through the treetops, a roiling white. Tonight though, the fog is thick and quiet as London pea soup fog that now and then obliterates the forest. My amateur guess is that there is warm and smokey air in the upper atmosphere pushing the fog into a ground level blanket. Air quality is as bad as it can be elsewhere, but here it is good to moderate. May it remain so. Speaking of fog horns, there is a famous Fresnel lens light atop the Point Cabrillo Light Station north of us. Built in 1909 and refurbished many times since its installation, still works today. The light station is one of the most complete working stations in the US. What I love about it is that it evokes a time so starkly different than our present.

Love,
Jane


*79 delightful degrees with breathable air and a gentle breeze at 5:45 on the 29th of August 2021. Feeling concerned for the folks in Louisiana and Mississippi on this auspicious 16th anniversary of Hurricane Katrina.*

Dear Jane,
Do you remember the blue single-page Air Mail products sold by the post office back in the day? I'm not sure these letters still exist, but it was an inexpensive way to write a long letter for a fixed price. Air Mail cost a fortune! When I lived in France, first Paris, then Nice, my mom used these to send letters to me. I wrote on postcards, notebook paper, France's version of the Aeropostale, sometimes daily over the course of that year. Instead of keeping a journal, these letters memorialized the exciting, the bizarre, the loves won and lost, the sights seen and experienced. I asked mom to hand them over once I was back home and she said, "Oh, I threw all of those away."

Fair enough, as I had not informed her of my makeshift journal plan, but I pitched an unholy fit anyway. And this is one of the acts that defines a "Good Mom"; when I graduated from college the following June, one of my graduation gifts, bulky and overstuffed, was a pair of scrapbooks with every letter, card, image and memento that I had sent home over those four years, including the French year. She kept that secret to herself for ten months, enduring my wrath and rage. Hers is "Selflessness" writ large.

(She and Daddy also wrapped a stuffed Cuban Tree Frog, a hideous beast about the size of a small basketball, knowing that frogs are my one phobia. After thirty years of consistent protestation upon receiving frog-themed gifts, I've finally convinced them that yes, I really do not like frogs.)

The gift in receiving letters in the mail is, for me anyway, the time it takes for the writer to sit down at a table, find a paper and pen, and craft a message, then fold it, place it in an envelope, address it, stamp it, mail it. It is not an insignificant act. Bruce chuckles that I get excited, every day, when I snatch the key from the key hook and walk to the mailbox on the curb. Most of the time, 99% of the mail never makes it inside but is tossed direct to recycle, like a bad film that goes straight to video. Yet I do maintain several friends who cherish a hand-written note as much as I do. When a letter from one of them arrives, my heart swells. No longer the love letters that Snoopy would hunt for because "the love letters always get stuck in the back," but letters that contain love nonetheless.

On a more immediately observant note, we walked today when the particulate matter measured only forty-one ppm. The birds remain cautious, yet more were flying and jumping and even calling more than we've seen in the past four days. The chickadees and titmice/mouses (apparently this indecision is an inside birder joke, I learned today) and nuthatches bustled all day around the feeders. The hummingbirds are *chipchipchipping* in the back yard. Even though the sky still looks a might hazy, the birds tell a more optimistic story.

One last observation. In our front yard, we planted a specimen cypress tree about twenty years ago. It's spring and forest green foliage dangle into the street, so every few months, it requires a haircut. As we left the house today, we noticed a silver tag nailed thorough its bark into its trunk. After all of the arboricide, my first thought is that my tree has been tagged for annihilation by some evil tree hater. But not wishing to jump to conclusions, we walked up and down a few other nearby streets and noticed other trees marred with tags. A redwood. A different species of cypress. More redwoods. A spruce. All evergreens. And only in our town.

Stay tuned.

Love,
Medea

P.S. Scores of scorched animals. Thirteen dead Marines. 147 dead Afghans. We have nothing to recommend us as a species this week.

*August 30, 2021 blue sky, sunshine, light cool breeze and clean air—this is what Elk used to be like in August, the little summer when the ocean was calm.*

Dear Medea,

Oh my! So much to respond to. First of all, I can't believe your mother did that! What a wicked thing, good thing she redeemed herself but what cost, the surprise. Yes, we used aerogrammes all the time, much as I hated them, they were cheaper and more likely to reach their destination. The ones we had in Iran in the 1960s were covered with Farsi on the outside, no idea what they said! Probably Yankee Go Home. My mother saved every scrap of letters and gave strict instructions to the folks at home to save all the letters. When it came time to write my memoir, it was such an amazing resource. My mother would have been furious had anyone thrown a letter away. From boarding school my letters were pages and pages of binder paper, or sometimes stationary if it was post-Christmas. We can both thank our writing determination to our time "away." When I went away to college, my parents moved house and my father threw away a box of letters, mostly from boys. Luckily he didn't throw away the box of letters from my oldest and closest friend. And she and I still have all the letters we have written over the past 60 years.

We have become a species of wants and egos and do not know how to find joy in quiet. Lately there is a push to get people outside. "Wild bathing" is a thing that has to be explained. How did that happen? "Forest bathing" is a form of meditation. Well, people had better hurry up and get out there into those forests before they are logged to piles of brush, or burn down. I remember how sad I was about a year ago to read that people of color don't often visit the National Parks. To climb into why that is is to really begin to understand the marginalization that exists for people of color and how important it is and will be in the future that we all learn that joy cannot be purchased, that it is there for us all. I know there are inner city issues, and poverty issues—that's all a part of the climb we must overcome. I would like to see the look on the face of a class full of LA inner-city kids if they were taken to Yellowstone to see the buffalo. Right? How can we learn to care for other animals than ourselves if we only see them behind bars. In many ways, we are all behind bars, punishment for this mess we have made of the environment.

Thinking of fire and scorched animals makes me physically ill.

Love,
Jane

P.S. I've moved the water trough to a better location, and built a brick ladder for the wee bitties who might fall in. I hope the deer find it. The ravens may as well.

They have been active today, very very early. I can recognize Tinker's voice now and he's learning to "bark" at Tweed. This morning he almost gained the wobbly clucking sound. I wonder if that's like boys' voices "changing"? He didn't show up during breakfast though. I think that's a good thing, it means he is with his tribe and not entirely dependent on me.

*30 August 2021, O What a Beautiful Day! 75 degrees. Sunny, blue skies. Fresh breeze. And the birds return to life!*

Dear Jane,

Is your sixty-year friend Kristi? What a treasure to have all of these letters. Returning to our words written when our minds were pliable, forming, questioning, discovering does offer a window into who we are now. We are a culmination of every wise and whack decision we've ever made, every revolutionary thought we've ever "thunk." I recently found a notepad from my sophomore year in college where I'd recorded details of my love life as well as my quest for a meaningful future career. The names of the man-boys did not ring a single bell. I had forgotten that I applied to the National Wildlife Federation for an internship. Once a tree-hugger...

It slays me to think about our lost connection to the wild. That's about as unthinkable a thing as can happen to, or be imposed upon, a person, a people. Building urban gardens might be a nice crumb; a concerted re-greening is long overdue. Immersion in wild landscapes connects us to the rest of our web. When we first visited our favorite diving spot in the Bahamas, the reefs and elasmobranchs welcomed us home. The warm aquamarine water bathes us in Gaia's amniotic fluid. But what keeps us going back is the fact our local Bahamians friends feel kinship to these reefs. We share a language.

These strike me as three critical keys to coexistence with nature: Know your land. Know your source. Know your soul.

South Lake Tahoe is under evacuation orders. Kirkwood and Heavenly, shuttered. As the surrounding forest burns, the structures in the historic town of Strawberry are saved. Lines of vehicles snake across roads that, for now, remain passable. The southeastern quadrant of Louisiana's boot drowns in rain and floodwater, cut off from power and cell service. Are these places where humans should build, putting more lives in peril every fire and hurricane season?

We are Americans. We never say "No."

We might wish to rethink this.

Love,
Medea

*August 31, 2021 finally this month is over. Sun, blue sky, cool breeze*

Dear Medea,

We are hafted to the land of our belonging the way sheep in the Lake District of England are hafted to their high country and wouldn't think of wandering off. They pass this genetic belonging on to their young and generations upon generations of wild yet minded animals know where to go and when to return without much more than a clear strong whistle. Your longing for Florida is your imprint to the land as much as it is to your family and history. I believe we are the collected experiences of our being over lifetimes of existence; those experiences bring us to this day and ask us to choose the next for ourselves. That is the true existential crisis. Do we have choice, and will we make them for ourselves or let others decide for us? I love your quote, "know your land, know your source."

In good wildlife news, today's local paper reports that Mendocino County has revised its laws on killing wildlife. It is no longer legal to kill any wild animal either by proxy through Fish and Game (I guess I'll have to stop calling them the Department of Kill and Maim), or through some right that ranchers think they have because they own livestock. It used to be that anyone could shoot a coyote if they thought it was a threat to their animals. I was not aware that there was an active lobby working toward revising the legalities of predators, but I am overjoyed to hear that the supervisors have agreed 3-2 to ban all killing of predators big and small and use relocation tactics to move animals who are a threat to humans and their livestock. The article further says that systems used elsewhere have been analyzed and statistically relocation works. I won't ruin your day by including here the numbers quoted of dead bear, mountain lions, bobcats etc. that Fish and Game and their trackers have killed in Mendocino alone. Just be happy along with me to celebrate the end of that.

My morning was scattered by the arrival of another caravan of tree trimmers and cutters and chipper machinery. This group apparently tasked with clearing beneath the lower power and phone lines. I know this makes no sense because those lines are directly below the big lines that unfortunately cut a corner of our land. PG&E contractor work is booming business. I was nearly undone at the thought of another day of chainsaws, another day without birdsong. I have not, perhaps, reached the bottom of my resilience, but I can see the bottom from here. It's not a day to even think of the fire in the Sierra, I guess having lived up there it's harder to ignore, harder not to soak up some of the turmoil and fear. It's definitely impossible to walk away. I suppose we must learn to compartmentalize if we are to survive. Meanwhile, a tsunami warning popped up on my phone but I figured, who cares, since I haven't heard a siren or the plane flying by as they do when we really have a tsunami. Surely we all realize there is a limit to what we can absorb? I have to wonder, why do I have a smartphone full of apps warning of dire consequences? Would oblivion be a sweeter state?

No, Kristi is my friend here in Elk, my soul mate for sure, but we've only known each other for fifteen years or so. Barbara is in Vermont but we write every day. It's good for me to have so much communication with my friends, it keeps the bubble plumb. You keep the bubble plumb.

Love,
Jane

P.S. The ravens made themselves scarce while the tree crews were here but they are back and rather agitated. I hope they don't think the trimming was my idea.

*31 August 2021. 72 degrees, per the Weather app, though I'd say closer to 65 with the very busy breeze. The sky is the color of a robin's egg for the first time in weeks, at least in the back yard; looking toward the north, the smoky haze lingers.*

Dear Jane,
As a frustrated, out-of-water mermaid in spirit, "bubble plumb" sounds like an identity I could embrace!

We are indeed hafted to the land, you and me and the salmon and the migrating birds. Another reason to cheer the insight and courage shown by your county commission for its decision to favor relocation over murder. The cynic in me has to wonder what precipitated their enlightenment? And the vote was close—will the next commission have the power to reverse?

Are you familiar with writer Mary Roach? She just published a book called *Fuzz, When Nature Breaks the Law*, in which she writes about her visits with local people in four different international locales and discusses how they manage annoying wildlife. *Annoying* in this case would apply to the coyotes that vex your local ranchers. Coexistence. It's a lesson that some humans are reluctant to learn.

Have you read any interviews with Dara McAnulty? I love this young man. The summer edition of *Orion* magazine published an excerpt from his *Diary of a Young Naturalist*. He's a Northern Irish teenager with Autism who writes with the insight, sensitivity and curiosity of someone who has lived decades longer. Here's a quote you will love, "We all have a place in this world...we must notice it, tend to it with grace and compassion." Dara also keeps the bubble plumb.

I've spent too much time half-listening to and monitoring video of Hurricane Ida and the Caldor fire, twin crises, far and near, at least in part attributable to our own insatiable need for more, our stubborn refusal to listen to the elders.

Do you think it might be time to excavate that commercial from the 1970s with the Native American crying over people tossing trash from their car windows?

Love,
Medea

*1 September 2021 70 degrees, breezy and sunny and brimming with birdsongs.*

Dear Jane,

We're twenty days from the onset of autumn. Who will visit the feeders in the fall months, then the winter months? As a newly-ardent observer, I will watch as the answers reveal themselves. We lack a great migration in this part of the Peninsula; you have to go up to Sacramento, and perhaps parts of the closer-in Delta to witness those spectacles. Spending another season tethered to the neighborhood, while survivable, does little for a heart yearning to see something new.

Though a junco will readily run off a smaller sparrow at the feeder, though the aerobatics of the hummingbirds displays their inner warriors, I don't think of birds as "hating." Yet, this thought has occurred to me the more time I spend in their blessed company. I read an article yesterday about an avowed vegan who married into the Niman Ranch family and after an osteoporosis diagnosis, commenced to eating meat again. Niman Ranch does support family farms and ranches. Many ranchers form alliances with organizations like Audubon and The Nature Conservancy, either donating some land to conservation easements or working with the organizations' scientists to devise best practices that encourage land stewardship. Some even dedicate their land to shared use with over-wintering of migratory birds. It's a solid start. Red meat, pork, veal, lamb, have all been off my menu for decades. Between the filth and inhumanity in factory farming and the unsavory idea of eating baby animals, there's no appeal. We do eat the occasional chicken breast, and I grapple with the decision every time. Bruce asked this morning whether I think the birdies would hate me if they knew I eat chicken. I've asked myself the same question.

You and I have the proscription against tofu and all manner of soy from our cancer days. I'm actually ok with that. A freshly-picked leaf lettuce and tomato salad satisfies for taste and hunger, at least during the summer. Legumes offer wide variety in texture, color and flavor. Will we wake up tomorrow to learn that growing legumes uses too much water as do our beloved almonds?

Awareness is a bitch.

Love,
Medea

P.S. Your description of the lighthouse and the Fresnel lens makes me think how romantic it would be to live in solitude as a lighthouse tender, watching for ships, flashing the warning, curling up with a fog-gray cat in my lap and a steaming mug of tea.


*September 3, 2021 (I had to look it up). Fog, blessed fog. 54 degrees would it be rude to start the gas fireplace?*

Dear Medea,

Catching up after being forced to leave the ocean and drive over the coast range to "civilization" yesterday for a few chores. It's been sixteen months since I entered a retail store, it was a bit of a shock. I can feel my psyche slipping into Hermit more and more. Even though I realize people are healthy diversions from solitude, I'm less and less able to engage and integrate in a setting like Costco. I know, I could have chosen a smaller venue, I didn't actually shop, I just went in for a wee before the drive home. On the way, we saw four young fawns, three safely behind a fence at one place, and farther on a fourth who was distraught and unable to find a way across the highway because of barbed wire everywhere. No sign of mother, but she was surely close by. On the way back, I looked for a dead fawn and was happy not to see one. But still, it added another layer of heaviness to my heart.

Speaking of shopping for meat, which is what we were doing, if I didn't eat red meat I might have to gnaw my own arm off every so often. Somehow I am genetically poor at converting protein and must compensate with a will. I'm allergic to fish. Boring subject but that is to say, the world of food is diverse. Fish feel pain. So do cows. Well, so does every living thing. It's a hard one for me to reconcile and if I had such animals in my care I would be a vegetarian by the end of the first cycle. You and Diane will get along great, she switched from omnivore to plant-based a little over a year ago and loves it. For her it was a matter of eating what she wanted to eat rather than the obligatory meat and two veg.

Meanwhile, several things have happened on the land. Monday brought another crew of tree trimmers. This crew has a bad reputation for making a mess and we have had "words" before. Gene went to interrogate them. They said they didn't have to inform us of when they were coming or what they were cutting. It is true that PG&E have a right of way easement under the power lines and a responsibility to keep the lines up and without threat. We're fine with that. What we don't like is their habit of cutting limbs, topping trees, cutting up logs, chipping slash and then leaving everything lying around—a perfect recipe for fire. Gene, not being one to like being told what can and can't happen came back inside perfectly livid. For some reason it seemed like the last straw to me as well.

There will be letters in the future. Truth is PG&E doesn't give a damn, they are so far alienated and in debt, they have lost any interest in community awareness.

A hawk –a lovely Red Tail who visits daily– just landed on the tree she prefers outside my window as if to remind me that all things move on, don't get bogged down in the ugly and ignorant.

Tinker found the water trough almost immediately. The past two mornings he can be found hopping in and out of the water while carrying on a running commentary, cooing, warbling, squawking and otherwise trying to get me out of bed. I think I will need to rebuild the brick "steps" in the trough. They might serve a mouse, but Tinker landing full weight on the top brick seems to throw it off center too easily. Would he float? Swim? When they take their turns at the dog's water bowl they perch on the edge and tip it to see if there is water, and how deep, and then hop off, hop back on and take a drink. Glug glug. Hop off. There's no chance they could drown. But the trough?

This morning when I put out food I noticed paw prints on the side of the Rubbermaid garbage can "garage." They are small, like a raccoon, but they are about 3 feet off the ground. Maybe a bobcat. Or maybe the prints are upside-down and a raccoon's efforts from the top edge? I'd like to install a night camera. Twice this week, Tweed has growled and sniffed the air with suspicion. Is it bear season?

I have bread in the oven, and a border collie staring at me. Time to play ball.

Love,
Jane

P.S. Further investigation on the footprints and it must be a fox. There is also scat in that prominent "look what I did" kind of way they love. There are prints both directions on the wall. I hadn't noticed before that there is a small sheet of plywood leaning up against the way. The perfect launch and grab spot.

*3 September 2021 7pm, the light shifts from summer's squawking parrot to a gentler cooing, like a dove. 64 degrees, as it was at 7 this morning.*

Dear Jane,
Despite your unpleasant foray into the blare of "civilization"–I'm loath to bestow that presumed compliment upon Costco—by the end of the afternoon you communed with deer, foxes, a collie, a raven, and a hawk. I'd call that "redemption."

I'm standing at the kitchen counter, watching the sun set over the western hills with my left eye, and watching my little cat Loki play with his treat Weeble with my right. The purpose of the treat Weeble is to force the kitty to work for his cookies, but the hole at the bottom of the device gets jammed, so I have to pound it on the floor a bit, dislodge the offending star of treat kibble, and then giggle as he uses his hand to draw a piece toward him and crunch. I know it defeats the purpose of the Weeble, but they try so hard. If Loki and Odin were human babies they would remain dependent upon their mama, and still live at home at age forty.

Bruce and I walked along the reservoir today, the first time we had been on an amble outside the neighborhood in weeks. The water level indicators scream "Don't Shower!" Typically, we would see scores of birds, including waterfowl. Flocks of turkeys. Families of deer. Today, we saw two deer, one at least a mile from the other, browsing for any remnant of green. Two black birds with bodies like footballs floating atop the water. A nuthatch foraging in the tree bark here, a junco hopping with his girlfriend on the ground there. I wanted to give them directions to my feeders.

As the East Coast drowns, we wonder whether it's selfish to flush the toilet.

Love,
Medea


*September 4, 2021. Saturday. Still it was chainsaws that woke me.*
*Overnight fog clearing to sun. It might hit 70 if it persists. AQ good.*

Dear Medea,
I do wonder where the birds go when the outdoors isn't Goldilocks perfect. Sometimes it seems they have an instinct about what's coming, surely the shore birds do—the gulls in particular hunker down all facing the same direction ahead of a storm–and won't that be a welcome sign that we've come through this dreadful season once again? You mentioned migrations, we see pelicans here in the right time, always just off the cliff line, and geese and ducks, Arctic Loons and mergansers in the river though I despair what they will think when they see the river now, clogged with toxic algae. I suppose they will keep moving, look for someplace new. Just south of Elk at the Garcia River there is a wintering spot for Arctic Swans. It is a bottom land of ripe grass, often flooded in the right season. I have made the pilgrimage a few times to watch at dusk when the whole flock rises to the sky as the sun sets, makes a few courses around the perimeter, and then resettles with much whooping. In the past few years the duration of their stay seems to have shortened. If there is no ice in the north, will they bother to come at all? Is it possible for it to already be too warm here?

Tinker knows where I sleep and has taken to muttering about outside the screened but open window, occasionally standing on the roof right above my window. The water trough is under the madrone tree, and he has figured out that he can perch on the wide lower trunk (the tree looks beautiful but suffers from having been rather brutally pruned twenty years ago). Tinker sits on the trunk where he can see into the living room to where I usually sit. He sits for a while and pecks insects from under the red flakey bark. Gene says the tree is too close to the house and is a fire hazard, especially because of the oily nature of the tree. Sigh. So another thing we can't enjoy but must add to the list of Things to Fear.

This morning, three of the juveniles came for breakfast along with mum and dad. Mum is looking rather the worse for wear, her feathers ruffled. I know the feeling. Are there two kinds of mothers? The ones who want to keep their chicks close by, and the ones who throw them to the wind to force them to fly? You are clearly the former.

I have rebuilt the brick steps in the trough. Only the dumbest of the wee creatures could fail to find safety. I have yet to see deer return to the front yard, but we did see them out the back the other day. We've noticed in previous years that September, hunting season, comes and they make themselves scarce. We have "No Hunting" signs up at the entrance to our lane, but the grazing land to the south is a massive area home to cows, deer, mountain lions. Anyway, the deer sense the season and the bucks make themselves scarce. They will be back when the coast is clear, literally, and full of the urge to breed.

September also brings the mountain lions, only coincidentally because that's when our area lands in their roaming itinerary, but also because the dry wild grasses are the same color as their fur. Now that it is dark at the time I take Tweed outside before bed, our first sign that they have returned will often be an eerie cry, like a woman with a broken heart, answered by another not far away. Even the dog understands the hungry warning and immediately heads for the door.

There was a whiff of skunk in the air this morning. It may be that my feeder pest is a skunk. I'm going to have to clean up the area and shift the feeding zone. I've de-skunked too many dogs to be cavalier about an encounter.

You know, if I didn't read the news, and stayed off computer feeds, it might be possible to think it was quite a nice day.

Love,
Jane


P.S. Redbeard the Burglar has been spotted again to the north of the river. 17 hrs. of police activity and he is still in the wind. He was seen stealing beets and onions from someone's garden. Most people would have sympathy for him if he weren't breaking into houses and stealing firearms.

*4 September 2021 A balmy dusk, the sky's pearl gray overhead, shading lighter and lighter toward the horizon, a dull white band, and then the cinnamon glow of smoky sunset at the western treeline. 78 degrees.*

Dear Jane,

I'm sitting on my front stoop in a sundress at nearly 8pm. The distant thrum of tires on the freeway that *clickclick, clickclick* as the cars cross the concrete sections of road. It's warm enough that cicadas are rubbing their burred legs together, offering a melodic accompaniment. Not a non-human creature is stirring. Every tree stands in silhouette. My very own Japanese woodblock world.

Redbeard the Burglar sure has a weird diet. Beets and onions. Is he a Bolshevik? Making borscht in some wilderness kettle? Maybe he steals firearms to take advantage of hunting season? Seventeen hours of police time and no perp, yet he's clearly a known felon. He is a danger to you, and that disturbs me. He knows the woods well enough to escape discovery, and an infinitesimal part of me cheers. The woods are his kin.

Mendocino's waterways are choking with toxic algae. The Chamber of Commerce for the State of California is blind to this reality. Everyone who stands to benefit financially from touting the flawless beauty of Mendo is blind to this reality. So, where does that leave you, aside from offering refuge to your local wildlife and taking PG&E to the mat? If the state rationed water, what would become of the weed and wine industries?

Some animal is making plaintive cries in the back yard. It almost sounds like a tiny bleating sheep. I must investigate.

Love,
Medea


*September 5, 2021 Dry, sun, warm, completely still. And did I say Dry? Seven weeks of Fire Season left.*

Dear Medea,

It's amazing how fast the relative humidity can plummet. From day after day of dense fog, welcome dense fog, to September's classic bone dry and warm sunshine that has chased the ravens into the trees for a much-needed snooze; and the only birds I've seen the last hour have been a pair of little birds in the water trough proving that, yes, indeed, the brick stairs are perfect! I don't know the birds, but one is mostly steel blue gray, the female, I bet, and the other is a gorgeous violet with a burnt orange flare to his wings. If I find my Sibley I will confirm and report back. They took the stairs, they splashed and primped, they fluttered and flirted. I think they don't mind the sticky madrone overhead either.

Speaking of trees, the madrone has a rusty plague on its leaves. It doesn't look as healthy as it often does, but there are seasons to its beauty. It never has the stark serenity of a deciduous tree at rest, it's always in the process of something: losing leaves, cringing leaves, flowering and then dropping the base leaves, and full bloom which doesn't seem to come at the peak of summer as one would expect. Someone else would make a study of this, but I'm content not to run to the library shelves for every speck of detail I don't know. I don't mind making assumptions.

In case you were wondering if my relationship with Tinker has gone too far and he is too dependent on me and my bucket of premium all-protein dog kibble, I'm proud to say my little guy has learned to eat berries! The other evening I saw a dark shape and a rustling in the bushes in the shadow of the woods. A bear? Sadly, no. It was Tinker, eating huckleberries, the dear. I admit, it's not so dear when he shits them onto the sidewalk, the roof, the BBQ and the patio chairs, but I'm a tolerant housekeeper, eventually we'll get it cleaned up. Along with washing the cars, the sidewalk and patio are suffering from the drought like the rest of us. The idea of full force hosing down of brickwork is enough to raise the blood pressure.

As to that, the water or lack of water, yesterday Gene picked up two 4K gallon plastic water tanks to add to the line, we already have one. The idea is to store water when the Rainy Season comes. Oh dear let it come. And then we would have water if the well runs dry in the summer–at least some water. With the configuration of the well we have, when the well pump can't find water, the faucet stops dead. No warning. It is amazing how much we assume from faucets. One year, the year of the girlfriend with very long hair and even longer showering habits, we ran out of water. In a panic and like true rookies we ran around like chickens in the next storm filling empty garbage cans with run off from the garage roof. Amazing how fast that would happen, the filling. We used the very gray water from the very new roof to do some laundry with predictable results. We were a little giddy with the effort, though, the way pioneers might have felt about hopping out of the prairie schooner and throwing a shoulder against the harness beside the oxen. And we learned we should plan ahead, just like the pioneers learned not to try to bring along Aunt Haddy's buffet.

Fair warning: the meat bees have been joined by the mud wasps, as 'tis the season for such things, be careful on your walks. Wasps are vicious little creatures. Just ask Tweed.

Love,
Jane

54

*5 September 2021 Happy me! 79 degrees at 6pm and the birds are singing their evensongs.*

Dear Jane,

I ventured outside last night with a flashlight and followed the sound of the bleating to no avail. It stopped as suddenly as it had started. My neighbor either has a new pet lamb, a very confused dog or a talented parrot. If I find out, I will let you know.

Gene lugged home 8000 gallons of water today? Behind a truck? How does that actually work? We take for granted that turning on the faucet always ushers forth water. You must appreciate the liquid even more when it's a pain in the ass to obtain. Seven more weeks of fire season. We do need a seriously wet November. I'm holding off cleaning out my closet until our first soaker. It's a valid excuse to procrastinate, my own attempt at a talisman.

I am so curious about your violet and burnt orange bird. Using Merlin Bird ID, I entered the parameters that were closest to your description and it returned "Western Bluebird." I hope you find that bird in the Sibley. It sounds like a luxurious bird. Do you know the Lilac-breasted Roller? This bird is an eye-popping confection in turquoise, rose, lemon, cinnamon and even Yves Klein Blue, and as fluffy as a cone of cotton candy. It reminds me of my favorite diving partner, the parrot fish.

Today, my birds defied the heat, and the air that is so dry that my insides feel like dust, and chirped and dived and swarmed and bathed while we fertilized our starving trees. The spectacle of movement kept us entertained. A big, fat Scrub Jay danced alongside, atop, beneath the feeder, succeeding only marginally at snatching some supper. The darling extended nuthatch clan took Sunday Supper together, six at the table, chattering between bites. Afterward, they took turns sipping water from the birdbath, feet hooked inside the chains, beaks down, like avian seahorses. Perhaps something exists in the garden, naturally, that they might feast upon, like Tinker and his new-found huckleberries.

For most of the six hours we tended our yard, those infernal yellowjacket/meat bees swarmed around my limbs, lighted on my thighs and forearms, buzzed the hose nozzle. I wanted to ask "are you thirsty? Then drink!" and then blast them into next week. But. One, that is not right. And two, knowing their temperament and tenacity, they would just, one by one, circle back to sting and bite me. Bruce suggests I stop flailing; it just inflames them and ensures an attack. "Just tell them to fuckoff," he says. Thank the stars we don't have murder hornets.

The advent of autumn gives the garden a chance to pause. The riots from spring and summer blooms give way to repose, even in our temperate climate. The fuchsia trees pump out their dancing ladies, a few rose buds feel the warm and offer one last show. The Hawaiian Ginger should send out its orange and yellow sparklers of sweet spicy flowers in a week or so. Spending so much time tending to my kids, which moments I would never trade for a billion dollars, distracted me from the subtle shifts in this garden.

Get grimy and sweaty and intimate with nature. You will thank yourself.

Love,
Medea

P.S. Last night, we watched "The Courier" with Benedict Cumberbatch, about Oleg Penkovsky and Greville Wynne and how they saved me, a tiny little girl living in Venice, Florida, from Khrushchev and the Cuban Missile Crisis. Well, not exactly. But, indirectly, yes. The big lesson? Two people *can* save the world.

*September 7, 2021 warm low 70s, sun, dry, but a hint of ocean cool air at least. Last night I used one of those thermal thermometers to check the skin temp beneath my breasts: 100.7. I hate summer in all its forms.*

Dear Medea,
The little Gray Jays, the sweet plain cousins of the bastard Stellar blues, came to the saw horse for kibble like boarding school girls in uniform at breakfast. The ravens were not amused, but didn't actually attack as I thought they might. There was some gentle nudging, but not a ruckus. I still haven't found my copy of Sibley. I thought it was by the window, next to the binoculars, and on top of the *Advanced Genetic Genealogy* course book I really really am going to work through sometime soon. "So many books, so little time" should be my epitaph. The true gift of the friendship of winged ones is that I have lifted my head from the page.

I remember the Cuban missile crisis, remember being scared. I was at boarding school in Beirut, Lebanon. At dinner we were told to pack a bag and be ready to evacuate. We did pack, but in the end did not evacuate. In the 60s, one couldn't pick up a telephone and call home. Information came by letter, or in this case, by way of the American Embassy in Beirut. Rumors beat out facts. In some ways, we were used to political uncertainty. Lebanon was constantly in crisis. Coups and revolts were daily occurrences sometimes prompting us to be "campused" while the streets were cleared and danger passed. Not for the first time I think about then and compare it to now and wonder "what's changed?"

We do have bluebirds here. I will make it my mission to find the bird book and figure this out. Stay tuned. There are a couple of tiny birds discussing sex (surely, because isn't that why they chirp?). I can't see them, but one has a simple descant, and the other one just hits one note, over and over. They are, I think, in the scrub of tightly packed new pine trees and water willow where the rabbits warren and where the quail nest. I suppose Mrs. One Note could be on alert and crying for help? The heat of the day as mid-day rises has put the predators to roost. I love to listen hard. So many layers. From close, to the distant fucking rooster who can't tell time, to sometimes, when we're lucky, the shore birds on a calm day like today.

Love,
Jane

P.S. How do we steel ourselves against knowing about bears with burned paws being euthanized? Breaks my heart.

Later:
I found Sibley right where he should have been. I must be blind. That said, I can't decide whether the birds I saw were Warblers, bluebirds (too small I think to be bluebirds), or Phoebes. I will have to wait for them to return!

I should have explained, the water tanks were empty. Empty they are about 400 lbs each. Full? I hate to think. We will fill from our well as we can once the rains come. Please Gaia let the rains come. Gene said on his bike ride Sunday they came across two 5k tanks next to the river, Big River, inland quite aways. The tanks were using a water pumper to fill out of the river and had massive exit ports for hooking up to fire water tenders. Nice to know they are there, but doesn't it seem like a drop in the bucket in today's "megafire" era?

*7 September 2021 7pm, blessedly warm, still as death. 79 or 80 degrees. A raven in the one remaining tree at the tree killer's house has a lot on its mind.*

Dear Jane,
Your water situation baffles me. The fire heroes must pump river water to save bears and forests. Weed growers get a pass. The water level at our local reservoir falls by the week, while Sacramento directs our towns to add thousands of new housing units. Who benefits? As usual, follow the money.

Your description of the violet bird sent me to my Sibley's as well. After forty-five minutes of careful examination, I have no clue which is your bird. My guess? Perhaps a kind of swallow? There is another jabberer in my spring green Curly Willow offering a soliloquy on a mystery topic. I've not heard this song before, and with the exception of the raven and last night's coven of Turkey Vultures, all of the birds in my garden must be too small to make this much racket. Upon investigation, it appears that Downy Woodpecker is reciting a love sonnet to his beloved. Lucky me, the unintended beneficiary.

The nuthatches and chickadees now believe that I am their mama. As I stood under the fuchsia tree to fill the feeder, two nuts and a chick buzzed my head, not more than two inches away. Then, the chickadee perched on a branch maybe a foot from the feeder. It would not shut up. The hungry nuthatches divebombed from the left, from the right, tiny blurs of gray, not at all concerned that I might pluck them from the air and close their bodies in my hand. (I read an essay once in which the author's uncle carefully snatched a hummingbird from its feeder, then purposely snapped it beak. Monsters walk among us.)

I think of you, alone with your classmates, in Lebanon. A cosmopolitan country. Limited communications. Pack your "go" bag—just like now, with the fires and floods.

Is it wisdom or blind nostalgia that leads a person to believe that "progress" is not all it's cracked up to be?

Love,
Medea

*September 8, 2021 fog gave way to sunshine, a light cool on-shore breeze so far but a Flex alert says something else is coming. How can we all live in fear when the sky is so blue?*

Dear Medea,
I was once told by a website developer who consulted for us and kissed my hand when we met that we had Hermit Thrushes and Townsends' Warblers that he spied on the driveway. I now know the thrush and the birds in question are smaller by far anyway. And I know we have Phoebes but I'm not sure of identifying them. We will just have to wait and see.

This morning three ravens came which means competition for poor Tinker. I tried to set food here and there so that no one bird can dominate. Tinker did get a bit. Later I was able to catch a photo with him on the step of the trough. Shortly after I was gifted with a doe and her fawn looking for green in the brown and brittle yard. They walked within four feet of the water trough without stopping.

Have you heard of the Land Conservancy? A few years ago a large land parcel was sold by one of those old-style lumber companies headquartered elsewhere, I think Louisiana in this case, to—of all people—the heirs to a teen fashion fortune. Much was made of their intentions with the newly formed Mendocino Redwoods Co. but as greed always wins, they have been logging redwoods ever since and the *thump thump thump* we hear as logging trucks hurtle down Navarro Grade and sway across the double yellow warning caps says nothing will stop them. What does this have to do with the Land Conservancy? That organization appears to be their charitable arm. To me it looks like carbon offset bait and switch time and only slightly more legit. Some of their projects seem great. The only one they have in California is here in Mendocino. Gene rode by the other day and says they are heavily logging the area, trash, slash, cans of motor oil, and stacks of debris everywhere. So much for Land Conservancy. They talk a good game. Their mandate claims to be forward thinking logging which preserves the forest but also preserves lumber industry jobs. That might have been a good plan twenty years ago, but no one in Mendocino thinks that's a viable future now. Preservation is the future; carbon sequestration is the future. The rest of it is bullshit blather meant to fool us into thinking good people are doing good works. Be careful who you align yourself with. Take a look at Land Conservancy's website. If Al Gore had contested the election results the way a candidate surely would do now, what would our world be like today? Would we have fought a twenty-year war we never could have won? Would we have started working for our planet instead of against it long ago? Oh Al, you don't deserve a sundress kind of day.

Yesterday I thought I should take a nap in the afternoon if only to not be tired if there were to be a sudden crisis or evacuation alert. Is this any way to live?

Love,
Jane


*8 September 2021 81 degrees and a dull blue sky. The tops of the trees dance like an aged, arthritic hoofer.*

Dear Jane,
Had Al Gore won, would the world be a different, better place? We'll never know the answer. Still, he was no oil man, nor an enviro-rapist. Rewriting the past is as impossible as spinning the world backward. Still, you have your go bag. That's your ammo. Take a nap.

The story about the Land Conservancy disheartens me. It seems like the entitlement aligns with Rockefeller's maxim that "enough" is "just a little bit more." I remember empathizing with the loggers when reading about the Land Conservancy originally, and again reading *The Overstory* this spring. Food, clothing and shelter don't fall from the sky. But blacksmiths retrained, didn't they?

This business of "offsetting," which allows a large landowner to exploit part of her acreage in exchange for granting conservation easements or outright gifting other part, does seem to provide convenient cover for some less-than-noble donations The question is who holds the carving knife? In Florida, it appears to be two families of notorious brothers, along with many others, both developers and industry owners. All dressed up in environmental green, they make grand spectacle of donating "critical habitat" while offloading fertilizer into the Everglades and other wetlands with impunity. In Florida, anyway, the governmental agencies are in bed with the landowners, or have been in years past, and refuse to enforce regulations against the powerful. A gripping, if depressing account of how nearly impossible it was, how insanely long it took, and how Swiss cheesy the ultimate protected area for Florida Panthers ended up being, is told by Craig Pittman's *Cat Tale: The Wild, Weird Battle to Save the Florida Panther*. I'd ask the manipulators—capitalist, bureaucrat, legislator—"Have you no shame?" But the answer is pretty clear.

We also need to talk about lithium and cobalt and the mining that is decimating aquifers from Australia to the Salton Sea in the name of electric car batteries. Groundwater poisoning. Habitat destruction. Desecration of tribal and state-owned lands. Electric cars may not save us from ourselves, either.

Love,
Medea


*September 9, 2021 blue sky with increasing cumulus clouds from the south, we could hope for rain but must bite our tongues because of red flag warnings for dry lightning and high winds inland. It seems so unfair. 66 degrees inside and out.*

Dear Medea,
It is a balm to be able to say that while I write this there are five deer in the yard. The pickings are slim but they are finding bits here and there, especially over the septic field. Two does and three spring fawns who have replaced spots with coats exactly the color of the dead grass so that when they lie down, they completely disappear. I don't feed them, but tomorrow I plan to clean out the produce bins in the fridge and will throw the lettuce out in the yard, they've earned it. Once again, they haven't noticed the trough of water. I wonder if they have better hearing than smell? The youngest fawn makes me cringe, she's so small and thin. The does are more a golden color but there is some change in coat here and there. I'm glad I have the woods for them to hide in. The last one down the trail heard Tweed inside and turned, turned to stone, so still, and disappears as if she is the woods itself.

Love,
Jane

*10 September 2021 8pm, 63 degrees. The horizon appears to have been appropriated by a miles-long ribbon of Burmese Python stretched out atop the Western hills. But it's just the evening's tawny glow.*

Dear Jane,

Today, another tiny lizard found itself in my sunroom. Thankfully, my glasses were clean enough to identify it as a lizard and not the brownish-gray oblong that usually presents as cat vomit. Using the time-honored tumbler tactic, I gently nudged little lizzie inside the cup and offered her safe passage away from the felines and into the garden.

One other discovery today to share with you: yellow jackets love the new bird food I found for the ever-growing flocks. Witness as the hungry chickadees alight on the larger feeder, twitch in surprise (and, I assume, pain) and dart away. After watching this for a few minutes, I asked Bruce to hang a yellow jacket trap, six feet away per internet directions. These yellow jackets must have AI, as they seem to have learned that the traps' sole purpose is to lure their deadly, articulated little bodies inside, forever, no exit. After a few hours, the trap swung forlornly from the nearby branch and the feeder hosted a swarm of these infernal stinging pests.

Do you know what yellow jackets hate? Spearmint. And the chemical reaction between cucumber and aluminum. The feeders are now baited. I will let you know whether The English Gardener, whose website recommends these remedies, knows her stuff.

Love,
Medea


*September 11, 2021 73 degrees, winds 17mph WNW. Sun's ablaze, suggestions of clouds over the western hills. It's blowing 25 in SF, the Central Valley's furnace sucking in the last of the summer's fog. Remembering 9/11/2001.*

Dear Jane,

The jury is still out on the efficacy of the mint cure for yellow jacket relief. The sprigs that I wove into the mesh late yesterday had worked free by this morning. The feeder swarmed with stingers, though we did capture a score or so that fell for the trap. I nestled a few more sprigs of mint into the mesh. After several minutes, a few insects buzzed back to the feeder, inspected the mint, flew around it. Two tucked inside, a few more circled around and landed near the mint but finally flew away. When I checked again thirty minutes later, two nuthatches had lighted on the mesh to peck away at the feed. An incomplete solution.

Meddling with nature's way, even this small-scale "dominion," is what we wrestle with; from thwarting meat bees to straightening rivers into submission. I have a theory that this word "dominion," the term used by many to justify injustice to the land, means something closer to *domicile* rather than *domination*. The earth emerged from chaos and evolved over billions of years, finally offering humans a place of beauty and bounty in which to co-exist; it seems wasteful and ungrateful to consider Earth like bottomless Bloody Mary, existing only for us to repeatedly suck dry.

Love,
Medea

*September 12, 2021 Warm, sun, dry. Reading Notes from Walnut Tree Farm by Roger Deakin.*

Dear Medea,
I'm comforted from the above weather by a thunderous ocean, occasional sea bird hysteria, and mare's tails against a searing blue sky. Dear goddess send rain immediately.

Tinker came to talk with me yesterday as I was upstairs reading. He sat on the porch roof outside my window and chatted and chortled and told tales, and laughed. I've never heard such variation in tone or texture. It was like being read a love letter. I find it easier to bear the craziness of our time if I narrow my perspective to what I can see and hear from my wrought iron bed. An afternoon nap in a quietly dimmed room after a few pages of inspiration and close observation by a writer like Deakin, and it's possible to allow sleep full sway.

Love,
Jane

P.S. I don't know how to get rid of yellowjackets but suggest you take the feeder down completely for a week and see what happens?

*13 September 2021 Another summery evening, 75 degrees, a light breeze and a clear, blue sky.*

Dear Jane,
Last week's silent, hidden birds emerged this week. It's like the first day of school for birds in the back yard. I've never heard so many *cheeps* and *chirps* and *haws* and

*graaacks.* The dark green pine trees, the pale green Curly Willow, the spring green Japanese Maple all ring with birds' voices. The foliage remains summer-lush. My song ID skills limp along, so I can't tell which birds sing in unison, and which belt out solos. A murder of over twenty crows appeared this afternoon, flying over the treetops before taking off again toward the west. They circle the canyon beyond the tree killer's house, then head east for the canyon at the end of our cul de sac, and then complete their circuit across the back yard again. Since the spring chicks have fully fledged, this is the crows' fall equivalent of dropping your incoming freshman off at the dorm and taking a road trip with your empty nester friends.

We welcomed two friends from Arizona this weekend, whom we met when our kids were toddlers. We walked them through our garden, picking berries and cherry tomatoes and apples. We pointed out the bromeliads, whose throats turn candy-apple red this time each year and are just blushing at their base. Together, we discovered a stand of white naked ladies that had perked up tall, (overnight?) to join their ruby and hot pink sisters in a floral can-can dance around a cluster of proteas. We introduced the gymnastic nuthatches. The lone Scrub Jay chose that perfect moment to show up and wrestle with the suet feeder. Even a garden this familiar to me undergoes a renaissance when seen through new eyes.

Did you know that Florida (and California and Arkansas and other states with cool, clear spring water) sells its spring water to Nestlé for bottling? A state with limestone netting cradling its sandy soil, and through which scarce fresh water flows. These springs are home to the manatee. So far this year, the dead manatee census equals 600. Manatees face threats from toxic red tide and toxic drunken power boaters. Is it too much to ask Florida's water management district to actually preserve water for *all* inhabitants of the state? The latest Nestlé extraction permit cost the company $115. It has pumped close to one million gallons per day.

Have we forgotten how to turn on a faucet and fill a glass? No, but the bottled water industry and cash-strapped counties bet your soul that it can convince you its spring water, in plastic, no less, hydrates you with a purity that tap water lacks. In Gilchrist County, Florida, Nestlé's bottling permit nets the county over $500,000 in ad valorem and personal property taxes. Seven percent of the county's annual tax revenue.

In Venice, our tap water came from wells. Liquid brimstone. It stunk of rotten eggs, the S-16 content so high that we had to hold our noses to fill the morning coffee pot. When I moved to Santa Barbara, the first thing my neighbor said to me was "you have to order Arrowhead because our tap water tastes terrible." Nestlé bottles under the Arrowhead label, too. Even then, over thirty years ago, the "golden" hills belied parched earth. The Chamber of Commerce should be ashamed. Instead, it urges people from the Bay Area to visit Mendocino while

Gene drives for hours to collect your water tanks. Our Arizona friends wait for Lake Mead to shrivel and their taps to run dry.

Meanwhile in Coachella Valley and Flint, residents rightly—and so wrongly—worry that their tap water will poison them.

Love,
Medea

*September 14, 2021 Sun, very light breeze, blue sky but a faint orange low glow to the eastern morning light, a reminder of autumn. The roar of logging trucks with jake brakes in full cry down the river grade.*

Dear Medea,

Wakened to the sound of many chainsaws in the distance, obliterating the ocean's constancy. Now and then, there is a thud as another tree falls. Men with saws clearing the power line course south over Kristofferson's pastureland. Fair enough, I suppose. We require electricity, we fear fire, and, as humans, what we need reigns. Gene consulted a land attorney last week. We can't stop them, but we can insist on a modicum of propriety, as in advance notice, and proper clean up, contrary to what happened last week when the contracted group showed up and declared they didn't need permission from us, nor did they need to take any mess with them. Thus, leaving great piles of slash and logs to dry nicely for an inferno. Yesterday, a supervisor arrived to see how last week's slashing went. He didn't bother to come to the door (why do I have a Border Collie instead of a German Shepard?). Thankfully Gene was home, so he talked with the super and newly empowered by the attorney's advice gave him a bit of "what for." I'm sure to no avail, but it made us feel better. We can't stop the cutting. But we can ask for what should seem perfectly obvious in the first place. Clean up the fucking mess, people, or you create a bigger fire danger!

Last night I dreamed I lived in a city, or the city as was probably the case since there were hills and for us both the city means San Francisco. In my dream there was a fire racing up the hillside and people were evacuating downhill, clogging the streets. Our car was a big black sedan and I was filling it with clothes and books and at some point in my dream I realized this wasn't either me or my dream but somehow I had dropped into someone else's nightmare scenario. We're all ghosted by the same fear, cutting and pasting it to fit our surface realities but in the end, we all live in fear, we all struggle to find a plane in our subconscious where we can find a moment of security and peace. Plague, fire, flood, and the torment we inflict upon each other...at some point it will all be too much. I've suddenly had the intuition that that moment will not come with a bang, but will creep up on us and one day we'll wake and realize our lives have been completely reduced to one sensation: Fight or Flight. The sun will be too bright, there will be no shadows in which to find nuance, no dusk where the wee ones come out, no veil to reach for where spirit resides in peace. Just endless days of this, all of this.

Yesterday, Tinker introduced his sibling to the trough, and after they splashed and drank and played in the water, up and down the brick steps, hop, stand on the edge, look right and left, more splashing, after all that Tinker spent some time cleaning up. Carefully picking leaves out of the water and dropping them onto the dry grass. What a good bird.

Love,
Jane


*14 September 2021 75 and sunny, blue and lightly breezy—it's a theme this week. The birds partied too liberally yesterday, hung over from too much song and sky dance, they've mostly confined themselves to the occasional nibble and sip, resting comfortably in the trees.*

Dear Jane,
I told my dad about Tinker, and how I think Tinker would score big if you build a YouTube channel for him. Daddy agrees. At nearly ninety years of age, my dad has questions about the way the world works these days. I can relate. Reading books from decades or even centuries ago, the thread that links us humans, the noble and the despicable, runs fairly constant. Saints and charlatans, wicked and wise, clever and simple; we have existed across eons and continents. Until the Industrial Revolution, I suppose people's quotidian lives remained largely unchanged. Wake up, tend the critters or the plot, cook and eat some food, go to sleep, repeat. Maybe read a book if you were fortunate enough to learn to read, or sing or go to a community gathering. City life of course offered more grit and dazzle. And new ideas and inventions—gravity, the printing press, Leonardo—injected food for thought and discourse.

Fight? Flight? Are these our only two options? I find that visualizing a place where all living things feel safe, protected, and at peace keeps me grounded in compassion and the demons of fear at bay. It's a blessing and curse to live far from urban life. The unscrupulous assume no one is watching. All too often, they are right.

Love,
Medea

*15 September 2021 Cool fog hushed the morning, kept the temp at 54 degrees. At almost noon, the sun is fighting for supremacy. A bit of blue, a bare breath of wind and only 64 degrees. Autumn looms.*

Dear Jane,

Today, the first falling leaves of the 2021 season dusted the small patch of grass under the Curly Willow. By the calendar, they dropped a week early. But their time—the time those attuned to the rhythms of the earth—lacks allegiance to Big Ag and school boards, so I believe it must be fall.

The black squirrel believes it to be so. After scouring the maple for seeds yesterday, this morning I noticed its furry self, crouched on a low branch of the fuchsia, studying one of the bird feeders. I watched from the bedroom window as she strategized, planning her attack. The feeder sways about sixty degrees when disturbed which could hurl the squirrel to the ground if her leap lands on the wrong edge of the feeder. She noticed me observing her, maybe unsure whether I would scold her, or worse, for raiding the bird's food. She took a chance, a fast-break along the perch, up the trunk, over to the branch underneath the feeder and executed a short hop up to the rim. The birds scattered. She picked out a cluster of peanuts and a few sunflower seeds, then looked back to see whether I might be approaching.

The titmouse stood on a branch the width of a small knitting needle, waiting for the squirrel to finish. The squirrel squatted on top the feed cylinder, leaving no room for any bird. Six of the chickadees formed a haphazard halo around the feeder. One buzzed the squirrel, chattering for her to hurry up already. One of the pecan-brown bunnies munched on fallen bits of nut and seed, oblivious to the stage play above its head. The inky raven appeared from nowhere; its *haw haw* sent the bunny scurrying for its den hidden under the nearby juniper.

To have an entire improv troupe right outside my window, the stories and actors changing daily, hourly—with this, I am rich beyond measure. Thankfully, Bird TV is free for everyone.

Many voices debate the effects of our relatively miniscule efforts to save the planet. Billions of families burn coal to cook every meal. Foreign fishing fleets fan out across the seven seas, decimating local food sources. Separating compost from cans and using a reusable rather than a single-use bottle can feel like bailing a sinking Titanic with a sterling silver soup spoon. And yet, our modest efforts lend optimism. Agency begets power. Losing faith in our capacity to influence leads to existential paralysis.

What do you think, Jane? I'm not sure an Environmental Revolution will auger anything but civil war—we can't even get half the country to take an FDA approved vaccine and wear a mask. While I admit to fantasizing about scaring the hell out of the chain saw gang with a warning wave of an unloaded shotgun, history makes it clear that using guns and other heavy artillery to resolve differences between us solves nothing and costs multitudes everything.

Our weapon of choice is words. May we wield them in service of the greater good.

Love,
Medea

P.S. You will rejoice with me in the latest news about the tree killer: A stop-work order is in place. Score one for small acts of the ornery and vigilant.

*September 16, 2021 Early morning fog and cool temps giving way to autumn sunlight. I like it.*

Dear Medea,

Well done you! I'm impressed and amazed that a/you got a response about the cut tree, and b/that anyone cares enough to act. It gives me hope.

Your squirrel mischief, they are, all species, such hogs. Hummingbirds can be the worst even to each other! While the squirrels are funny, they are also happy to make messes. Even the field mice do that—once a section of insulation fell out of the ceiling in the garage and it was full of about 20 lbs. of dog kibble! Needless to say, we bin the kibble now.

Not to add too much to the gloomy environmental news but I heard yesterday about the slaughter of 1400 dolphins off the Faroe Islands. The "tradition" of bird and fish slaughters must stop. Once again I am reminded of John Lewis's advice to "make good trouble." The time has come. Or passed, actually.

For the first time in weeks, we have a morning visit from the primary deer herd. Two fawns probably born in June or July are quite brown in color to match the dried grass and dirt of their environment. The adults are caramel colored. They range the dead fescue grass looking for dandelions and small shoots, there isn't much. As far as I can tell, they haven't discovered the water trough yet. At this minute they are within ten feet of it. The young deer look hungry, and perhaps are no longer nursing from their mothers. They come out of our woods, their woods, and munch their way across the yard at the edges where water willow signals moister soil though, truly, there is very little moisture anywhere. They move, eat, and are ever watchful, keep look out for their mothers and mates, and for danger. The ones who do this well are the ones who will survive. From my window seat I'm so close to the fawns that I don't dare move or they will spot me. I'm mentally urging them toward the water. It may just be too close to the house for day time, perhaps they do come at night. Even as the creek dries, there are wet area ferns and other delectables– horsetail, nettles, saw grass still alive, but I heard today that Noyo River to the north is stationary, no longer high enough to gain tidal flow inland. This is terrifying. Noyo is a deep channeled harbor with a major fishery and a substantial fishing fleet moored there as well as the Coast Guard. Sea lions patrol the water in front of the fishery processing plant alongside harbor seals. Inland, sea otters and river otters nest and make their families. I've never heard of the water being so low as to delete a tide without a sandbar. It's time for some research.

The deer have decided to bide a while, folding their legs under them, still chewing the last bite. One of the does is drooling, she must have eaten some star thistle. Seriously, they are only ten feet from the water! I want to shout at them, "Look! Sillies!" Some twisted version of "you can lead a horse to water…" Sigh.

This feels like a Robert Frost moment. We are just observers after all.

While I sit here as very still as possible and enjoy the 180-degree meanderings of hungry deer, it is making me reflect on the human need to "fix" things even, or often, when that fix makes everything off kilter: rabbits to Australia, capybara digging up the neighborhood in Brazil. "Culling" isn't even a nice word, never mind a nice activity. We have no room to allow nature to take its course. We have stepped into the middle of the flow and sat our big asses down right center stage. What you and I do, my friend, in our little patch, is help the creatures we have learned to know, and surely without affecting them one way or the other. Even Tinker knows how to peck around for bugs and disappear for a day or two with his mates. Maybe I'm wrong. What I do know is that putting out rat bait kills rats, but it also kills dogs and cats. Culling hooved animals, predators, and even rabbits alters the natural course of a balance we have already shifted. If you and I draw the line at ants and flies, how can we enlarge that feeling without also impacting the ebb and flow of Life? I suppose, for us, it's one back yard at a time, one palm tree. As I write, one fawn is now less than ten feet from the water trough having a bit of a lie down.

Love,
Jane


P.S. the trough must be considered a failure. The fawn walked up to it, sniffed, and walked on. I think she objects to drinking out of a plastic container. And rightly so.

*17 September 2021 Barely 6pm and the sun is so low. Wind at 13mph, 63 degrees, feels like 59.*

Dear Jane,

We've walked each afternoon, one of the same tired routes we've trod each day for the past Covid months. Again. Still. It's selfish and spoiled to wish for different scenery. Today, I carried binoculars.

The black squirrel apparently spread the word about the fine menu here in the backyard. Again, looking through the bedroom window, I noticed a brown furball perched on top of the cylinder of seed. Too large for a junco or even a robin. I opened the shutter and it started, stared at me, then lunged for the fence. It scrambled to the top, and froze. Its fur is the same pale brown as the weathered redwood. It does get points for attempted camouflage. The black squirrel also came back round today—it saw me sneaking around the corner with my camera. It jumped onto the Windmill Palm behind the feeders, pointed head-down, a very convincing attempt to disappear. Had I not seen the leap, I'd have spotted him only when looking at the photos I snapped of the birds posed on the branches above the feeder.

The brown squirrel returned to the feeder two different times. I shooed it away twice. I considered sprinkling the seeds with cayenne pepper. I found some peanuts in the snack drawer, and lined them along the fence top where he'd tried to hide. One of the squirrels found them. Or maybe it was the raven.

I read about the dolphins. The UN claims the sea will rise by .3 to .6 meters by the close of the century. That temperatures will rise .9 to 1.8 degrees Celsius within the coming five years. Before I understood the dire consequences to all creatures, this warming thrilled me. You have heard me bitch about the cold for years. But your deer lack even a trickle of river water. What do you think wards them off the trough, where fresh water waits? How can low water levels eliminate a tide? You draw a picture of your verdant, pastoral surroundings, your Robert Frost moment. A snippet of peace. Forget the chaos. Until the chain saws start up again.

I read this editorial headline today in the *NYTimes*: "Do We Need to Shrink the Economy to Stop Climate Change?" It concludes with a link to a Wired article from 2020 entitled "Why Degrowth is the Worst Idea on the Planet." Reading these in tandem, it's clear that polarization reigns supreme, even when the goal is saving Mother Earth. Max had to cancel plans to spend the day by the water with me after his team called an "emergency" meeting. As wise ones who can see life's horizon a bit more closely than we could thirty years ago, spending Sunday in the fresh air bests a Sunday on a command Zoom call. No one will remember that call a year from now. I recommend that Wired writer take a thought-clearing walk on the beach.

Love,
Medea


*September 18, 2021 "Rain! Oh rain! Kiss me Everywhere! There's not a moment to Lose!"*

Dear Medea,
You are the sun to my moon, the light to my dark, we would make intolerable roommates, and yet, we agree on everything else. What a joyful thing!

Yes, indeed, it is raining. I wrote that little poem a few years ago on a day like today, rain began falling mid-morning and while it is still just a light rain, it isn't mist, and it isn't heavy fog, IT'S REAL RAIN. And, it is a bit ahead of schedule, not just today's rain which is forecast to be a decent amount though nothing to write home about (though here I am doing the next best thing). It is a bit early in this endless summer season we are subjected to. Generally, for coastal northern California, the rainy season begins on Halloween. I've always said that was Mother Earth's witchy revenge on children and parents everywhere. Poor wet children with their dreadful costumes wandering up and down the three blocks that make up this village, Hwy 1 deserted of traffic, parents compensating with a gathering in the community center afterwards where, so I hear, there is wine. Kids and parents love it. Now, sadly, there are fewer real residents in the village. The west side of the highway bought up by the Jackson Rancheria who have remodeled and spruced up and oh please god don't let them bring busloads of tourists. One of the last of the old timers died recently, the absolutely splendid Prue Wilcox, unofficial mayor, who welcomed everyone with open arms and a sense of wisdom and wit that this town needs. Who will replace her? The leader of the Jackson Miwok apparently spent his summers on the coast and loves it the way I love Wisconsin and you love Florida's Gulf Coast. When two old inn establishments came up for sale at the same time—he jumped. The "tribe" has been generous, friendly, and inclusive, something that cannot be said for the reverse when 19th century gold rush and then lumber rush easterners ravaged not only the land, but deliberately killed every indigenous person they could find. And so here is another shift, another little fold in the landscape and her people. We shuffle down the bench and, hopefully, accommodate and welcome each other. Welcome back. Or just welcome. And yet tiny villages aren't classically very welcoming. It's an interesting microcosm of an earth too crowded with humans. I want to share with you a few sentences from Tove Jansson's wonderful little book, *The Summer Book*.

*Here you come headlong into a tight little group of people who have always lived together, who have the habit of moving around each other on land they know and own and understand, and every threat to what they're used to only makes them still more compact and self-assured. An island can be dreadful for someone from outside. Everything is complete, and everyone has his obstinate, sure, and self-sufficient place. Within their shores, everything functions according to rituals that are as hard as rock from repetition, and at the same time they amble through their days as whimsically and casually as if the world ended at the horizon.*

Isn't this all humans everywhere, and isn't this exactly the fucking problem? Isn't this how it must feel for every immigrant? Whether the Afghan refugees coming to Europe or the US are excited to be here/there or not, whether their lives have been saved, their children rescued from ignorance and poverty, what faces them now? What immense barriers, invisible and economic, religious and racist will stop them yet again from the privilege of creating a safe and satisfying life? Why aren't there more people who understand inclusivity than those who practice the opposite, those who are trained from childhood to exclude, trained in the hallways of their schools, the locker rooms, the club meetings, their churches? How can we change?

Well. Or as one of my favorite Irish phrases goes, "Oh now." Back to the rain. The deer are under the trees to the east of the garage. I saw them before I let Tweed out, so avoided that moment. Their coats are dark brown with the rain, just like the tree trunks and like your squirrels, they were invisible until one of them moved: reached for some grass, took a step or two so as not to be left behind.

The turkeys appeared, oh dear they are ugly now they are grown. All eleven of them still strutting their stuff. Tweed did chase them and they flew into the trees to safety, all but one who was addled and ran around the edge of the swale looking like a naked old man, long gray legs and red feet. It did find the others, no harm done. Thankfully they do not want to roost here—because of Tweed, I suppose. I'd just as soon they didn't.

The rain doesn't bother Tinker who came to breakfast on schedule and seems to be taking advantage of becoming soaking wet to do some much needed grooming as recently one of his siblings apparently shit on him and he's had a patch of white guano on his wing ever since.

Love,
Jane

*18 September 2021 Happy Birthday, Nana Sasser, 106 today. 66 degrees under skies the color of oyster nacre.*

Dear Jane,

Rain. RAIN! Well, you had rain, which I will share with you in spirit. The weather map shows parts north of SF dappled in green waves, moving ever eastward. Too warm yet for the rain to become the snow that may relieve us from this drought. Let it dampen you now, in September, in technical summer. Prepare the cisterns. There's not a moment to lose, not a drop to waste.

I'm going to try to be more like you and less like me this season. Banished are worries about autumn's approach and my annual Fall Funk. Does NorCal have room for two moons glowing in the dark?

When we humans finally realize that we hold the magic wand over our emotions and our reactions, a volcano erupts. I can bitch and moan about short days and frigid nights. Or I can hitch up my pony to the autumnal hay wagon, cozy up with the teetering stack of books next to the sofa, notice which trees go naked and which offer pears and persimmons, light a fire and piece together the 1000-piece Paris puzzle. No succumbing to the Second Arrow. Hibernation is for bears.

Your Tove Jansson quote describes the insularity of some "homes" with precision. For me, there is comfort in sharing your den with those who know that a thunderstorm will pass over in half an hour. That if you head to San Francisco on a sunny summer day from San Jose, you'd better pack a parka. That your 85-year-old neighbor, Mrs. Smith, wanders sometimes, and if you approach her face to face, you can escort her back to her son's house. And Billy Smith will grip your hand in a thanks that bathes your heart. What is wrong with that? It's when you exclude the "other" that things get ugly.

A small town is supposed to be a warm, inviting place. What safer spot to get to know? Within a week, you're on a first-name basis with the cashier at the market and the coffee shop. Some people prefer the anonymity of a metropolis to test different versions of themselves. Yet wherever you go, there you are. We might be happier in one spot versus another if our soul demands a daily climb of snow-capped peaks or a weekly wander among VanGoghs and Lichtensteins. The Afghan refugees lack the luxury of such a choice

How can we change, Jane? The number of corrupt, inept, venal governments across the planet means, in my mind, that "we" accept that our power is limited by the schism in our country, so that voting in many cases becomes irrelevant. We can boycott Haitian rum or Guatemalan textiles or even Texas grapefruit until the regimes feel economic pain, but the truth is that those in power are insulated from any small acts of defiance we might unleash. Is it too naïve to believe that we can use our words to encourage others to show compassion, to light the world around them with grace?

One person, one act, one step at a time.

Though turkeys have flocked through our neighborhood, it's been awhile. We followed that flock, sauntering down our road, wondering where they were headed. As if they had an invitation for tea, they turned in unison into our neighbor's driveway, blustered to the top of her fence, then plopped over into her back yard. When she arrived home soon after, they had helped themselves to the last of her garden's blackberries.

Love,
Medea


*September 19, 2021 Mild, overcast*

Dear Medea,

Your comment about voting becoming irrelevant gave me a sinking feeling as I realized that's where we are now, not where we might get to. How do we stop a tide of people who have figured out that the way to get what they want is to destroy this "experiment in Democracy'? Voting, the right to do so and the obligation to do it with consideration is all there is. If we don't make the act available to all, if we don't defend the right to vote, the safety to cast one's personal opinion into the mix of where does this country go next, if we don't do that, all is lost.

Here's some news: the main herd of deer has just trotted across the yard, skirting the brush and literally hightailed it into the wood. What's amiss? This reminds me that as I was falling asleep last night I heard a gunshot. Poachers? Very possibly. Something has upset them, that's for sure. Now I see them down by the barn, still in a hurry. As I've mentioned before, this is the season we see the mountain lions return. They have a wide area of range but appear to be consistent in their travels. May/Jun and Sept/Oct are the times we have seen them here, but since that makes no sense, I imagine they are here in February as well. One of the things we assume is that Tweed has a tolerant relationship with the deer. They know his limits and he knows theirs. There is an occasional show of whimsy rather than force on Tweed's part as he reminds them he is aware of being a predator. It keeps them from being too comfortable and therefore too easily preyed upon by the real enemy. On the other hand, I have seen a buck corner one of our dogs on the front porch, the dog cowering by the door while the buck stood on the path and snorted and stamped its hoof. It was clear the buck won. Tweed hasn't been out, and now he's older–he's nine–he doesn't spend time outside on his own, so he's not the alarm but they are definitely alarmed.

I promised elsewhere to write about the General Sherman sequoia. This morning's news is that the tree, so far, is safe. Let's not give too much credit to the news that there has been fifty years of grove management using controlled burns on the forest floor, or to the twenty-foot-high wrap of foil. The tree is the tallest single stem tree in the world (probably, this is debated) and is estimated at 2500 years old. General WT Sherman is an ancestor of mine, for better or worse, so it was fun to read the comment section of the SF Chronicle article. Sherman was to the Civil War what the atom bomb was to WWII. Opinions range according to birthplace mostly about Sherman's march across the south. I have letters from another Sherman ancestor who was part of that march. It was, for northern soldiers, as if they marched across another country. They pointed at and mocked the women who chewed tobacco and spat. Many of them had never seen plantations or the slaves who labored there, and often the soldiers when they were at home, labored as hard and lived as poorly but were free to do so or not. It was an education in boots that rotted and guns that misfired and lines of warfare where you could call back and forth to the enemy and ask them "what up." I think my point though is this, are we similar enough to be one country, or has this experiment in states united been a mistake? If it weren't a mistake, how would we explain the determination with which some ideologies persist 100 years later? Would it be better for everyone if these united states were divided up into cultural countries and loosely networked the way Europe is? I couldn't be more of a Yankee in ancestry and mindset, so I want to know what you think from a southern point of view. People love to joke about California becoming its own country, but is it such a bad idea? And, not to poke you with a stick at all, but with Florida overrun with northern snowbirds, has the melting pot method worked at all? And why is there unrest now?

Love,
Jane

P.S. Tinker came to breakfast with the shit all cleaned off his wings.


*19 September 2021 74 and clear, breezy, calm. Judging from their nattering all day, the birds approve.*

Dear Jane,
Do you remember the letter in which I wrote of the TV commercial from the 1970s with the Native American crying over the bag of fast food tossed at his

feet from a passing car? That ad had a name: "Crying Indian." I read an article in *Business Insider* yesterday about how manipulated we are by Big Everything (this one was about Big Oil), and how it systematically, through advertising and corporate messaging, seeks to pin the blame for climate change based upon fuel consumption on the driving public. The article references the Crying Indian commercial. All part of the plan to make us feel like shit about ourselves while the CEOs laugh all the way to their private islands on their private jets. Big Coal. Big Oil. Big Tech. It doesn't leave much space for Big Democracy.

You have poachers shooting deer? Can't they wait until season if they have to engage in mammal murder? Tweed defends and the deer know he's a bit of a paper tiger, and the dance goes on and on. There you are with a front-row seat for "Tweed in the Bambiverse," endless entertainment. Odin and Loki need to up their game. They spent the last eight hours or so snoring on top of the cat condo. Odin did leap to the window early this morning when he spotted a nuthatch in the rhododendron outside the family room. The bird flew away, the curtain fell. If I moved the squirrel and bird stage to trees outside the family room window, how long would it be before an alpha critter emerged? Given the likelihood of violence or injury or death, we'll let sleeping cats lie.

We could go on forever about Texas and the abortion laws. How is it that a group of people who believe their opinion about another person's body is unassailable change their tune immediately when someone utters the words "vaccine mandate"? I know many Texans, good people, smart and reasonable, so I won't disparage by tossing the lot of them in the same pot of stupid. But their duly elected "leaders" surely belong there, on a slow boil, until their nuts shrivel to raisins.

I'm not sure the fix rests in drawing new boundaries, though that may minimize the prospect of an ugly, bloody civil war. Your Sherman relations marveled at folks who were surely relations of mine. My mom's people, the men anyway, and my Poppa's mama, definitely, spat "snuff juice" into disposable paper cups while rocking on the front porch after a long, hot, hard day in the fields. Little Grammy was in her late 80s when I was a little girl in the early 60s, so not Civil War era herself, but she learned that nasty habit from someone. You're pure "Yankee" but what does that mean now? I don't think, fundamentally, we are all that different.

The melting pot, though is a fairy tale. Big Government looking for more votes, perhaps? Florida suffers not necessarily because of the influx of new residents, but because so many of the newcomers are not invested in the community. Their time is limited; either because they are seasonal residents, or because they believe they are too old to care about voting for school bond measures that will increase their property taxes and ensure that the public-school kids grow up to speak proper English, know how to estimate, and at least possess passing familiarity with the Bill of Rights. Not that this is a hot-button issue for me.

The unrest appears uncontrollable now not because people are any more or less tolerant than we were fifty or a hundred years ago. It's because "if it bleeds, it leads" guides not only the network news but the hundreds of other media outlets on offer. And if nothing is bleeding, well, let's make something up! A large percentage of people today learn the latest news stories from social media. Much of that "news" is algorithmically slotted in to their feeds to stoke their confirmation bias. The sources of this "news" remain unchecked. It's a wonder we're not already in a full-scale conflagration.

Which is why we hew to our animals, our trees, our understanding of the innate goodness inherent in these. Today, two Nuttall's Woodpeckers visited the suet feeder, one a black and white female, the second a male with a rich, full red head cap. What I believe to be a family of three ravens, perhaps spiritual friends of the newly-groomed Tinker, also passed by. A Scrub Jay came looking for peanuts. And the usual assortment of tinies. During our walk this afternoon, I heard a hellacious commotion, deep, throaty vocalizations, and looked up to see two Red-tailed Hawks crossing paths, diving, one chasing the other. One of the hawks seemed to clutch a long object in its talons. A snake? A black rat? Whatever it had, the other hawk demanded she hand it over. And, I found a dime on the street!

Though this is one of our five well-worn routes, novelty favors the curious mind.

Love,
Medea


*September 20, 2021 Sun, warm, on shore very light breeze Summer returns*

Dear Medea,
I find the selective memory or definable ignorance of younger generations about their elders really annoying. In the case of Baby Boomers which includes me, I would like to know if they would prefer to serve in a draft army? Wear a coat and tie to work? Be educated in a segregated system? Not have reproductive autonomy? The opinions of the young are not based on any reality. When there is meat to eat, everyone gets fat. Post war generations always thrived, but it took a global uptick in economy to pay for the rebuilding of the devastation from two World Wars. My parents and grandparents all believed in ZPG and kept their families to two children. They recognized in the 60s that the problems of population growth would bring all of us down. The advances of technology in the past fifty Baby Boomer years lack any comparison in previous generations. I say, "you're welcome. Now get off my back." The problem seems to be that while all this great stuff was happening, the grifters and opportunists were also

thriving. The few Fat Cats became many and institutionalized greed. That's not a generation, that's the unfortunate human condition. And in some sort of inevitable "fall"—here we go, the Roman Empire, Sodom and Gomorrah, the Dark Ages. Everything has an ebb and flow. Human survival is no exception. When I was a junior and senior in high school in suburban Chicago, I took a bus one night a week to a boxing gym in inner city Chicago where upstairs in the break room I tutored inner city middle school kids in English and writing skills. No one said I should do that so my college application would look fuller, no one said it was required for a diploma, no one said competition for slots means you have to do tons of extracurricular stuff. Someone said, hey, we've organized a school bus to do this good thing, who wants to go?

I have strayed too far from our mandate and I apologize for the rant. What we do in ignorance we often have to regret at length. Any time we refuse to think critically, we lose. Isn't this the purpose of college education?

Yesterday Tinker tried to pick up and fly away with the blue plastic watering can. He worked at it for a while. Then he dug up a small polished quartz stone, one of those you buy in a bag to decorate a walkway or garden area, he perched himself on the garden fence solar light with the stone in his beak looking forever like some sort of totemic image. What can I learn from him? He dropped the stone with intent and watched where it landed. A gift. I've noticed the past few days he is braver and more willing to get close. When Tweed and I are outside he is there, sometimes only a few feet away either perched or flying overhead. Watching, and watching out for me. Even just writing about him calms me, refreshes my heart from the angst of ranting about what a generation thinks of me, when, I'm not sure I care. Maybe this is the cycle of age for every generation. And so it goes.

Did you know that the woodpecker is a totemic sign of the need to get to work? I heard one here yesterday but wasn't able to find him so not sure what kind he was. I like it when they peck the wood phone poles and they ring hollow and loud.

About culture, Southern culture in particular, my Yankee-ness, it is surely our being hafted to the land, as we've talked about before. It's why I long for four seasons. I'm sure the chewing and spitting in the south was a direct result of tobacco growing and use and, sadly, addiction. Not that northerners didn't smoke, but it was a male habit. But tobacco use must have staved off hunger, don't you think? Who wouldn't chew it if it made the pangs soften? It reminds me of the Q'ero in Peru who would dip into the little string bags of coca leaves they carried and hand them out to us. The first day we were with them, they showed us how to take three leaves and fold them and chew, like gum. This was how we dealt with altitude. We drank coca tea as well and put it in our water bottles, but chewing the leaves was more potent. There were times when I really wanted to spit.

Love,
Jane


*20 September 2021 Last day of summer. 81 degrees, sunny and blue. A perfect send off for my favorite season.*

Dear Jane,
This will be a brief letter. It's essential for me to eke out the last couple of hours of summer with a walk. The woodpeckers must be my totem avifauna; that they are redheaded (at least the males) honors our kinship. These Nuttall's must peck the pine, but they do so quietly; only the Downys make that kind of Tommy gun *ratatattat* that gives them away. Kind of like a really good exhaust system on a car.

As far as the Millennials thinking poorly of our generation, they will be so stunned when Gen Z turns thirty and blames them for all of society's ill. Every generation is convinced it invented sex. Every generation basks in the certainty of its moral superiority over its forbears. Were we this annoying with our parent's generation? God, I hope not, although I do recall taking my dad to extreme task for leaving the water running while he shaved. I shudder to recall this now, but I told him I hoped he was first in line when the world runs out of water. He was standing at the bathroom mirror at a hotel, probably in Miami or the Keys. He wore his undershirt and a pair of trousers, getting ready for a Florida Bar meeting. His face turned pale gray. His eyes lost their usual light. That was forty-five years ago. His bewilderment and pain stay with me.

Every society has its intoxicant, does it not? Opium, kava, chaat, coca, tobacco, alcohol, ayahuasca. Not knowing why we are here feeds a bottomless fear that these things numb. The practical uses—staving off hunger, combatting altitude sickness—perhaps these are legitimate. Micro dosing LSD and ingesting magic mushrooms obliterate consciousness barriers, apparently. We have one friend who claims that mushrooms opened a door nailed shut by an overbearing father and a soul-crushing divorce, allowing him a life-affirming clarity of mind. And Cedar Waxwings get drunk on berries and weave in flight to the point of crashing into trees.

Universal Life Church has confirmed my appointment as a Minister. Now, I have the power to marry two consenting adults; this offers backup, should Dylan, the official officiant for Max and Haley's wedding, somehow be waylaid in April. I'd thought of going to seminary at one point, and have considered following a Buddhist path of ministering. Where I've come to rest is upon the pew of compassionate attention and equanimity. Though the ire that wells up inside me from Gates and his spyware, Elon and his carnival in the sky and Bezos—just writing his name inflames me—shows me that I am far, far away from enlightenment, with or without a mind-altering boost. As with law and medicine, this continuing, evolving, quest to abide in bodhicitta and offer to others unequivocal compassion is why we call it "practice."

Love,
Medea


*September 21, 2021 blue sky, warmth soothed by a slight off shore breeze*

Dear Medea,
And Happy Equinox to you as well. There was a time when I would spend the day in ritual and ceremony. I like to think now that the spiritual part of me is always in ceremony, in a state of receptivity and, dare I say, power, at least I hope that's true. My friend, Baba, asked me yesterday if I would also call myself mystical, or a mystic. I'm not sure what that really means, but I think I would say "yes." I honor my power in all its manifestations. I think of our relationships with our wild partners in life as mystical, don't you? Speaking of mystical, last night I dreamed a white raven was perched on the roof peak, and its feathers were covered in words. Sadly, I cannot remember what the words were. Tonight, I'll try to get back there.

I might also have been good for the seminarian life except that in my early schooling years I didn't believe in god. Pretty funny to go from no gods to many gods but there you are, one of the mysteries of life. I've never been pulled to Buddhist ideas because it is such a male dominated ideology, as they so often are. More should be made of the First Nations beliefs in matrilineal society, recognition of neutral sexual identification as something to be honored and revered, female leaders and shaman. Congratulations on your ministry elevation. What does that cost these days? There was a time when I was going to do that, but the Hermit/Mystic in me decided I wasn't enough of a showman. I think I missed something along the way, I didn't realize Max was getting married. Congrats to them both.

Yes, all generations do this bitching, I have an uncomfortable memory of a similar problem with my own father at the dinner table. I guess that's required for learning one's place.

I'm not good at using mind altering substances but I am aware of people who have had life altering experiences, and also know people who have worked with micro dosing LSD for bipolar disorders. All of them say it changed their lives. Many shamanic practices avail themselves of the local "weed" whether it's peyote or ayahuasca–I think sure it's a faster way to the gate, but it's better to get there through meditation. My teachers, the Q'ero, didn't use anything but the heady altitude of the high Andes. Though there was/is access to and use of San Pedro (trumpet vine) on the dark side. Trumpet vine grows so big in Peru! It's amazing. We were taught that the vine is very protective. If you plant it near your door it will keep people away. The vine can be jealous.

I'm disgusted and heart sick at the killing of the dolphin pod in the Faroe Islands. I signed the petition you sent. Perhaps the thing that will change those old habits fastest is for tourists to stay away.

If you were to exile to some remote monastery or place, where would it be?

Love,
Jane


*21 September 2021, the REAL last day of summer. Hot, so hot the blue is afraid to appear in the sky.*

Dear Jane,
I jumped the gun declaring yesterday the last day of summer. Today promises to bake the entire Bay Area. The annual Flower Piano event at the San Francisco Botanical Garden plays this time of year—the garden imports a dozen pianos and scatters the instruments throughout the fifty-six acres of green and bloom. Professionals play at intervals, melodies waft over and between the trees. But the pianos are open to everyone in between. That is where the magic happens. Gray-haired ladies, (maybe former piano teachers?) take a seat at the bench, close their eyes, and let their fingers remember a Rachmaninoff concerto. Tattooed and pierced teenagers tickle an experimental melody from the ivories. I've seen a six-year-old boy play with the same reverence from the gathered public as it offers to the pros.

It's no wonder that certain religions ban music. Playing, dancing to, and feeling music is a revolutionary act that confirms our shared humanity.

My friend Lisa and I are volunteering as greeters at the Garden this afternoon. The weather forecast calls for the usually fog-shrouded grounds to hit a sunny 81 degrees. Expect the crickets that have been out partying on these warm evenings to join in, chirping along with the pianos in tonight's finale.

This morning, I saw two birds that I thought were jays chasing each other, finally landing in the pines across the court. They chattered like mad, then one uttered a sound like a long *buzzzzz*. It sounded almost like a bullfrog. The Cornell Lab, harnesses citizen scientists to record all manner of bird songs, calls and "other sounds." Jays are much like mockingbirds in the sheer number of calls they make, mimicking ducks, other nearby birds, and even dogs. That's some evolutionary genius. The only similar call on the site was recorded in Maryland, so not a Western Scrub Jay, but the sounds are identical. And this was a pair—the jay that comes to my feeder comes alone. I guess the word is out among the jays too. Bruce suggested I might want to get a part-time job to pay for suet and seed; he offers that both CVS and the Post Office are hiring.

Today, I am grateful for the summer that was, the autumn that will be, and the gift of this blessedly broiling day.

What remote place would I choose for my remote monastery? Fakarava, hands-down.

Love,
Medea

P.S. I watched a raven go after a hawk at the Botanical Garden. Feathers scattered across the Great Meadow. I had a moment with a dad who was with his kids in a blue tent under a tree, listening to the pianos. We locked eyes after we watched the harrowing spectacle overhead, left speechless by this pursuit set to music.


*September 21, 2021 nice symmetry to the date. Earthquake weather. Hot baking soil, the sun sucking every bit of that beautiful rain away. I can't get cool, my body temp just goes up. And up.*
*Reading* The New Yorker *magazine,* Where Do Species Come From, *Ben Crair.*

Dear Medea,
What a lovely way to spend an afternoon! I took many piano lessons in my youth and still own the baby grand that was my last piano but I never play it any more, my little fingers won't cooperate and flex out of joint if I try. My father was an amazing extemporaneous player and would have loved your garden setting. He was never shy and couldn't resist a piano with an empty bench. He was a skilled classical player, but I think he loved just wandering around the keyboard more. I hope it is a beautiful day for you. Wear a hat.

I was reading a New Yorker piece this morning about species and how they split. In part it is a criticism of Darwin for implying he had nailed "the origin" of species when he had not actually done so. The article is about a German biologist and his work with Crows. Close enough, but my mind wandered and I started thinking about human evolution now that we know Neanderthal interrelated with Homo sapiens, and then there's the other new species recently found but I can't remember if we have found evidence of overlap there. And of course, this should be no surprise to anyone with a brain. The new people wandered into a camp of the old people and two of them thought, "ah ha! I'd like some of that sweet thing." Humans are so silly, so intent on being special we miss the in between joys that growth and evolution can bring. Without a geographic barrier to force a species to keep itself to itself, the default is usually some kind of blending eventually. Now we are learning that contrary to historical beliefs, Neanderthal had bigger brains than we do and there is evidence of social structure and culture that even incudes ritual—which is the archaeologists sneaking up on the idea of a spirituality without having to commit themselves.

The last few days Tinker has brought Ma and Pa to mealtime. I have no idea where the other four siblings are. Ma came this morning with a feather half off her wing. She kept tugging at it and finally wrenched it free and flung it on the ground, re-refluffled, and settled down to some kibble. She always seems to have fluffier feathers than her partner. She could be the cartoon image of the German housefrau, portly and a little bit bossy but loving and wise. Tinker brought Ma and Pa to the trough and showed them the steps. He has been pecking around a lot on the ground and eating whatever he finds so I can feel less guilty and concerned at making him too tame to survive.

We have jays here who mostly *squak squak squak*, probably in alarm at something. Once I was swimming and watching the trees at the same time and the jays were going wild. I looked at a nearby tree and there was an owl, at noon, sitting in the tree. No wonder the jays were crazy. The quail also have a big vocabulary but I don't think they are mimics at all. I love the rising trill. They are at least one gift of warm weather.

A good cool swim brought my renegade body back to normal and I have turned on the AC. All the birds except the buzzards have retreated someplace cool as well.

Love,
Jane

P.S. Have you noticed that the written equivalent of bird sounds in bird books never equates to what you've just heard?

P.P.S. I looked it up. Denisovans do share DNA with some modern humans, most closely with a group of indigenous people from the Philippines. Science appears to prefer to refer to these Paleolithic people as subspecies of archaic humans. Like us but not so tech savvy. (And who knew savvy has two v's? Seems greedy.)

*23 September 2021 Summer returns with a vengeance. 81, hazy, still. Only two of the ravens and one jay are squawking today.*

Dear Jane,

When Bruce was leaving for work this morning, I heard him moan, "Oh god it's all yellow." The sky? Did someone paint our driveway in the dead of night? "What's yellow?" I asked.

"All of the leaves. It's really fall."

So, it appears that I will be learning to love fall for the both of us.

I have noticed this about the sound descriptions in bird books. But I love The Cornell Lab's book, *The Backyard Birdsong Guide*. It's an audio field guide for Western North America. With its push button sounds, it reminds me of the song books the boys loved when they were little. I refer to it constantly. Not only does it give interesting tidbits about the birds in the yard, it makes me feel like I'm among little kids again.

You bring up a point about Buddhism and paternalistic religiosity that incites a pang of guilt. I never did "get" feminism, much to the chagrin of my mom and her friends. I guess because my dad is so kind and I couldn't understand why I should be angry with him and assume he would not be supportive of my or any woman's professional aspirations. But the key thing is that I took reproductive freedom for granted. *Eisenstadt v Baird* allowed contraception for unmarried couples when I was in the ninth grade, before I'd even had a date. When the *Roe* decision came down the following year, intercourse was not on my radar. So, I didn't understand what all the ruckus was about. I only heard the true horror stories much later. If the Supremes overturn *Roe*, they will face an eternity of karmic torture for all of the uteruses scraped clean on a dirty kitchen table by a beady-eyed stranger, and for every death of a woman who must resort to a self-service abortion. When Dylan left for college, my raison d'être left along with him. I thought Buddhism might offer some light, or direction. If I was no longer functioning as Mom, my role for the past quarter-century, what was the point of going on? My primary teacher, Thich Nhat Hanh, (known by his devotees as Thay) encourages respect for all beings equally. The male domination—from the Pope to the Taliban to the Baptists—is meant to keep us submissive and pregnant. No thanks. Anyway, with deep study and much meditation, I got over myself. And seven years on, after all that initial hand-wringing, I remain "Mom" to two loving, tolerant adult sons.

The Cathars, who I still harbor visions of tracing through the Languedoc region of France one day, espoused, among other heresies, equality among the sexes. In the 1200s. According to one account, the Cathars were a "collection of freethinkers, cranks, and rabble-rousing preachers, with a fair smattering of ...cunning women." The problem with hewing to dogma is that it relegates the mind to nothing more than a bulletin board, with its cork drying out as the years wear on. I can't think of anything more antithetical to our capacity for limitless thought.

So, we end up either accepting blindly, which some call "faith," or we reject any imposed belief system, which some call "anarchy." I think the Cathars, and the Buddhist writers that I've studied (and there surely are writers from other disciplines) adopt a path that swerves with the rhythms of the sun and moon and seasons, accepting that we are literally just passing through. So, let's leave good works in our wakes. Defy greed and corruption wherever it attempts to impose. Does such a belief system have a name?

You and I have an overwhelming amount of Neanderthal, which I would not have been so keen to admit a decade ago. Large brains, living in harmony with the land. Welcoming to the tiny-brained Homo-sapiens, the poor dears. Our ancestors lay down with the curious, more upright brutes, and the tree of evolution budded yet another branch. It seems that every biological discipline is discovering new species, merging species, extinct species. I read this morning in *The Guardian* about how we are rapidly specializing our staple crops into dangerous homogeneity. A goodly portion of the world's seeds rest in the control of just four corporations. Think about that for a moment.

My friend Bobby told me that his girlfriend refuses to cut back their bolted lettuces because she is harvesting the seeds. *Garden and Gun* magazine frequently runs articles about regeneration of forgotten foods, from ramps to certain kinds of rice grains to pawpaws. We will not go quietly into Big Ags good night.

Love,
Medea


*September 24, 2021 warm, dry, blue sky. Very typical for fall on the coast*

Dear Medea,
Various times over the years people have gifted books of Buddhist teachings to me, often the "American" versions invariably written by converted Jewish Americans, a subject I know nothing at all about but seems to be a "thing." Jack Kornfield was my favorite and I respect him for not taking on a name other than his own. I did read his book about "after the laundry" cover to cover. I confess to have only grazed around in the other titles on my shelf. My mother collected Buddha sculptures and on her death the pieces were divided among us. I have a 3-foot wooden Buddha on the stair landing which is supposed to stop all our wealth from rolling down the stairs and out the front door. I did place a mirror

next to the door as well, to throw off the inclination. All children who visit are drawn to the little man who is the same size as they are and so his belly has been rubbed many times for luck. Just the other night I gave him a pat as I walked by on my way to bed. My point being, sometimes these things of a spiritual nature are sentient and elusive but we find them in our own way. As for the Cathars, you mentioned them to me when we first met. You are clearly drawn to them. I would like to know more.

What strikes me in reading about feminism and abortion rights is two-fold. First, isn't it always the case that we are subjective beings? We fight for what we have been deprived of, we are loath to engage where we have no anchor. This is going to be a bad thing for us as a species. It so succinctly explains why we are at "code red" for climate change. The oldest among us don't care because they will be dead, the youngest don't care because either they want to have some of what their elders had first, or they see the future as nonexistent. The middle of the subjective sandwich is the generation with the most on its plate: racism, police brutality, climate change, war, and personal rights including abortion. How can they fix all that?

For you, abortion rights and the feminism brigade of bra burners and political activism had peaked leaving you with all rights intact and perhaps your self-esteem as full formed as possible. For me, abortion rights came six years too late. I became pregnant at 18, last year of high school, and, importantly, the first time I had intercourse. What a different life I would have lived in penance for that one mistake. I traveled to Japan with my mother and found a back alley abortion, an experience I wouldn't wish on anyone, and an experience that will become the norm again if this country allows *Roe v. Wade* to fall. I don't regret my choice. I want all women to have complete dominion over their own minds and bodies. What worries me is that women think they have control, but we must look around, because the truth is, we are still being held back and manipulated by misogyny. There are so many important and terrifying crises happening today and in our immediate future, we roll along and put ourselves at the back when that's the last thing we should do. Without full power in our own determination, we cannot help anyone else.

I have strayed again from the natural world, wound myself up in a knot, frustrated and angry with border guards on horseback and Texas laws and stupid people who won't get vaccinated. Let me shift and tell you about Tinker's morning. He found me in my window seat and in order to be close by he landed on the front porch where he discovered the 3-inch-tall temperature gauge which he proceeded to knock down and then take apart. When I finally got up to see what the clatter was about, he had taken the lid off–no mean feat since it was a sliding thing, I'm not sure how he managed–and he had one battery half out. The whole time he was doing this he was muttering and chirping to himself.

I put the gauge back together and distracted him by tending to watering my lettuce seedlings. These little buds aren't going to make it if Tinker doesn't stop landing in the grow bag where I planted them. About half the seeds are left. Then I emptied the trough which was dirty and smelly with tannic water from the madrone leaves which fell from the tree above. I rinsed the trough and refilled it, and rebuilt the brick ledge. Tinker hopped around about 4 feet away, watching my every move. Next on the agenda is to give Tweed a brush and bath.

If lifetimes come and go and, in some way, (to tie this all back to Buddhism etc.), perhaps karma, we chose the life we get/need/deserve it is fascinating to look at a life like yours compared to a life like mine and wonder at the plan. I'm not at all sure any of us humans has it right about the universe and the Order of it all.

Love,
Jane


*24 September 2021 73 and dull here. Fall can't make up its mind.*

Dear Jane,
You are right about the importance self-determination and agency. And my own spoiled upbringing, during which free sex and love with an (un)healthy dose of great drugs mixed in was only brought to an abrupt, traumatic halt with the AIDS epidemic. You had to endure the worst of all indignities. And it's happening again. Dumb as stones, we humans are.

Max phoned as I was writing to you. Max knows things. "The Bible gives instructions on how to induce an abortion," he said. Hmm. I had to look this up. "It's in the Old Testament, though," he claimed. And indeed, passages exist in Numbers that talk of "bitter water that brings a curse." And passages that discuss multi-centenarian men impregnating their wives. I remember a conversation with an anthropologist, a specialist in Polynesian culture, who explained the social structure of the pre-Missionary Polynesians. They did not believe that a fetus became a person until it took its first breath outside the womb. There's a certain wisdom there.

Tinker and her antics give me pause about the ravens in my yard. Is my yard boring? Thankfully you were on hand to remove the batteries from her clutches before she pecked them open and swallowed the innards. The only shiny objects in my yard are the old CDs that swing from bamboo poles to keep the hungry ones from my crops. The tomato plants will need to come out this week. The necessary heat to turn the remaining green fruit to red eludes us. Before I plant fall lettuces, which I know the sparrows here love to munch, I'll find a shiny something to stir their imaginations.

Bruce says we get the spouse we deserve. There's a karmic temptation to extend that sentiment to life in general. But I'm with you. The Order of the universe holds its cards close.

Love,
Medea


*September 25, 2021 fog, light mist, cool. My kind of morning*

Dear Medea,
It is true that there is herbal lore about many abortifacient herbs which can sometimes produce early term miscarriage. In general, though, it's not as simple as a cup of tea. Too bad. Of greater concern to me is why Max is reading the Old Testament and whether he thinks that information is sufficient to replace constitutional laws on behalf of women's right to agency? This sort of thing is how OWM (Old White Men) in Congress think women can choose not to get pregnant, like cats, and so they deserve it when they do if they are raped. A+B=Stupid. I will assume that Max, being yours, knows better and is only digging out bits of knowledge he has accumulated along the way of life. Any decent herbalist will note herbs that should not be ingested while pregnant. That doesn't mean they will successfully unhinge a fetus. Some are blood thinners so strong that surviving the massive bleed out is unlikely.

Funny, but I think of Tinker as male. Damned if I know for sure though. For a while I thought the male raven had a Cathar's hood capped on his head but now I'm not at all sure. Sibley's wasn't illuminating either. When Tinker finds a mate we might find out. The only way I could tell the difference between Ma and Pa was that Ma's feathers were always ruffled and frenzied as if she just took off her apron after cooking Thanksgiving dinner and, hot and frazzled, stepped into the frame of the family photo.

I was thinking about where I would go if I went in search of the monastic life, and surely it would be some quiet place in France where they served wine and good food at the table, and had a beautiful chapel where a choir of angelic voices rang out daily. That made me think about the fact that the farther north you travel, the more austere and unwelcoming, in fact painful, the houses of god are. Scotland? Norway? Iceland? No thanks. But why is that the case? Calvin and his pinched up sense of ritual. Took all the beauty out of observance. Ritual is theater. As shaman we learn that early. We don't need the dramatic paraphernalia but it helps get the supplicant in the right frame of mind to accept what we're about to do. Sometimes religions take it too far, but who's to say eating a cracker or taping a little black box to your forehead is or isn't the way to find god? I think the more ritual, the better.

Back to karma. The existential thinkers would say that the "existential threat" often cited in the media today is actually this: we all have a choice to make, to not make that choice is the threat. To allow someone else the agency over our Being is the error. Choice. Choice is the solution. We must all think as if we are the ones we have been waiting for. Only we can save the planet. Only each one of us can decide to act. The existential threat comes not from without, it comes from within, from the ennui that kills our desire to act.

It's apple season. I hear that the bears have been in various orchards up the road. It makes me very happy to imagine a bear full of apples, snoozing beneath the branches of a heavy tree.

Love,
Jane

*25 September 2021 65 degrees, overcast all the way up. Humid, at least according to my hair. But it looks like fire weather to me.*

Dear Jane,
Though there are many more important issues to discuss today, first let me assure you that Max's familiarity with the Old Testament—with any Testament for that matter—is purely intellectual. When he was a tiny boy, he would willingly accompany me to St. Bede's Episcopal in Menlo Park on Sunday mornings. Our priest, Kitty Lehman, spoke in honeyed tones of forgiveness and grace. Her Southern drawl, her dark hair that slowly turned gray in a loose bun at the nape of her neck, her easy laugh all reflected my notion of how a person of God should look and act. Kitty performed the "Thanksgiving for the Birth of a Child" for both Max and Dylan. I wrote the script based on a similar service in my deep maroon Book of Common Prayer. We located a big-hearted and open-minded rabbi from Stanford to co-officiate. When Kitty retired a few years ago and went home to Texas, the magic moved with her. Max very likely indulged me so that we could have punch and cookies in the Great Hall after church. But he can still recite The Lord's Prayer, and I think there is some small part of him that finds comfort in those words.

Which place might offer you the best monastic retreat? You love the chill and gray. What about Brittany? Those churches, cold, gray stone pierced with brilliant stained glass, offer quiet refuge. Smaller towns, smaller sites. In Aquitaine, a compact maize-hued stone chapel with a terra cotta barrel tile roof sits in a field near a national park just outside of Labastide-d'Armagnac called "Notre Dame des Cyclistes." It used to serve as a chapel for the Knights Templar fortress that sat nearby, but the Black Prince took care of that in the 1300s. Since the 1960s it's served as a cycling museum and bicyclists who have competed in the Tour de France donate their jerseys. We tried to visit a few years ago, but the caretaker was picnicking on the grounds nearby, a sacred ritual not to be disturbed, and my travel companions were anxious to reach our hotel. Americans' eternal ritual of chasing the next moment, ignoring the present. When ritual offers framework that allows the practitioner to dwell in the spirit of what she seeks, I agree that it can serve a purpose. Some rituals, like live sacrifices, are best forgotten.

Choice. I read a piece by Jerry Saltz about Jasper Johns today that I can only describe as "epic." (An over-wrought word.) But Salz met Johns at the upper floor of the Guggenheim in 1986 and that chance encounter haunted him ever since. The reverence for Johns the man and Johns the artist ooze from this essay. He quotes Johns as insisting that his art comes from a place of helplessness: "I decided to stop becoming, and to be an artist," he said. "If you avoid everything you can avoid, then you do what you can't avoid doing … You do what is helpless, and unavoidable."

You and I would likely agree that being part of this existentially threatening "now" demands that that we do what must be unavoidably done. Saltz goes on to dissect many of Johns' most iconic work. The inevitable conclusion is that Jasper Johns notices things. Small things, things that should be obvious to every sentient person but rarely are. The choice is to see. Right action flows from the conscious act of noticing.

I'm happy for the freedom of your apple-munching bears.

Love,
Medea

P.S. Bruce is outside brushing Loki. Loki cries like a little human baby, so much so that when I talk on the phone and he meows, my communicant fears I've dropped an infant. His yowls scatter the birds.


*September 25, 2021 overcast cleared to sunshine of the autumnal kind*

Dear Medea,
We're on a similar schedule apparently. I brushed Tweed and chopped off a great big pile of hair from the aft end. In his old age his coat grows really long and luxurious down the mid-section, with a ruff of white curling locks. The

tendency for burrs to hitch on is at its peak about now, those small round ones being the worst. He's very patient with the process, but that isn't to say that he likes it. We followed the brushing with a bath, or more accurately a shower in the purpose-built mudroom. Now he smells strongly of lavender which must really annoy him. But he does look healthier and slimmer without all that rear end hair. We are noticing that Tweed is having a harder and harder time with the stairs. I'm worried about the future. Will we buy a sling and haul him up every evening? Or give in to his preference to stay downstairs. I always feel safer with him nearby, but logic would say I should prefer he be on guard, at least give me a running start on escape.

I read a little about raven sexing. It appears I may have it backwards and my assumption about the disheveled feathers might indicate a male. I just can't bring myself to think of Tinker as female, yet. I'm not sure we'll ever know. After reading around a bit I started to worry about Tinker thinking I might be a suitable mate and thus not go find one of his/her own. I should have more confidence in Mother Nature, no?

Today the quail were more a passel than a covey and appeared to be eating deer poop but who knows, I wasn't close enough, and didn't want to startle them into the bushes.

The hawthorn tree, surviving another season, is full of red berries. A magazine from England says one can make cordial, jellies, even ketchup with the berries. But I know that as an herbal medicine it is a heart regulator. Would it be wise to make ketchup? More research. Again. This time of year the *Country Living* magazine UK version always talks about sloe gin. If I lived where there were sloes in the hedgerows, I would make sloe gin. My *Country Living* UK is probably akin to your *Garden and Gun*. Reading it always makes me want to paint my kitchen cabinets, have a wild swim, or put on wellies and take a long walk in the wood with Tweed.

Is zucchini chocolate cake really worth making or just a way to disguise a vegetable long past being interesting?

Love,
Jane


*27 September 2021 What is that gray puffy stuff obscuring the sky? Rainclouds!*

Dear Jane,
I walked outside to deliver the recycling to the bin and felt a soft prickle on my skin. Rain! Well, drizzle, but a welcome relief for all of the flora and fauna in these parts. Let's hope it portends well for a monsoon winter, *sans* mudslides.

Tweed smells of lavender while Loki and Odin smell of fish. I've tried bathing them. They object with fierce swipes at my forearms. The older they get, the more they tolerate brushing, which helps with kitties since the self-grooming leads to hair balls. Not an issue for pups. I imagine you sitting next to a sweet-scented Tweed on the porch stair, thinking of the lavender fields in Provence, waiting for the deer to come by for their evening quaff of water, watching the gray autumn sky, listening for the mischievous Tinker.

I wonder about Tweed's burrs. Are they sandspurs? We swore at them when I was growing up, particularly once they turned black; one misplaced step and the bastards embedded themselves in your sole, only extractable with soaking, a needle, and a bullet to bite on. The G.Os who work at the Club Med in the Bahamas where we love to dive call them "foot fuckers." If you've had your foot fucked by one of nature's miniature mace plants, the name makes sense. Far more poetic than "sandspurs."

The tree wars may be resuming. The town sent a notice that the neighbor is requesting permission to remove "trees and stumps" and install artificial turf. The only remaining trees are the palms. According to the county website, if the circumference of the trees exceeds thirty-eight inches at four and a half feet above the ground, they are considered "significant" and cannot be removed. I walked across the street carrying a tape measure and eyeballed the trunk—careful to avoid trespassing. My guess is that the trees are safe. And yet the owner of the property is a Master of the Universe. People like that are not accustomed to being told "No."

And who installs artificial turf these days? It melts in a fire. How do you clean up melted plastic grass? What if it oozes into the house that sits below it on the hill? What toxins does Astroturf brulée emit? It lasts ten to fifteen years on site, then the tattered remnants wind up in the landfill. Whose genius idea was that?

Have you tasted a hawthorn berry? How can the fruit become ketchup *and* cordial? Do let me know what you decide. My pineapple sage, aka pineapple salvia, is blooming in a riot of magenta blossoms. It sits between the lemon tree and the regular sage. Following a *Garden and Gun* recipe for fried eggplant with butternut squash salsa, fresh tomatoes and sage sent me into the garden to harvest. The hummingbirds came at my head from every direction as I had the audacity to position said head between their pointy beaks and the juicy salvia. I stuffed my pockets with as much sage as I could grab in a fist and dashed for the garden gate. They really do sound like tiny jet engines.

The last time I drank sloe gin was in high school. The last time I drank any gin was in high school. The mere mention of juniper berries gives me a headache.

Love,
Medea


*September 27, 2021 Rain! Oh lovely rain. Mild temps and soft Irish rain*

Dear Medea,
Such a lovely thing to wake up to the sound of rain hitting the leaves on the madrone outside my open window. It is a steady rain, soft the way the Irish describe it in their ironic kind of way. We noticed this morning that there is a slight green cast to the yard as tiny green shoots begin to push through the dirt. It has excited the quail to cover the yard, pecking all the time. I love their coloring, the stripes of black and gray and now and then tan. Their funny calls and bobbing manner with the spearhead top knot on the males. They are endlessly entertaining to watch. I went out to the mailbox and came upon the deer herd, almost right on top of them before I even saw them. They weren't interested in me, or at least not in a panic sort of way. They did slowly rise to their feet and prepare to move, but decided I wasn't a threat. Their coats have gone bark colored gray which blends in so perfectly with the dirt and the trees that I didn't know they were there and as they rose, each one surprised me. Seven in all. On the way back in the house I saw that Tweed had been outside and stepped on a slug. He left most of the slime on the kitchen floor. Have you ever stepped on a slug? It's like wet gum and harder to get off.

Love,
Jane


*28 September 2021 66 and breezy, wispy clouds, setting sun. It's fall.*

Dear Jane,
When Max was little, he loved a program on Nickelodeon called *Doug*. Doug was a sweet, sincere kid of maybe twelve whose alter-ego was Quail-Man. Doug dressed in his tightie-whities, wearing a cape and a belt wrapped around his head, the tongue propped upward like your quail's spearhead topknot. We used to have a covey that lived in the canyon, and everyone squealed with joy to see ten or fifteen of them bobbling across the street, crossing from one canyon to

another. The quail disappeared for several years, but a few returned in 2020; this year, though, nary a quail. In Florida, we loved the sound of the Bobwhite Quail when I was growing up. Unlike the descriptions in the bird books, this quail really did squawk "*bob WHITE bob WHITE.*" The sound, and the striking brown and black streaks flecked with white, melded with the landscape, as though each belonged to the other. The Bobwhites largely disappeared with the advent of the razing of the piney woods (for the f***ing condos!) but one of my friends who remained loyal to our town tells me that they are, slowly, retaking the neighborhood.

My landscaper friend tells me that while I might love the Canary Island palm, it is not indigenous so I should not get all worked up about losing this tree. I told him that, after reading Richard Powers' *The Overstory*, the trees now talk to me. This one tells me it's happy where it lives.

We spent a small fortune trying to save a Bay Laurel that shaded most of our front yard. That tree fought so hard to survive. Its old, gray stump remains, now stubbled in fungi and shoots of euphorbia. And there is a mysteriously similar volunteer growing, hidden, inside a nearby thatch of bamboo.

The Nuttall's Woodpecker perched on the branch above my head and clucked at me when I replaced its suet this evening. Rather than fly away and hide as it usually does, though, it remained in full view, hopping up the trunk of the adjacent pine tree, peering down to chart my progress. Is it becoming used to me? Like your deer and Tinker?

Love,
Medea

P.S. At the pet store today, the adoption cases showed three cats—two siblings with adoption pending and one skittish amber-eyed calico. I had a calico as a kid, Cleo, who we rescued as a kitten from a dumpster in the Keys. She lived to be twenty-five.

*September 29, 2021 a perfect autumn day if you like sunshine. Cool. Light breeze, slant sunlight, crunchy leaves falling*

Dear Medea,
As to whether your bird recognizes you, I'm sure he does, even with the caveat about "bird brains." I mean, why not? There is the argument that we all should have with ourselves about whether and which animals have processual logic. My cousin Jimmy says cows don't have processual logic, meaning I guess that he believes they only think in the moment. But more recently it has been shown

that cows do exhibit anticipatory fear to a degree bigger than just the smell of blood. Sorry, I think I've strayed here into a subject many of us, myself included, don't care to dwell on. Back to birds, if they arrive when you step outside, surely they connect you with food, and thus "recognize" you.

Yesterday as you know we traveled two hours inland to Santa Rosa. While I sat in the car I watched the steep hillside to the east of the offices where we parked. There was one dead tree containing eight or so buzzards and another half dozen crows. (I read that the difference between ravens and crows is mostly size, but also crows don't soar, they only flap their wings). Every so often the birds would be disturbed from their perch and use the warming thermals to circle (the buzzards) or flap around and play, perhaps mate (the crows). There must have been something dead up there. The old tree was completely bare but there was evidence on the ground of a fire and perhaps some homeless occupation up there. Since I was sitting in the car waiting and waiting, I had plenty of time to imagine a few possible plots. I also had plenty of time to be very grateful that I don't live there in the middle of the cars and asphalt and trash. Trash! California highway maintenance should be ashamed but the residents should be even more ashamed. Recent mowing of the verge on the freeway reveals so much trash it's heartbreaking. Back to crying Indian level. And did we ever settle the question of whether the actor who did that commercial was really a Native American? I would have to say to people who think they want to come here for vacation and she what California is boasting about—well, don't. It's embarrassing, but our roadways and parking lots and public places look like Spain in the 60s where I once saw a teenager finish her giant soda drink and just let it drop on the terrace floor of the outdoor restaurant. And she hadn't even bought it there. Have you ever had tapas at a bar in Spain? All the little squares of wax paper building up to a foot deep around your shoes? Ugh. We're no better now and now Spain has learned and cleaned up their act. Today's headline ads for the *NY Times* are supported by the Plastic manufacturers against reductions in plastic use. Grass roots campaigns are the thing that will work. If only we could find some green grass.

Here's some joy. As we returned to the coast yesterday afternoon and crossed the Navarro River bridge back onto Hwy One we saw at least 75 brown pelicans floating in the river! What a treat! I would have loved to stick around and watch if they took off—and surely they will, or did, because there are no fish for them in the river. I will check and see if they are planning to spend the winter with us, that would be splendid indeed. We do often see them traveling south along the cliff edge in groups of a dozen or so, but so many together and in the water, was heartwarming.

And a poem I wrote in 2010 about a pelican on Manasota Key in Florida.

**Brown Pelican**
The gulf sea, agitated and grey, still settles us,
the pelican and me,
into a cadence of energy, a rising…

a falling, and I imagine his great gullet
filling with the words I'm rolling around my mouth
not yet certain of their order or importance,

words that glimmer like the sun on the wave crest
words that run deeply like the fish he dearly wishes.
And now and then he carries my words up into the sky

banking, a flick of unsteady wing trembles, he hesitates
and dives, so certain, and I turn back to the strewn pages,
myself hoping for fish.

Have you noticed the moon all day? Watching us.

Love,
Jane


*29 September 2021 75, clear, sunny. All of the birds sing in avian harmony—
except the hummingbirds, who can't get through a day without divebombing my
head. No moon visible here—it must be hiding behind a tree.*

Dear Jane,
Today the earth around me feels like she's offering every treasure; the sun warms,
the trees whisper, the birds delight, even the tomatoes are fighting to redden.
But the news. Oh, the news. The Ivory Woodpecker, gone. Multiple species of
mussels, gone. Several nectar-loving Hawaiian songbirds, gone. Not rarely seen.
Never to be seen again. Species loss is sad in itself; but what happens to the
insects these birds ate? The fresh water the mussels filtered? The plants, terrestrial
and aquatic, that shared symbiosis with these lost creatures? Listening to the
recording of the extinct birds reduced me to tears. Me, and nearly everyone who
wrote a comment for the *Times* article. Many of us have recognized for years if
not decades that the trajectory of unchecked consumption and reproduction
would spell the demise of humankind. Between Covid and Forever, a glimmer
of acceptance appears to be forming.

After wiping my bird and mussel tears, I found a link to an article in *Current Biology* my friend Bill sent entitled "Overfishing drives over one-third of all sharks and rays toward global extinction." Overfishing sits on top of habitat loss, pollution and climate change. What a sorry stew. So, we take out the birds, plants, crustaceans then go gunning for the apex predators and rays. Let's build more "affordable housing" while we're at it, getting rid of ever more acres of trees, shrubs, coyotes, deer, banana slugs. Big Fun! The billionaire space cowboys will be living in lavacrete tiny homes on Mars, breathing God-knows-what. If Bezos relocates to Space, is Amazon still on the hook to deliver plastic "must-haves" in a single day?

You noticed the same thing that I did when we drove to Alameda on Sunday, to San Francisco last week: Our highways look like garbage dumps. Under the overpass that leads from Jack London Square to the tunnel into Alameda, the trash clustered in impenetrable hillocks, plastered to fences and abutments. I have been to a Spanish tapas bar, but not in the 60s—by 1989 when I was there, the Spanish had gotten their eco-act together. That's thirty-three years ago. It occurs to me that it might improve the lot and mental health of the tent dwellers that sleep nearby, in the midst of all of this filth, to be hired by the town to clean it up. It's a job that does not require a lot of training, it would improve the community, and they would have a purpose and a paycheck. As I write that, I can hear the howls. I guess it's more humane to allow people to destroy themselves and their dignity?

Your pelicans (Oh Happy Day!) are my call from the Town, which came in as I was about to write to the *Times* to ask what the hell they are doing, taking an ad from the Plastics Coalition asking readers to oppose the Plastics tax (But it looks like someone beat me to it—that banner is now replaced with an ad for Pratt Industries that makes 100% Recycled Boxes.) The woman from town hall called to talk about my neighbor's plot plan. She's a landscape architect who shares my bewilderment over the use of Astroturf in the 21st century. She is overseeing the project. She expressed disbelief, then surprise, then relief that fresh green fronds are shooting out of the decapitated palm's head. And all plans for all projects within the town must pass muster with her office.

I'm going outside to check on that moon again.

Love,
Medea

P.S. More good news: The 400,000 acre Daintree Rainforest in Queensland is now back under the control of the Aboriginals.

*30 September 2021 82 degrees, clear blue sky, not a single cloud. Yup, as we say goodbye to Q3, it's summer again.*

Dear Jane,

In a radical act of self-love (a phrase I hear more frequently but have never spoken) I skipped my usual Thursday housecleaning in favor of a six-miler with a dear friend and an afternoon with a stack of environmental and literary interviews and articles. The sheets are clean and the bed is made, the rest will have to wait. It's sometimes healthy to goof off.

Richard Power's latest is called *Bewilderment.* On a parallel track with *The Overstory*, this new book looks at our inner life in relation to nature, the whole concept of interbeing. One of the book's threads considers how we have muted individuals' differences, particularly kids', with labels and drugs. Ever since Max's elementary school principal suggested I put him on ADD drugs, it has occurred to me that taking the curious and intelligent mind of a sometimes-disruptive child and wrapping the gifts in chemicals so as not to annoy—or challenge—the teacher is a dangerous approach. Of course, there are undeniably some children (and adults) who benefit greatly from certain pharmaceutical interventions. And there are others who do better with latitude and encouragement and patience.

What I do love about Powers is his veneration for every living thing, a bona fide Biophile. He lives in the Great Smoky Mountains, a place near my grandparent's house in North Carolina. We would visit them, then strike off for the Smokies in our camper. I remember colors, mostly—blue-grays, bright greens, and deep ruddy reds. Oddly cool mornings and evenings, so much different from our sticky, stormy Florida summers. Inky nights with billions of blinking lights, so many more than we can see these days. Lightening bugs by the hundreds, tiny yellow flying lanterns. The creeks where we hopped boulders across frigid water to explore what might be hiding on the other side. We never saw a bear, only traces of their pads and expended lunch. It would have been so cool to see a bear.

Anthony Doerr writes about the Hubble Deep Field in *Orion Magazine* and it reminded me of the Smokies's skies, all those stars. When I was little, maybe six or seven, I'd slip out of the house in my pajamas while the neighborhood slept, carrying my telescope, and set it up in the driveway. Even looking at our ordinary companion moon felt like taking a forbidden trip to a secret spot. Doerr describes the immensity of the universe: trillions of celestial bodies, billions of galaxies, too many planets too far afield to begin to count. Some galaxies resemble the flying spaghetti monster, others look more like the Trinacria, a three-legged Medusa head, symbol of Sardinia. He describes the earth as a "chickpea" compared to the "beach ball" sun.

I pondered these writers' incisive brilliance this afternoon while wandering along the reservoir, the warmth of that beach ball on my skin, an indistinguishable mote on our chick pea home. We may be careening head-long into the worst extinction event the world has ever seen, but all of those stars will still sparkle plenty.

Love,
Medea

# *October 2021*

*October 1, 2021 Indian Summer—where did that come from, and is that appropriate?*

Dear Medea,

Oh my! Leaving you to your own devices for a day has produced a year's worth of things to think about. We will never be bored as we go not so gentle into this good night.

I mostly read non-fiction as well. Occasionally I find myself deep into a novel but the older I get, the more difficult it is to immerse in such a way as to commit to fiction. The exception being Niall Williams newest novel *This is Happiness* which is in the top five of the best novels I've ever read. My nonfiction stacks are almost always related to the natural world, never related to politics.

I've only been to the Great Smokey Mountains briefly. Gene's favorite aunt and uncle lived just south of Asheville for the last two decades of their lives. They are beautiful, though the steady stream of folks in and out and up and down is a crisis in the making. When I was a little girl, my grandmother bought me a beautiful pewter bracelet of a dogwood blossom. It was the first piece of jewelry I had, and I still have it, the treasure. I realized on our first trip to North Carolina that she bought it in the Smokies, and the Arts and Crafts Movement art studio where it was made is still there, still making dogwood blossom jewelry. I'm a big fan of Arts and Crafts period style, and it was a special connection to make as I was writing a couple of articles for *Piecework* magazine at the time.

I'll see if I can find a way to read the Doerr piece. I'm sorry you don't have a dark sky every single night to engage with. I love the magnificent sky at night. I have a telescope but no really good place to set it up. Too many trees and no permanent place that suits. Once a few years ago we took a guided outrigger canoe trip in a dark sky in August in order to see the bioluminescence in Big River which happens most years. We were treated to a meteor shower at the same time making it hard to decide whether to look down or up! And have you been to the Andes? The southern sky at night, oh my, it's disorienting and magnificent at the same time. We camped out with the Q'ero shaman, and they pointed out their pantheon in the constellations. Of course, the stars couldn't have been any brighter.

Finished the Pico Iyer piece about Handel, and other music. I find his writing mood altering and this piece was no different. I love listening to music but don't do it often. It sometimes tangles up my emotions and I can't break free of the melancholy I have brought myself to. I like my music loud. All-encompassing and embracing. Have you listened to the Islandic band Sigur Rós? The lead singer invents the language he sings in as he goes along. It's truly a gift of the angels, as Iyer says. Can you imagine singing words no one has ever heard before?

The world is full of wonder. Best we leave the housecleaning aside and roll around under the deep forest canopy while we can.

Love,
Jane


*2 October 2021 78, clear, and mild in the shade, animating all the critters.*

Dear Jane,
Does "Indigenous People summer" sound like pandering, or trying too hard? If it's offensive, it's unintentional, but either way, opinions will abound.

Another faunal clamor outside sent me running—this one sounded like a cross between an old bullfrog and a duck. I expected one of the woodpeckers, but the Nutall's kept quiet, except for the signature *taptaptapping* on the scraggly pine. Looking in the direction of this odd noise, there sat the brown squirrel, on a lower limb. It didn't exactly tell me what got its goat, but did keep chattering for several minutes, sending me indoors for peanuts. I set the treat on the fence rail—whether squirrel or raven or jay will get there first is today's garden mystery.

I will send a link to the Doerr piece. Though I've not had the good fortune to visit the Andes, I've stared at the black and silver sky from my tent in Uluru, from the bow of a runabout off Florida's Marquesas Islands, and from a field beyond the edge of habitation on Maui. No mystics or sages to point out the pantheon, but the gods imparted their wisdom just the same. Will young people today see the night skies as we have seen them, sparkling and endless? How many of Elon's satellites hover up there, polluting the heavens between earth and eternity? What happens to the pantheon when somebody actually inks a contract to shoot our plastics and other garbage into space?

Sigur Rós played Outside Lands a few years back. Opposite Metallica, both on the schedule and on the fields. After singing yacht rock anthems with Mustache Harbor at GastroLands, I wended my way past ChocoLands toward the long field that led to the Twin Peaks stage where Sigur Rós would soon start performing. As I rounded the corner, a literal tsunami of humanity tumbled toward me, so many bodies that I jumped behind a mature and beamy pine tree to avoid being trampled. This wave of Metallica fans, like a dangerous driftnet streaming in the opposite direction toward the Land's End stage, scared the hell out of me.

Those of us at Twin Peaks formed a comparatively small but mighty group of loyalists, ready to be swept away by Jónsi and the band's gauzy music. Some describe their sound as post-punk. To me, it sounds like immersion inside golden, lacy fog, a little bit high, disoriented but not frightened, guided by the promise of love in a distant place. Holding hands with a stranger. Is this what life in Iceland is like? The band's latest is called "Odin's Raven Magic." The title track opens with vibes, and reminds me of the ravens that hop around my yard and neighborhood, observing, weighing options, *hawing*, deciding. A soundtrack for our letters.

For decades, my dad insisted our name is Icelandic. "It's a version of 'Isafjordur,'" he claimed. I can pass, physically, so I wore my Icelandic and Viking heritage like a horned helmet. Alas, 23andMe blasted that fantasy wide open. I am a run-of-the-mill Euro-mongrel, heavy on the Franco-Swiss and peppered with Gambian. But still, if my parents had thought to name me Medea Rogersdottir, I might have pulled "Icelandic" off. (As it was, zany parents that they are, one of the top five names in contention was "Rogerina Osmondina." Mom's memories of her role in the stage production of "Medea" during her college career won over the tribute to my dad and his mother, maiden name "Osmond.") I've grown into my name over the years. But I was careful to keep D'Aulaire's *Book of Greek Myths* hidden until my two sons understood that, no matter how deeply Bruce might rile me, their chances of becoming meat loaf were nil.

Pico Iyer worked with my secret crush, Leonard Cohen. Imagine the dreams they dreamed together. When Cohen sings "Dance Me to the End of Love" in his tobacco-stippled, gritty voice, there is no choice but to surrender, to fall into his arms and swirl around the floor, lost in this ephemeral moment. Though the song originated with an image Cohen saw of musicians pressed into service to play outside the crematoria of the WWII death camps, the passion, the surrender to beauty—it's here, then it ends. The Jewish Museum in NYC ran a Cohen exhibition a couple of years ago; video, photos, audio, interviews with the master, his family, his intimates. His spirit permeated the entire building, spilled out into the street and followed me home.

Singing words no one has sung before. The same ideas from the time people began to write words for songs, albeit with slightly altered lyrics. When Jónsi or Cohen or Joni Mitchell or Aretha gift their originality, another crack opens in the universe and the light flows.

Love,
Medea

*October 3, 2021 Indian summer. I looked it up. Surprisingly, it refers to the hazy sky warm days of fall when fields were burned off before snow came. Reading Leonard Cohen, The Flame. Rereading Pico Iyer, such sentences!*

Dear Medea,

A musical posting and once again we are so alike! I love Leonard Cohen! One of my favorites is *The Stranger Song* which became the soundtrack to one of my favorite movies: McCabe & Mrs. Miller. I love Cohen's poetry, his lyrics, his sense of ironic humor. His rich sherry voice as he aged. Pico Iyer was his friend in Buddhism originally, I guess, but after Cohen left (he said once because cheerfulness kept seeping through or words to that effect) about both his Buddhism and his use of antidepressants. Do you have the book of his poetry and various things that came out after his death? Cohen's that is. I also have a fondness for Aretha. So much music brings me to my knees, I have to be careful about listening. I've written poems about how music shifted a day, an entire way of thinking, of life. Such hefty triggers. I'm so happy you got to see Sigur Rós live. I think I prefer the solitary experience, something headphones has gifted us. I'll have to get their latest release.

In natural world news, I heard a fox screaming in the dark of night. That classic scream you hear on British tv murder shows. Hair raising in person. I suppose either mating, or hunting. Recently he/she shit in the dog bowl I use for one of the raven feeding sites. Then the ravens knocked the bowl to the ground, just to make sure I did something about it. Yesterday I was sitting in the bay window in my oversized chair where I usually read and write, and suddenly there was a flash of shadow and a bang as a hawk crashed into the window shadowed by Tinker. The hawk made it into the madrone tree where she looked shaken but ok. I only know she was ok by the fact that she had a shit, and then flew across into the wood, perhaps a little ruffled but not badly injured. Tinker followed and a short while later they were sky larking and I think Tinker was winning, but how could I tell? In the afternoon I was upstairs folding laundry and Tinker threw himself/herself* at the nearest window several times. I'm quite sure she/he doesn't want to come in, really.

*I've noticed the last few days that there is more of a difference between ravens' plumage. Therefore, based on the bird books I'm going to admit that Tinker may be female. And if that is so, won't it be fun when she has chicks in a few years? The males apparently have the fluffy plumage that I mistook and possibly anthropomorphized into a harried mama look, and the females are sleek and unruffled. Well, just wait, Tinker, in a year or two you will be soaring in the sky with some mate harrying after you. I hope I will have made life interesting.

As for "Indian Summer" a quick Google search turned up similar inquiries from people trying to be politically correct. Fair enough. One description I read was something I'd never heard, that is, that the phrase refers to the end of one's life, sort of like the autumn of our years. New one on me. The consensus seems to be that it's ok to still use the term for weather.

I was meaning to ask you about your name and your ancestry. I have a friend who is jealous that I have someone named "Medea" in my life. We were both saddled with strange names, my "Galer" is, of course, my actual given name. Jane is my easy name. Not given but intended. I'm nearly entirely Irish and British. My maiden name is Britton. Can't get more ancient British than that. But I do have a little bit of Finn which is pretty nice, fun to be unusual. And German and French. All in all, nearly 100% Celt. Daughter of ancient kings. Why not? Recently, 23&Me has indicated a tiny bit of Icelandic but since there is no Scandinavian to support that, I wonder. I do have fun with it all though.

The hawk is squawking. She must be nesting or at least territorial about the stand of trees closest to her hunting ground which is the "grass" (using the term very loosely to mean the gopher ridden expanse between the house and the edge of the 8-acre wood). She perches every evening before dusk to try her chances and I wish her all good hunting.

Love,
Jane

P.S. In a note on Indian summer and Harvest season, we tried some new squash last night, spaghetti squash shaped but very small. Not worth the effort but I did think that alongside a huge zucchini a pair of them would make perfect testicles for a Straw Man.


*3 October 2021 79 degrees, and with no speck of breeze, feels like 90. Ahhhh....*

Dear Jane,
The Giants won the National League West Division Title for the first time in ages. It took a World Series title back in 2010, and the ever-agile Tim Lincecum for me to notice that baseball is a sport that entails more than adults clobbering a white threaded ball and running around a red clay diamond, aiming for dusty fabric squares. We went to one of the playoff games when Timmy still pitched for the team, and sat near the pitching practice box. When Timmy arrived to warm up, I squealed and giggled, which was apparently caught by the news camera as my phone immediately blew up with messages from friends congratulating me on my fifteen milliseconds of fame.

Orange October, here we come! Discovering new passions never gets old.

This excitement for my hometown team was quickly tempered when I read about the Huntington Beach/Newport oil spill. Gallons and gallons of fuel gushing from a busted pipe three miles offshore. Boaters report witnessing dolphins slogging through the muck. They will surely drown. The pelicans and seagulls, rockfish and leopard sharks, starfish and seals, all will suffer, many will die. That oil derrick was erected in 1980. Forty-one years ago. It's the Surfside condo collapse all over again, because greedy people refuse to take responsibility. One of the drilling derricks malfunctioned near UC Santa Barbara in 2015. Refugio State Beach quickly became thick with oil. The snowy plovers, endangered and beginning to recover population, stuck in the slime. I was, ironically, driving my gas-powered car down to visit my son when the traffic on the 101 South ground to a halt because clean-up vehicles needed clear access to this rock-studded, glittering crescent of beach. This is not new; the oil spill off Santa Barbara in the 1970s that launched Earth Day left residual tar that sticks to bare feet. All of the hotels offer Tar Off towelettes to preserve shoes, socks and sheets. Here we go. Again.

Did you know that all of us, everyone, is urged to reduce our carbon footprints to 2.5 tons/year? The U.N. Climate Change newsletter reported today on a Swedish company called *Doconomy* that offers a Lifestyle Calculator, a fifty-question survey, which allows an individual to measure her carbon footprint. My usage of elements, so I thought, was pretty modest. According to the calculator, my annual carbon footprint is 26.94 tons. Short of staying home, in the dark, and eating only what I grow, I have no clue how to decrease this to the aspirational 2.5 tons.

The Scrub Jay is cackling like a blissed-out Giants fan. Bruce thinks I will soon know whether it is happy, sad, hungry, horny or satisfied.

Love,
Medea

P.S. Beyoncé celebrated a major birthday aboard Bezos' private monolith of a yacht. No word about that event's carbon footprint. And upon further study, it appears that this initiative to encourage the conscientious, non-jetsetters among us to monitor and reduce our comparatively microscopic footprints originated in the boardrooms of Big Oil to deflect blame. I should pivot to a study of Leonard Cohen's post-mortem poetry where the gloom of cynicism can't touch me.

*October 4, 2021 Indian summer. Aka Fire Season continues. New moon.*

Dear Medea,

Oil spill off Huntington Beach, warm water luring sharks to surfing bays, bears enjoying grapes in Napa. It's been a week of news. Of course, the one I will dwell on is the bear story. People are mystified as to why bears are moving into Bay Area counties. Really? Take a drive, a meander, to the North Bay, Sonoma, Napa, Mendocino...what do you see? Wire. Wire everywhere. Not an acre of undevelopable land is left to the wild. We have no water for all this wine growing, and what is it all for? I mean, I like wine, but do we need all this? Do we need expensive, high alcohol wines that compete for the attention of a very few wealthy people? We do not. The bears, the mountain lions, the foxes, the bobcats, the pigs, boars, and tiny wee ones need space, need us to move the fuck over and stop fencing every single acre. And if you do fence and plant and control then you'd better be prepared to help and share with the wild ones.

Fort Bragg has purchased desalination equipment in order to find a way to survive the drought. Probably a good idea, even one that should have been taken many years ago since this isn't the first ever drought. But what are the ramifications of desalination? What is the future of a state without water resources? Clearly major portions of California's agriculture systems need a complete rethink. We keep putting Band-Aids on every problem, robbing one area to bolster another. Let's start by mandating how many acres of any given county can be put to vineyards, and demand that those vineyards be self-watering without dipping into the major watersheds.

I might do better than you in that carbon quiz, but not if I have to count ordering from Amazon. No matter how hard I try to order a lot of stuff at once so that only one box arrives it never ever works out that way. But still I don't fly anymore, and I rarely drive, so perhaps I would come out ok? And here's a problem. We get electric cars and rely on PG&E for charging them? We already have sky high electric rates, what will happen when that broken company controls the charging stations? Without massive solar development electric cars are going to cost far more than anyone expects, especially in this state with our current utilities systems.

Facebook has crashed globally. I can't help but be a little glad. Read a book people, one with words and a plot, and a message. My father used to refer to the tv screen as "that damn glass face'—kind of applies nicely to FB, no?

Love,
Jane

*4 October 2021 Packing for NYC*

Dear Jane,

Three ravens decided to come for a walk with me in the hot, dry afternoon. The sky looked like skim milk—The air was dry, definitely fire weather. They made so much noise. I spotted them perched on a phone wire above me, two touching beaks and the other looking on like a peeved chaperone. Then the *hawing* started. First the chaperone, scolding the kissing kids? He flew off and they followed, along my path, performing an aerial dance of the veils, then stopping in a tree just ahead of me. More insanely loud *hawing*. I asked, as I do, whether they would like to chat, or visit my feeders, upon which cue they resumed aerials overhead, then found rest in another tall pine. This family always stops its pursuit just as the street starts a steep decline. Do they dislike the neighbors in that area? Thinking about Tinker again, I am going to learn about the territories of the ravens. In terms of square miles, this family sticks to one. If the area were more wooded and less densely populated with people, I wonder whether they'd wander further afield?

A friend visited last night who has lived most of her life in the square miles between Port Washington and Brooklyn, with a detour to Vermont, and to Nice, which is where we met. Driving to my house from the BART station along the 280, she said, "so this is the road to your house?!" I'd never thought about it that way, but yes, it is; a freeway lined in greenery with a shimmering reservoir below and low hills beyond, not a skyscraper in sight. We sat on my front porch in glow of the late-afternoon when the sun illuminates the silvery fluff on the native grasses and the charm of hummingbirds rumbles in to feed. The photos she took, elements rather than landscapes, reminded me of the geometry in small things. Once the sun dipped below those hills, the Monterey Pine across the street stood in silhouette with Venus winking behind its shoulder. The world looks different through the eyes of another.

Love,
Medea

P.S. FB note: how about writing a letter?! Bring back poetry and lyricism in daily discourse. Read the letters between Anaïs Nin and Henry Miller, both married, both crazed with passion that ignites the pages. Twenty years of unrelenting overflow. They dwelled inside each other, body, mind, spirit. If you have read *A Literate Passion*, don't tell me how it ends. In my head, they float, like escaped embers from a decades' long fire, into eternity.

*6 October 2021 Dateline: Brooklyn, Williamsburg to be precise. Overcast skies, 63 degrees rising to 70 later today.*

Dear Jane,

The hipsters are stirring at 9:45 in the morning. Man buns abound. The cafe where I'm writing to you is owned by a Frenchman. He's playing perky classic French songs, reimagined by the new generation, full of "joie" and "oo-pah." It has always tickled me that a culture that is known for its embrace of art masters and cutting-edge philosophers has such profoundly kitschy pop music. Looking out at the sidewalk with its orange bistro tables, skinny women walking tiny dogs, drivers ignoring all the rules, I'm not on Berry Street in Brooklyn but on Rue Jacob in the Sixth Arrondisement.

Three million people live in Brooklyn. That's four times the population of San Francisco. Maybe because this part of town is filled with recent college grads launching their first careers, the atmosphere feels ionized. It's impossible to walk down the sidewalk without noticing. You can almost see the ideas floating through the air, the sense of limitlessness. Even the graffiti looks curated. In fact, there is one artist, an Ecuadorian named "Kobra" who paints faces ten feet tall on the brick facades of random buildings. One near the Driggs Ave. shows a young Warhol, looking at you from behind his wire-rims, and his friend Basquiat sizing you up from his right. The animate portraits, surrounded by garlands, give you a feeling that these two will start a conversation with you if you only give them an opening.

I can't wait to savor, again, the kale Caesar at The Bedford. It has haunted my memory since I first tasted one two years ago. This modest white storefront, warmed inside with wooden floors and walls, must have a hundred years of stories ground into its grain. As it has across the world, the pandemic opened the windows and streets here to restaurants as well, and The Bedford's outside tables form a right-angle in the neighborhood. We half-watched the Mets game playing on a big-screen TV across the street. A man walked by while we were munching on fried artichokes carrying a small Tortoiseshell cat in a blanket. This cat had a scrunchy face, similar to the famed Grumpy Cat who died last year after becoming an internet sensation. I of course had to hop up to pet the cat. Its owner obliged, as one does in a small town tucked inside a megalopolis. "His name is Bedford. He's named for this place. He's a little under the weather today so I am taking him out to get some air." We learned that Bedford hails from Colombia. Sitting outside in October at 11pm on a Tuesday, feasting on the best kale salad in the world in the most electric town in my world petting an immigrant kitty beloved by his concerned papa and in the company of my fearless son, I'm torn between longing to be 25 again and vowing to cram as much life as I can into what remains after these 62 years. Form is emptiness, emptiness is form. Every breath contains an entire life.

Love,
Medea


*October 6, 2021 very odd but at some point this week my Word program caught up with the calendar and started auto suggesting the right date. Beautiful cool Fall Day, Bring me more of this please. Very light misting rain last night.*

Dear Medea,
It does sound like Paris, except perhaps for the population density. I'm afraid NYC will never be high on my list of anything but places to avoid. I have always found it curiously offensive for a people to boast about how rude they are. I wonder what the population of Paris is if the tourists are subtracted? Perhaps your love of the city is more to do with your immense pride and love for your Dylan. In any case, enjoy!

I think I might be becoming a germaphobe—my reaction to your cat story was "oh no! you TOUCHED the cat?"

Yesterday Chris did a perfect imitation of a screech owl—the phrase that is almost a yodel like the loons make—a repeating "oooooooo" followed by a descant. Coincidentally, early this morning I heard the same sounds. I always identified this as a shore bird. I will have to try and find some audio to compare. It is the season to begin hearing owls, and we do usually have at least three species of owl here: Great Horned—the most common—Spotted Owl—the most protected—and another small owl who often is seen standing on solid ground instead of up in a tree, but I'm not sure of the kind of owl he is. Less Wise? I do love owls and usually think of them as my favorite bird, don't tell this to Tinker. The ravens are certainly more fun.

The deer are very happy that the winter grass is sprouting, and the previously hay-dead dirt isn't looking so pathetic. They have a lot of catching up to do, calorie-wise, some of them with ribs pushing at their skin.

I missed posting yesterday due to an animal emergency; Tweed is lame on his back left leg, hopping three-legged for 36 hrs. This morning after several doses of anti-inflammatories, he is much better which is a big relief. While we have a terrific vet 30 minutes away, any surgeries or serious ER canine emergencies require a two-hour drive inland. Another of the downsides to living coastal. The rise in pet adoptions during the pandemic has led to a shortage in veterinary care, with many new pet owners unable to find care. The average duration of vet assistants and staff on the job is five years. Could you be a vet? I couldn't bear the sorrow of it. A good vet, like ours, deals with a great amount of sadness.

Love,
Jane

*October 7, 2021 temps in the 40s overnight and a distinct air of Fall. Dare we hope Fire Season is over? I almost couldn't bring myself to tempt fate by typing that.*

Dear Medea,
While you adjust to the bustle of New York for a week, I'm enjoying the heartbeat pattern of the Albion foghorn. It's a splendid way to calm for sleep at night. We don't always hear it, but when the ocean goes still or in swell, the electronic foghorn a few miles to the north is startlingly noticeable. Suddenly it is as if there is no ocean. The trees are allowed their say without background commentary. We humans hear everything in a new way, without picking apart various sounds to find the dominant or dangerous voices. Sometimes the ocean can sound like traffic. Sometimes there isn't a whisper of sound, but usually there is a steady cadence—that key of A I have mentioned before. Yesterday the crash of surf gave over to quiet, the fog came in, the foghorn took up its place. Once again, I heard the owl that Chris says is Screech. He called, but I did not hear a reply. In the early hours I had to get up and close my windows against the dreaded garbage trucks and the horrible empty logging trucks roaring and rattling to be first in line, first in line to load up the newest cuts of poor old redwoods. It makes even seasoned soldiers of emotional ambivalence cringe. Something has to be done, for "too late" has arrived and it's roaring and rolling down the road.

Love,
Jane

P.S. For the first time in months there was no Tinker, no Tinker's friends waiting on the rooftop for morning talk and kibble. What's afoot? Perhaps the cold overnight?

*October 8, 2021 cool morning, narrow temp range for today from 48–54. Sunshine and maybe rain showers this afternoon. Snow in the Sierra. This is not particularly unusual, but we will grasp at whatever Fall straws we are offered.*

Dear Medea,

Tinker came to eat in the evening on her own last night. Later I saw several of the ravens flying back and forth from south to north, flying so fast through the trees, how do they do that without crashing when their eyes are on the sides of their heads? I wonder if they are roosting in a new spot, or preparing nests. I also wonder does only the mating pair make and settle the nest or are the juveniles included?

I have not seen Tinker this morning, but there were active ravens at dawn making a racket so they are around. The weather shift seems to have made their habits shift.

We had one small young female deer grazing by the pool house when I got up. She settled down and in clever disguise blended right in with the dead branches of a rosemary bush where she sat and chewed her cud. She was there for about an hour when I happened to see her looking intently toward the woods. Here comes a big buck. Three points and a monster compared to the little doe. She got up and quickly loped away toward the denser part of the forest The buck didn't see her. He had his nose to the ground, nostrils flaring, trotting along a well-worn deer path edging the brush. On the make! He's a big brute of a buck, out to make a name for himself. I'm glad the little doe chose her escape wisely. He disappeared over the edge of the swale and headed toward the creek. She returned to the meadow grass. She must not smell of estrus. Lucky girl. We wondered why she was alone from the herd or her mother, but probably it is because of the buck being on the hunt.

Speaking of mating, I read a news article about the mating habits of some dinosaur that involved clamping their teeth in the skulls of the mate. Not exactly foreplay.

I hope you learned a thing or two at the Botanical Gardens. My new Sibley book says that ravens remember people's faces and by their actions and even five years later will steer clear of someone who didn't treat them well. Corvids in captivity never survive in the wild. An important message about keeping things simple. According to Sibley, I haven't crossed a line. It's a good sign that Tinker and her mates are off doing new things and not standing around waiting for me.

Love,
Jane

P.S. Did you know that there actually is an elk in Elk? A lone bull Elk the town has named Elvis. I saw him up close a few years ago when he walked across the highway in front of my car one evening at dusk. I was amazed, thinking they had long ago been pushed north. Then I saw another one about ten miles north of us. Then this guy in Elk. He must be interbreeding with the deer. Or very lonely. Early in the 20th century, the herds of Roosevelt elk that were common here were moved north into Humboldt County where they are protected now and make for a fun day trip for visitors into the Sinkyone Wilderness. Because they are protected, they are very calm. Not tame at all, and one needs caution, but they put up with being observed.

It's very calming for me to think and write about the animals and ignore the chaos of humans for a while.

*October 11, 2021 Sun, wind, cold and extremely low humidity*
*Happy Indigenous Peoples Days—surely it should be several years long?*

Dear Medea,

The weather has turned, or perhaps twisted is a better word, into the October nightmare fire season of the past few years except we are blessed with cold temps–even freeze warnings for tonight–. High winds began last night, very high inland and peaks. It is picking up here with gale warnings and red flag warnings in effect through tomorrow. It's better to think of this as Mother Nature shaking out the rugs as seeds shower down off the trees, the needles of pine, the oak spinners, anything not firmly attached is coming down. PG&E has shut off power to 26k customers in the Bay Area proactively trying to avert another disaster like the Santa Rosa fires of two years ago. It seems strange to worry even more about fire right now, and still light a fire in the fireplace to take off the morning chill. Of course, for us, "lighting a fire" means flipping a switch since we removed the wood fireplace and installed propane a few years ago. If we had a wood fireplace now, we wouldn't be able to use it for fear of terrifying the neighbors and bringing the volunteer fire department down, bells ringing. Maybe I'm suffering battle fatigue, but I actually slept well last night as the windows rattled and the hum of the humidifier canceled out any awareness of impending danger.

Tinker seems to have settled on a "friend," surely too young to call him a mate, and likely her sibling. He's a bit bossy and tends to take Tinker's food. I guess this is why she's the runt. I try to outfox him by putting food in at least three places. If it's just the two of them, he only manages to monopolize two by the time Tinker gets the third. This morning it was leftover pork chop. "Burt" as I'm calling him, got the pieces and the larger bone and flew off with all of it jammed in his mouth. Tinker got a decent size piece, but I felt sorry for her and came back out with another piece of bone well attached with more meat. Fair is fair. I have committed to Tinker being female. Burt is therefore male, having fluffier feathers.

The females and the young deer are skittish and definitely hounded by the buck who we saw again this morning, nosing around. As far as I can tell, no one wants him, but boy oh boy is he determined.

I had a funny dream last night about a well drilling gang who showed up. They were a ragtag bunch of hillbillies who arrived to a chorus of loud and poorly out of tune hymns. I asked them if they had dowsing rods. They did. They told me the neighbor said it was ok to drill on her land because she wouldn't go against God's will. (Honestly, these dreams are wacky). When I woke up, I decided to order dowsing rods. I think that was the point, don't you? I was at a prehistoric monument site in Wiltshire, England a few years ago and we ran into two nerdy old guys who had built a contraption to track ley lines. We stopped to talk to them, and they explained their machine and then pulled out dowsing rods and let us try them. Of the three of us, I was the one who really "got" it. It's rather amazing really (nb: Have you noticed that because we all use the word "amazing" all the time now, nothing really is?). I found all sorts for sale on Amazon (that word again in another form) and ordered a pair. This is going to be fun.

Between you off in NYC and Diane in the Amazon, I'm feeling a bit lonely. I'll look forward to your returns on Wednesday. I'm trying to figure out how you could stand to leave SF during Fleet Week and the play offs. Go Giants.

Love,
Jane

P.S. Headlines about the 8 wolf pups the Feds killed. I hope there is massive response to this horror. It's a despicable thing.


*13 October 2021 Sunny with wispy clouds after a mostly gray day. Temperature, 55 degrees, as it was at your house on 26 July.*

Dear Jane,
I have missed you. Your wit, your words, your ineffable knack for saying something that hurls me into such laughter that Bruce thinks I'm watching *South Park*. Something about being away from the familiar flips a maniacal switch inside, forces me into the streets, neck craned up, down and sideways. I took four books to New York. I bought a fifth from my favorite Brooklyn bookstore called *Word* on Franklin. This book is called *Names of New York*, written by Joshua Jelly-Shapiro, in collaboration with Rebecca Solnit. The

small hardback with a map of the city on its cover tells the histories behind the names of boulevards, boroughs, and beaches. The beach where we whiled away an afternoon, Rockaway, comes from the Munsee word "leekuwahkuy", which means "sandy place." And Bowery Street, renowned for drunks and the Boys in my memory, is actually an Anglicization of a Dutch word, "bouwerji," which means "road leading to a farm," the farm in question belonging to none other than Peter Stuyvesant, whose name now graces not only the formerly sketchy Brooklyn neighborhood that abuts Williamsburg, Bedford-Stuyvesant, or Bed-Stuy, but also Stuyvesant Town. Stuyvesant Town houses hundreds of NYU students, old guys with dogs (I watched one hairy man wearing a wife-beater and stubble exit his basement flat leading two brown dogs on worn webbed leashes up chipped concrete stairs to a patch of grass) and families with young kids who yearn for access to green space and a view of the water. I have it on solid authority that this is a coveted address, at least for NYU students. The East River, East River Park and green spaces between the buildings offer breathing room. (I wonder if the students know about the gangsters who concreted boots upon their foes and tossed them over the railing? Do the Gangs of New York merit a mention in history classes these days?) From the shores of Marsha P. Johnson Park (named for the LGBTQ activist, drag queen and AIDS activist né Malcolm Michaels, Jr.) in Williamsburg, though, these endless blocks of red brick mid-rises look like so many inhospitable boxes, not bereft like housing projects but dreary nonetheless.

I did meet a teacher in line with me waiting for the ferry from Manhattan to Williamsburg who suggested strangling de Blasio for eliminating gifted and talented programs might be too soft a punishment. As a gifted and talented teacher in the Bronx, she spoke with authority when she said, "We've got to hold our kids to a higher standard! What is this? A race to the bottom?!" Yeah. Maybe.

Where was I?

Nature exists in New York City. It abounds, in fact. What I observed during these past seven days will seem risible to New Yorkers. Well, maybe not to the guys riding illegal dirt bikes on a side street in East New York, whose presence caused our driver to shake, and say, again, that this is a "bad area" and to please only take a car to JFK before 2pm and after 6pm because you get caught in this mess and you might get popped. But Jane. If those guys lived among leafy greens and not in houses or apartments with barred windows and doors, they might not feel so mean.

I digress. Again.

New York does parks. It has to, or maybe it doesn't given footage I've seen of concrete apartment blocks with not a tree in sight. The point is that New York is a city on steroids until you stop. Look. Listen. A Wood Thrush in a sycamore tree in McCarren Park. This bird is listed as "threatened." It winters in Central

America. Yet it's hanging with the sparrows and grackles on a 72-degree October afternoon, watching the joggers and the U.N.-worthy contingent of nannies and the fucking tough as hell little old Jewish people ambling down Lorimer, leaned against their walkers, talking trash about their know-nothing kids who think they can't live alone.

Brooklyn breathes.

Love,
Medea

P.S. I did not see the story about the wolf pups. I thought Biden beat Trump. Who kills baby animals?
P.P.S. I promise to respond to your letters, and update you on my critters, as well as the "Canary Island Palm formerly known as Headless." I must draw a symbol for that.
P.P.P.S. The Brooklyn Botanical Garden gave us a full day of fresh air entertainment.

*October 14, 2021 warm, still, earthquake weather*

Dear Medea,

I'm so glad you're back, at least here on paper, though your pure joy at traveling and enjoying NYC is energizing to me here in my woods, I sense that your return home holds conflicting emotions, your heart divided. It is a gift to be able to see, really see, your surroundings rather than cataloging your expectations and coming away disappointed—because that would always be the case. Being open to every breath, every whisper, is what makes you such a great essayist.

You might want to read *Golden Hill: A Novel of Old New York* by Francis Spufford (now there's an old-fashioned Yankee surname if there ever was one). I confess I have only read part of it. I bought it because I have an interest in the history of immigrants to the colonies, including the Pennsylvania Dutch who weren't Dutch at all, but rather German who came by way of the kindness of Dutch and English politicians. A story in itself. What reminded me of this book is your fascination with place name origins. There's plenty of that in this novel.

It has been quiet here. There are regular visits from Tinker and her friend. Usually three times a day, or whenever I am outside. Obviously, they are watching my every move through the big windows. Yesterday Gene came home from the feed store with a new bag of kibble (*Taste of the Wild* small dog Pacific Salmon) and offered to feed the ravens. Not knowing my routine, he gave them about ten times what I do and I think they were startled at the opulence of their table. As a result, I think, the little gray jays have jumped in and cleared up the leftovers. They are cheeky devils and not at all afraid of the ravens, or these ravens anyway. Jays and ravens are members of the same family of corvids. Hard to imagine.

My dowsing rods arrived today. I'm looking forward to sharpening my water finding skills. I am interested in map skills as well. They use the pendulum instead of the rods, and I have a lot of practice with the pendulum. 'Tis the season to be witchy.

Love,
Jane

*14 October 2021 Backyard, setting sun, clear sky. A frozen (well, 49 degree) morning decided to behave in the afternoon and warm to the low 70s.*

Dear Jane,

You had me worried about Tinker with her absences, yet it appears Sibley would call you a fine steward and Tinker a maturing young lady. Will she (and Burt) nest with you and raise a brood? That sounds like a welcome spring surprise. And if Burt tries to penetrate Tinker's head with his hard, black cone of a beak, let's hope Tinker has enough sense of self to tell him to sod off.

It was a warm enough afternoon to walk the College route, and I added the extra two-mile loop down to my friend Paul's house. It sits on a canyon with a view of the Bay. Always quiet on this street, with the occasional hawk sighting. Today a bird I could not identify nestled in a tall oak behind Paul's neighbor's house trilling like crazy. The moment I activated my Merlin Birdsong app, it stopped singing. As I've learned, the size of the voice does not betray the size of the bird, so I'll have to keep an ear out when I walk tomorrow. Maybe it was an owl?

Your ground owl I suspect is a Burrowing Owl. We have them in profusion here, so they say, though I've yet to see one. Tiny, with huge eyes, they resemble those kids in the Margaret/Walter Keane paintings from the 1960s that appealed to ladies who wore full aprons over their calico dresses. I guess the allure of the faraway gaze in the subjects' eyes took them to a more romantic place than the kitchen sink.

We had a mountain lion sighting in the neighborhood overnight. It killed a raccoon in someone's backyard. The homeowner rudely interrupted the kitty's dinner, so it stared at the howler before leaping the fence into the half-dark. Poor raccoon, poor mountain lion. I looked out for any sign as I walked, but the wild creatures see more than we. The foxes and coyotes must have drifted down to the reservoir since the canyon's lost all of its water in the heat and dry. If La Niña comes this winter as predicted, you and I will wish we were veterinarians, or at least stewards of a large, wet, fruited plain where the wild things could drink and roam.

You and Bruce share similar sentiments about New York, and Paris to a degree. He is good for about four days in either metropolis before the crush of the world's tired, poor and huddled close in on him. Car's blaring horns deafen. The air reeks of a savory blend of dog poop, every single human effluent, weed, and exhaust. I'm busy imagining what it would have been like to live in the apartment next door to Charlie Parker, in the brownstone across from Tompkins Square Park, to listen to the wail of his horn in the dark. Or stumble into Kevin Kline and Phoebe Cates on the Upper East Side, whereupon I politely ask her to leave so that I can tell Kevin how his performance in "French Kiss" made me believe in impossible, fated love. Or discovering a coral reef scene in carved sandstone and ringing the façade of a 1940s-era office building, hoping it remains fully leased so that XYZ Partners resists the all-cash offer from LMN Equity whose only objective is to raze it and build another super-tall. Just like Paris in winter, these stories keep me warm, and immune to the stench of the street.

I don't have a symbol for the palm yet, but it's sprouted four new pale-yellow fronds while we were away. Yay! And the crown fronds grew another seven inches or so. That tree could in no way be declared a "stump" ripe for grinding. Tiny victories.

Love,
Medea

*October 15th. Earthquake weather, still.*

Dear Medea,
Cities, San Francisco, NY, Paris to some degree, all suffer the same problems with smells. I suppose we should be glad we don't live in the 17th c. with a matron tossing the pot's contents out the window yelling "Gardez-loo!" to the poor sods below. Maybe I can blame my dislike of cities on my acute sense of smell which is often a terrible curse. Telegraph Ave in Berkeley smells like Beirut, Lebanon in the 60s and that's not a good thing. Although, I will say that Beirut probably smelled better since it had roasted chestnut carts and lamb kabab vendors which did a lot to cover the smell of piss and shit, and then there was the Mediterranean. More recently I remember being disgusted by Amsterdam in the 90s, awash in dog shit so prevalent that there was no way to look up, no way to enjoy the four-story narrow houses with their hook roofs and modest paint fronts. I wonder if that city has cleaned up at all? Many things these days remind me that humans

are the only species I can think of who don't have a sense of pride about their waste removal, we want it to be someone else's problem. Isn't it odd that the worst offenders are campers? Have you ever found an outhouse you could stand to use? This issue will be the downfall of San Francisco, which used to be such a clean and beautiful city, and then what happened? Vietnam? Hippies? Reagan as governor? Or some natural degradation? Who ran off with all the tax revenue meant to keep our world clean, pristine, and safe?

Tinker and Burt are pals for sure, but I confess I know nothing of whether siblings will mate or not. I do know that they do not find mates for a couple of years, so there is time for them to learn about their world and for it to widen. I hope when Tinker does have chicks, she will be close by.

Mountain lions! Excellent. Not for them, though, sadly because dipping into some human's backyard for a snack is a risky business. It is the time of year here that we usually have sightings–being on their rounds over a vast ranging area–and bears. And the owls are late in beginning their courtships. I think you're right about the burrowing owls.

The leaders of the many Pomo bands gathered together to implore a bureaucrat named Wade Crowfoot to stop redwood old and second growth logging and sit down to discuss returning the lands back to their native Pomo owners. There is a YouTube video which will make you angry. Between the excessive politeness of the Pomo Chief constantly saying 'Sir...' begging for understanding and more than once choking up with passion as he asked to be understood, and the obtuse repetition of the state 'line' 'as far as I know...' fill in the blank with the appropriate bullshit nothingness. It makes me furious, but I bet you can tell that. Mr. Crowfoot, who is apparently not a Native American himself in spite of his name, is the top of the food chain of state parks, forest management, Cal Fire etc. The single minute in the 30-minute session where the Pomo Chief describes dancing his feather dances among the redwoods of Jackson State Forest will bring you to your knees. Or maybe to your feet.

That reminds me, I should send you a link (do you do Instagram?) where you can see my acupuncturist Jessica Curl dancing her acrobatics high up in the redwoods. Before she took herself off to the circus to learn the silks, I told her in a tarot reading she needed to find a way to escape people and have some peace on her own. She took me literally.

Love,
Jane

*16 October 2021 82 degrees, clear, bright and still. The weatherman promises rain all week. I'll finally have to clean my closet.*

Dear Jane,

No Orange October for the Giants, and, if the meteorologists speak the truth, no Orange October due to fire weather either. At least the latter is a positive.

Tinker flew to mind yesterday as I was walking a different path and saw a raven at a construction site. It hopped around a discarded lunch bag, pecking and poking, before deciding to abscond with a plastic water bottle. Odd choice as the bottle was empty, but light, and shiny. The bird flew about three hundred feet with the bottle in its beak before it lost its grip and the bottle fell into the culvert, where it may wash into the sewers with the coming rains. I could rage on about reusable water bottles again, but I won't. The raven didn't choke on PET particles. That's a plus.

Rebecca Solnit has written a book about George Orwell's roses called, aptly, *Orwell's Roses*. I've known Orwell for his political and social prescience, but he also understood the sanctity and saeculum of the other living things on our planet. During a leasehold stay in 1936, Orwell planted roses and fruit trees on the grounds. During the days leading up to World War II, he planted flowers, more than a victory garden; a pure act of bringing forth beauty from ugliness. He only lived to be forty-seven. Imagine what he'd be writing today. One of my favorite Orwell-isms that Solnit includes in her book is his admonition to plant an acorn every time you commit an "antisocial act." Beauty from ugliness. Imagine the gardens that might bloom in Washington, Orlando, Sandy Hook, Louisville.

Not to give anything away, because it's written in *The Guardian's* excerpt, but Orwell's seven rose bushes continue to profuse in salmon and in pink at age eighty-five. May we fare as bountifully and enduringly as those roses.

Scents carry memories for us both, it appears. The first time I visited Paris was with my family as an incoming high school sophomore. The thing about Paris in 1972 that stayed with me was not the preponderance of *merde de chien* in the *rue*. It was the unmistakable, musky odor of a half-smoked Gauloises. Six years later, I moved to France and took up the Gauloises habit. The tobaccos shreds stick in your teeth. The unfiltered ends turn your index and middle finger top joints a sulphury yellow. Disgusting habit. I can still smell the remnants of those cigarettes on my fingertips. France infiltrates a person in the most peculiar ways.

And Amsterdam? In 1978, my friend, Linda, and I landed in a hash hostel there over Spring break. The owner delivered brownies to us for Easter breakfast in our garret, where we slept on the floor with twenty other bodies. He threw a disco party at the bar next door for the fifty of us staying in his house. Good people. Good times. I've never been to Beirut.

Love,
Medea

P.S. We saw a Horseshoe Crab while walking along Rockaway Beach. Do you remember these prehistoric crustaceans? Dylan had neither seen nor heard of them. They crawled all over the beach near my house when I was a kid. Spotting this one, I realized I had not seen one in at least a year of Sundays. A single, small Horseshoe Crab corpse on an autumn beach; another spectral reminder of what we had and what we've lost.
P.P.S. I Googled "Jessica Curl" and find ten listings for a hair product called "jessiecurl," which I should probably try. But no silks dancers high in the redwoods. Do you think bureaucrats display such arrogance because, deep down, they understand that, in the end, they are inconsequential?


*October 17, 2021 mild. dare I say rain is coming?*
*Reading Richard Powers essay* A Little More than Kin, *Emergence Magazine*

Dear Medea,
Thanks to your link, I read the Rebecca Solnit piece on Orwell's roses. How wonderful that at least one bush is still not only live, but blooming? Orwell, I found, died young from tuberculosis. Such a pity. He and so many others. Wasn't it Emerson who not only died but first suffered with the disease in his eyes, and suffered terribly. Did I ever tell you I have TB? It's dormant now, but I was so ill in high school that we selected colleges based on dry air. Once in college—in Denver—I was subjected to inhalation therapy every two weeks at hospital. On the bright side, it was my ticket out of field hockey class. TB was, and still is, endemic in the Middle East. The gift that keeps on giving. The constant snot and spitting and public evacuations of all kinds of fleshly juices by the native population makes me gag even today. Here's a spooky connection, seeing as it's October, my name's sake—my 2nd great grandmother, Jennie Galer—had tuberculosis. This was during and just after the Civil War. Her husband took her off to Colorado for the cure where they pitched a tent along with a few hundred other caretakers and invalids up in the mountains above Colorado Springs. No backpackers' skint was this, but a regulation army tent complete with camp bed, and candle lamps, and trunks of clothing. Can you imagine wandering out among the red rocks dressed in yards of cottons and silks? Jennie could, and

did. I have one of her dresses, and underclothes, and a nightdress stained with ancient blood. Was this a curse? Was I destined to follow her path? Seems like it.

Now, where were we? Oh, right, Orwell, poor thing. He looks so sensitive and thoughtful in the photo. I'm amazed his writing was as unyielding as it was. He looks like he would be more of a romantic. Perhaps he was until his wife died. I wonder if that was the 'consumption' as well. The description of his croft on the island of Jura is in Roger Deakin's excellent book, *Waterlog*. Chapter 23, titled "Orwell's Whirlpool." Deakin says that Orwell had planned to move there (Scotland's isles) but postponed because of the sudden death of his wife. It was just the end of the war (I suppose there may be a time when a generation coming will interrupt here and say, 'which war?' but you know what I mean). He wanted his small son to grow up in the country. In retrospect I imagine this was a common impulse, much like today's exodus from cities– 'if I'm going to die, damn it, I'm going to live someplace beautiful while I'm doing it.' Orwell farmed, fished, and quieted himself with his own brilliance. He also almost drowned in a skiff with some friends and his son when they got into the famous whirlpool effect of Corryvrekan. (See also *The Summer Isles* about sailing the treacherous passage.) After the horrors of war, there was a sudden rush to escape, camp, build a cottage, unhook, unplug…my own family did that in northern Wisconsin. I think now Orwell would have to say with all banality, 'I told you so.'

Richard Powers has captured my mood today, literally, after reading his fine essay, my mood completely changed. There is much to think about in his essay, but what I will worry at now is the idea that while we are made to care for our fellowman, and we know now that we must also care for all things be they animate or inanimate, they live. But somehow, rather than evolve, we are losing ground. We have miscalculated that algorithm of who would you give your life for? Not only is it starkly true that an extreme of our species wouldn't give a fig for anyone or any cause other than themselves, but at the other end of the spectrum, the pendulum sways in a truly 'quoth the raven, nevermore' kind of way to a mutation of human who would sacrifice all of us to rid themselves of principle. Strangely, in the middle we find the caretakers, the tree sitters, the protestors, the recorders, those of us who's sensitivities are brightened to an acuteness that is painful and yet impossible to deny. I have the feeling an entire generation or two will be lost because they cannot bring themselves to fight for all of us and have instead, retreated to game play and the irrelevant release of urgency in front of a blue screen.

It's that kind of day.

Tweed and I walked in the woods. I wanted to visit the pet cemetery and speak with the little ones. Give them my grief before it becomes too heavy again to bear. The drought has nearly destroyed the largest wetland in the wood, a place that always had some squishy ground is now dry, fine dust with a few of the marsh grasses left doing their best to survive. We did find two of Tweed's balls. Upon our return, Tinker and Burt were on the garage roof peak, speaking in low and loving tones as they took turns grooming. At one point Tinker had to stop and wipe something off her beak on the edge of the roof shingle. Then Burt seemed to sniff her beak. I have no idea if this is just siblings being useful or if this the formation of something bigger. Perhaps I have misconstrued all of it. I kind of like being unsure.

Love,
Jane

P.S. While I've been writing to you, the very light breeze has brought the smell of rain, put ripples on the water surface of the trough, and darkened the sky. Please rain goddess, don't pass over us now.
P.P.S. Not 30 minutes later…it is pouring down rain and suddenly, a storm! Perhaps there is a goddess after all?


*17 October 2021 What's that pattering on the pebbles outside?! YES! It's RAIN!*

Dear Jane,
The ground looks so strange, dark and slick and spongy. It feels like years since the rain's been gone. A tease, this short shower. And yet I hear a faint hallelujah chorus coming from the trees. Yes, there is a goddess, after all.

You did not tell me you have TB, nor that your great-grandmother was a TB patient with nerves of steel. I guess everyone back then had nerves of steel, but back then, traveling across acres and miles in a wagon and sleeping among snakes and bandits and varmints was just everyday life. Lordy. Did she stay in that tent during the winter? Double Lordy. I'm relieved that your disease lies dormant and all that spitting and snorting lives on only in your memory. Where do you keep Grandma Jennie's garments, bloodied and otherwise? Is she keeping watch over you through the cotton and DNA?

These writers with their too-short lives remind me of the curse of twenty-six for rock stars. It's as though the fates want to make sure you know that, at any second, your date with eternity may come knocking. We have two friends who died at age fifty-two about a year apart, both gorgeous, accomplished, edgy, hilarious, irreplaceable men. I visit both of them, one at his grave and the other at the bench his wife and daughters placed for him at the reservoir. They remind me.

I also read the Richard Powers essay. You mention the two extremes of selfishness, and the great empathic middle. If you think about those inside a bell curve, the average Josephine who will pick up groceries for her shut-in neighbor or yell at the PG&E tree cutters whose failure to sweep the forest floor threatens to incinerate her neighborhood form the big fat middle. Those selfish cads on the left and amoral loudmouths on the right amount to nothing more than flatlines. Yes, they may control eighty or ninety percent of the wealth in the U.S. and beyond. I won't discount that. But when revolution comes and you pull up a potato from your garden and decide who deserves to eat, who will that person be? There will always exist fringes of people who prefer alt-realities, or the latest update from an "influencer" or rocket-propelled phalluses. But I honestly don't think homo sapiens could have survived this long without that big fat bell curve middle of people for whom rB>C.*

I was talking with my best friend, also Jane, this morning when I looked out at the front door and an adolescent deer tapped its nose on the glass. We've seen deer scat in the front garden, but this was a first live encounter. I'm not sure what prompted it to wander up and knock. I hoped to snap a close picture, but it sensed movement and meandered down the driveway and into the neighbor's front yard. Jane said, "Oh no! Now I have to worry about the deer too!" as one does when one is a part of the big fat bell curve middle.

Love,
Medea

P.S. When you master your dowsing rod, could you please visit? We really need to sink a well.

*Hamilton's Rule attempts to quantify an altruism gene. It declares that "genes tend to increase in frequency when the degree of genetic relatedness between a giver and a receiver of an altruistic act, multiplied by the benefit to the receiver, is greater than the reproductive cost to the giver." In giving, we all receive.

*October 18, 2021 cool, sunshine. The world is cleansed. almost an inch of rain over the last 24 hrs.*

Dear Medea,
The goddess of rain deserves a name. While I think of her as capricious, I admit that she must have some objective in mind. A chilling thought. I too seek out water to cleanse my soul. What would you call a power such as this?

You really did have a close encounter with deer this morning! Fantastic! When I came downstairs to make a cup of tea the house was surrounded. I first saw two young deer being guided hurriedly across the front yard by a female. I wondered why she was in such a mood—even chasing one of the kids. Then I looked out the kitchen windows to the south and saw the reason for her urgency. Two bucks, my how they've grown since they were teens in the pack last year. One was stamping his hooves, snorting and sniffing the air as he avidly followed behind a female who was ignoring him, her tail tucked snugly. He followed her around to the side of the house and for a moment I thought we were going to have a coupling display, but she diverted her track and squatted to pee. I think that was a signal, but yea or nay? No idea. The other buck displayed no aggression. He has one antler and only a short bud on the other side. I wonder if he lost it or it's a malformation. This reminds me that a few years ago there was a young buck with only one visible antler and from a distance he could be mistaken for a unicorn. Perhaps it's a mutation. Within a short period of time the herd of seven had made their way into the wood. If I were to follow them, I'd probably find them in the outside meadow, a spot Tweed never visits, where the grass is fine, and they are protected, though they don't know it, by a fence between them and the road.

Speaking of grass. Suddenly, it is green. The forecast is for rain for the next ten days. How much only the goddess knows.

Horseshoe crabs! Yes indeed. In fact, my biggest memory of them is on my honeymoon on Manasota Key just south of your homeland. I confess the scrabbling masses of crabs startled me the first time we walked down to the shore. There were crabs in Wisconsin as well, not sure what sort they were called though. Perhaps it's wrong to say 'were', and yet, who knows whether these creatures are still common when we look at the morning news and hear that wild salmon are threatened with extinction?

In a short follow-up about my ancestor. I have her letters and diaries as well. They traveled (post war) to Colorado from Vermont by railroad. Along the way, the train was harassed by Native Americans on the plains who, my guess is, probably wanted to discourage random shooting of their buffalo. Anyway, the idea to convalesce in the high dry air of Colorado was much advertised back east, thus the California gold rush of the 40s and 50s was followed in the 70s by an 'air rush'. Mostly, the patients were women. For two reasons: first, when men were diagnosed with consumption they were told to go adventuring–sail away, visit the continent, climb a peak. And second, because women were encouraged to gather together in a household, they were far more likely to spread the disease to their own sex. And so, the trains west must have been filled with pale, consumptive waifs laced into their corsets and bustled under yards of cloth. The graveyards of Colorado Springs were soon populated with the beloved, mostly young women. Jennie was thirty-six and left three children behind. Her husband built a business in the town and never left it, remarried, and died there at a reasonable age. His two daughters were raised in Quebec by their grandmother, while the young son grew up in Colorado. The telegram announcing her death almost reeks of relief in its clipped, spare prose. My connection to her is so palpable, it should be thought of as an ancestral curse to be exorcised, but of course, I can't do that. Funny you should ask where the clothing is. I was advised a while back to get all her things out of the attic and the house: that having it hanging over my own head was a problem. It's stored in the barn, but I have recently planned to send the archives to the women of the next generation. It's time.

As the rain came down yesterday a parade of cars brought probably a hundred people, mostly Pomo and their supporters, to Jackson State Forest. We don't know yet why. Were they there to pray for the redwoods or to continue to implore the state government to open their eyes and ears and listen to the graceful singing of the giants? The rain, their tears.

Love,
Jane


***18 October 2021. Cold.***

Dear Jane,
My intentions were to write deeply this evening about the rain, the deer, the Pomo. But my culinary skills are required in the kitchen. The condensed version, then:

Max also saw a deer when he arrived home today, at his front door, just like mine yesterday. He failed to see the symmetry but thought it cute that I did. It's weird to be perceived as a wacky old lady, but better wacky than grumpy.

Your description of the herd in your yard sounds like a frat party, right down to the asymmetric buck and the shy doe behind the bush.The Pomo. From December through April, the De Young will have on loan from the Met a painting by Jules Tavernier, 1878, called *Dance in a Subterranean Roundhouse at Clear Lake, California*. It depicts a ceremonial dance of the Elem Pomo that Tavernier witnessed with his patron and others—who look out of place in their suits and mustaches. The White men do not appear to be anything but rapt by the ceremony and dancing. Is it wrong to lose oneself in the joy of another culture? Or to find oneself cowed by curiosity in this practice that diverges so from one's own? What are the Pomo doing in the forest now? I'm finding more and more references, particularly in the literature for public gardens, that reference the fact that they rest upon indigenous homelands.

Rain gods and goddesses populate almost every culture. Freyr, the Norse rain god, also covers the sun and summer. "Dylan" (in Welsh) means "son of the sea" or "born from the ocean." Integral to the rain cycle. You know which one gets my vote.

Love,
Medea


*October 19, 2021 overcast. Rain coming. Gale warnings. yippee! Reading* **Animal Speak,** *Ted Andrews, entry* **"Deer."**

Dear Medea,
Dylan can be god of rain if he can make it rain. Do you think he can if he puts his mind to it? I'm convinced some people have the power to govern such things. If we believe the world is ordered and synchronous then we must also believe that all things are connected. It would be a messy universe if we all were active on all levels all the time, so why not assume that if I can call down the thunder, Dylan can call down the rain? Besides, my Welsh ancestors would be pleased. "Dylan" could also be female? You know how I resist sharing power with the masculine.

Perhaps because of the impending storm, the wildlife have been pretty quiet this morning. A short visit for breakfast from Tinker and Burt, but no bittie little birds, and no deer. I'm shocked that Max doesn't see with glaring urgency that both of you having deer at your door MEANS SOMETHING! Have I been talking to myself all this time?! ha-ha! Of course it means something. Question is, what? Deer, according to Andrews (see above) represent gentleness and innocence and their power comes on in autumn and spring. They remind us to pay attention to our intuition, that something significant could be overlooked. Deer showing up suddenly tell us to move back into the family unit and traditions, you have gotten too far away from the role that would be most beneficial for you at this time. Be gentle with yourself. Clearly all this relates to wedding plans, *n'est pas*?

I'm sorry this is brief; the morning was wasted fixing email passwords because someone of the opposite sex was too oblivious to recognize phishing when it bit him. Joy arrived in the attention of the kind support team at our lovely local server.

Love,
Jane

*19 October 2021 Cloudy, windy, cold, I'd say the "feels like" temperature is around 20, though I don't think I've ever felt 20. But, anyway, it's damn cold.*

Dear Jane,

Your day sounds much like mine. I'd elaborate, but I'd either sound like a cranky bitch or a Luddite, or both, so I'll leave it at that. There was joy as well, when a fat brown bunny appeared to scavenge from under the bird feeders outside the bedroom. A new pair of birds arrived this morning—grosbeaks? Pine Siskins? The suspense was killing me! These chubsters out-girth the chickadees and nuthatches, and their muted caramel, gray and dark brown color scheme might strike some as boring, but the pattern on the wings looks like it was conceived by a sedate Milton Glaser. What are they? Merlin knows. After listing all the important parameters, it appears that my mystery birds are...

House Sparrows.

This is why I love nature. Ordinary blossoms into extraordinary at least once every day.

There were three kids named "Dylan" in my son's class. Two boys. One girl. So, yes, our rain goddess can be female. My son is the finder of lost things. No matter how small or buried an item might be, within usually fifteen minutes, given a perimeter, he can locate it. Sort of like a Dowser. So, yes, Dylan can conjure rain, though he might not realize it yet.

Max is going to receive your paragraph about the Deer. He's an engineer, so the connections to family and intuitions, gentleness and traditions may strike him as "woo woo." But he is his mother's son. It's in there. I am looking up *Animal Speaks*. That feels urgent.

The wedding planning gives all of us hives. What was Chris and Michri's wedding like? (I assumed they are married, and what a fuddy-duddy that makes me!) As the mother-of-the-groom, my role is limited. Well, not really. But I'm excluded from all the girly stuff, dress selection and hair designs and whatever else brides do these days. First Look? What?? Is Hallmark involved?

All I want is for my kids to go to sleep each night and hold someone who loves him. To wake up with a kitty at the foot of the bed. To walk in their neighborhoods and see, no, SEE, every brilliant bud, every *thing* that wasn't there yesterday, every brave weed poking through the cracks in the sidewalk with a person who sees those things too. To feel fully alive.

Love,
Medea

Dear Medea,

Today I am baking: bread from ancient Yecora Roja, bolted, and ordinary cinnamon rolls the old school way. It's that kind of day where the sun is hidden and so the temporal aspect of the time, the day's progress, is null. I wonder while I knead the bread dough how many people from the pandemic quarantine are still baking. It was such a perfect visceral respond to an invisible threat. When life gets difficult, we cook, and then we eat.

I was expecting your new bird visitors to be equally prosaic, but robins, which come here all of a sudden and dig up the yard. Since we don't have much of a "lawn," we don't care, but I have heard people complain about the damn birds in a flock, digging. What I do complain about is the single male robin who sees himself in the landing window and pecks and pecks. This always frightens the dog and cascades into a trauma. The past two years I have taped strips of foil to the window which has helped but not completely eradicated the problem. Those bird brains are creatures of determination and habit. Speaking of fat, the quail are growing like crazy, plump and nearly as big as their parents they can still lift off into the bushes when necessary, but barely.

I'm looking forward to hearing Max's response to the totem animal. I'm used to skeptical engineers, they don't bother me, and in fact, I'm rather good at converting the skeptical mind. Yes, Chris and Michri are married…maybe fifteen years or so? They chose what to do, but I was more involved than the usual MOG. Chris wore a kilt and loved it so much that he has since worn a kilt at most party events. We found the perfect and most beautiful dress locally for Michri and they really looked wonderful and I think everyone had a fine time. The wedding was presided over by an old friend, Virginia, who, like you, was ordained, in her case while studying with the Berkeley Psychic Institute. It was Virginia who taught me how to manage my clairvoyance, how to use it. And for a number of years she was my traveling companion to Ireland. We spent a lot of time among the portal tombs and standing stones at all hours of the day and night. Back in the 90s that wasn't such a common sight as it is today. One midsummer eve, we climbed the top of a mound at midnight, the light had only just faded, and we were having a moment with the faeries when a young man wandered down the farmer's path. He was quite startled to see us on top of the mound. We invited him up, but he declined. He said he'd been at the pub, and just wanted a moment with the ancient ones. I felt like such a hag, but thinking back I was only mid 40s. It's strange but I have always felt "old."

I do need to work on my weather skills. You have a good point. I've heard it's always better to call in good than try to banish bad. Step One. We did get rain yesterday, no thanks to me, but not as much as just north of us, every time I looked at the weather radar we were at the bottom tail of the body of the storm. The fun went north as it passed inland. Today is quiet, but tomorrow is to be what they now call an "atmospheric river." Predicting up to 2 inches of rain which is a lot, especially for here.

As for cold, you've never been in subzero temps? Not even for skiing or some holiday? When Chris was a baby there were times when we couldn't go outside, the prairie winds and subzero temps would have frozen his breath in his little lungs. Lighting a match to heat up the car door lock? Starting the car and letting it idle while you go back inside to wait for it to warm up? You've been deprived. What about hurricanes, how many of those have you survived? It's all Kansas everywhere now, Dorothy, everywhere.

Love,
Jane

P.S. What if your boys end up dog lovers?


*20 October 2021 Gray, damp, looks forbidding outdoors, but upon gathering the mail, the 64 degrees declared by the weather app feels closer to 70. Blessed humidity. It's 75 in New York.*

Dear Jane,
Max has already declared that he intends to add a dog to his current three-cat menagerie. I bite my tongue. They bought an automatic litter box to reduce chore-time. They have foxes wandering their back yard. What is the equivalent of an automatic cat box for an indoor dog? It doesn't exist? That's what I thought. Dylan and his roommate would love to have a cat, but the landlord is pet party pooper. I would love to have a dog too, if only to snuggle and to keep company on errands. Bruce is opposed on freedom grounds; it's hard to argue, unless we abandon tropical dive travel, buy a trailer or trawler, and take the pets along. Which sounds like a travel blog in the making to me.

The furthest north I've ever lived is Lynchburg, Virginia, for three years during college. The weather made no sense to me, coming from a single-season state. I fought the chill autumn winds in shorts, because who ever heard of wearing pants in October? The one time I went skiing, a wet, dark bus ride to some godforsaken ski resort in West Virginia, I fell on the first run, disconnecting my ski. I couldn't right myself. For the next two hours, I sat against a tree, shivering, waiting for the ski patrol to help me down the mountain. Rather than reattaching the ski, he clicked off the other one and told me to walk back to the bus. I've tried skiing in Tahoe a couple of times. I've tried hot cocoa by a roaring fire, hot tubs under the stars and lightly falling snow, buying a puffy Bogner après-ski parka. There's no denying it. I was not built for the winter.

Max would look great in a kilt. I'll have to suggest that. Chris and other men who wear kilts, self-possessed and iconoclastic, should really run the country. Imagine that class picture.

Did you know that the US and the Vatican are the only two powers that failed to sign on for the latest biodiversity conference, the one at which the attendees learned of the rapid eradication of insects and fungus, birds and fish and mammals by humans? It's a companion to Glasgow, but less glamorous, or maybe the media glossed over it because the administration is too mired in budget talks to attend and didn't want to draw attention? Most everyone can do one thing to help stem this degradation, whether it's reducing meat consumption or planting milkweed to attract butterflies. But anything that requires action, that takes us away from wringing hands over our holiday gifts languishing in stacked containers, that diverts attention from watching a parrot emptying a utensil drawer on TikTok, the media prefers to ignore. Maybe we're just not terrified enough. Yet.

With all of the rain, I wonder whether the bird seed and suet will become too soggy for the birds to consume. Then I remember that they've managed to survive on seeds stowed underneath tree bark or buried behind damp mats of fallen leaves. That's the thing about birds: they're resourceful.

I can see you and Virginia, atop an emerald cnoc, divining ancient secrets from portal tombs. That pub crawler missed his chance for a double epiphany. Does Virginia believe that all people possess the power to see beyond? How did she instruct you to harness your vision? Bruce would say it's genetic, that only people with a "God gene" believe in things unseen, intuited. He has not met you yet, though. I recommend taking leave of one's own burning house, to experience the limitation in perception for what it is: fear of the unknown.

You're a champ for baking. The gray outside that blocks the sense of time lends itself to that. I adore the feel of the spongy dough, the sour tang of the yeast, and the house filled with the aroma of baking bread. The anticipation of that first bite of warm bread slathered in pale yellow butter. Making a grilled cheese sandwich to pair with freshly made tomato soup. Hmmm. Thank you for the inspiration.

Instead, of baking, though, I'm cleaning. My "spring cleaning" occurs in the shorter, colder days of fall, readying my den for the hibernating hours ahead. After refreshing the bedclothes, I'll start purging from the closet skirts and dresses whose fashionable days expired a few years ago, taking stock of small appliances and serving pieces that have lived in the pantry, untouched, for even longer. But not the books. John Waters once said if you ever go home with someone and they don't have books in their house, don't fuck them. After

I took the kids to see *Hairspray* at the Curran, we were moved to memorize the soundtrack. All summer long, by the pool, in the car, while making scrambled eggs, we sang like it was 1962, hamming it up like Corny Collins, cheering for Penny and Seaweed. Imagine John Waters in a kilt, serving as the Secretary of Education, or as the Senator from Maryland. Please help me visualize that.

I just caught the raven trying to access the too-small-for-him suet feeder. For such a majestic bird, it looks like it's wearing the wrong size of every body part. Do you ever feel that way sometimes?

Love,
Medea

P.S. The Lenape in NJ, the tribe that traded away its land in Manhattan so many fateful years ago, is granted fifty-four acres adjacent to Spirit Rock, one of its sacred sites. Saved from developers by a wise town council. The area is home to over ten miles of trails, which the interviewed tribe member, Owl, said will remain open to all.

*October 21, 2021 "Atmospheric River"—which we used to just call rain. Either way I'm happy. 60 degrees. I wonder if it's more the fact that the temp hasn't varied for the last 24 hrs.*

Dear Medea,
See, the trouble is that we can't possibly run away to France together if your ambient temperature needs to be above 75" and mine needs to be below 60. How will we solve this dilemma?

I had a cat as a child, and we have had many cats over our fifty years of married life. Around here cats need to come inside at night, or they will quickly disappear. I got tired of litter boxes and trails of cat litter, and even more I got tired of the cat fur everywhere. About 25 years into our marriage, we got a dog. She was a great starter dog for us, and she taught us a lot about how to be good humans. Poor thing. Then when we moved to the coast, we got our first border collie and have had joy and tragedy mixed ever since, but I absolutely love having a dog. Strangely, the neediness of cats began to wear on me. People would normally say it should be the other way around, but I think the key is how much more devoted dogs are to figuring out what we need emotionally at the moment and giving it. All of that said, sometimes I wonder about the heartbreak. As you know, it's been very hard, loving these housemates, very hard to lose them. Having a dog makes me get up in the morning and want to live another day.

I have exciting news! Yesterday I was sitting in the window-seat reading and looked up to see a beautiful bobcat! He/she (no idea) was having a bath but then froze. Fascinating how easily it faded into the background. I realized it had seen Tweed who was sitting on the front porch. I watch with my binoculars for a long time before it moved (binocs because my eyesight is poor and I wanted to see all the detail, not because he was that far away). I think it ran under the pool house deck, but I couldn't be sure. His coloring was splendid. The ears had the usual black tuft at the tips but had horizontal wide bars of black and white, a bar each, on the ear itself. The short tail was the usual tiger coloring but for the very end which mimicked the ears exactly. He was medium size and very healthy looking with thick sturdy legs and body. Of course, we know they are around, but we don't often get to see them. The only downside is that he was right near the thicket where the quail nest and the rabbits have their den. I hope the bobcat is happy enough with the profusion of gophers not to bother the bunnies or the quail.

This morning I was going to bag up my breads to put away and realized I'm almost out of plastic bread bags. I want you to know that I have purchased a beeswax reusable bag to try. I hope it works. Of course, it is the right thing to do whether it works or not. I had a bread box, but the bread seemed to get moldy awfully fast. I also bought a linen bread bag, same theory, reusable, washable, and handmade in Cornwall, England. What I like about that is that it has a tab for hanging it up. What a great idea! Take that you kitchen critters! Speaking of breadmaking, I've made bread my whole married life, but took a break when wonderful local bakeries proliferated. I like getting back to making ours now that it's just the two of us consuming. I love the smell of baking bread, but I must say I hate having sticky yeasty hands, I don't like being dirty in general but bread dough all over the sink and on my cuffs and under my nails. Ugh. That mess is only slightly improved by a stand mixer. The real gem tool added during this pandemic baking frenzy is a bench knife. How did I ever get along without that before?

My own belief is that we all have the nascent ability to use our senses far more than we normally do. If there is a "gift" involved, it is perhaps that the sense in question is developed without our working at it. Maybe it is genetic but not in the way Bruce means. That the Irish are known for having the "second sight" might be more genes than mythology. Why shouldn't it be? My opinion is, and my advice is, to everyone: Evolve or Die out. Scorning and denying what might be possible is a sign of insecurity. Almost anyone can learn to be more intuitive, and with intuition comes grace and generosity. We need that now. We will need it even more in the very real and very near future.

The full moon last night was lovely. I watched from bed for a long while. As the moon shifts, her light walks through the branches of the trees and sometimes it seems there must be sprites or fairies as a glow or sparkle finds space. It's no wonder dogs and their wild counterparts bark and yap and howl at the moon.

Love,
Jane


*2110 2021 Patterns in the date. Dylan would call that more of my pareidolia. Gray, humid, 64, singing plants, again.*

Dear Jane,
A meteor shower, twenty per second, is promised by meteor forecasters tonight. The cloud cover may prohibit a viewing. But knowing they're there means the universe is going about its business, ignoring the quotidian mundanities of we humans.

Today, the beasts of the world revealed themselves in muted splendor. We drove to Golden Gate Park with friends, on an explore. The Bison, which in thirty-two years I've never seen, stood shaggy and grazing behind the grounds of what was in the early 1950's the grandstand of a three-mile race track. This track saw competitors for four years. Badasses, barreling around the middle roads of the Park, until at some point the Commissioners or the Park and Rec decided this was way too *too*. The Commissioners did not predict what 1968 would bring.

A bobcat! You're enchanted. On our way back from the city, almost home, I spotted a streak of fur running westward. This coyote seemed worried. It looked back toward the road after it stopped a few meters in, as though it were waiting for its friend. Or its mom. Or its baby. Once the boundaries between species burst, anthropomorphizing disappears. This pup looked to be about three feet tall. Mostly gray fur, a smattering of chestnut, black tips at the ears and tail. And bright eyes. Please don't cross that road again, coyote. I told Bruce that I want to bring all of the animals to live in our yard. Then, I remembered that some of them might eat each other. Yikes. He said, "You already have all of the animals in the back yard." Which is kind of true. But instead of coyotes, we have gophers.

Speaking of gophers, Max told me that the ASPCA allows you to adopt a cat(s) to live outside as mousers. His house suffers gophers and rats and the aforementioned foxes. Ethically, is it ok to adopt a working cat, knowing the chance that it will perish in the fangs of a wild one? You live in the wild. I'd appreciate knowing your take. I think every living thing should only eat vegetables. But after you nurture the vegetables yourself, ethics take a turn toward the tricky. Biology dictates that cats and canines live as carnivores. Diet for us humans is more fluid, fraught. I talked to a man today whose eyes twinkled as he recalled gigging big, juicy frogs in the Delta when he was a kid, carving out the legs, and barbequing up those suckers off the stern of his dad's 43" Hatteras. He and his dad shot doves, too; his job after the bird fell was to row out to where it landed in the slough and ferry it back for "dressing." All of this talk gave me a sick feeling. Is remembering fondly the taking of a life for your nourishment the equivalent of reverence? I do always thank my tomatoes before I slice them. I hope that's adequate gratitude.

What is a bench knife? Will having one give me a reason to make bread?

Love,
Medea


*October 22, 2021 beautiful day, sun (I'm making an exception), everything is new*

Dear Medea,
Sitting in the window the ocean makes her presence known with crashing surf that makes the windows shiver and rattle. I couldn't resist. I got in the car and drove north along the coast. Oh my, what a spectacle. It never gets old and is so often breath-taking. Today, between storms and in advance of what is coming, the ocean churns grays and silvers and the mist shines with the sun and blends the sea into the sky. The beaches are already littered with new logs, huge trees tossed like joss sticks up onto the beach. I wonder if anyone has ever seen it happen? The shore birds are on the move and the cliff line was full of shifting pelicans. The Navarro River was full, and the algae bloom is gone. It's a miracle how it can change so fast. The grass is green, and we can all exhale. I can't see the ocean from my house, but to feel it shudder is such an amazing thing, to be aware of how fragile we are by comparison.

I've had a question searching for an answer lately, it has two parts. First, where have the raven children gone? And second, is Tinker actually the mom of this brood? Because now she comes with Burt, and they come alone. There are other ravens around, next door, across the street, up in the field, but only Tinker and Burt come to beg for food. I don't like to use that word "beg" because it seems as if they are needy and resourceless when it is surely I who am needy and resourceless. I've decided I should look back through my photographs and see if I can match mom with Tinker.

Yes! You absolutely must own a bench knife even if you never make bread because surely you do make pastry? I use it to cut pie dough in ½ and clean the residue from the countertop surface. It's more of a scraper than a knife though the edge is sharp. I have found that bakers are very fond of their secret language:

"bolted" as in bolted flour just means sifted but how would you ever know that? In the same way that a bench knife is a scraper (think putty knife without a handle). Bolted conjures up the image of a 20th c. farm mother running from her house (burned bread loaves smoking on the stove) with her flour sack kitchen towel flying in the wind. Bolted. Will she return? Or leave her worthless man high and dry to bake his own damn bread?

Barn cats are all well and good where two factors exist at the same time: 1) a safe barn 24/7, and 2) a human who is fairly lax about their well-being. I don't think either of us qualifies. I would love to fill my house with puppies and my yard with every wild thing, and I'm doing my damnedest, but the worry does catch up to me too often. I would make a terrible scientist, but I guess that's obvious.

Love,
Jane


*22 October 2021 The sky shows personality today, cottony clouds the colors of snow and oyster shells waft east, carrying the front inland. All the West must have some of this blessed rain. Mercury reads 64, though without much wind it's warm enough to open the doors and windows and welcome the fresh air.*

Dear Jane,
Outside my sunroom sliding door, the Japanese Maple's leaves have turned the color of a tropical sunset. It's a funny juxtaposition for this tree, which is flanked by three species of towering palms on one side and two on the other. While most of them rustle a soothing accompaniment to the ravens and the chickadees, my favorite is the quiet Shaving Brush Palm. This tree favors the shade and the quadrant of the back yard where the maple sits offers the most shade in the garden. Unlike most palm with their trunks that resemble a vertical stegosaurus, the Shaving Brush Palm's trunk sits low in the ground, only a foot or two above the soil, so most of what is visible are the fronds. These stretch skyward, over the roof line, about fifteen feet. We have three in the front that used to rest peacefully underneath the boughs of a heritage Bay Laurel tree. When that tree succumbed to an unknown parasite or disease after many years and dollars spent to save it, those palms became victims of the abundant sunshine, and their once-olive green fronds turned a sickly yellow and the tips scorched to dark brown. We've planted three other supposedly fast-growing shade trees to protect them, but between the eternal water shortage and the dense clay soil, those trees themselves are fighting for their own lives, and not in any shape to save the palms.

Feeling connection to the trees adds dimension to loving the garden. Not quite maternal, not exactly friendship. More akin to the complete loss of an independent self and consequent merger of the with the rest of the living world that one senses when planting seedlings in rich, wormy soil, or skimming along a reef wall at one hundred and twenty feet, feeling warm sand and foamy saltwater underneath bare toes, or reaching an alpha state during meditation. All boundaries melt away. We're one, massive, breathing, living whole.

Beyond the maple and palms, a trio of ravens and a pair of black squirrels are up to no good. The new cylinder of birdseed that I mounted yesterday I found occupied by a hungry squirrel, who used the top of the feed as its throne, and twisted its furry body into a candy-cane shape so it could peck at the food. I can't blame it, really, but that's expensive squirrel food. I tapped on the glass and it leapt away; but the sneaky little dickens returned for more. The ravens seem vexed by the power tools the workers have deployed next door. The same low roar of sawblade on wood has gone on for the past over an hour, amplified by the clouds pressing down from above. It causes my ears to ring; what damage might it do to the more sensitive birds?

Love,
Medea


*October 23, 2021 rain and rain showers, but the big storm remains offshore for the moment. 51 degrees at dawn. Reading* Hakai *magazine,* Why Salmon Need Trees, *October 2021.*

Dear Medea,
It's funny how you'll find palm trees in a strangest of places, including the south coast of Ireland where there is an ironic banana belt where sailors and would be yacht owners love to live for the friendly harbors (not that common in Ireland in general) and the mild weather. Take a right (west) off the mooring though and it gets problematic real fast. Back to palms, they always remind me of the date palms in Iran. When the dates were ready, groups of chador clad women and children would come down the road. They would bang their sickles along the fence to get the attention of memsahib for permission to harvest. I don't know of anyone who would deny these very, very poor women, but it was the accepted practice to ask before the most agile child was sent aloft to bring down the fruit onto large cloths spread about underneath. I love dates. Don't you?

Keeping a tree alive can be a challenge. I failed completely with the apple tree my neighbor gave me for my birthday. My favorite tree is a hawthorn where I tie "clooties," scraps of cloth imbued with intention, like Buddhist prayer flag scraps. A few years ago, we had so much rain (that seems like forever ago) that the tree started to fall over. I read that once it's uprooted that's that. Give up. We pushed it back in place and even dug underneath the roots which are classically shallow anyway and packed in more dirt under and above and then rigged a support line to hold it up. Two years have passed and while it's not the most opulent or happy of trees, it is alive. This summer when I watered it, I told it to imagine rainfall. I hope you can save your palms. I definitely support you not giving up or giving in too quickly. Either way, in the end, we will have tried our best with all of our creatures.

I read an article in Hakai magazine about the symbiotic relationship between salmon and trees. Salmon, our newest endangered species, and redwoods, the trees men are determined to make endangered. For fuck's sake. Every year someone from Fish and Game comes and counts the salmonid population in the rivers, including the Navarro. I wonder, will they tell us when they come up with zero? Will they change their title to just Game and concentrate on eliminating all those next? I'm in a bad mood, yes, it seems impossible that we can shift all this at all, never mind in time to make a difference. Speaking of hooved beasts, the deer seem to be wandering in circles today and I wondered why until I saw a massive buck with a regular hood ornament of rack. He shook his head and raindrops showered down. I'm surprised he didn't fall over.

Still waiting for the major storm to come onshore. The rainfall predictions are great news. The water trough is up by about 4 inches already. I suggested to Gene that he fire up the generator and see if it still works. It appears he would rather have it be a surprise.

I hope Windsong was tightly moored, whoever had her out last (talking to you, Max) and that you enjoy the storm, you do love storms, yes? How could you not, being from hurricane country?

Love,
Jane

P.S. Update, the generator works. I take it all back.


*25 October 2021 63 degrees, the remnants of the Atmospheric River/Bomb Cyclone scuttle across the sky. The ground sports a carpet of auburn maple leaves.*

Dear Jane,
The weekend delivered its promised deluge. You're right—I love storms, the darker and wilder, the better. Coming from hurricane country, the weather people on local news and their storm hysteria raises my maternal urge to

pat them on the head and remind them to fill the bathtub with water. Not to minimize the damage, God no. Flooding and mudslides and any number of trucks blown sideways by great gusts of wind on open bridges. The point is not that storms wreak havoc. The point is that we, like the birds that bolted to hidey holes in a quiet area in my garden, have the innate smarts to avoid being destroyed by them. Like a wave is the ocean, we are the storm. And the consequent calm.

Palm trees manage storms too, with that supple trunk and fronds that wave like hypnotized concert fans. I have seen palm trees that, over time and through stormy weather, reform from straight and tall to a little bit bent to the shape of a crooked elbow. Nature, the master sculptor. The palm across the street, which sprouted three new fuzzy fronds over the weekend, may not be native to California, but this species has been here, minding its water intake and offering shade and splendor for so many decades that, like other transplants, it can claim residency. The messy, shedding, fire-prone eucalyptus trees simply don't belong. I read this morning that two towns in Florida, Miami and West Palm Beach, will not plant any more palm trees because they don't provide enough shade. Now, mind you, palm tree groves covered South Florida before most of those decision-makers' parents were born. They survived hurricanes and droughts and developers. But, who studies history, natural or otherwise, before pronouncing a tree unsuitable?

I do love dates. Mom used to stuff them with peanut butter and roll the log in confectioner's sugar (Overkill. But so delicious.) When Bruce and I would take the kids to Arizona, we'd stop for date shakes at Hadley Fruit Orchards in Cabazon; when the mercury threatens to burst out of the top of the thermometer, a straw full of date shake cools the core.

The cylinder of seed, all eight by four inches of it, disappeared on Saturday afternoon. When I saw it last, Saturday morning before my foray to the Delta, it still measured a good six and a half by three and three-quarters inches. The only squirrel in sight that morning looked runtish; unless it called its extended family to the feeder for the mother of all squirrel parties, only one explanation remains: the ravens banded together and levitated it up and out.

There is a woman in England who tends birds and has taught "her" raven, whose name is Fable, to speak, chortle and kiss. Fable's fifty-word vocabulary includes "Hello," "Hi" and "Wow." She speaks in the voice of her "owner." Putting aside for a moment the ethical question involved in keeping a raven in a pen, when a wild bird comes to a person to have her head rubbed, that's evidence of our shared existence, right? Or perhaps Fable transforms into a fair-haired child after dark, sits at her learning desk, then returns to her preferred shape at daybreak. Could you please ask Tinker and Burt when they come to politely ask for food?

The Navarro River runs clear again. It must be shouting as it tumbles over rocks and across fallen trees. You have that river, and the ocean, both close enough to recharge you. My quick trip to the Delta did likewise. Skimming over the flat, agate-colored water demands attention to all, small things. Golden dragonflies perched on the tule reeds. A Great Blue Heron standing sentry atop a weathered navigation aid. Two (two!) different, solitary ospreys, white feathers dipped in chocolate dots, alert, talons poised for fishing. A Cattle Egret, elegant and erect and almost glowing against the tule. This time of year, the roar of power boats and jet skis gives way to the rustle of reeds and the lapping of water against shore. The birds, too, seem to understand the restorative power of silence.

Love,
Medea

P.S. *Orion's* Autumn edition contains an article about slime molds called "What Slime Knows," by Lacy M. Johnson. I had no idea. And like sharks and rats and cockroaches, slime will live on to repopulate the planet after the sixth extinction. Tesla is now the first company with a trillion-dollar market cap. Bring on the slime. P.P.S. California only captures 20% of our rain.


*October 25, 2021 sun, cool, calm. Raging surf.*

Dear Medea,
It was a good storm, not a great one. Still, I guess we got around 5 inches of rain, and we'll take it with gratitude. At this moment, the high surf warnings of possible 35 ft cresting waves seem to have come true. The windows are rattling, and the ocean is quite audibly raging. The beaches are closed against stupid humans, and there is some roadway detritus, but the Navarro has not yet overflowed her banks. I bet the hundreds of brown pelicans (a group of pelicans is apparently a squadron) are hunkered down on shore, surely fishing in high surf is a fool's errand.

One tree does not a windbreak make. The poor palms planted in some concrete meridian in a hotel parking lot struggling to hang on. I'm shocked about the fruit stealers, but then recall that a tourist in the village was once accosted for having picked flowers from someone's garden and replied, "flowers are for everyone!"

This morning I saw the two male deer from last summer's herd for the first time in ages, they both have starts of antlers, and are still in company with two young females. I wonder if the herd will come together after mating season. It seems more likely that the interference of the master buck will disrupt the herd. If it does come together it will increase by at least three.

Tinker and Burt stayed quiet and hidden through the heavier rainfall but showed up the moment I appeared in the kitchen this morning and were more fearless that ever before about approaching me while I set out food. Everyone feels better with routine, right? As to teaching them words, that might be a bit across the line right along with kisses. Kisses? Yikes! That woman is braver than I am. A few feet between that beak and those talon feet is fine by me. Also, need I remind us that those are bugs they keeping picking out of each other's feathers? Our shared existence has its boundaries for a reason. At some point, one has stepped across but in doing so has chipped off a bit of sanity or maybe even wisdom. None of us intentionally become the crazy cat lady down the road whose house smells of decades of litter boxes; but a few losses, a few missed steps, a few disappointments coupled with a heavy dose of giving up, and there we are: the village oddity. I try to remind my friends to be sure to let me know if I've missed a chin hair and suddenly there's an inch long hair sticking out of my beak, I mean, nose. Trouble is, their eyesight is only marginally keener than my own. I saw an old woman on a sidewalk in Ireland one day who had several thick and long hairs jutting from chin and nose and I had to conclude with some envy that she clearly was aware, and clearly didn't care. I would like to be that self-contained.

Interestingly, I put on my new-last-year raincoat and pulled up the hood and I think the ravens didn't recognize me at first. They held their perch at least (Burt on the top of the Verizon signal extender on the house roof peak–30 feet up–, and Tinker in a tree) and waited until I had put out food before descending. I pulled my hood down and said, "hey, see, it's just me!"

My dowsing rods did arrive. I haven't tried them out yet. They are on my altar soaking up the invisible world. Very important to "charge" them before use. This is also true of husbands.

Slime. I saw that also. Slime and the bugs that live on our eye lids will rule the world someday.

Love,
Jane

P.S. It occurs to me to wonder if I will ever need to shop for a new raincoat or wellies again?

*26 October 2021 63 degrees, humid and overcast. The sun lost the race today.*

Dear Jane,

Your raincoat question reminds me about a time perhaps fifteen years ago when my mom in full melancholy told me she and daddy were shopping for "their last house." That was three houses ago. I would say buy a raincoat and wellies if your current raingear either scares Tinker and Burt, springs a leak, or fails to bring a smile to your lips. Raingear should encourage you to splash in a puddle no matter how old or new you might be. You can always give the old ones to "Buy Nothing." If people can offload used fish tank water or the pickle juice left in the jar after the last gherkin is crunched, you'll have a welcome line of takers.

I did not know you need to charge the dowsing rods. The idea of installing a cistern appeals, until the nitty gritty details of chlorinating and scooping out drowned rats and whatever else might be required to ensure quality intrude. Don't bother me with facts when I'm trying to save my tiny corner of the world.

The power and water situation during the fires and floods force our attention to conservation. I've told you about my comment to my dad years ago, which still haunts me. It's impossible to run hot water into a coffee mug to warm it and then toss the warm remnants into the sink. Any ice that has fused in the freezer I offer to the potted plants. Every appliance not used must be unplugged. My friend Doug, who lived in Noe Valley, once cut off the heat in his home for the winter. His wife told me that the average temperature hovered at 55. Now that we have a power wall, the Tesla app will disclose whether we are generating our own energy and at what rate. Bruce sat glued to the app during the power outage on Sunday. Imagine telling someone now that they had to wait for a sunny day to do their laundry so that they could hang it out back on the clothesline. Then imagine giving that person a scratch-and-sniff of sheets blown and baked dry by Mr. Sun. If that person were blessed with sensory memory, she might conjure her grandpa carrying pegs in his teeth while he strung the wet sheets up tight.

I did know that it's not illegal to pick poppies but stealing flowers from a person's garden, well that's plain rude. And illegal. Flowers may "belong" to everyone just as air "belongs" to everyone. But if those flowers bud from a rosebush that I have tended gently for weeks and years, and my wish is for everyone to enjoy them, who is the flower snatcher to defy? As you said, boundaries exist for a reason. Tweezers also exist for a reason. And mirrors. Boldly parading about the town with chin whiskers trailing in the breeze could evidence self-containment, a fearless "fuck you" to those who travel great distances to visit the perfect brow shaping salon. Maybe she didn't care. Maybe she lost her tweezers. I promise to always tell you, as I hope you will tell me. The skin on my arms already gives me a feeling of elderliness that does not match either my *esprit* or the rest of me. The illusion of youth withers in the presence of obvious facial hair.

The new additions to the bird sanctuary fit right in. House Sparrows at the window, in the bushes, on the feeders—front and back—, hopping and pecking around in the mulch and singing as though they intend to show the chickadees how it's done. How long will they remain here? Will they build a nest come spring? All of the birds act super-animated after the rain. Even the decapitated palm tree shot its fronds up another two feet! There exists a slight sense of drought reprieve; though the water pundits declare the Sunday storm a mere drop in the bucket, the birds and we know when to shut up and dance.

Love,
Medea

P.S. The Hairy Woodpecker accosts the nuthatches. The sparrows appear to scare off the chickadees. The bold black squirrel continues to cross the feed line. Sprinkling the seed square with cayenne pepper, which the lady at the bird store promised would ward off all non-avians, did not deter that squirrel. Did the cayenne embolden the woodpecker to warrior status? It seemed dazed after grazing at the feeder; after it attacked the tinies, it drilled deep and multiple holes in our wooden fence. Is cayenne a bird hallucinogen? What is the hierarchy here? When the population consisted of chickadees, nuthatches and the occasional Scrub Jay, cooperation and peaceful coexistence ruled.


*October 26, 2021 light rain, occasionally. mild*

Dear Medea,
Cayenne? Oh my, that sounds like torture. I'm not sure that's a nice thing to do. Afterall, squirrels are opportunists. There's no sign "no squirrels allowed." I have to think the pepper burns like crazy, no?

Seems like all the species are assembling in groups: the quail always have, but the wee tinies are all in the hypericum hedge refusing to come out. I'm not sure where the robins have gone to but they are gone, along with the Mourning doves. Yesterday I heard a bird sing a song I've never heard before, loud and clear, but I wasn't able to spot the bird itself.

My active day was mostly standing around watching Gene remove the ceiling fan and replace it with a light fixture. Is there anything more boring than being the audience and occasional gofer for a husband? I think not. Why does everything take forever, require a pile of tools and numerous trips to the tool shed, and then, finally, the job is never quite finished? Afterwards, I rearranged the furniture. It's some psychological thing with me, surely there's a name for it, but I rearrange furniture in order to calm my mind. A messy house is a reflection of clutter in my head. Even if the mess is of my own making. I feel better now.

Love,
Jane


*27 October 2021 Blue-sky sunny and a cool 62.*

Dear Jane,
Yesterday marked three months of our correspondence. I've learned much from the birds, the trees, the weather and from you. Eyes wide open to all possibilities. A now-deceased relation once told me that she could not tolerate a life lived without continual external stimulation. I wonder whether she would find a daily chickadee census life-affirming or soul-numbing?

Your deer situation concerns me. You've observed this herd for some time, so you have a sense for what the bucks want, what the does evade. Is this common deer behavior? Biology compels all creature to mate, and also to self-preserve. Where will the does ultimately fall?

My heart is heavy this morning with a discovery about a person close to me who appears to be losing a grip on reality, failing to correctly identify members of her own family. What is memory? Where does it reside? The birds remember the position of each feeder, and when one is empty, they fly to one of the others. The Bay Laurel tree that we tried in vain to save remembered how to shoot a runner up through the soil toward the sun. Salmon famously return to the same spawning grounds each year, like the turtles that lay eggs on the same patch of sand. When I was in school, this behavior was described, or maybe dismissed as "intuition." Even slime mold has memory. Slime mold, unlike birds and fish, lacks an organism that we might recognize as a brain. Does this mean that memory may not always require a wrinkled nut in which to percolate?

Accepting impermanence, when it happens to someone else's familiar moves us to offer compassion and broad shoulders. When impermanence manifests in the supernova of a realization that your own clan faces rupture, are we able to offer that same compassion and strength to ourselves?

They say it takes a human three weeks after you move, say, your garbage can to internalize its new location. I wonder whether that holds true for memories as well.

Love,
Medea

*October 27, 2021 fog, sun, mild, still*

Dear Medea,

Oh no! This news is so disturbing. It's everyone's greatest fear, isn't it? No matter what the cause, losing our minds is the unacceptable evil of aging. I hope you don't keep it to yourself–tell the people who need to know, need to step in and help.

Yesterday evening one of the raven pair, I'm pretty sure it was Tinker, but they are much easier to tell apart when they are side by side–anyway, Tinker was up a tree cawing *"caw caw caw" "caw caw caw"* over and over. No reply. She became agitated and added a *"caw."* Called and called. I went outside and got food and put it out on the sawhorse and on the sheet of wood on the ground and then stood by. She called and called. I started to fear something unfortunate had happened to Burt. Then, there was a reply from a long way away. Tinker called again. Nothing. She flew to the food and stood by, as if guarding it, but kept calling. Finally (and I'm going to admit maybe it was only ten minutes, but it seemed like forever), Burt arrived. A bit of drama. It worries me that I was so worried. I'm not sure I can deal with tragedy. The edge on which I dance still seems steep, and uncontrollable. It has been almost two years since we lost our young dog and I fell into this sadness, and I still can't heal those wounds. Can't take them in stride. Humans only survive because they become expert at reconciling and moving forward, right? I need a pathway. And one that isn't at the cliff's edge. Like the tarot card 0 The Fool, dancing at the edge without regard for society, dog yapping protectively at her feet. The Fool is the first card of the journey we make over and over from birth to death. Repeating our mistakes sometimes, fixing them other times, finding our way. Dancing on the edge is a very hard place to stay for long.

What makes us sensitive and inquisitive in the first place is the same response mechanism that makes us vulnerable to sadness, to accumulating cares and forgetting how to move past the worry. Finding a way to catalog the escalating global traumas we are experiencing in this world is the new work of life. We can't fix it all. We can't pretend it doesn't exist. We can only put the things we can do something about at the top of the list and set to work. It's pretty clear many people have abandoned all pretense of sympathy in favor of greed. Our government politicians for example. Does there exist a more blatantly ignorant and self-serving body? How did we, the voting public, let this happen?

It's no wonder I'd rather watch the deer do their mating rituals. This morning the younger doe of the herd trotted by at a good clip followed closely by the young buck, literally hot on her heels. I suppose it's inevitable. And at least it's not the big old man buck. 'Round and 'round they go.

Tinker had to call Burt again this morning. She used some other calls besides the tradition *"caw caw caw"* this time. Something is up. I don't know what. If they are siblings, then perhaps Burt is off finding a mate. If they are mates, then where is he off to?

Sending you love and compassionate energy for what is to come.
Jane

*28 October 2021 Dusk, stillness, the sound of crickets in the perhaps final warm evening of 2021.*

Dear Jane,
Reading your letter, it's evident that our thoughts are once again in sync. This afternoon, after learning that the reason for my familiar's loss of memory stems from a fall that left her with a brain bleed and a respectable shiner, the only place that felt hopeful was beside the water. So, I headed down to the reservoir (time not permitting a drive to the best water for me, the ocean) and unloaded on Mother Earth. Not that she wears a "kick me" sign; she simply seems capable of absorbing pain and uncertainty and using it to feed trees and nurture waterfowl.

What strikes me about this brain issue is how very different is my reaction from the sufferer's. My familiar's choice is magical thinking. Nothing to worry about. Is my concern an unnecessary overreaction? My original family lives in the neighborhood of eternal sunshine. Bruce's pessimism defines the house where I live now. The nexus? That's the edge where I dance.

Losing a pet who was so young reminds us that our control over pretty much everything is nil. That dog did nothing to deserve such a fate. You certainly did not deserve to feel that heartache. In a broader context, what does it signify? Life may be beautiful and wonderful, and it is also grossly unfair. I'm not sure that humans' ability to move forward, to reconcile is what keeps us moving forward. Perhaps it is instead a willingness to accept that what or whom we love we must cherish every second that we're graced with its presence. That the bad things that happen are not any more unusual than the good. Who becomes expert at reconciling heartache? Forgive yourself your grieving. Is the Fool who thumbs her nose at convention really foolish? Or does she dance on the edge to remind us we have power to decide on which side our feet will fall?

I'm relieved that Burt showed up. And Tinker. Attachment is a bitch, and so let's call it "interest" instead, shall we? Your deer will bring forth fawns, who will repeat the mating ritual all over again. My squirrels, who I do not wish to call "my" squirrels though they've adopted the feeder, played slap and tickle after I shooed the smaller one from the feeder; the larger (male?) waited at the fence rail. Much mating ensued. Squirrels screwing on top of a fence while trying to remain horizontal on a space about three inches wide defies the laws of physics. They tumbled over the lattice. They clawed their way back to the level and resumed. They dashed a few more feet forward, attached at the pelvis. They finally finished or decided the fence railing lacked the comfort and stability of a bed of pine needles. The world is replete with singing whales and chariot clouds and bodies of water that reflect fire in autumn leaves. I don't trust anyone who rebuffs nature's wonderous distractions.

As for how we allowed such craven leaders to grace the halls of our Nation's Capital and behave with such disregard for civility, cooperation, and compromise, I think the first place we must look is our fractured, feckless education system. I think the second place we must look is in the mirror.

I feel your love and compassionate energy and carry it with me with much gratitude.

Love,
Medea


*October 28, 2021 warm sun, humid, is this California? `Tis the season of the Dead.*

Dear Medea,
While I might not be able to control my grief, I have had plenty of time to figure it out. Does that help? Probably not. In fact, in this case I think the knowing has prolonged the experience. The problem is far bigger than the loss of the sweetest dog I've ever had in my life. But he was very ill with severe epilepsy, and it was the only compassionate act to let him go. I don't want a new puppy (and neither does Tweed), I want Tosh back, I want to take back the whole experience, drill down and find some place in it where I could have done something different. It's a fool's errand. Where it has led me is to the realization which you reference. We have no control. I would say, we not only have no control, but when we do act in a truly existential way, we are in for a ride of conscience that we aren't in any way prepared for. Tosh's death and the helplessness that I felt returned me to the core of my experience of the deaths of the three humans in my life I have had to let go, literally. It was my responsibility to release my parents and my grandfather to Death. Guess what? It's impossible to "deal" with that existential moment and get past it. I will never recover from absorbing that energy, even though it was absolutely the right thing, the right time for them to die. How then should we manage this grief? I haven't a clue. I know that losing this sweet puppy has put me at the finishing line, at the edge, and there is no more room for such extremes of existence unless I can shift. Unless I can shift, or jump. A part of me is preparing for that in a way that is more immediate than the usual thought process implicit in "getting old." The need to control the uncontrollable. These

times of desperation, of pandemic, really start to force us to focus. There seem to be two kinds of people: those who can't help but micromanage their futures, and those who have danced at the edge, fallen off, but not been hurt. It worked for them so far, so screw vaccines, screw being polite and careful.

There is nothing I could have done differently for my parents or my grandfather or any of the cats and dogs in my life. Carrying grief is, I guess, a part of being wise, at least I hope I am gaining wisdom through all this heartbreak. The problem remains, how do I step back from the edge where emotions are simply too ragged. The Q'ero believe that our core, our center is our solar plexus. They call it the cuzco, like the city. It's the third chakra, where we get our gut instincts. For the Q'ero it is where the archetype of the Hummingbird resides. In hummingbird we are reminded that the journey is long and very difficult, and inevitable. Take the sweetness where we can. I'm trying to let that wisdom outweigh sadness. And yet, is there any point in preparing for what's to come?

I know I've written a lot about Hummingbirds, but I don't really like them-mean spirited wee shits really. Is it the sugar? I'd rather put ravens in that third chakra place, or swans. I love birds who mate for life but then that's another problem to grieve over. Tinker and Burt are back to normal. This time.

Love,
Jane


*29 October 2021 73 degrees under a robin's egg sky, a few thin clouds, a mere whisper of breeze. Almost November at 5:30 pm. A gift from our Mother.*

Dear Jane,
Where I should be right now is tromping through muddy grounds at Golden Gate Park. Today is the first day of Outside Lands. Glass Animals and The Strokes both perform this evening. Bruce said I'm free to go as long as I come home and quarantine for two weeks. Does that mean I'm free from kitchen duty for a fortnight? It's tempting. Yet, the educated part of me that listens to the Cassandra in Bruce can acknowledge that despite vaccine requirements for entry and encouragement for social distancing, after a few hours of swaying to strains of multiple guitars, sampling wares in Chocolands and quaffing a tequila or two in a crowd of 100,000, precious little room between respirating, probably Covid-positive bodies will remain.

Ugh. I resent my grown-up sensibilities sometimes.

As we walked past our sad, spindly, coney pine tree at the start of today's walk, Bruce said "I see death everywhere." This struck me as wildly hilarious—he's prone to drama—but my laughter met with a disapproving, or maybe perplexed look. When does the birthday switch flip and render an upcoming anniversary of YOU cause for morosity? Don't you remember being five or sixteen and thinking "Wow! Today I get presents and cake and my driver's license!" Eighteen elicits this glee. Twenty-one, when official adulthood tied to the legal consumption of mood-altering substances, does too. I turned twenty-five in Paris after a botched attempt to sail the canals of France with a man who claimed to have invented the Pringle's potato chip can when he worked for Proctor and Gamble. He (and I, to be fair) neglected to conduct research, or to use our heads and factor in winter and its attendant ice blankets over the waterways in France between October and March. We left muggy Ft. Lauderdale at the end of September. We bought a 26-foot sailboat in England, he transported it to St. Helier, Jersey (how? I have no idea—I rode over on the ferry) and we lived aboard in the luxurious (seriously—hot showers, always clean. SF has much to learn) municipal harbor for two months while he tinkered with the engine. I joined the public library, discovered the Financial Times, learned to make kedgeree in a pressure cooker, walked the perimeter of the island, kept the boat tidy, and met a local lawyer's wife who spent her days on their cabin cruiser drinking Calvados (and who loaned us a heater in mid-November when the weather turned.) St. Helier. A fine place to be marooned.

By Thanksgiving, the canals had fully frozen over. Our dream died, adventure aborted. My bank account (a sock in the cubby underneath my bunk) would support a frugal couple of weeks. The engine remained out of commission. I called my folks warning them I'd be home for Christmas. They helped me to secure a job with a law firm in Naples. I bought a ferry ticket for St. Malo, and bid the captain adieu around the seventh of December. Sitting toasty in the glassed-in patio of Le Gentilhomme bistro at Place St Michel, where I'd spent time as a student only seven years earlier, I spotted a girl with a journal and chewed pen, sitting alone in the corner, recording. "I'm so lucky that may parents could afford this junior year abroad in Paris, the City of Light!" or "Why am I in this bar when I should be boffing a sexy Frenchman?" or "Death. It haunts me." We exchanged glances. She must be 55 now. I don't feel, inside, one bit different. I wish the same for her.

Bruce turns 72 on Wednesday. We met in Martinique in 1977. Inside, he's that same bronze, blonde scuba god. But now, Death curls its finger, beckoning, from the desiccated branches of a pine tree that we've nurtured for 22 years.

Love,
Medea


P.S. Despite a paralyzing fog this morning that messed with their IFR, all the birds rallied round the feeders for another day of warm.

*October 30, 2021 light rain early. sun and light clouds. mild. getting used to smoke in the air not being a reason to panic*

Dear Medea,

I guess it must be the Scorpio in our spouses because Gene is exactly the same morose depressing human for weeks before and after his birthday, insisting he doesn't want presents or any acknowledgement of the event. I always ignore that. What's a birthday without presents and some fun? Gene's birthday is the 7th. Isn't that funny? People should come with owner's manuals that detail these things as required reading in advance of commitment because frankly "love at first sight" is a blinding experience. Poor Bruce. He's right. Death is everywhere. But that doesn't mean no birthday!

I love hearing about your adventures. Living on a boat in France! I know what you mean about feeling the same inside. I think everyone does. It's a mean little party trick of human nature.

This morning I neglected to check out the window and make sure the coast was clear, so Tweed and I went out the back door and he spotted the doe and her juvenile and took off after them. We try to avoid this. The routine when it happens is that they are far faster than Tweed and he is giving it only a cursory go and stops halfway down the driveway. His "border." This time the doe must have felt she didn't have enough of a lead, so she turned on Tweed and they both reversed course! Tweed pulled out all stops and took off for the front porch. The doe must have caught him because there was a squealing from Tweed– I didn't see it, but I think she probably bumped him or nipped his butt. Tweed flew up the steps but when the doe turned around, he came back down and went after her. She was still faster, and Tweed still stopped at his invisible border line. Tweed's lucky it wasn't a buck. I have seen bucks be pretty aggressive toward other dogs in the past. And so that was the morning entertainment.

Love,
Jane


*31 October 2021 61 and gloomy in the suburbs.*

Dear Jane,

Your love of this weather encourages me to keep trying to find the positive in cold, gray days. So far, I have the advent of the sparrow couple. And the appearance of mold on the cocoa mulch so that it resembles permafrost on the shady parts of the ground. This is positive only because it means the mulch continues to feed the plants. We have another week before the clock falls back, when waiting for a civilized hour to have dinner feels like we're eating in the middle of the night. No, that's not positive. Shoot.

I've never had a Border Collie, but Tweed's antics tempt me mightily. Would the Border Collie torment the cats by trying to herd them? I suspect it would. When Tweed and the doe mix it up, will Tweed then hesitate to go out later in the day? A buck with a full rack could do some damage to your pup. I'm also glad it was only a nipping doe in the yard.

The little birds thrilled me when I reloaded the feeders. They flew so close to my head that I could hear the beating of their wings, a low "fltttddddd" that grazed my hair. I'm not sure whether the air is particularly still, or they were so excited by the suet that they were flying faster, or whether they were really that much closer than ever before. Am I a cheap date or what?

Are you watching *Squid Game*? I finished season one while making black bean chili last night. We humans are a confounding, repulsive species capable of unexpected acts of pure compassion.

Happy Halloween!

Love,
Medea

*November 1, 2021 rain. sweet rain. temperature hovering at 60 night or day Day of the Dead*

Dear Medea,

Happy Samhain, the Celtic New Year's Eve. In ancient times the crops would be in the storehouses and the cattle would be culled, the vulnerable among them slaughtered and prepared: some feasted on right then, parts rendered into oil, hides hung and scraped. It was a busy time of year. The big fires cleansed the world, removing ticks from the cattle before they came inside, and burning thatched roof material that had seen the last of a winter deluge.

New roofs, sometimes new structures, and a cleaned hearth prepared the family for the coming winter when the comfort of a fire around which famous and familiar stories were told and retold until the children began to know them by heart. Rain, snow, the coming of calm to the moors and forests let the wild beasts relax and find their mates without as much caution. The people had indoor tasks to keep them busy. Making clothing, carving weapons, and growing the winter child in their bellies. The clan gatherings of Lammas in early August bringing together more than the harvest but an opportunity for alliances to be made and fortunes joined. Being pregnant in winter, with soft rain falling and easier tasks to perform made sense for all beasts, even the human kind.

Why am I telling you this? First, it is to give you another perspective on this lovely season that you dread. Now is the time to grow new ideas, seed them and feed them over winter, giving them time to ripen in the gentleness that is rainfall, a time when the world outside suggests a stasis of physical energy, and a weaving in. And so, as we tend the Samhain fire, cooking a great joint of beef, or aurochs, or the giant version of deer from that time, we bring everyone to the fire to sit and listen to stories of warriors and goddesses and magic cows and rivers of blood and now and then we will feel a stirring in the belly, a quickening, and maybe we will think beyond this time we're in now, and begin to color a new world for ourselves and our grandchildren with a small spark of something, anything, positive.

I wish for you a winter time, and a new year of creativity and fertility of the kind only sought and only obtained behind the protective veil of the rain.

Love,
Jane

*1 November 2021 The sky offers cold, gray rain, igniting rather than dousing my mood for a rant. But I'll spare you that.*

Dear Jane,

COP26 started today. India vows to attain Net Zero emissions by 2070, an improvement over yesterday, when Modi refused to come out and play with the rest of the world. Biden claims we'll reach this milestone by 2050. Twenty-nine years from now. Meanwhile, the Dems are promising to give more childcare dollars to families, in the hope of spurring families to have even more children. I have whiplash.

I've read some encouraging op-eds and articles written by and about religious leaders vowing a commitment to the planet. Only Thich Nhat Hanh, so far as I've read, has called affirmatively for ZPG. Most of the people walking to the Texas border, who will need jobs, food, shelter, carry two to five kids in tow. What are all of those people going to do? How do you convince an entire faith community that being fruitful and multiplying directly conflicts with God's wish that we serve as faithful stewards of Her bounty?

If the Amazon Rainforest were a harem of beautiful, mute, raven-haired virgins being brutally raped and mutilated on a daily basis and they lived only to provide fun for their torturers, rescue operations would abound from multiple quarters. The cogent, data-based warnings from scientists get buried under the weight of celebrity gossip, ads for pharmaceuticals most people don't need, avalanches of fake news. These keep us distracted, much like that Keep America Beautiful campaign from the 1970s.

And what is one person, faced with this horror, supposed to do to save the earth? Jane Goodall claims that gentle persuasion rather than angry scolding will change people's minds. She has decades of success to prove the point.

Toward the end of the documentary, *Breaking Boundaries*, David Attenborough speaks to me with his comforting blue eyes. He tells me that my plant-based diet, efforts to eliminate plastics from my daily life, planting trees wherever trees might grow, that these small acts create planet-saving agency. Sir Attenborough believes that "we have the capacity to act as earth's consciousness, its brain... to ensure that earth remains our perfect home."

I'd like to harness this consciousness, to rewire this brain, to go to sleep tonight secure in the knowledge that all of our great-grandchildren may marvel at the blinking of lightening bugs on a warm summer's night.

Love,
Medea

*November 2, 2021 Sun.*

Dear Medea,

If I analyze my intellectual and emotional response to your beautiful words, I'm sad to say I think we are powerless in the face of a planet out of control. Yes, it's entirely humans' fault. We are the pest. I don't think ZPG is going to be a problem, since generations after us seem to be skipping children of their own accord. And who can blame them? I want to tell my own son to take his little family and sail away someplace safe. But where would that be? And I would only continue to worry, so it's best to let them figure it out. Isn't it?

Here's what might be one shining light: the two years we have been forced to change the way we live has, apparently, prompted a whole bunch of people (consumers) to change their lifestyles toward less consumption, more meaningful time spent. Will this last? There is no way to know. It must be a thrilling time to be a sociologist. We don't need to eat out constantly, we don't need to buy cheap crap at Bed, Bath and Beyond, or Costco simply because it's there. Shopping is an addiction. It can be kicked. We don't need multiple homes, plane trips, cars, and we really don't need to cut down more trees, send more islands of trash out to sea, or suck out the last of the earth's oil. Will it help if you or I change one or two of our bad habits? I have no way to know. Feeling responsible comes naturally to me, and to you, but it clearly doesn't to much of the world. It will only make a difference if we act on our beliefs: vote, yes, but more than that. Donate, activate, hell—run for office. Why not? I'd vote for you in a heartbeat.

The place we are as individuals and as a species makes me incredibly discouraged. I wish getting angry mattered, we have enough anger to create a new world. But even poor little Greta Thunberg giving world leaders a tongue lashing isn't really going to change anything. The only change will come when those old white men aren't in charge anymore. I don't know why or how, but they seem invincible. Are we angry enough to torch the world we have without knowing what will come after?

Love,
Jane

*3 November 2021 Well, it's summer again! 72 degrees and sunny. The small planes are flying about, which is typically a sign of the advent of spring. More whiplash.*

Dear Jane,

Thank you again for the soothing words about Celtic traditions and the regenerating power of this time of year that I historically dread. Communal repair of home and hearth, the forging of swords and alliances, instilling in the children a sense of kinship and history, these fill darker days with purpose. Planting idea seeds for spring harvest sounds like a capital idea.

Yeah, the manifesto I emailed to you. I was on a tear. You are a tried-and-true friend for wading through it all. Like you, I believed that the privations of Covid would reveal our overstuffed lifestyles for the soul-numbing deceptions that they are. It worked, for a while, just like everyone you met after 9/11 smiled and opened the door for you or waved you ahead at the stop sign. How long did that last? For some, the awakening of our vulnerability and reliance on the sacrifices of others endures. There is a new generation among us since then, one more attuned to the mess we are making of our planet. Will we prove to be an immovable force against which the twin tides of greed and denial are rendered impotent?

Yesterday, duty called me to the Marina in SF to check on my ancient sailboat after Monday's heavy rains. The cockpit felt toasty in the afternoon sun. With no wind to rile it, the basin lay flat as glass. A sea lion stopped by to chat. The gulls shrieked over God knows what. I plucked an empty oyster shell from the stern rail, some bird's discarded dinnerplate. A Great Blue Heron, more chocolate-gray than blue, cruised in for a landing on the finger dock next to Windsong. Scores of people walked, biked, and scootered along Marina Boulevard. I thought about our water words. Rather than drive back from SF along choked, frenetic 19th avenue, I ambled along the Great Highway. I watched the Pacific Ocean cresting, resting, cresting again, regaining my blue mind.

Do you know about the young Dutch man who invented a device to extract plastic, sixty or so tons at a time, from the Pacific Gyre several years ago? He celebrated his first real victory this past week. He's labored since his late teens on the extraction device, formed a nonprofit, landed partners, and delivered sixty-six tons of junk to British Colombia for repurposing. The Pacific Gyre would fill an area equal to three perimeters of France, so his efforts are laudable though it may seem like a task equivalent to emptying an Olympic swimming pool with an eye dropper. He thinks beyond the *now*. His optimism in the face of these daunting odds acts as a life jacket for those who may despair.

Love,
Medea

P.S. Thanks for the vote of confidence, but I'll demur on running for office!

*November 5, 2021 just beginning to rain*

Dear Medea,

While I am disheartened by the obstinate place-holding nonsense that is mostly what the Glasgow climate summit has produced, I do place hope and send energy toward people like the inventor with his garbage converting gizmo. I wish him well. Is there any point to reiterating that we are the pestilence when it's only you and I listening?

Your afternoon with Windsong sounds like it soothed your soul in ways only the sound of gently lapping water against a wooden boat can. I'm glad all was well with her, and that you felt better surrounded by people enjoying the warm sun.

This morning I carved up some leftover beef roast and took the trimmings out to the ravens. It is clear to me that if I spent even an hour a day tempting them with meat, they would soon be happy to take it right from my fingers, but I'd rather not. They're very big, for one thing. But there is also something unapproachable about their wildness that I know needs to remain wild. Lately when I take them special treats (e.g., raw meat) they have outsmarted me in my efforts to divide it up evenly between them. I'm not sure Tinker quite gets the strategy I have in mind, and she tends to follow Burt to the sawhorse and sometimes manages to snag a bit, but then Burt either beats her to the platform on the ground and gorges himself, or she flaps enough that he lets her get a piece or two. When it's only kibble, he's not as avaricious. I am more and more thinking that these two are the mated parents from last year. Revelation! Talk about burying the lead. After today's feast they perched on the roof of the garage and groomed each other pleasantly as the light rain began to fall. The more I deduce, the more I realize I simply don't know. Every day thus becomes an adventure. Screw Google, this way is more fun.

Love,
Jane

*5 November 2021 60 degrees, but winds light enough for a long-ish walk. Night falls earlier each day; still, the sun fights for the last scraps of space in the sky, pale gold against the lost tropical clouds.*

Dear Jane,

What does one wear when rending beef roast and carrying it outside to large black birds with beaks the size of a baby carrot? Anything she wants! Tinker and Burt would not peck your eyes out. They will behave.

Right?

Google, Sibley, and the book, *Beaks, Bones & Birdsongs* by Roger J. Lederer that Bruce gave me last Christmas surely offer clues. The ravens here are talking a blue streak, still, which means...it's not a seasonal shift? They are pissed off about shorter daylight hours? They still can't readily access the suet feeder? When I went out to collect the mail at midday, the wail from one of them frightened me. It sounded like the cry an old man would make if he had lost his direction and didn't recognize his surroundings. Not eerie as bird sounds often do but a heart-tugging cry for attention. I tiptoed across the street; the sound came from a neighbor's tree. Two ravens stood on a branch and the sad raven flapped and flapped its wings, inching closer to the stoic raven, who held its ground. When the weeping one moved too close, the other hopped away, but didn't flee the tree. A third swept in from a different tree and perched on a branch above, just watching. I guess the stoic raven finally tired of the haranguing and it hopped to a parallel branch. Then, I saw it: the crying bird began to gorge itself on something it had situated in the crook of the branch. Something else to learn— under what circumstances will a raven stop fighting for food? I didn't see the kill. Did the carcass rightly belong to the plaintive bird or was this agonizing cry coming from a starving bird begging for the stronger to show mercy and share?

I read today that ravens are *aves non grata* in Joshua Tree National Park. Ravens love to feast upon the babies of the Desert Tortoise, California's state reptile since 1972. The Desert Tortoise plays an integral role in maintaining the health of the close-to-endangered Joshua Tree (43,000 acres of desert burned earlier this year taking out a critical mass of the ancient trees.) Some desert-studying biologist teamed up with an engineer to produce a decoy baby tortoise. The plastic foil tastes not like tender baby tortoise and so ravens habituate to seek other prey. The article failed to mention whether the baby tortoises constitute the ravens' main food source. Either the decoy saves the desert or it institutes a butterfly effect: the ravens leave and the weevils that evaded the scientists' study multiply and eat the newly-planted Joshua Tree seeds to replace the hundreds of trees hacked down during you-know-who's administration, when funding to watch over parklands dried up or was diverted to wall construction.

Love,
Medea


*November 6, 2021 light rain overnight. overcast and cool.*

Dear Medea,

I'm trying to train myself to sleep more deeply. Doing this involves closing the windows and shutting out the night noises of ocean, owls, and wind, and turning on an air filtered fan for white noise and temperature control. I can't tell you how sad this makes me, but I can't deny that it is working. There is something about sleeping by an open window–it's an invitation to fly the night sky, free the spirit to the wild unknown, dance under the stars and, with the creatures of the night, find new paths of awakening. Perhaps I am better off behind closed and darkened windows; perhaps allowing my spirit the night world was just too stimulating (I've written poems about this). I need deeper sleep, fewer dreams, less restless awareness. The wilderness can manage just fine without my witness. But the darkness is also what gives me a feeling of endlessness, of expansive imagination. In the shadows there are no boundaries. Maybe one night a week, I can sleep with open windows?

I'm sorry about the baby tortoises, but I think we've meddled enough in the natural order of things, surely? My own meddling aside, I don't know of a single instance where introducing some obstacle (whether it be rabbits to Australia, or some other pest or restraint) has worked out in the long run. The predators have their place in the cycle. What are turtles doing in the desert in the first place? Did you read about the "virgin" birth condor chicks? They died, and their parthenogenetic birth is still a little bit of a mystery, but maybe it's also a big red flag about how far we can manage wildlife. Isn't that a contradiction in terms? Managed forests, managed wilderness, managed wildlife! I'm in the kind of mood that leads to the conclusion that the sooner we are wiped from the face of the earth, the better for every other species.

Last night I observed the little deer herd come together for the first time in many weeks. It must be a sign that the rutting season is over. Some of these females are surely pregnant now. There are three in the herd, and two juveniles. I still see the solo female and her single fawn, so they are well, but have not joined back to the herd. Since that female was watched closely by one of the bucks, she is probably also pregnant and perhaps will form her own multi-generation herd.

The ravens would never hurt me, I don't think, but they have long claws and sharp beaks and, frankly, trying to see where you're going when you have eyes on either side of your head must make accuracy a challenge. I'd rather not risk it. I also don't want to teach them to say words or otherwise "parrot" back non-raven behavior. They gift me with the opportunity to watch them as individual ravens, but they will always be ravens, not dogs with feathers. As for your plaintive bird begging for or protecting her food: I've not seen them be much for sharing in the kill, but I do think they "share" later whether it is with chicks or in teaching food sourcing skills or sharing with mates. Hard to say what was going on with those three but I have the impression that "three's a crowd" so someone in that trio wasn't wanted.

Love,
Jane

### Open Windows
Within a rattled night of dreaming
carried on the breathing ocean
wanderers come.
It is that roaming energy,
lost and grieving, seeking.
Open windows egress to spirit.
Sleeping, we are bare:
any fey creature can join in,
muddling our history,
mingling our truths
until we lose the backstory
and agree to meet deep in the wood
take the moon filled night walk.

Open windows
we should know better.

*7 November 2021 Sunny day. Dark afternoon. Cold, for me; for Bruce, "this feels just perfect!"*

Dear Jane,
Closing the window to sleep better, turning on a white noise machine, does not sound like the Hummingbird I know. Your dreams are telling you something, disruptive though they may be. Please do try one night per week with the

window open until your sleep returns to restful; the spirits in the shadows will wait. Still, something out in the wilderness beckons. Do you dare not heed?

Bruce prefers to sleep with the blinds closed and the demon air conditioner fan on high, white noise that deadens the ambient night sound. As I sleep, I gaze out over various oceans, walk beaches familiar and foreign, occasionally find myself facing a tsunami, scooping up the boys (whose tiny legs could never outrun the wave) and scrambling toward the dune before my racing heart wakes me up. On the very few nights when he's not home, or when I elect to spend the night on the sofa with the cats, I open the window and meld with that roaming energy outdoors, the rustling raccoons, rats and mice, gophers, voles and listen to the quiet conversation of the trees.

Ravens typically live twenty-five to thirty years, sometimes to age forty. How old do you think Tinker and Burt might be? Condors average sixty years. Parthenogenesis failed in the lab, but in the wild? It might explain their hearty constitutions. Some sharks have been known to experience parthenogenetic births as well. Managed life? More like mismanaged meddling in nature's rather perfect designs. We spend so much time lauding innovation, worshiping at the altar of the new, deifying disrupters while the natural world does its best to adapt. What about just taking care of what we have? How about refurbishing, restoring, repairing? When we learn to muster the humility to grant equal respect to the people who take care of our infrastructure, think plumbers and pothole fillers, as we do to those who gain great wealth from inventing dating apps, when we trust that love will find us rather than swiping left and right, we may discover the secret to peaceful coexistence with the universe.

Love,
Medea

P.S. I read an article about water quality assurance law in Florida that began with this sentence: "Florida has long prioritized the preservation of its coastal waters and lands, ground water, and surface waters." After I stopped laughing, I checked the date on the cover of the magazine to make sure it was not the April edition, lost in the mail. Nope. November/December.


*November 8, 2021 waning morning sun giving way to overcast. Gale warnings for Pt Arena to Cape Mendocino—here's hoping. Calm before the storm.*

Dear Medea,
You're absolutely right and thank you for reminding me that hiding in bed with the world at bay is not living, not feeding whatever gifts I might have. Night

flying might be the best of my abilities. Shutting the windows now and then—especially against fire smoke—may be a required respite, but I miss the world that is alive in the dark of the woods. Last night when Tweed and I went out for a short walk in the dark we heard a Great Horned Owl, far off, and then a bark and cry from either a fox or a coyote. And that moon! Oh, how glad I am to have seen her in this aspect! The golden glow crescent and the brightest of bright stars. "Bright star" always reminds me of Keats' poem which I confess I am fond of more because I enjoyed the little period drama movie produced about ten years ago of the same name. Poor Keats, another consumptive poet. I guess that's the good side of being an invalid, we become poets. The moon and her star were truly inspirational. What phase were you born under? I was born under a new moon. (It's easy to find out, Google it).

This morning as Tweed and I walked our circuit I heard what I thought was a cow. For a moment, I was overjoyed (and is that possible? Being "over'joyed? Is this another problem of language like "disgruntled': as my brother pointed out once, can someone be "gruntled'?). When we first moved here there were cows in Kristofferson's fields next door, but the fences deteriorated in stormy weather, the cows were moved over the hill south and west toward the ocean, and while the caretakers promised cows would return, they haven't. Most people don't want cows pastured next to their houses. Not me, I love cows. The sound of their lowing, the rustling as they get a good scratch on the fence post. Companions in spirit. As it turned out, what I heard this morning was a badly run chain saw, off in the distance. Oh Snap!

Love,
Jane


*8 November 2021 65 and clear. Still waiting for the rain that was promised by Weatherbug.*

Dear Jane,
Do you remember any particular reliable weather phenomena when you were growing up? In Florida, during the summers, every single afternoon at 4:55, angry charcoal cumulus clouds scuttled across the sky and unleashed buckets full of rain in drops the size of quarters. The raindrops plopped into themselves fast, making puddles that invited dragonflies and toads to frolic. You could set your watch; I worked summers at my dad's office, if I did not start walking the short mile home by 4:40, I had to wait until 5:15 for the clouds to pass over and continue watering the Gulf.

When I moved to Santa Barbara, summer mornings started cool and foggy. I walked the ten blocks to work, wiping the damp from my hair so I'd enter the office looking like the professional AVP my boss hired. By the time I'd step out at lunchtime, the fog lifted and the sun shone. Every day. Even when I moved here to SF in 1989, Carl Sandburg's fog still came in on little cat feet. Do you recall a time when Eastern Australia burned for days on end? When Western Canada broiled under a heat dome? The only thing constant may be change, and it appears that our $CO_2$ output has really fucked with the weather prognostications.

Moon phases, however, are safe, at least for now. My birth moon phase is New Moon. Just like you! According to Astrocal, my date of birth put me zero to forty-five degrees ahead of the Sun. That feels auspicious. "You are a cosmic new baby; you are a young soul with much to learn in this lifetime," Astrocal claims. Born into beginner's mind.

The owls appear to avoid our neighborhood. The only large birds we see aside from ravens are the occasional hawks. We spotted one yesterday, alone as always, gliding over the pines, minding its business, probably hunting, when two nebbish, obviously disgruntled, crows crashed in out of nowhere to nip at its wingtips. We watched the attack for a minute until the trio flew over the ridge, out of sight. Poor hawk.

Welcome back to the night, Jane.

Love,
Medea


*November 9, 2021 overcast. calm.*

Dear Medea,
We did have a good storm last night with decent rainfall and a little wind, nothing to stay up and experience, mind, but decent.

I was playing ball with Tweed earlier and suddenly there was an outcry of birdlife somewhere at a distance. I wasn't sure it was ravens, but Tinker and Burt were sure, and began calling urgently and flew off north in a big hurry. More noise ensued. I couldn't begin to guess the cause, but an encounter with a hawk is certainly a possibility. Interesting that they flew immediately to the rescue, or to join in.

As for weather, forecasters have lost their edge in the face of climate change. I remember in northern Wisconsin it was common for the lake to kick up in the late afternoon as the wind from the north blew across the open water. I suppose that meant fishing wasn't good either. After sunset, the fishermen would reappear in their skiffs and continue trying to catch "Scarface," the mean northern pike. There was a story that once he rolled up next to the boat when my aunt was out in it and gave her the once over. She said he was as long as the boat. Not sure why, but this did nothing to deter any of us from swimming.

Love,
Jane


*10 November 2021 65 degrees and sunny, birdies are chirping, the rest of the land is still. Today is my parents' 65th anniversary.*

Dear Jane,
Do you have an opinion about the Canada Goose? The Canada Goose migrates in its "V" formation to Foster City every autumn. The mostly vegetarian birds keep the grasses mowed on the acres of open space that T. Jack Foster carved out of the waterways when he founded Foster City.

The geese know nothing of human land domination. They just like wintering in Foster City, much like human Canadians this time of year fly south to their condos on the golf courses in Southwest Florida. Most local, year-round Floridians bitch and moan about the Canadians, their migration in throngs of thousands goose the economy by usurping all the best restaurant reservations and gridlocking every asphalt artery. The Canada Goose that winters in Foster City sports handsome taupe coverts, a white chinstrap above its elegant black neck, and Sibley describes its call as "resonant", "musical", and "mellow." Audubon.org relates that "many geese in urban areas...are permanent residents." You might pass a pair-for-life on your evening lagoon paddle or hear a happy honk while strolling by the water's edge at Leo J. Ryan Park.

It seems that the residents of Foster City feel about their snowbirds similarly to the way the residents of SW Florida feel about theirs. But the inconvenience of stepping over tidy mounds of goose poop on their sidewalks and in their parks has exposed amongst those Foster City-zens a murderous rage. Despite the fact that the Canada Goose enjoys federal protection, they have issued a call to cull. (I won't venture a guess as to whether certain Gulf Coast locals don't dream about such a culling call.)

Because of protection under the International Migratory Bird Treaty Act of 1918 (which presumably lay fallow between 1918 and the early 1960s) the nearly-extinct Canada Goose population now approaches four million. It's not only Foster City that seeks to trim the flocks; one community in New York slaughtered the birds, dressed them, and added the carcasses to its indigent food delivery larders. (On a scale of one to ten, the recipients rated the fatter, autumn birds a solid nine.)

This rebound in goose numbers, success that has repeated with endangered wolves, deer, alligators, should be cause for celebration. And indeed, as concerns the Canada Goose, very likely would be, but for the insertion of a manufactured town on the reeds of their wetlands. Three pounds of goose poo per bird per day requires much patience to navigate, no doubt. Yet, when we monkey around with nature's way, we interfere like the rudest caricature of a nightmare mother-in-law. Who rightfully roosts on this land?

Love,
Medea

*10 November 2021 mild, overcast*

Dear Medea,
I absolutely think you need to trim your goose letter down and send it into the closest editorial newspaper to Foster City. Those people need to be educated in tolerance! There is not a moment to lose!

Today would be the perfect day to open that wound, pick that scab, or fight. The stars are aligned for the words to come out sword sharp!

That said, I'm going to try staying mum myself and not get into any trouble. I'll hold your parking place for you though.

Love,
Jane

*Veteran's Day 2021 Blue skies above, stillness below. Temperature heading toward 70 today.*

Dear Jane,
On Veteran's Day I'd like to recognize one of the thousands of people who sacrificed for our freedom to speak, travel, worship and live in an open and democratic society: my friend Terri, a helicopter pilot in Iraq and Afghanistan. Thank you. The families who send parents and children and aunts and uncles to defend our country also deserve our eternal gratitude.

You make a valid point about disappearing into books. How would we have navigated our way through puberty without *Little Women* and *Everything You Always Wanted to Know About Sex*? I voraciously consumed and imagined my life as every of famous woman's biography our library carried, from Queen Liliuokalani to Amelia Earhart. The power of a book to lift a person out of her drab or dangerous existence, to live for a time in different skin draws a parallel with gaming.

Max advised today that this rage against the machine is a canonical reaction to the new and the next-gen. He extrapolated from "books" to "the printing press" and how that invention met with similar suspicion. When I suggested that Guttenberg certainly was not twiddling his hands and narrowing his eyes as he hunched over his new creation dreaming of manipulation and riches, Max replied, "the first thing he printed was the Bible!" Word.

What happened with the hawk and the ravens? I heard a hawk in the old pine tree near the feeders this morning, its "*eeeee*" "*eeeee*" seemed to come from a bough that hangs over the front fence. I stood for ten minutes, immobile, hoping to spot it. There is something fierce and vulnerable about a hawk's face, its large yellow eye above the piercing curved beak, and slicked back ruddy head feathers, like it primped for a party, but decided there would be too many ravens and no one to talk to. It stopped vocalizing, but I still feel its gaze.

Love,
Medea


*November 11, 2021 Sun. warm. Is winter over already?*

Dear Medea,
And a "Happy" Veteran's Day to you as well. My father and his three brothers all served in WWII and all, incredibly, returned home at least superficially intact. The alcohol and in some cases the cigarettes and the shuddering fear of actual battle–that seems to be the shame of it all still to this day. What will it take for us to shun war and, moreover, to truly care for those who have fought for us in the past? It takes more than flowers on a tomb. My crazy Uncle Jim was crazy because of serving in WWII. He was like James Garner's character in The Great Escape. "The Scrounger"—his job was to chase into villages and towns after the battle but ahead of the troops and round up anything useable. His letters often included long lists of alcoholic beverages scarpered into the Willys Jeep and spirited off to the camp. Along the way, though, he saw what no one wants to see. My father served on a destroyer at Okinawa, my Uncle Bob in the army at Guadalcanal. My Aunt Margie was a WAC and is buried in the military cemetery in Dallas—her war service was one of the things in her life she was most proud of.

One evening midway through the war, my grandfather took my grandmother out for a special dinner to celebrate their wedding anniversary. The dinner club in Chicago had a resident artist who table hopped and drew caricatures of some of the patrons while the diners nearby watched and chuckled. He stopped and drew a quick sketch of my grandfather, mostly his prominent hook of a nose. Easy. Then he turned to my tiny grandmother and started to draw, chatting with her. How many children did she have? Five, four boys and a girl. The artist drew her face without exaggeration, and while she talked to him about her boys, he drew her dress. He spent so much time with my grandmother that people nearby became quiet and tried to hear. She talked and he drew one star on her dress. A few people smiled encouragement. He drew a second star, and there was a smattering of applause and "thank you for your sacrifice," the artist drew a third star, and the restaurant became quiet. The artist drew the fourth and final star and everyone in the restaurant stood and applauded my tiny grandmother.

The ravens have been enjoying leftover chicken. It's back to dog kibble today though. It's quite clear they prefer the meat, raw or cooked and somehow can tell the minute I walk out the door. Probably simply because either there's something in my hands or there isn't. Meanwhile, the problem between Tweed and the deer has escalated. Last night, Tweed and I went out before bed, and he took off. My fault for forgetting the leash—I won't forget again. He ran around the garage and then down the driveway toward the barn, barking—with me yelling at him. Then he came running toward me and I suddenly saw that two deer were after him, one was the buck with the single antler, the other the mother of the single juvenile who chased Tweed last week. Tweed squealed but I don't think they made contact. That said I grabbed the ball chucker and heaved a ball between the deer to distract them, otherwise they might have run right over me. Let's hope Tweed was sufficiently scared this time to curb his appetite for this game. He is more likely to get hurt than the deer. Leash on at night from now on. I promise.

Love,
Jane


*12 November 2021 Yeah, what the hell?! 72 in SF today. I'm not complaining.*

Dear Jane,
Your tiny grandmother sounds fierce and funny and loveable. No wonder Uncle Jim spoke "Bird." War scrambles peoples' brains. It severs their limbs and blows out their eyeballs and surely makes them question their own and everyone else's sanity. Bruce's dad didn't smoke, so he traded all of his Red Cross cigarettes

with his fellow POW inmates for Vitamin C during WWII. At age nineteen, his wisdom belied his age. The other prisoners called him "Rabbi."

Ok, so dogs, particularly Tweed, presumably possess a second sense regarding other animals. The deer have him on the run, which concerns me and I hope you won't take offense but gives me a tiny frisson for the wild ones. And I thank you for promising about the leash—I've grown quite fond of Tweed.

The Marina this afternoon hummed with scooter and bicycle tires, *screed* with seagull songs and offered me a moment to absorb some Vitamin D. A Great Blue Heron alighted on the finger dock one slip down. This bird had a circle of black on its shoulder—I've been observing Great Blue Herons for decades and this is the first such marking I've ever seen. The bird stood at the end of the finger, watching, waiting. I invited it to come for a visit, but with no fish to offer, it politely declined. Its beak I swear measured nine inches. Would it pierce my hand were I to offer a sardine? The heron, like the hawk, lives a solitary life. Do you think that makes them sad? Are the tinies in their fluttery communities happier? This heron seemed absorbed in the to and fro of the boulevard. No fish up there. What was it watching for?

Rather than fighting my way down 19th Avenue to return home, I pointed the car to Ocean Beach, with a wedge of time to watch the sun melt into the sea. I walked to the edge of the sand, still warm from this balmy day. The globe of sun shape-shifted into a pumpkin with vertical ribs. Then a cat's head, complete with pointy ears. Then a Craftsman house. A block of cheddar cheese. And, finally, a little red caboose. I swear I saw a green flash, which no one will confirm.

Love,
Medea


*November 12, 2021 warm, 60s, sun*

Dear Medea,
I slept with the windows open last night, and woke this morning to the rumble of the loudest logging truck ever. I really do think he (they) do this on purpose. They know the "Jake Brake" isn't allowed on the grade (illegal on new trucks), they know everyone else is still at home and in bed. The older trucks have terrible mufflers. It's their "fuck you" to the world as their way of life heads into history. The world is against them, the trees are against them. I don't know how they can stand themselves–the truckers and the loggers, not the trees. The trees rise tall in solidarity with each other, we must rise tall and stand with them.

I got out of bed and went downstairs to find trash strewn across the yard behind the garage. Uh oh. I filled the kettle with water for tea and went out to assess. I can't be sure it was a bear, but I suspect it was. The "bear resistant" can that was emptied was non-food, but it might have smelled like food (wrappers) enough to attract a hungry mammal. It was also loaded with some heavy scrap that would have made the can hard to tip over. Raccoon? Maybe. I got a rake and cleaned up the mess. Put my tea on to steep and took a walk around briefly to look for foot/paw prints. I didn't see anything definitive but there is something strange in front of the garage—what could be a bear print. Four claws and a pad depression. Or just my imagination, but I can't think what else would make such a mark. Since the recycle cans are full of things like empty tuna cans and empty dog food, I suspect we will be visited again. The actual food waste garbage is inside the garage.

The other night I thought I heard snuffling outside. Maybe it was a bear? Tweed has been actively sniffing everywhere outside. I assumed he was following the deer. Perhaps not! It was this time last year that we were visited repeatedly by a bear. I'd better alert the neighbors. We have wonderful new people who are here to build, up from the LA area. I don't want to scare them, but better to be prepared.

Quinn got his kid vaccine today! Let the holiday Solstice celebration planning begin!

Love,
Jane


*14 November 2021 Sunny and mild, toasty even outside of the shade.*

Dear Jane,
Hooray for Quinn! That's a relief for everyone, no doubt. You'll have even more reason to celebrate this holiday season.

It might be time to invest in a critter cam? I'm kind of surprised the new people from LA don't have one, being from LA and all. Did you see the news report a couple of weeks ago where the bear broke into a man's home, not far from LA, and found his bag of KFC? He, the man, followed the trail of destruction wrought by the bear (who somehow figured out how to open the front door, which was bolstered with a key pad) from the foyer, through the living room, down the hall and into the kitchen. The bear had ranged through the cabinets, pulled items from shelves, raided the fridge, and plopped himself atop the counter, where he happily munched on every delicacy he found inside the Colonel's paper bag. If you discover that your beast is a bear, let me know so I can watch for you on the 10 o'clock news.

Of course, the critter cam can serve double duty. The loggers do evoke certain sympathy, as they may lack skills outside the contract murder of trees.

Is that too inflammatory? We all bear responsibility for the logging dilemma, unless we live in stone castles or mud huts and burn straw or dung to keep us warm and cook our food. The passive-aggressive, heavy on the aggressive, illegal Jake Brake behavior sounds much like the toddler hurling his body against the wall rather than going quietly to bed. I root for the trees, yet the loggers' battle to remain relevant—and solvent—elicits compassion as well.

We took full advantage of the Summer-in-November weather yesterday to (finally) run Windsong after her extensive, expensive engine repair. She started right up, and after warming her oil to temperature, we set off for a cruise to nowhere. She's an old gal, feisty, tired, deserving of whatever pampering will see her through the rest of her life. We passed a family of sea lions lolling in the harbor, to the delight of throngs of tourists, who have suddenly reappeared.

Love,
Medea


*November 15, 2021 overcast, cool*

Dear Medea,
More bear stories popping up in the news with yesterday's large male who scampered up a tree, way way up a tree, in a Petaluma neighborhood. The poor guy was traumatized by the flashing lights of the police and fire responders, and the reporters' vans, and the neighborhood camera and cell phone users. By the end of the day, a "shelter in place" order was put forth and people were sent home in hopes the bear would come down and go home himself. Which he did. sigh. Poor thing.

We got our booster jabs this morning and feel tired, happy, and free. Will life go back to normal? Not a chance. Too many stupid people out there insisting they actually are islands "entire unto themselves." The drive north to town to the Public Health Dept seemingly housed in a repurposed motel or something, we couldn't quite figure it out, anyway, the drive was a bit of a shock for me as the passenger with a chance to look out the window. The trees are dying! I mean, so so many trees are already dead, or are clearly dying. The bark beetles and the drought strain, it is truly shocking. Couple that with the deliberate execution of trees that dared to grow near power lines, often topped at 20 ft and left to die like criminals at the crossroads. A disgraceful business. I'm sputtering with distress, and with fear. Where we are as far as climate change is right here on the roadside, scarecrow tree trunks, rusty downed branches and rolls upon rolls of cut limbs. While we drove up the coast, our county Board of Supervisors was hearing testimony about Jackson State Demonstration Forest's mismanagement of their mandate. "Follow the science, People!" is the rallying cry of the protestors. Let's hope the supes have a care.

Meanwhile, with no one coming up for Thanksgiving dinner, do we bother with it at all? Make some half-assed attempt, or pretense? I'm torn. And sadly, I also don't care as much as I would have thought I would.

Let's hear it for bears everywhere. Hurrah! Hurrah! Hurrah!

Love,
Jane

*15 November 2021 61 degrees and gloomy. The hangover payback for a brilliant and warm weekend.*

Dear Jane,

Hurrah for the bears indeed! The Petaluma bear looks bewildered up in the tree, as in "what the hell is wrong with you people? Haven't you ever seen a bear taking a snooze twenty feet in the sky?" The police parked an SUV to block ingress and egress on the adjacent town road and I thought "seriously? The bear is going to turn around when it sees the car and slink back to its den?" People. As a species, we seem to grow more disconnected by the day.

And what shall become of the trees? We see the fallout from PG&E's lame efforts, and the drought, which brings on the beetles that feast on the pine trees, turning them a morbid brown. The birds don't care about the color of the pine trees as long as enough bark remains for them to hide their bits of seeds and nuts.

Both of the woodpeckers spent the weekend at the feeder tree. The markings on their coverts, bright white speckles on onyx feathers, give them star status since the juncos and sparrows blend in with the scenery—I only see them when they hop or dart from limb to limb. The chickadees, nuthatches and titmouses (titmice) stand out more starkly than the sparrows but require closer inspection of subtle line and hue variations to elevate them to the gasp-inducing level of the woodpeckers. Max had a run-in with a woodpecker that mistook his wood siding for a tree. He's not sure that "star" aptly describes the bird that tried to peck his house to death.

Three thousand Sandhill Cranes descended upon Staten Island in the Delta a couple of weeks ago and will dine and dance there until February. I'd never heard of the Cosumnes River Preserve, nor the Lodi Bird Festival and its annual celebration of the coming of the Cranes until yesterday. Emerging from life under this very comfortable family rock is revealing the most magnificent spectacles. For every time there is a season, right?

Thanksgiving. Have whatever makes yours and Gene's mouths water. Invite Tinker and Burt. Cavort around a blazing fire. Or you could come to my house. We'll have conversations about pets and careers, diving and gardens, Paris and weddings. And we'll pour Champagne.

Love,
Medea

P.S. Hurrah for your third jab! We're safe for another few months, anyway.


*November 16, 2021 partial sun but cool, or maybe it's just my booster jab reaction*

Dear Medea,
Your Thanksgiving sounds like bliss. Especially the polished silver and the Champagne. Some future day, my friend, we will drink together.

The pine trees shouldn't be removed entirely or just pruned now? I'm curious about the rules. There is no end to the trees in danger of pine beetle here but the arbor expert from the state said it didn't matter about getting the infested ones cut and burned–too late for that. I find that even more frightening.

Tell Max that woodpeckers are about "getting to work," as a totem animal they remind us to keep at it. You can also tell him that the ravens are "repairing" our shingled roof in ways that have gone too far. Gene bought a car port from Costco in which to park all his tractor implements and as soon as it was up, the ravens started ripping it apart. I wonder, did it smell bad to them? Gene then bought a roll of shingle material and spent two days covering up the damage with what he hopes will be an impermeable barrier. Bets may be placed at the door.

About the moon, we have an eclipse coming on Friday. Duck.

Love,
Jane


*16 November 2021 Gloomy and 63. Won't it just rain again, already?*

Dear Jane,
Max may already have received the woodpecker's message, since he is using his week off to prep most all of the Thanksgiving meal. I'll ask!

The Cornell Lab presented a winter bird feeder seminar today. Over four hundred participants listened to various recommendations for choosing the right food, feeder cleaning tips, directions for recording observations for the Lab's annual Feeder Watch. The three young ornithologist panelists assured us that feeding wild birds is, on balance, the right thing to do. Best inexpensive but nourishing food source? Black sunflower seeds.

As I was thinking about the earnestness of these three delightful avian enthusiasts, the conversation took a weird turn. A huge quantity of questions posed by the audience concerned the voracious appetites of House Sparrows. My beloved newcomer! While I have noticed that the feeders seem to be empty far faster since they appeared, well, so what? If you put out a pile of books with a note that says "free," do you fret when one or two people cart away the whole lot?

One panelist said, "Well, if you don't want the sparrows to come to the feeders, I guess you can take the feeders down." Touché. Then, she reminded us that many House Sparrows, as well as other birds, visit only seasonally. Maybe we could simply appreciate the limited time we have to watch the hoppy birds with feathers that look like Harris Tweed mingle with the regulars.

Imagine taking a trip to Greenland and telling your traveling companion "I only want to see a narwal today. No polar bears. No walruses. Don't even point them out." If you accept the premise that we expect nature to bend to our every whim, it's easy to understand how the sparrow-haters felt justified asking the experts to help them ensure that only the "pretty birds" visit their back yards and feast at their seed banquets. I do admit to my own faunal chauvinism, preferring birds over yellow jackets, for example. But if I offer the birds food impregnated with mealy worms and mealy worms attract yellow jackets, that's how nature works. Railing against it won't alter reality.

Ravens as roofers. Of course. I'll put $100 on Tinker and Burt.

Love,
Medea


*November 16, 2021 another day just like the other day*

Dear Medea,
As the human race hurtles toward extinction it does seem clear that the worst of humanity amplifies. The insistence on photographing oneself as proof of some narcissistic urge, the landscape and any creature around being just so many props, this is the mechanism by which we will implode, very likely not even knowing we have done so, as the world flashes by one last time in the background of some vapid teen, eyes glazed, mouth open, the bright gleam of unnaturally white teeth outshining everything else. Then, perhaps the sharks and the whales and the seals will make a ring of leftover nets and swim all of our

plastic trash islands into one large ocean monument to the Great Devastation, and we will be done.

Yesterday when I went out to put kibble on the sawhorse for the ravens I noticed a tidy placement of fox scat under the platform. I have tried to be careful not to let the kibble roll off onto the ground for fear of attracting raccoons, rats, and mice, but hadn't thought about the foxes who have been audible and clearly roaming around the outside of the house and garage, at least this is what Tweed says every time we go out at night.

Love,
Jane


*17 November 2021 63, still, but sunny with a light breeze.*

Dear Jane,
It's a bird parade out there today. Do birds prefer the sun or am I projecting again?

It occurs to me that when the birds sing it's much like listening to a band. The woodpeckers with their *ratatatat* are the drummers, and like Charlie Watts, dress the dapper part. The *cheeeping* chickadees and juncos are the backup singers, in complementary tan, chocolate and storm cloud gray suits. The sparrows, leaping and strutting all over the place, are the guitar players. Blue jays, in the background but keeping the beat, on bass. The ravens? They're the lead singers. Of course.

We are now up to twenty for Thanksgiving. My high school friends' son and new wife who recently moved to the area from Northern Virginia will join the crowd. My brother-in-law, whose wife and daughter are visiting relatives in Brazil for the next several months, makes the world's best pies, south of Elk, anyway. He offered to bake pumpkin (he uses fresh sugar pie pumpkins) pecan and apple-quince. I bought a new tablecloth, and will count forks and knives this afternoon. Our tradition is to start the savory herb stuffing first thing in the morning to set the sensory mood with this signature scent. We watch the Macy's Day Parade and watch for Snoopy and Pikachu and Santa and Bart. Then, the National Dog Show. By this time, most of the sides are simmering or otherwise in process. Our taste in dogs will preclude us from second careers as National Dog Show judges, but we love the unusual breeds, especially the dog that looks like a Rastafarian. What would happen if you give a dog a cannabis gummy? Or a cat? I saw Meowijuana at PetSmart last week. Who thought that was a good idea?

The fact that a turkey is a bird is not lost on me.

Love,
Medea

P.S. Headline news this morning: The "biologically dead" Thames River, after years of renovation effort, now counts sharks, seahorses and seals among its living. A pearl of hope...

*November 18, 2021 overcast, rain coming*
*Beaver full moon tonight. 97% lunar eclipse*

Dear Medea,
I'm never quite sure whether to say "here it comes" in anticipation of an eclipse or "there it goes" afterwards. The latter smacks of enjoying the comeuppance which surely counts against the unaware. This eclipse tonight is a big event, a Taurus full moon, not sure really what that means but I think of Taurus as a big stubborn bull in a china shop sort of moment. My instinct is always to "duck" an eclipse, perhaps this one is a "duck and cover." That it will be overcast and invisible might be a good thing. By the time November hands us over to December, I think we will all be glad to see the back of 'em.

Meanwhile, The National Dog Show! Thanks for reminding me! We've been wondering what we'll mainline for the day–god forbid we should spend the day talking. Kidding, of course. Watching the dog show is kind of like watching 4H competitions at the county fair: it's such an alien and fascinating world. What makes these people into fanatical show people? And what do the dogs really think? We have a deep prejudice against small yappy dogs that is not improved by watching. Like car enthusiasts with their brand of auto, we are complete snobs about our own favored border collies. We are all grasping for ways to set ourselves apart from the "other." Tribal to the very bitter end.

This year of no entertaining has me floating toward the end of November without enough of an agenda. I realize that deep cleaning the house happens twice a year but only because of the anticipation of one of my more fastidious friend's arrival. How to keep motivated? Maybe I should offer myself a treat, a piece of gold jewelry or some special book. One good result is that the habitual nagging of the man of the house to help with this or that won't happen and thus won't result in tempers flaring, like clockwork, on Thanksgiving morning infusing the resulting day with a light frisson of incomprehensible energy as we pass around the table and give thanks for the love we find there.

Turkeys are birds. Yummy with mayo and crunchy lettuce on white bread the day after, standing at the kitchen window watching absolutely nothing happen. I admit, if they were pretty, even a little, we would be eating a squash casserole instead. You are a better person than I. And yet, the fact that they are disagreeable birds, entertaining enough to watch but not a good idea to have roosting on the porch unless there are ice skates handy for navigating the slick of gray-black shit that quickly accumulates. I don't want to sound like your Foster City people, but birds are best kept off the porch, and off the BBQ grill and patio table for that matter. I'm sure they would agree, if asked. The birds, that is, not the people from Foster City.

Love,
Jane

P.S. Pot for pets is a "thing." I even considered trying it for Tweed's epilepsy but sourcing it and dosing it properly is a very risky proposition, so I wasn't willing to experiment on my sweet dog. Definitely wouldn't buy it at a store. As for other alternative medications, I have used acupuncture for both my dogs and cats. Cats seem especially to love it. If either of your sweeties have joint pain, it's a great thing to try. Best if you can find an acupuncturist who will come to your house.


*18 November 2021 The sky is back to gray. Only the chickadees venture to the feeders today. Small, but mighty...hungry.*

Dear Jane,
Should I find an acupuncturist for Loki, who I believe might benefit from such treatment, you'll please do me the favor of telling Bruce that we are paying an Eastern Medicine Healer to visit the house with a box full of needles to puncture the cat. Thank you!

Today is our 32nd wedding anniversary. How did we get here? At about year twelve, Bruce gifted me with a card in which he'd written "It's been interminable." Interminable. Well, that is a loaded word. So far, at least, our marriage has, by the grace of a god with a very weird sense of humor, proven impossible to terminate. It has also, from time to rare, occasional time, seemed like living in a cold, windowless room where a sadist is piping in "Feelings" on an endless loop. Whoa, whoa, whoa.

To be honest, we both feel triumphant to have endured together for as long as we have. Staying together is hard as hell. The first blush of new love addicts like the best cocaine. The patina that colors a lasting love sometimes feels like dirty, flaky, rust on an old pair of pruning shears. Sometimes, it feels like the soft, ancient, celadon sheen on a Paris rooftop. We've veered dangerously close to calling it quits. But we know each other's foibles. We mostly tolerate those at this point. When you've been married for so long that you can tell your mate to sod off and he knows he deserved that, or when your mate feels secure enough to go full nerd and spend the weekend chasing radio signals across the globe in hopes of securing his ten-thousandth QSL card (a ham radio confirmation of contact highly sought by operators), you've attained true Interminability.

While celebrating our marital stamina, I'm interrupted with wonder at how, on the heels of COP26, the Biden administration could open my beloved Gulf of Mexico to the most immense oil and gas lease auction in the history of the universe. Cynically, I think it has to be a reaction to stratospheric gas prices. If you can't trust your President to use his office to protect the Gulf from oil drilling, then is that another ecosystem we simply write off?

See you after midnight at the hidden moon party. Will homo sapiens survive to marvel at the next such eclipse in 600 years? Not at this rate. But today, we dance!

Love,
Medea

P.S. Both of my sons are partnered with women whose parents remain married. Tenacity, patience and a sense of humor serve as powerful role models.

*November 19, 2021 overcast*

Dear Medea,
The eclipsing moon was elusive last night. Now and then there was light, but not in the right time frame. It's ok. I know to hide under the covers.

Marriage. Currently working through year 52 of my own, sometimes I wonder if I've just been a coward, or if I have created the persona for my half of this endeavor on a false premise. And other times I look over at my husband and feel such an upwelling of tenderness and spine-chilling good fortune at having just happened to run into the one person who could get me through this lifetime in one piece. Of course, I highly recommend separate bathrooms and bedrooms at this point. It's lovely that your boys have found partners who also have the role models of tenacity and compromise before them. I'm sure it helps. Once when asked how long we'd been married, Gene said "it seems like yesterday," at exactly the same time I said, "it seems like forever." Couch cushion needlepoint? "Interminable."

This morning, in a perfect example of just how little we know about anything at all, I was feeling happy watching the five deer remaining of the original herd–the two bucks being off on their own still. They were grazing on the lush clover and grass of the front yard and while not inclined to move into the woods, they heard Tweed inside and started to wander down the drive occasionally nudging a young one to move it along. Suddenly one of the females charged at another female and she scampered a few hasty steps distance, but the angry female was having none of it and reared up on her back legs and lunged, holding her two legged upright position in balance for a moment before landing and lunging again. I guess I was wrong about the happy families deer herd.

I'm speechless about Gulf oil production. I don't have much faith in Biden, and I think the lack of conservationist political pressure from Florida has a lot to do with it, but seriously people? The dirty laundry from the trip to Scotland hasn't even gone through the wash, and we are the ones making things worse?

Love,
Jane


*19 November 2021 Thunderstorms threatened all day but delivered only mist. With the effect the humidity has on my hair, I could pass for Don King.*

Dear Jane,
Dylan arrives for the holiday weekend in three hours. Who's counting?

What's up with your does? Do does do jealousy? Turf wars? Did the angry one sense a threat to self or fawn? It's anthropomorphic to suggest deer motivation, but you've seen this herd behave as a mild-mannered family. I could go further and point out that Thanksgiving is right around the corner. Wouldn't that be a stitch if they're arguing over who has to host this year. That ignites verbal lunging from coast to coast. I hope they make up. It's disturbing to stand by and witness wild animals behaving badly. That's what CNN is for.

We saw a glimpse of the eclipse, sort of a hazy, ruddy moon with a bite taken from its chin. Given the cloud cover, I'm claiming the sighting.

The oil lease sell-out lost news space to the Build Back Better squeak-through vote. That the House and President's crew claim this a victory in extending climate protections strikes me as the epitome of hypocrisy. All you had to do was challenge the lower court's ruling, Joe.

Love,
Medea

Dear Medea,

Your Bruce appears to be a master of one-liners which may be taken as insults or compliments but it's impossible to tell which. Perhaps it is less complicated to describe relationships that are successful as perfect compromises. It is true that I am well matched, and that life support goes both ways. It's also true that if asked, Gene would say he made all the concessions and I always got my way, while I would say the opposite. When I point out that that must mean we are 50/50, he looks baffled. Secret to success? Like I said the other day, separate bathrooms.

As for the does, I have been thinking about that a lot. My guess is that one or both of them is now pregnant. As the herd comes back together after rutting season, the hierarchy must be reestablished. The younger doe with the younger single fawn was always an outlier tagging on to the group. She needs to find her place in the group if she's pregnant so that when she leaves again to isolate herself to give birth, she will leave her juvenile young one with the group herd for protection. The primary doe has the same problem. If they are both pregnant, and both will find solitude and safety in which to give birth and protect the fawns until it is safe to rejoin, the juveniles from last year will be with the young males "leftover" from the rut. All this is speculation. Watching nature at work is so stressful.

I'm sad and embarrassed for Wisconsin. Stupid and insular behavior. It is a place I love, but the people? What century are they in? I agree about shotguns and vests. I already have the former. Who would have thought 25 years ago that we would be thinking about self-defense strategies in this way? We've spent several generations starting and fighting wars in other countries and all the time what we were really doing was training young mostly men of inadequate intelligence how to kill without thinking. We reap what we have sown. That little punk is now a role model for who knows how many other little punks who have no concept of death beyond the one their fingers create on a video game.

Are we heading toward Civil War, or is it already begun? So much road rage, airplane rage, racist rage. The other day when we drove north on beautiful highway One, some guy in a huge pickup truck passed us at speed on a double yellow line. Ok, it does happen now and then, but why? We weren't dawdling, and there was a passing lane coming up. I think people have forsaken the law and channeled their pandemic fears into rage. I told Gene to mind his manners when he gets in his cute sports car with its artwork bike rack and expensive bicycle. He's a prime target for a disappointed and angry man. Do I think we really are headed for Civil War? I do. Would we miss the south if it were another country? I wouldn't, but I guess you would disagree so I'd love to hear your opinion.

Love,
Jane


*20 November 2021 67 degrees and sunny. Warm enough to walk in shorts, the long walk today.*

Dear Jane,
The small cup feeder at the front door hosted the party today. The revolving door welcomed the female woodpecker and a titmouse, then three chickadees, who have taken to perching on the tall sword of pandanas leaf beneath the feeder, defying my grasp of physics, then a junco and a couple of sparrows. Out back? Only a very vociferous black squirrel, hanging upside down by its back toes, holding seeds in its hands and chomping away. I reluctantly shooed it away—twice—then returned outside to refill the suet square and heard a new sound: a metallic-toned chattering coming from the big pine tree. Mr. Noisy perched on a high branch, looking down at me and blathering on, very likely scolding me for my inappropriate squirrel discrimination. I engaged in conversation with him, ignorant as I am about squirrel language, but he was so upset. So, I capitulated and invited him to come for dinner any time.

Dylan's home and gone to SF to visit friends whose parents have wisely fled the Bay Area for less dysfunctional pastures. Having close friends here draws him back, so while I'd prefer to be walking on the beach with him, that can wait until next week. While not exactly a "Cat's in the Cradle" moment, it does take Herculean effort to remember that he's a separate person with a life that spins in its own orbit, sometimes coming near enough to light my world and sometimes disappearing to the edge of his unique universe.

The decapitated palm across the street is growing so many new heads it looks like a leafy Medusa. Ha! His downhill neighbor has taken out his two eucalyptus trees, opening a vista clear through to the reservoir. I may have to put a lawn chair on the roof.

We're now squarely in our year-end party season—from Halloween through New Year's Eve, our friend and family group celebrates two anniversaries and sixteen birthdays in addition to Thanksgiving, Hanukkah and Christmas. Moderation is key.

Love,
Medea

*November 21, 2021 sunshine, warmth*

Dear Medea,

Now you've got me stuck with "Cat's Cradle" in my head. Speaking of music, have you heard the latest Robert Plant Alison Krause album? I just bought it. I really like their combo. I also bought the latest Adele but so far, I am disappointed for the first time ever. (Oh! Roberta Flack "The First Time Ever I saw Your Face'— it's our song—Gene's and mine.)

I'm so glad you have such affectionate men in your house who are mindful, it appears, of what you need as well as what their own needs are. I hear it's a thing now for young couples to adjourn to their own parents' houses for holiday dinners, figuring they have had enough of each other? How does that make for cross family ties? Seems odd to me. There is also a trend for the younger couple to marathon both dinner tables in a single day. That just sounds like a prescription for disaster! These things get tricky, especially if there are small children involved. We have made accommodation here over the years, fair's fair. I find I care less and less. Connecting isn't really about some calendrical notation.

Today I finally dug out my fancy camera in order to try to get decent shots of the ravens for Kim to use in her cover illustration. Interestingly, the moment I took a few shots and the camera made its typical clicking shutter sounds they panicked and took off! What do they know about that sound that I don't know? The funny thing is, I'm pretty sure it's an electronic sound that can be turned off, so I'll find the instruction manual and do that before the next attempt at a photo shoot.

Your squirrel is persistent, and you are surely stuck with him/her barring violence. I read recently about the gray squirrel versus red squirrel problems in the UK. Intervention attempts abound but the incomer gray is winning. Why is it that the native species is always the vulnerable one? Was the vulnerability there in the first place and the replacer simply following survival guidelines? Perhaps what you can do is slow them down, make a feeder that's a bit harder to access and also doesn't make the squirrel the sole winner over the little birds?

We have some eucalyptus trees on our property. A small grove planted by my neighbor many years ago. They are not natural to this region and are known to be flammable and a big mess. We have talked about taking them down. The trees make the ground beneath them difficult to plant with anything that will overcome the oil, and the nuts smell like cat piss. Do you think your neighbor had good reasons for removing the trees and if so, does he have plans to plant something else? Or are we all so terrified of fire than the landscape du jour is tarmac? Trust me, that battle goes on in my living room. Managing ten acres of mixed conifers and oaks (a clear historic Pomo acorn grove of seasonal use) has become a matter of living room battles with Gene on the one hand antsy to cut down any tree limbs closer than 20 feet off the ground, and many entire trees, while I cringe at the clearing, the exposure, the frustration of the birds, especially the tinies who can't understand why their nests have just crashed to the ground. I understand the reason for clearing dead brush and limbs and removing the slash; but I love the wild wood and the creatures in it. I don't think, in the event of fire, it will have made a difference. To expand to the greater issue, surely the answer is to put electric power lines underground. Full stop.

Love,
Jane


*22 November 2021 61 and sunny today, unlike yesterday, when summer returned, and the 70 degrees called me to the coast.*

Dear Jane,
After another late night on Saturday (two nights in one week where we came home after midnight—it's like we're in NYC again!) we spent the morning in the back yard having our friend Bobby cut our hair. When Bobby visits, he brings warmth and laughter. He loves women, so takes extra, tender time styling my hair. We talk boats and gardens, birds and drum circles. He's a gem. After he left, I checked Google maps and found that no one was driving to Half Moon Bay. No one. Not a speck of red or even orange to indicate a pile up. Who could resist?

The beach brings out the happy kid in people. A pair of ladies grooved to what sounded like Aretha Franklin—timeless and soulful, much like your Roberta Flack. Scores of parents stood by or sat in the sand with their little ones, digging in the sand or collecting hands full of lime green seaweed. To be a child and see slimy seaweed as an object of curiosity that merits carrying down the shore to show your big sister; this is the gift of being a kid and watching a kid, gushing over every new thing in the world.

Teenagers in swimsuits played volleyball. Teenagers in wetsuits rode waves. Young couples and older couples tossed balls and frisbees to dogs, some pups better at finding the toy than others, one old yellow lab ignored his human's efforts to play entirely. "He's the worst at fetch," his man told me, smiling at his friend. A lone blue heron stood on a rock crop staring at the horizon as though he, like the assembled crowd, was waiting for sunset. Have I mentioned how the beach is the place I feel most at home?

The tidepools look healthier than they have in decades, teeming with anemones and hermit crabs. A man squatted next to his daughter in a foot of water, gently pointing out the different critters that make their home here. It may take intervention to save the native red squirrels from the interloping grays, as it did with volunteers who watched over the vulnerable habitat that slow-witted people love to trample, crushing the anemones, starfish and sometimes plucking out anything living as a souvenir, or poaching sea cucumbers for dinner.

I watched an animated Italian couple marvel at and then photograph a Monterey Cypress that I've walked past a hundred times with barely a second glance. The sunset drew dozens of clusters of friends, standing quietly like a church congregation waiting for the Good Word. The sun delivered. It was clear enough to gift a green flash; instead, it flattened into a golden ingot on the surface of the sea, where it perched, unchanging, for a good six minutes.

Your eucalyptus would worry me, too. It appears that after our soggy fall, we're in for a dry winter. The birds might lose their nests if you take the trees out, but they would decamp for the oaks. If their nests' trees burn to the ground and the tinder takes out the rest of your forest, where would they live then?

My parents have celebrated Thanksgiving and sometimes Christmas alone for decades. Flying over the holidays reminds me of my 8am Contracts class. Or chewing glass. If Dylan stays in New York long-term, he'll soon tire of these back-to-back trips to SFO. My Nana's wise words, "don't borrow trouble" ring in my ears. Perhaps, like you, I'll not care, not live as a slave to a man-made chronology. This Thanksgiving, my sons are with me. That's real.

Please share your photos, once you can take them without scaring the subjects! A pair of Black Phoebes showed up at the front feeder today, then repaired to the dead pine. They symbolize hope and new beginnings. The ravens spent most of the afternoon chatting at the top of that same tree. Ravens can symbolize change. The tree guy is supposed to come next week. Is there a chance for redemption for that crispy, brittle tree?

Love,
Medea


*November 23, 2021 sun, but cold with some wind that bothers my ears*

Dear Medea,

Your description of the beach, the sensations, the variety of people and activities was so vivid, it reminded me of Aptos in Santa Cruz when we lived there. Of course, now there's no swimming, I assume, since the concrete boat is a nursery for sharks, your pals. When I was a kid, we occasionally went to the beach on the north shore of Chicago. Lake Michigan was perpetually cold, but the sand was blistering hot, so you ran fast and stopped frequently throwing down a towel to stand on for a minute. The beach was crowded with people, and I remember the stone steps smelling of fish, piss, and suntan oil. Aren't we lucky that northern

CA beaches are never crowded? I hate the beach. I hate wind, sand, and sun. We're such a pair! I love a quiet north woods lakeshore though, clear water, a dock with a skiff, water lapping. An overhang of leafy deciduous trees, green ferns, true dappled sun. That's my idea of heaven. It sucks that neither of us have our heavens. I didn't see your green flash sunset, but I did see a very red sky as the sun went down through the trees and I thought of you.

The ravens are on the roof today apparently trying to pry off the chimney cap flashing. At least that's what it sounds like. They can be destructive little buggers. The deer herd is back to three, so apparently the kerfuffle of the other day was about more than social hierarchy. The three are quite bold. The two does seem to be expanding in their girth, so I think they are pregnant. The bigger and older (my calculations being that the younger one is pregnant for the second year, so the big girl is older than that, at least) is I think the one who chased after Tweed. I went outside to try to get them to move along away from the house. My friend was coming by, and Tweed wanted to be outside, so it was time. But she stood her ground, perhaps even more than stood her ground, she seemed challenging, and I didn't risk approaching her for fear of being charged myself! I wonder how often that happens? I don't want to find out. Finally, my friend drove up and Tweed started barking from inside so that convinced the deer to move on into the woods.

At the feeding sawhorse this morning the cheeky Gray Jays were the first on the scene gobbling up the small kibble bits, not a bit afraid of me standing right by them. As the bittie cousins, I think the ravens are tolerant of them to a degree, but there was a limit and eventually they were scattered by a close fly-over from Burt.

I don't want to talk about the way humans are losing control. The news is terrible in so many ways and from so many places. I can't help but wonder if they are being egged on by their media, Facebook, Fox, whatever. But there I go, making assumptions on who is doing this lawless stuff. Now we have new words for things, like "side show'—since fucking when does that mean hundreds of people at an intersection watching stupid guys spin donuts in their cars? I feel like we are all in some terrible dystopian movie. And yet, so far, not much of it happens here, not much of it touches me directly. If we didn't have 24/7 computer news, what would we know? Would there be rumors that eclipse today's truths? Or would we be living in our own little bubbles finding the day in what presents outside the door. I could unplug and do that, but it feels like there is an obligation to hold space for those trapped in bad places. It will all get worse before it gets better.

Yesterday I canceled our satellite dish subscription. As usual, the customer service person, a woman, started to offer all kinds of discounts if I would stay. On and on she went, being very pleasant. Finally, I said, "truthfully, if we needed to go back to a sat dish, I wouldn't return to AT&T. I don't approve of their politics." She stopped her good-natured chatter, rushed through the threats and disclaimers, and hung up on me! I wonder how many other customers have left. Doesn't matter. We're thrilled to be wireless. Afterwards, I wondered if Tony (that was her name) thought to herself, "gee, she was so nice, I never would have guessed she was a Democrat."

Love,
Jane

P.S. Good news, my organic Diestel turkey fits in the fridge for once. Bad news, it cost $75 and it's only 16 lbs.! My mother would have heart failure.


*November 24, 2021 sun, cold (upper 30s overnight) and very dry*

Dear Medea,
I read with dismay that the Santa Ana winds are attacking southern CA and so we must admit now that fire season never ends.

Speaking of attacks, a very healthy-looking mountain lion killed a couple of goats at the Boonville Farm School inland. Now there is an uproar of hysteria and I'm trying to avoid local news. I don't want to know about it when Fish & Game (aka Kill & Maim) hunt the lion down and kill it. This shouldn't ever be legal. Now and then, there is an upsurge of discussion about revising the laws protecting predator animals like mountain lions, but have you noticed? They never go anywhere. We'll see if they relocate the lions as they are now supposed to do by law. It's animal cruelty to tie up or pen up domestic animals outside up here, it's like offering hors d'oeuvres to the coyotes and lions. If a sheep or goat or dog or cat is killed, that's on the owners, not the wild animal. What do people expect? They fence off every acre of wild land and plant it with grapes, pushing animals together and reducing available food in the wild. Where are the bigger animals supposed to go?

Speaking of bigger animals, the little deer herd stayed in the front yard all day yesterday grazing on the clover and red fescue well into dusk when they finally meandered off. No sign of them today. Tinker and Burt have been around all morning and when I go outside, they are very talkative. I watched them for a while on the roof peak grooming each other and chatting. Ain't love grand?

Love,
Jane

*24 November 2021 63, sunny, horizon haze. My birds dislike the cold mornings (46 today) and refuse to emerge until some warming occurs.*

Dear Jane,

Aptos has a concrete pond? This is news to me. And if someone thinks he can deter the ocean's apex predator with a roped off swimming area, I've got some bad news for him. The sharks have lived here forever, though the Great Whites move in closer to shore now, up and down the coast. Until we kill off the last of them, they'll swim where and when they please. You're a lake person, and that verdant, leafy tranquility connects you to the earth the way the beach does me; though there were random hot as hell days in Florida when I ran faster than the wind to the water's edge because the sand burned so hot on my feet it felt cold. And wet sand mixed with shell shards and wedged into the body's crevices beneath a bathing suit feels like sandpaper torture. Lakes the way you describe them appeal. The lakes I know grew monsters in their black water. Alligators. Water moccasins. Inedible and homely fish. My favorite law school boyfriend lived across the lake from Greg Allman. RG spotted Greg and friends on their lawn when he canoed on his lake. Even a chance encounter with Greg couldn't convince me to swim in it.

We are reprobates for assuming that a mountain lion must be put down because it needs to feed. Again, I wonder about the hierarchy amongst living things. A mentality that leads three men to corner and trap a jogger and shoot him for being in the wrong place at the wrong time. A values conceit that advocates for finning a shark and tossing it back into the sea, still alive, with no chance of survival. I started to write about the Nazi recruits and their assigned cats, but I can't commit that atrocity to writing. Matt Groening and friends cast dolphins as the heroes in The Simpson's episode about environmental revenge against interloping humans. Art imitating life, one can hope.

Without the Dish, will you have access to *Hell on Wheels*? Or is that the dish equivalent of television only? So many channels and nothing to watch. This is why people go to the lake, the beach, the woods. Even in Central Park, that fifty-one block long patch of green in the midst of New York City, screens disappear unless a photo demands its use. Human Tech CEOs, take nothing for granted. We don't need you as much as you need us.

While your deer may not menace, you show wisdom in your restraint. Even the squirrels may bite if they feel hungry or threatened enough. A magenta and gray Galah with a Pepto-pink pompadour a dive bombed my head when I walked too close to its nest in Canberra. I'd never seen a bird wearing plumage perfect for the disco before. But it cared not a whit about my flattery. Lack of awareness about appearances separates most other creatures from humans, except perhaps cats whose owners force them to wear a spider costume for Halloween. That cat, with eyes at half-staff and its chin tucked into its breast, told me exactly what it thought of such indignity.

The news cycle today raises this probing question: what if people had to wait until 5, 6 and 11 o'clock to hear the latest? If you were to take a wild guess, how much footage of arms jabbed with vaccine needles have you seen since January? How many close-ups of Gabby Petito's sun-kissed face? How many stories that repeat not every hour but every fifteen minutes? Or that six interrupting heads debate for thirty? The endless droning on of the twenty-four-hour news cycle. As if we clamor for its noise. Another excuse for a brain bath by the sea, or lake. The idea that injustice encompasses redlining certain urban areas or building only public housing in treeless, airless concrete plains did not register with me until the past decade. I'm ashamed of that. If your hard-of-hearing neighbor on the fifth floor tunes in to Fox or MSNBC all day while you're trying to work or cook or play with your kids (because outside offers only a rusty slide and dust where a garden used to grow), where do you find your piece of beach?

You found a sixteen-pound turkey for $75? Mine topped that by two, including the brining. Max picked up the bird and took it home for dismantling, sous-viding, and herbing. He first plans to slather it in duck fat. Then, after its eight-hours under water, he'll sear it and crisp it up on the grill. Since I don't eat duck, he is concerned about my offense level, but he forgot my secret weapon: I never eat bird skin.

Love, and Happy Thanksgiving to you and yours,
Medea


*November 25, 2021 clear. still clear. This is not good news.*

Dear Medea,
Duck fat! Max is a genius. Not only do you have loving and adorable men, but they are also talented as well. I will have to remember the duck fat idea for the future. I have some, of course, what self-respecting fridge doesn't? Since we don't have guests this holiday, I have the leisure to do the minimum. That said, we are spending most of the day packing up my jewelry making tool collection, four huge boxes of great stuff, to send off to the Zuni people for any budding jeweler who would want to continue the artistic traditions of the Zuni people. It felt great to clear the bench, and free up some much-needed space at the same time. The truth is, I love jewelry, but I have no talent for making it, just for wearing it.

Aptos's concrete ship is a hull which sank long ago, perhaps post WWII? I can't remember the history. The bay has always been a warm spot along the coast but with climate change, it has become warmer and the attraction for sharks and their young is obvious. Still, the beach at Rio del Mar was a popular surfing spot and now teams with nursery attendees. It seems fair for the sharks to push and reclaim in much the way the gray whales have done the same up and down the coast from Baja to the Arctic. We interfere, we malign, we deliberately and accidentally cause death wherever we go. It will stop, some day. Perhaps someday soon. You and I are not the only ones speaking about how the Earth will shake us off soon enough, and she will move on.

I hope your holiday dinner is splendid and filled with friends and family.

Love,
Jane


*26 November 2021 Warm-ish today, though post-Thanksgiving clean-up lasted until almost 3 o'clock, so I felt the sun through the windows, and while replenishing the feeders. Tomorrow, the beach?*

Dear Jane,
How did you enjoy your low-key Thanksgiving? While I know we went way overboard with both dishes and quantities on offer, our guests have been texting and phoning all day with words of praise and gratitude. The stragglers bid "goodnight" after midnight. We have left-over turkey and broccoli, though the ravenous ones finished off all three pies, which is just as well as we are not even half-way through this party season.

Max outdid himself once again. When he decides he's had it with space systems, the consensus among all who have tasted his wizardry is that his destiny lies in creating intimate tasting menus for discriminating diners. His cranberry chiffon with caramelized ginger kisses and orange slices required three people (in shifts) and two hours to produce: cranberries, fresh ginger and a hint of lemon are simmered to a soft, crimson mélange. We on the assembly line then pushed the small quantities of the mixture through a Chinois with a wooden muddler. We plucked out woody bits of ginger before adding more puree and starting again. The tart flavor of the fresh cranberries reigned, with a dusting of sweetness from baker's sugar and a squeeze of juice from two oranges. The ginger offered a kick of excitement for the taste buds. Best of all, he arranged the candied ginger and orange in a half-moon that looked like a spray of flowers against the carmine-colored cranberries.

As the Santa Anas decimate SoCal, Seattle's next deluge approaches. The temp in Riverside on the first of December is slated to hit the mid-80s. The Colorado River's allocation contract, written a hundred years ago, must submit to renegotiation within the next five years or...water wars? Why are they building more golf-course housing developments in Arizona? (One of the investors in this folly is our own beloved Bill Gates, who pitched in $80 million to build 80,000 homes west of town.) Have you ever driven to Phoenix? About one hour outside of town you spot the first street number sign, something like 160th street. Not bad for a city that measures five hundred and seventeen square miles. That's a space closer to our SF Peninsula than an actual town. A *Guardian* article warns that if the city doesn't wake up, it could go the way of the "original irrigators" of the Phoenix region, the Hohokam people, all 40,000 of whom likely perished because of disputes over water. In 1500.

At our dinner, we didn't talk about the Santa Anas, water wars, ZPG, or the crisis of over-consumption. One guest helping in the kitchen kept the tap running continually. Another quipped about expecting to one day travel by private jet. A third mentioned buying a second home in another land (reachable by non-private jet.) Talking with a young friend who lives a low-impact life this morning, I mentioned that while it is obvious what has to occur for humans not to kill ourselves off, I live in a beautiful single-family home and drive a fossil fueled car. I've benefitted for decades from the advent of reasonably-priced jet travel. It's the argument made by developing countries for years—you first-worlders screw up the planet for the rest of us then ask us to go without? No fucking way! Could this explain the sclerotic pace of essential change?

The birds didn't think much of Thanksgiving as it kept me from refilling their feeders in a timely manner. The cats, on the other hand, are thankful for hand-fed shreds of fresh turkey.

Love,
Medea


*November 29, 2021 sun and occasional dense fog. warm.*

Dear Medea,
Your dinner sounds lovely. I confess that I am a well-mannered dinner table guest with all proper behaviors in place, but I might not have been able to resist sticking a pin in the contest of overabundance bragging. That said, I'd love to hitch a ride to Scotland on a private jet some time. Did the water running constantly drive you crazy? I know people who would have let loose and ruined the event with their ire.

Your Max and my Chris should cook together some time. Chris graduated from culinary school and never fails to amaze me with his easy knowledge of things cooked. I forgot to mention on Thanksgiving that I fed the ravens bits of raw giblets. Now they are finishing off a bag of various cooked bits, skin and flesh. They have been *chortling* and *cooing* whenever I step outside. Burt was perched on the garage roof peak post prandially *squawking* and *rasping* and then suddenly upchucked a piece of previously eaten turkey. Put it between his claws, tore it into small pieces, and ate it again. How's that for leftovers?

Do you observe Hannukah? Or Christmas? Or both? How about the Solstice? Reminds me, I have to mail your birthday present.

Love,
Jane


*30 November 2021 Low to mid-60s today, enough sunshine to scare away any atmospheric river that might threaten to drown us.*

Dear Jane,
We found a new beach! "Found" might overstate the truth. This beach coasts between Poplar Beach in Half Moon Bay and the Ritz Carlton. Had we infinite time, I think we could walk to Santa Cruz from here. The wide, honey-colored sand sits below tall cliffs at a two-hundred-acre open space preserve managed by POST and the Coastside Land Trust. Most visitors come for the shorebirds; we saw a single White Heron, a few seagulls and scores of sparrows, which are not shorebirds. One small Red-tailed Hawk scanned the ground for prey. The half-mile walk to the cliff's edge passes through coyote brush that smells like pancakes.

We reached the edge, and this beach demanded our presence—looking north and south, we saw that very few heads had scampered down these wind and rain-scalloped bluffs. Alluvium and steep, narrow chines in the rock, rather than stairs or dedicated trails carved by volunteers, convinced some visitors to simply stand at the edge and enjoy the view. But this sand looked too inviting. The paucity of people here, unlike the walk further north that we usually take made the trek down the cliff irresistible. Shoes off, toes in the warm, nubby sand, and off we set. Two equestrian couples cantered past. (No horse waste bags in sight...and the hoof prints dig deep enough to twist an ankle if you're not careful.) Dogs chased balls into the surf. One snake-blooded woman wore only a bikini and headphones. The ocean waves broke like crashing cymbals, sometimes into each other sending up a geyser of seafoam tens of feet into the blue. We even talked about moving. We do need a dog.

Today is night two of Hanukkah, which we think about and occasionally light a candle to celebrate. When the boys were little, we observed more consistently, spun dreidels, distributed gelt. I know where the menorah is but have yet to pull it out. After the Thanksgiving extravaganza, the next holiday is up to Bruce to organize! Christmas we all love, though decoration remains my domain. As for

Solstice? The shortest day of the year? You will find me dancing in the back yard and double-checking that the next day offers a few extra minutes of daylight and thanking the sun for every extra minute thereafter.

How many hats can a person wear in a day? Yesterday, I counted fourteen. Plumber. Tax attorney. Laundress. CFO. Chef. Errand runner. Cat whisperer. Counselor. Personal shopper. Comedian. Anti-bigot activist. Bookkeeper. Travel agent. Writer. Whenever the shadow of insecurity sneaks up behind, lists like this one act as a force field to fend it off. My dynamic octogenarian friend, Fran, who reminds me that age is number best told to fuck off, is publishing a book of her short stories in addition to relaunching her website and contributing periodically to Medium. Sylvia Weinstock, who just died at ninety-one, started her career as a celebrity wedding cake baker in her early fifties. Some people bloom early and flame out spectacularly before they reach twenty-five (like the legendary captain of the high school football team whose light burns bright until graduation and never reignites.) Others live like moss-gathering stones, rolling through different terrains, trying on swan's neck thyme and ditching that for tamarisk, divining the secrets whispered by each and every one.

Fran quotes Martin Luther in her most recent *Medium* post. Given our occasional tumble into despair over the miserable state of the environment and the ineptitude that defines most global governments, we are wise to take heed: "Even if I knew that tomorrow the world would go to pieces," Martin Luther said, "I would still plant my apple tree." As Fran suggests, "Maybe we should all go out and plant a tree." Or watch the sunset from a new beach.

Love,
Medea

P.S. Tonight the beach teemed with endangered Snowy Plovers, seagulls and a flock of Canada Geese. A group of women carrying a pack of tiny dogs carried a surprise as well—a marmalade Tabby Cat. Bruce said, "That cat must have thought it found the world's biggest litter box." And the sun sets on November.


*November 30, 2021 sun.*

Dear Medea,
So many beautiful phrases to your last post. I had to just stop and sit with it, soak it in. Reflect. Reflecting for one thing on why "writer" was last on your list of fifteen occupations for the day. And that makes me again come to terms with the uphill slog that is a woman's life. That said, you are many things, and all of those things require intellect and talent, none of them are throw away trades,

easy come, easy go. Your personal resume would consume pages and far top any man's you know. I'll lay money on it.

If you walked from Half Moon Bay to Santa Cruz, you could stop and say hello to the Elephant Seals at Año Nuevo. You've surely been? It was one of our first adventures back in 1975 when we moved to California.

A dog? Really? With two grown cats? I guess that's exactly what we did, now I think about it. There are puppies with Santa at Macy's. It's a huge job, having a puppy. But grown dogs need to already be used to cats. Having a dog ties you down to one place the way cats don't. Just so you know. But then, you have Max so perhaps he could be trained to be the designated dog-sitter. I used to do that for Diane's huskie. It was known as coming to "auntie" for camp. He loved it, and once tried to refuse to go home with her. I think what he loved most about being here was that he was able to really run off-lead, and that's what huskies do best.

And, with that, we have dispensed with the month of November.

Love,
Jane

P.S. Bruce seems to have that dour pessimistic world view akin to Eeyore, who was a donkey, not an ass.

*December 1, 2021 warm, sun. Is this winter?*

Dear Medea,

I've torn up and parceled out the last bits of turkey scraps for the ravens. Probably just as well because it seems to my eyes that they have grown perceptibly over the past week and at this rate would surely be unable to fly and have to waddle like ducks instead. They won't like going back to kibble, but it's for the best.

Our little neighborhood is a bit uneasy once again. This time my next door neighbor has reported that it appears someone tried to steal her tractor. They started it up but seemed to be in reverse, rammed into the rowboat in the back of the carport and then stuck onto the structure and drove it for about ten feet before giving up. What in the world? And how far did they think they would get, driving her tractor up the lane and down the county road onto highway 1? There are possibilities for how someone knew where she kept it, none of them are reassuring, so once again we are conferencing about security cameras and locked gates. I'm surprised whoever it was, assuming it wasn't a prank, didn't try to steal Gene's two new 4k gallon water tanks. Far more valuable and theft worthy than a John Deere. A few years back someone did steal a similar water tank that was ready for installation up the road for the fire department. The stolen tank was discovered down in Gualala, identified by the big red letters EVFD on the side. No one says thieves are bright. Redbeard, by the way, is safely tucked in jail, telling his tales to the press, and to his attorney—court appointed. Of course, drugs are at the root of his path of destruction. Drugs, and lack of smarts.

The pandemic has revved up and refuses to give us any sort of grace period for the holidays. This state of fear we are all supposed to be in causes all sorts of chaos. Will it impact your travel plans?

Love,
Jane

*1 December 2021 Thirty days left of this warped year. 79 in Santa Cruz, the same temp as in Venice, FL. Not a cloud in the sky.*

Dear Jane,

Who steals a tractor? Who steals a water tank? Brazen or brainless? We had a friend whose power was running on generator during a PGE outage. His lights suddenly went out. He ran outside to find two gents attempting to hoist his generator into the bed of their pickup. He yelled at them to stop. They dropped the device, thankfully not far enough to do damage. Thieves, like the gang that blasted into Home Depot and stole the hammers and crowbars they use to smash jewelry cases and storefront windows, know that the de-funded police can't catch every miscreant.

The tree guy will be here first thing tomorrow to discuss removing the beetle-infested pine. I stood near that tree for fifteen minutes today, watching the comings and goings of the phoebe, the woodpecker, the junco, and a new bird with a call I didn't recognize. Where will they go? In proximity sit a ginko, multiple pittosporums, ample oleander and a few palms. I'll attach a feeder or two to show remorse and love. Maybe they'll stay. I draw the line at serving gizzards.

Love,
Medea

P.S. Eeyore and Bruce. Tigger and me. Sun and moon.


*December 2, 2021 sun. depressing sun. We (meaning women everywhere) are mad as hell and sick of the Supreme Court in particular and all bossy white men in general.*

Dear Medea,

This morning, Tweed went outside and lay down on the grass outside the back door. I was making tea and could see him through the kitchen window. Then Tinker showed up and flew down, landing on the grass not 3 feet behind Tweed. And there they were, aware of each other, and tolerant, if not companionable. If ravens and dogs can stand together, why can't humans? I took photos and sent you one. If we could figure out a way to get a chickadee or a phoebe into the frame, we might have a cover in the making!

Love,
Jane

*2 December 2021 Sun, giving way to broad brush stroked clouds in a pale sky. Warm early, then fall descended in brisk air. "Brisk." A word that best defines iced tea. Otherwise, it's just cold.*

Dear Jane,

For the first time ever, we stood vigil while the tree guys disassembled our deceased pine. The hatchet man wore crampons and crabbed up the trunk, a rope over his shoulder and a chainsaw in his hand. His five helpers stood on the ground below to catch falling limbs before they flattened our mature agave. As serious as it is to climb a tree holding a live chainsaw, with every severed limb a collective "whoop!" let rip from all of us. This either demonstrates the power of chainsaws to evoke glee, or two years of virus-induced psychosis. You be the judge.

As the tree slowly disappeared, I absently leafed through one of the thousands of catalogues that litter the mailbox year-round and particularly during the holidays. How many trees like this poor pine sacrifice their lives each year to produce circulars, pleas, impossible offers and wish books urging us to buy yet more overpriced plastic, manufactured crap that, ultimately, ends up in the landfill? (Cue the Grinch.) Jane, we have many problems to solve.

During today's hike, I spotted the elusive hawk on a bough just above my head. It seemed so intent, like a race car driver at the line. It allowed me to snap a couple of photos, then it flew toward the canyon where the smorgasbord lives. When I pressed the "Live" button on the picture later, the hawk already airborne, returned to the branch and the sequence of movements unfolded. Tech has its moments.

Tweed and Tinker together on the lawn, setting an example for humanity. Is anyone listening? Is that a rainbow above their heads?

Love,
Medea


*December 3, 2021 fog, cool.*

Dear Medea,

As I wandered in to the living room with my first cup of tea this morning, after having taken Tweed out for his first pee, fed him his food, and said good morning to my love as politely as is possible for a woman of a certain age who is definitely not a morning person.....anyway, as I was about to sit down in the window of my private world I noticed an orange hard hat bobbing along through my woods. Glad I didn't run into him when I was outside. He must have just walked on scene as I came back inside. Rather than completely ruin my morning confronting yet another PG&E contract worker chalking trees for destruction, I passed the buck to Gene, who dressed and went out to ask why it was that they seemed to refuse to respect our privacy with the small and simple courtesy of a phone call before they arrive? The man left with an apology and a promise to call first next time. This is what they always say, and they never do.

I began my morning chores, folding laundry, changing sheets. Stripped down to the bare minimum, I gave myself a haircut, and then stepped to the window because that was where the vacuum lay, in time to see another contract worker PG&E truck pull in and tuck itself hidden in the brush. This time, Gene wasn't home to take the "man of the house" approach. The harridan came. I threw on a sweatshirt, ample breasts barely contained in a tank top beneath, leggings, and clogs, grabbed Tweed and flew on my broomstick out the door. The poor man didn't know what was coming and gave a cheerful, "good morning!" I said various things, including, "go away," "don't come back without calling ahead," "have you not heard we are all on edge after 25 weeks of a prowler?" "don't you dare spray my dog with that pepper spray clipped to your shirt."

"Oh, it's for bears." he replied, as if that was going to make me happy. I can tell you that my blood pressure, usually low, skyrocketed. By the time he left and I went back inside the sight in my left eye was feeling wobbly and I was amped up enough to invent a recipe for chocolate pudding right on the spot, nothing like whisking egg yolks to calm the fuck down. I should add that before I let him go, at least 8 or 9 minutes of rant preceded, but I did say something about "This isn't directed at your personally, but you do have to understand how frustrated we are." He said he did, backed away, remounted his oversized work truck (have you noticed all the crews are sporting brand new trucks? Guess where that money came from?) and drove off.

Tweed was his usual friendly self. I might need a German shepherd or some such. Ok, not really. Escalating situations is easy enough when you're a witch in harridan mode. Tinker and Burt watched and observed in awe. They had no idea I could fly.

On the nature of nature, I have realized that Tinker and Burt have no concept of Pacific Standard Time but they do have a real grasp of time, and being on it. They used to come for dinner at 4. Now they come at 3. Right now they are feasting on the egg whites and shells. Shouldn't they be called egg clears instead of whites?

Love,
Jane

P.S. Quinn gets his second jab of Pfizer vaccine today. Hooray!

*3 December 2021 Evening all day from the Peninsula to Land's End and as far as the eye can see, 360 degrees around. 55 degrees*

Dear Jane,

The sea and sky merged today in a pearly gray gouache. Only man-made structures, white wisps of sea foam and a few intrepid paddleboarders in black neoprene stood out. Today I met a friend to see a small environmental art installation at the Cliff House. Each work told a sad tale of the mess we've made, except one. An art-loving surfer named Kevin, who died at age sixty-two a couple of years ago, kept a collection of kitschy surfboards, crafted from well-worn blades, and collages incorporating bits of boards and photos. Kevin elongated a photo of the Southern Lau Islands in Fiji so that it fit one board to end to end. One artist created a photo wall in cyan of the lionfish unleased by unscrupulous aquarium owners in her Jamaican home waters. A couple from Marin collected bits of white plastic and Styrofoam from a beach near their home for over two years. They mounted the litter on ceramic buffet plates that were placed throughout the Cliff House's kitchen. The effects of man's abuse to our Mother from the Baltic to Bolinas wrapped us in shame and awe.

After the exhibit, we stepped into the former gift shop, now transformed into a museum about Outside Lands, which, before my favorite music festival was born, is what this westernmost part of SF was called. According to the marvelously chatty and informed docent, in the early days of the City, the area west of Divisidero was considered uninhabitable—except by Adolph Sutro, who built his estate above the Cliff House. The historic photos show that even then the beach drew throngs, fog and chill be damned. And with the auto came gridlock on the Great Highway. Is there anything new under the sun that doesn't involve penis rockets or crypto-anything?

PG&E is paying out big for the Camp Fire, but obviously not big enough to bankrupt the division in charge of buying shiny new trucks. Those orange helmeted ones had better leave Tweed the hell alone.

Love,
Medea


*December 4, 2021 chilly, fog*

Dear Medea,

The weatherman on San Francisco's ABC news said NOAA had invented a new term, "aggressive drizzle" and applied it to the "not rain" we can expect today and tomorrow. I wouldn't call what we're having even drizzle, or the lovely "soft rain" of a typical Irish day, but it is true that when I took Tweed out last night in the dark, the flashlight showed the mist falling well enough. The warm temperatures that made you happy last week have been replaced with low 40s and wet enough that even I might have to reach for a coat when I go outside to feed the ravens.

Did you survive the solar eclipse last night? It was a truly astrologically chaotic day, as predicted, and my tongue was not held as you have already heard, but there was more, and then more, and then more so that by the time I went to bed I was cross-eyed with fatigue and "beside myself" with frustration. Since 73 years of life and 52 years of marriage have proved to me that all things really do pass, this morning the world is calmer and as far as I know, no one new has committed a mass murder. But then, there is Putin and his army massing at the Ukrainian border to consider. Can't forget about him while we shake our heads over the Michigan idiots who goaded their son into committing yet another high school atrocity.

I would like to know why all those other Greek letters were skipped in favor of omicron. Were they worried the others sounded like frats? Or Star Wars? Or did they just go for the one the current democrat was sure to stumble over? Will Pi be next? I doubt it.

Good news. Quinn has had no side effects at all to his second jab. Or is that bad news because it means his immune system said, "eh, no biggie."?

Love,
Jane


*5 December 2021 Sunny and 61, with no breeze, temperate enough to clean and water the bird baths and to pin the giant Christmas balls onto the pittosporum boughs wearing only a sundress.*

Dear Jane,
Eclipse?! How did I miss that? It's probably for the best. Today, I debated these truths: "Ignorance is Bliss." "Knowledge is Power." Are those complementary or mutually exclusive? Had I known about a chaotic eclipse, it may have clouded the purely ecstatic experience of walking down Santa Cruz Avenue in Los Gatos with my family, dancing and singing with the street band to "Let's Go Crazy" and "Best of My Love" and "September." Max and I know the lyrics to every song, for crying out loud!

Tonight, the moon has covered all but the top of its head in its weighted blanket. Only the smallest of crescents shines almost pink beneath a blazing Venus. Oh, to be on a sailboat in the middle of the sea!

An avian encampment down at the Safeway caught my attention today. Management decorated the parking lot with concrete squares in which it planted trees of indeterminate species. It's a big parking lot, so twenty-four or so trees, probably Bay Laurel. One spotty, iridescent starling, squawked a blue streak, probably issuing commands, or invitations. His friends, other starlings and glossy blackbirds with pinhead-sized yellow eyes, chattered back at him. Or her. In that first tree nearest the door, I counted thirty blackbirds and starlings. Twenty that I could discern in the next tree, and fewer, perhaps twelve, in the third tree. Thinking it weird that out of twenty-four trees only three interested the birds, I drove the lot looking for other bird parties and found none. Some mysteries remain locked.

I'm happy to hear of Quinn's mild reaction. Ah, the resilience of youth.

Love,
Medea

P.S. I suppose there is some reason for failure to just follow the Greek alphabet in naming the Covid variants, but given the terminal laziness and lack of academic rigor these days, I doubt it. Since Biden and others have taken to calling Omicron "Omnichron," it could probably have been named "ComiCon" and no one would have batted an eyelash.

*December 6, 2021 cold (for here, meaning 50 maybe) and tiny rainfall*

Dear Medea,
I went to feed the ravens in my usual attire, pjs, and realized it was not only cold but also beginning to rain. Excellent surprise! When I took Tweed out to play ball I got dressed first and even put on a rain jacket but had to call a halt to play on account of still being cold. This is very unusual. I will have to shake the spiders out of my wool stadium coat, a 25 yr old Jones New York treasure I bought in self-defense when my wicked step mother insisted we go shopping at Marshall Field's one autumn when I visited my father in Chicago. Love the coat. Not the step mother. Today is quite dark and overcast, and there is more rain predicted but we know from experience how elusive that particular god is, so I will hope for the best and try to act like I don't care so much, in case that's critical in attracting god's attention.

The PG&E contract worker checking trees to remove (kill, let's call it what it is) actually called this morning to make an appointment! The man must be new. He is supposed to arrive any minute now. It's Gene's job to mind him. These things are better not left to the witch. Speaking of witches, this is the moon period known as the Birch moon, the first sacred tree of the Celtic alphabet. Birch trees are perfect trees to make the brush part of a "besom broom" as in "get back in the house, you wicked old besom!" Thwak. Thwak. When I first noticed my calendar notation of the Birch moon I misread birch for bitch (I should wear glasses 24/7, obviously). That started me thinking, shouldn't all names of the various 12 moons be words that relate to women? For better or worse, don't we really own the moon? I nominate December as the Bitch moon. I'll let you take January, which I might as well warn you in advance is not my favorite month.

Love,
Jane


*6 December 2021 51 degrees and a cocoon of fog. It's 79 in Venice, and my Poppa Sasser's birthday.*

Dear Jane,
Riding a hickory or hazel broom to the market cures so many ills. No fossil fuel burn. Parking problems solved. An effective whacker against a thicket of thieves. Where does the hazel tree grow? Both of my neighbor's birch trees died of thirst while the family directed their home remodel from afar. Shall I steal over under cover of the Birch moon and lop off a branch and start forming the bristles? Birch bristles traditionally *thwack* the evil out of miscreants and mischievous schoolkids, replacing that evil with a purity imputed to the silvery bark. Wishful thinking. But the ritual gathering of twigs of the resilient birch tree in recognition of the promise offered by a new season sounds like a gesture most respectful to the earth.

In Celtic astrology and lore, the Rowan tree follows the Birch tree in January. My grandparents lived in Rowan County, North Carolina. January and I rarely get along, but the feisty Rowan tree symbolizes perseverance. If ever a month demanded perseverance, it's January. According to Celtic lore, the color white links with the Rowan tree and the month of January, so consuming white food (potatoes and turnips are seasonally appropriate) and wearing white, burning white candles gives the spirit a clean place to rest, and prepare for the flurry of activity augured by Spring. In honor of Nana and Poppa, I'm happy to take the Rowan Tree.

If every month-name related to women, which it should, given our tether to the moon, some misogynist in Congress would find a reason to rename all the months. Bob Dole nailed it when he wrote, "When we prioritize principles over party and humanity over personal legacy, we accomplish far more as a nation." I'm tempted to riff and rant about the degeneration of civility since Dole's official retirement in the 1990's; then, I recall that my mother wore white gloves and sensible heels with her shirtdress to Florida Gator football games in the early 1960s. The urge to tell the opposing team's fans to go fuck themselves dissipates when one dresses respectably. When I went to Gator games in the early 80s, we wore Dolphin shorts and crop t-shirts. (Skin cancer did not exist yet.) Today, cameras pan over bare chests painted in team colors. Seems we've come full circle to the barbarian days of Braveheart.

We need a Broom Brigade. Stat.

Love,
Medea


*December 7, 2021 mist, fog, sun repeat. A day of infamy, of remembering Pearl Harbor 80 years later*

Dear Medea,
I think hazel trees live in northern climates with four seasons but could be coaxed into living with a caring gardener like you, surely. It's a great idea to collect birch branches and bind them together as a last gift from that poor dead birch tree. Birches are another tree than do better with snow and distinct seasons. As for naming moon months, other names for January are Ice moon and Wolf moon. Pretty hard to beat Wolf Moon, but Perseverance moon would certainly be more feminine, unless we think of the Wolf the way the Romans did, the wolf mother with her heavy teats and hungry cubs. I like thinking about the moon this way, in all her angles.

Bob Dole was a gentleman. He was 98! Oh my.

It might be my imagination but it seems like Tinker is getting big. How does a raven, or any bird for that matter, produce eggs. How fast do they develop and enter the world? Does Tinker have five hard shelled eggs in her gut now? I recall learning that eggs are quite soft as they are laid. Perhaps she lays one at a time over several days? I'm tempted to break my rule and look it up.

My father just missed being at Pearl Harbor on that day. Young and wet behind the ears, he had just received his posting out of San Diego on a destroyer. He wrote my mother a letter, excited to get out into the Pacific on his ship and fight. It took him a while, but eventually he realized what a horror war is. All war.

Love,
Jane

*"December 7th, 1941. A date which will live in infamy." 2021 today, 59 degrees, fog, sun, fog, nightfall. Two weeks 'til Solstice.*

Dear Jane,

Can you hear in your mind those words Roosevelt pronounced, the calm, but steely address to Congress that crackled across the radio at 12:30pm December the 8? I can see the microphone, his dark gray suit, his silver hair. These are memories from newsreels, since my dad was just about to turn ten on the day the Japanese divebombed Pearl Harbor. But the sound of Roosevelt's voice, strong, stable, trustworthy, remains with me still.

Hazel trees. When I was a kid, a show called "Hazel" aired. Hazel was a maid, in a maid's uniform, who of course knew more than anyone in the household. Like Alice in The Brady Bunch. The actress Shirley Booth played Hazel. She was a red-haired TV star. Her role model status seemed more approachable for me, as a geeky redhead, than, say, Rita Hayworth's. What odd things we remember.

Love,
Medea


*December 9, 2021 cold, windy, sunshine, dry, very unpleasant outside*

Dear Medea,

I spent the morning cleaning but in the spirit of a solstice sort of preparation which meant cleaning my altar, dusting each crystal votive candle holder and each totem animal and realigning them in the traditional six directions. There are three bears and two dogs at the altar, Zuni carved fetishes from various stones, all beautiful. The littlest black jet dog is in howling pose, a thin heartline of turquoise lifts his voice to the upper world. This is Tosh, and his place is in the center of the circle. The bright yellow sulphur marble mama bear stands with her black picture marble cub, keeping vigil. On the far side is a carved black agate dog, this is Tweed, but it is also all dogs, and God, at the same time. Dog is backed by a jasper small bear, one of the first I bought from the Zuni, he is traditionally dressed with a sinew thread holding a quartz arrow head and a small turquoise stone on his back. I cried while I lit the candles. They will burn themselves down, and carry my tears to be composted by the earth. Imagine the smell of piñon pine incense, and you have a full picture. Think of this as an advent moment, witch style.

Something's up with Tinker. Perhaps it's just the evil wind. They seem rather "het" up today and at one point she found a stone, picked it up in her beak and flew up onto the roof with it where she dropped it near Burt. Maybe she couldn't figure out how to squawk at him and keep the stone at the same time, but the stone rolled down the roof and back onto the ground. She hopped around a bit and tore some pieces off the shingles and discussed these things with Burt as only ravens can, and then suddenly they both flew off in close formation. But they came back almost right away and remain close by, lots of chirping and flying around going on.

Here's something funny. I thought you had blond hair? Strawberry blond? Back before it turned gray, my natural hair color was dark auburn, a lot of red in the sunshine, so when it did begin to turn gray, I leaned toward red. Matches my freckles. Well, not anymore, but it did. My father's legacy.

I know it's not your birthday until next week but you are quite right to celebrate for as many days as you possibly can wrangle.

A team of scientists in Switzerland is nearing completion on a suicide machine. It looks like....hmmm....a large vibrator? A giant forehead thermometer? A tanning bed? Probably all of the above. I'm not sure I want to get into a coffin and then proceed to die, but I like the promise and intent of the project.

The twin fawns from last year seem to be on their own. Hopefully mama is busy with a pregnancy and has pushed them on. The group I had been seeing together last month has split and dispersed but I'm going to blame that on Gene's tractoring and brush clearing rather than something dire (as in with four legs, a very long tail, and a voracious appetite).

Good for you to balk at the obnoxious car rental person when you arrived in Tampa. Stand your ground!

Love,
Jane


*9 December 2021 Casey Key, Florida. 79 degrees and breezy by the water, still and (some would say) stifling inland. My heaven on earth.*

Dear Jane,
In Florida, "stand your ground" entitles you to shoot and kill someone. When the car rental woman at the airport suggested that I was a racist, rather than just accepting responsibility for wearing her Federally-mandated mask as a chin diaper, I let it go rather than standing my ground.

We flew over the Mississippi River yesterday as I was reading about meanders in *Home Ground*. I could make out the meander scars and oxbow lakes that tattoo most of the landscape between Arkansas and Louisiana. I imagine they extend further north to the mouth of the river that twins with the

Missouri at St. Louis. The Big Muddy rolls south to the Gulf of Mexico, my home waters, alluvium and all. The Army Corps puts up dikes and dams and berms and seawalls. Rivers and oceans laugh.

The air smells markedly different today than it did when I woke up yesterday in NorCal. There, the air bit like December in Paris, the chill had a distinctive scent, a mix of pine and fireplace, minus the baking baguette at the boulangerie., Here, the seaside carries the scent of brine across the Gulf. You can sense the signatures of the organism that live under the surface, from the bait fish that are running right now to the crustaceans that scuttle along the seafloor. When I awoke this morning, after sleeping like the dead to the sound of the lapping waves, the birds were feeding elsewhere—only a pair of gulls waddled along the shore. Now, chevrons of Brown Pelicans are divebombing for dinner, fighting it out between two different flocks of seagulls, one closer to shore and one about a hundred feet out. Cute little skimmers skitter along the swash zone nibbling on minnows and pecking the animals from the tiny coquinas. The pelicans look like photos I've seen from kamikaze flights—they ascend to the perfect hunting height, then narrow their round bodies into bullet form, wings tucked in tight, then with a *pweeew* and a splash, they dive, beak first, into the sea. Another of nature's ballets. The dolphin ambled by earlier; these would form my token animals, along with the osprey that cries alone from the top of a power line.

That you cry while you assemble this altar speaks to the power of these animals, the Zuni, the memories of Tosh and the companionship of Tweed, mama bears, winter's light.

I heard a pair of blue jays, the east coast version with the Mondrian patterned tails, calling in some kind of code across several lots. One stood on a power like above me—the other must have been several blocks away, invisible but audible. I imagined one saying "come here!" The other one saying "no, you come here!" The reference books say they are alerting each other to the presence of food with a single chirp, danger with percussive chatter. Like your liberated fawns, we have one less living thing to worry about today.

Twelve days until solstice. Seven until my dad celebrates the end of his ninth decade. We formalize these constructs, throw parties, light candles, ritualize the passing of time and seasons. Meanwhile, solitary cloud mountains float overhead, vapor monadnocks reflecting the rose gold of a setting sun.

Love,
Medea

*December 10, 2021 dry, sun. light breeze.*

Dear Medea,

There is excellent news in the local paper today that Gov. Newsom and his team have sided with the Pomo and directed that Jackson State Forest be reorganized to honor and reflect the governing participation of the Native American residents of coastal California, partly in reparations but also in awareness of the value of native land stewardship practices and the mess that has been perpetrated by the commercial logging industry. It's a big step, and so very welcome to have something positive in our collective pockets. It is supposed to be a collaborative effort, people will have to work together and there will be a lot of oversight, arguing, and dissent yet to sort through, but I am, for once, pleased about a government action.

Happy Birthday to my beloved grandfather, Howard Payne, who would want all of us to remain curious no matter what else falls away. Born in 1895 in mid-state NY, he experienced the transition from outhouses to indoor plumbing, from horses to cars, from airplanes to spaceships, but when asked at age 100, what the most important event in his life was, he said the day women got the right to vote. He would not be pleased at the current supreme court who have, in my book, lost the right to caps in their job title, and the challenges to Roe and women's right to choose.

While reading your lovingly rendered posting from your homeland I was suddenly struck by one thing: that you slept well and deeply. It all became crystal clear to me then, we will not sleep peacefully unless we sleep in our native land. I'm doomed, but I am so happy you have these opportunities to revisit the "mountain of your beginning."

The ravens seem to be busy, not sure what with. Yesterday I was looking at the madrone tree outside my bedroom window and wondering if the branches were about to crash through the glass, when I noticed a robin, facing west and buffeted by the 25 mph winds, and yet doing an amazing job of maintaining its position on the branch. The four remaining deer who are still together¬–one juvenile and her mother, and the mother of the twins– were skittish, grazing in the front yard on the bright clover and grass, starting occasionally as if about to leap off into the woods, but then realizing it was just the wind. Eventually they curled their legs under themselves and had a rest, chewing the last mouthful of greens. At this point I can tell them apart because the juvenile and her mother are lighter in color and still sticking close to each other, the young one very much still wanting her mother's protection and guidance. The other female is very pregnant and so I am assuming she has pushed the twins off on their own while she grows new life. It's nice to have seen all of them in one day, if not together. The pregnant female has a much darker coat than the others and I wonder if that's a part of the hormonal changes she is experiencing in pregnancy, and if the darker coat will help her hide when her time comes. Some things we will never know.

OK, watch out for creepy crawlies, alligators, and, most of all, Republicans with guns. Does your curly hair like Floridian humidity?

Love,
Jane


*11 December 2021 Casey Key, FL. 72 degrees, going up to 79, sashes of thin, white clouds, and a marine layer hanging over the horizon. Almost a green flash moment at sunset last night.*

Dear Jane,
Thank you for asking about my hair. It is disheveled, wreaked to havoc by the blanketing humidity. Did you see *Young Frankenstein*? You thought I was going to say it resembles Madeline Kahn with the pointy updo. But no. I look like Gene Wilder in the lab. Thank the stars for hair elastics.

If the first thing you see in the morning is the sea, the rest of the day promises to follow a similar, gentle rhythm. I'll walk after I write, and look for that pair of ospreys. Will they be nestling in the Australian pines, or headed out to join the pelicans and seagulls at the bait ball brunch bar?

I did witness a fracas yesterday morning. Two flat-bottomed fishing boats tucked up against the beach, three guys in wet t-shirts fighting with a tremendous cast net while being filmed by two guys standing on shore on their respective stairs to the sea. My first thought was that the fishermen were delivering square grouper to their land-based dealers. But nothing came up from the nets. Then, I thought maybe it was some kind of edgy movie filmed on two iPhones. But instead of collaboration, the air seemed tinged with acrimony. After several minutes of net wrangling, the captain (I presume) began shouting at the "cameramen": "It's mean high water mark! We have the right to be on the beach up to mean high water!" And then "Go ahead and report me! My permit number is *****" So, as is the habit of rich fucks everywhere, the guys on shore were pissed off that the lowly fishermen were using "their" beach to try and reorganize their nets to start their fishing day. Those fishermen did not wrap until after sunset. They put in a long, honest day's work. The homeowners have lost their beach due to the shifting sands and unknowable intention of the Gulf. Where there once was a walkable strip of beach, the Gulf has swallowed everything up to the rip rap installed to keep the sea from reclaiming the land on which their stupid expensive monuments to themselves rest. What this Key really needs to put things back to right is a series of strategically-situated sink holes.

Your grandfather Howard sure did see changes, as did mine—my grandpa Edward T. Sasser. I often wonder how they rolled on with the changes. My poppa loved his car. He only drove Mustangs. We never talked politics at all. May Grandpa Payne rain down a shower of sense on the Supremes. If you read *The Guardian* today, you'll see an op-ed that warns that not only is the right to abortion in jeopardy but also the right to contraception, equal marriage, and other rights we take largely for granted, because they are not based in actual Constitutional language (I.e., "right to bear arms," "right to freedom from unlawful search and seizure") but from a "right to privacy" that is implied. If this court has its way, we'll all be uptight, committing sin and breaking the law daily.

One of the ospreys caught breakfast, and a tiny gnatcatcher is flitting inside the seagrape tree just outside my window. A Snowy Egret continues doing what shorebirds do all day. Just in time to save me, and you, from more ranting against the Supremes. At least Gavin has redeemed part of his reputation with this ruling on the Pomos and the Jackson State Forest. How will Cal Fire and PG&E cope now? Is this a test case for returning other state forests to indigenous co-management with the other stakeholders? You're right that battles remain to be fought. Let's hope some semblance of sanity can emerge for everyone's sake, not the least of which are the trees and forest creatures.

The tenacity of those skinny little bird legs in the face of gale-force winds always inspires awe for me. Fire is different, but the winds and rain don't seem to cause much lasting concern for the birds. It's raining all week at my house in CA, and I hope my friend is keeping the feeders full so the birds can cross "finding nuts and seeds" off their to-do lists. I've never seen a dark brown deer but your theory makes sense.

This place is most definitely "home" for me. Max feels so uncomfortably hot he won't even come to the beach; but I love him still! I have photo proof that he passed many happy hours here digging in the warm sand as a kid, but now both his feet are planted firmly in the California redwoods. Dylan took a swim this morning and chatted with the fishermen. His feet are happy wherever he roams.

Heading out to search for gators in the Myakka River today. They stayed out of view yesterday; not even their hemispheric eyes visible above the waterline. Wish us luck!

Love,
Medea

*13 December 2021 Casey Key, FL, 73 rising to 82 today, a happy birthday gift to me and the two ladies swimming in the Gulf! Sunny day, all day long.*

Dear Jane,
Short post today—my best friend is arriving shortly to celebrate my birthday. Our first time together on this day in about forty years.

I walked the beach with a pair of ospreys *piu-ing* this morning, flying from pine to power pole, a sonorous reminder of nature's tenacity in the face of man-made dangers. Yesterday, I gleefully counted seventeen individual ospreys in the space of an hour. Not so long ago, the osprey faced certain extinction.

On this latest anniversary of another turn around the sun, I remember with gratitude and awe all of the people, especially my parents and their forebears, responsible for this kaleidoscopic life of mine. The beaches. The cats and dogs and my one iguana. France. All the boys and girls, women and men who held me to a standard I was unaware I could attain. My three men, who give me wings. Madame Jankowski, my college French professor. Shorebirds, willets and ospreys and sandpipers and the Great Blue Heron. Flamingoes!

This list could fill a book.

Love,
Medea


*December 13, 2021 rain. snow above 1000'. (we are at 650'). perfect weather.*

Dear Medea,
Happy Birthday! it sounds like you are in heaven. I feel for poor Max, what sacrifices he makes for his mama! I have mixed impulses about the alligator search. Did you see the news report of the woman who fell off a Carnival Cruise ship and they can't find her? I think that happens more than we know. The stuff of a bad romance novel, or crime fiction. Anyway, back to you, I was sure you were going to relate that there was a movie being filmed. It's unnerving that there are so many acts of aggression happening everywhere, as if we're in some dystopian movie about end of days–. Keep good care, and remember that snow birds with money are just as likely to be armed and dangerous as locals.

The darker pregnant female deer is very skittish. I'm chalking that into the same category as the darker fur: up to pregnancy. Do you know about "mother's mask" in humans? Maybe the darker fur is a hormonal response similar to the skin shading some women experience. When I was pregnant I suddenly became so tan, in Illinois in April, that when I went to the hospital they asked me if I'd been to Florida. I'd never had a tan in my life, just lots of sunburn and freckles.

Erratic use of birth control pills causes the same response but localized to my neck. Apparently this is common. So my supposition about the pregnant doe has a bit of basis perhaps. She has been spending the night in the seclusion of some bushes– blackberry and elderberry as well as other stuff. She blends in so well that unless she moves, she is wisely invisible. I wish she would move farther into the woods, but then perhaps that isn't the safest place, perhaps being closer to the house, and to the dog, actually is more protection from mountain lions than risk. Tweed barks and makes a pretense of chase but he stays 50% distant from the deer, wherever they are. He's good practice for them, particularly the juveniles. There is some bit of symbiosis between them that helps with how vulnerable they are to the mountain lions who are definitely here.

Don't you think all this action on the part of violent men, Supreme Court justices, and, well, just about everyone else who isn't female is backlash against #MeToo and women's right to choose and equal voting rights for women and, well, all marginalized people. In 2021, should we even have to say that? That women today, as always, are marginalized, brutalized, controlled, and objectified and that's exactly the way men want them? Seriously depressing to me. And I confess that this depression, in me and in many women everywhere, is long past turning into anger. Men know they are wrong, this is that domestic backlash scene where the gaslighting escalates as they try to regain their power. It's very sad how very little they have evolved.

Have you noticed the latest fashion trends? Women are covering up. Take that men! Head to toe in gingham Prairie dresses. Reminds me of the 80s. I'm long past it, but I would have been first in line to buy a prairie dress.

Have a lovely birthday with your bestie! May you have a new year filled with joy and sweet peace, and much love.
Jane

.

*December 14, 2021 chilly, sunshine, building cumulus clouds over the Pacific, it's a pretty day if you like that sort of thing*

Dear Medea,
It must be beautiful inland, the fall vines of Anderson Valley sparkling with raindrops against snow on the coast range beyond. I can't see it from here, of course. We have had snow here once or twice in the 20 yrs. we've lived here, and snow not a mile or two uphill that thrills the children and then melts. I wonder if snow will be a distant memory for everyone in 50 or 60 years? What falls will be dirt and dust and toxic winds. A remake of "Dune."

My post yesterday was too gloomy for your birthday and for that I send my apologies. I should have kept myself in check. I'm not sure why it was such a gloomy day, but it only got worse as the day progressed until I was nearly mute with fatigue and sadness and disappointment by the end of the day as the news of the world* just goes on and on. Democracy itself is on the line. What can we do?

Today I'm going to have a cup of sadness tea and then drive north along the coast and try to fill myself with the beauty of this gorgeous landscape where, I admit, Gene's right when he says we are so lucky to live here as we do. A couple of errands and a check in with the kids for a few minutes will perk me up nicely. I promise a decent sense of humor back in place by tomorrow.

Love,
Jane

P.S. *Speaking of: *News of the World* is a lovely book by Paulette Jiles about a post-Civil War soldier who travels around Texas reading the newspaper to gatherings of people for a penny a listen. Do you think sometime soon we will have to have a redefinition of "Civil War" to accommodate a second? At some point these phrases and snarky comments are starting to feel too real, too likely.

*16 December 2021 78 degrees here on the Key gentle breeze, the water looks like sheets of glass in hues of blue and silver. Going up to 82 today. Heaven.*

Dear Jane,
One of the blessings of changing scene is changing routine. Bruce fills me in on certain horrors, and my parents leave Fox Business on continually, but I'm blissfully ignorant of the gloom you mention, save the poor folks in Kentucky being blasted out of house and home. Tornadoes in December. Mother is really screwing with us.

Your pregnant deer with the "mask" is like the heron Dylan had to point out because its gray plumage matched the sand cliff against which it stood. Animals' super-power. Speaking of herons, our favorite restaurant here, the fish house where Stephen King wrote when he had a place on the Key, attracts six resident Black-crowned Night Herons. We had dinner here on my birthday. Some of the diners decided to feed French fries to one of the birds. Bird abuse! These birds look so soft and cuddly; I reached my hand toward one of them and it mistook my finger for another fry. According to *Beaks, Bones and Bird Songs*, birds lost their teeth as they evolved, replacing that enamel with serrations akin to razors. Perfect for grinding fish bones and fingertips. (Fun fact: the sheath of the beak that grows throughout the year and in some birds changes color is called the "rhamphotheca." You'll thank me the next time you play Scrabble.)

The night herons remind me of the Boat-billed Heron that I fell hard for when I first saw one at the National Aviary in Pittsburgh a couple of years ago. Each of these herons has eyes that seem to cover most of their face. And the night heron's iris is a blood red. We were back at the fish house last night, and I saved some snapper for one insistent little guy who screeched for his supper. Many fish swam in the water beneath the dock adjacent to the restaurant, but why put yourself out when you're the main attraction and dinner is but a *squawk* and a beguiling glance away?

My dad turns ninety today. That's a lot of birthdays. If you saw him, you'd swear he's in his early seventies. It's an illusion that gives me, and my mom, much comfort. The year of his birth is the year they broke ground on Rockefeller Center, where Dylan works. What are the odds?

You're right about the ongoing marginalization of women, and the stubborn insistence on subjugation of us by certain men. Though I will gently disagree that covering up with prairie dresses marks our sartorial victory. Are we so fearful of predatory men who can't control their anger that we have to suffer inside yards of fabric? What's next? Chastity belts? I do fear for all of our kids. The calm here on the deserted beach offers its own comfortable illusion.

If you would kindly arrange for a heat wave to hit the Peninsula on Saturday and remain in place until, oh, April or May when it arrives naturally, I'd be most obliged. Going back to cold, dark and wet gives me hives.

Love,
Medea


*December 16, 2021 cold, rain showers, sunshine decidedly wet outside*

Dear Medea,
My powers don't usually, or naturally I should say, lie with controlling the weather, but I will do what I can. That said, the ramifications of added extra heat to your environs could make us responsible for more off season tornados and we don't really want that, do we? Mother Nature's "besom" sweep of trailer parks and old warehouses aside, we should be calling for calm in all places. I read about hurricane force winds across the interior in places where there is no such thing as a hurricane, so I think we're not done with erratic weather. For us, we had a serious amount of rain yesterday which will go far to quench the thirst of the deep, the previous storm having basically missed us. Fickle, that woman.

Happy Birthday to your dad! Excellent genes he has given you. Longevity genes run in my family as well but only among the men. I'm pretty sure the perils of childbirth have had the deciding impact on that trend. May your dad see triple digits without a single misstep. (of course, your mother too, but as it's dad's birthday—he gets the prime energy).

Herons are so common and yet everyone talks about them as such a treat, because they are. When we kayaked the local rivers we would always see them, and they would mark our progress as we moved along. Pelagic herons here, gray ones. Such ancient birds. They are, along with owls, among the first birds I became aware of as a child as they featured prominently in the landscape of my summers in Wisconsin.

Enjoy the celebrations, the warmth and the love of your family.

Love,
Jane


*18 December 2021 Cold. Gray. Except for the ray of sunshine who flew in yesterday from NYC.*

Dear Jane,
If any human possessed the power to control the weather, we would either escape this mess or that person would be a nefarious type who would use the power as blackmail. So, let's go with Gaia's plan. I own sweaters, and a very cute pair of Santa kitten leggings that will come out of the closet to celebrate Christmas week. Our plants nearly doubled in size while we were away thanks to the rains and absence of that unseasonal blazing sun. It's best to remember the interconnection of all living things and not selfishly yearn for endless summer in a location that reveals surprises with the unfolding of each season.

After spending time at my home beach walking and socializing with family and friends, reentry usually feels like a cold-cock to the jaw. Particularly with the temperature differential. But this trip, the Gulf exacted its influence in a more permanent way. When the kids were small, I'd take my "last walk" before driving to the airport and weep with grief for the place and people left behind.

But, with time comes perspective. The beach is still there. My sweet parents are like the rodents of the human world, which sounds disrespectful superficially but their steadfast insistence on living out loud, damn cancer, damn malaria, damn the Tamil Separatists that held them hostage and the Covid that threatened to do the same, and double damn the thousand other Italian Oreo Box perils that conspired to interrupt the adventure that defines their lives elevates them to that lauded level of Survivor.

So, my birds fattened up while we were away, especially the sparrows. The raven still visits the feeder, still flies away the moment he senses my presence. The black squirrel remains convinced of its invisibility. The bunnies huddle under the feeders, nibbling bits of whatever happens to fall to the ground. The rain coaxed out many species of fungi, frilly golden clusters and solitary dark chocolate specimens the size of bread plates.

And guess what? The palm tree across the street sprouted five new fronds, a middle finger to the failed executioner. Another survivor. It almost looks like its old self again.

Love,
Medea


*December 18, 2021 cold, overcast, frost warnings overnight*

Dear Medea,
I was startled yesterday by the whole raven family flying overhead–Tinker, Burt, and the five children now just as big as ma and pa. Where have they been? I have no idea. They came from the southwest when I saw them, but I think they have been to the north Never mind, it was heartwarming to see them playing tag, chatting, skydiving, and dominating the sky, a little family reunion. I did notice that Tinker and Burt kept them on the move and they didn't stop for tea or a breath, no begging for kibble, no perching on the rooftop; they flew around a bit, flapped, and soared off. I do know that they won't be breeding or nesting, but does that mean that neither will Tinker? Will she get a much-deserved year off? She and Burt have been coming around for food more often, is that because of the cold? The approach of a nest of eggs which will prevent them from coming as often? Do I actually know anything more than I did before? I'm content finding my knowledge from observation, it's a fine thing to be curious and need to make and disprove assumptions. Science was sure a slow process before the internet. Slow knowledge. Like "slow food" maybe we could start a new trend. It's definitely meditative to simply watch and wonder. There is value for me in the learning process itself, the figuring out of what to assume, and what to wonder–really wonder– about.

The full moon overnight woke Tweed who seemed to think there was a slow moving intruder make his way across the yard. Or something like that. Once he stared out the window long enough I guess he figured out at least that it wasn't a human or other predator. He has been quite agitated every evening when we go out for a pee before bedtime. An agitation requiring a leash. It seems clear there is a fox who does his foxy things, meanders down the sidewalk, has a drink from the dog bowl, checks for leftover kibbles and then, always, shits creatively on either the saw horse or the palette where I feed the ravens. Tweed would love to catch him. I would love for him not to do that. It does amaze me that the moment there is the cover of the night sky, the creatures come close without fear.

With the fire lit, fairy lights in the windows, and a lowering sun casting a pale pale glow through the trees to the south west, it is truly the gloaming. Completely still, we wait for what will come next.

Love,
Jane


*20 December 2021 Cold. Gray. The full moon last night shone so brightly it felt almost like daylight. Winter looms.*

Dear Jane,
Tomorrow at 7:58 am comes the Solstice. You love this day for its extended darkness. I love this day as a marker of longer days to come. For two people who share so much, we stand as opposite sides of the same coin in this. I see you, with Tweed, absorbing the deep stillness of the winter wood, standing on the porch, quiet in the gloaming, anticipating the moonrise, and whatever comes next.

The ritual of stopping to admire, appreciate and acknowledge the sunset is a little bit harder for me to schedule this time of year; it happens early in the day compared to summer sunsets. Like mastering a Shostakovich piece, it's the intentional effort that amplifies the melody, that sharpens the tones of amber and amethyst against a slate blue sky. Even against the gloom that holds us hostage this week in Northern California, the shifting colors of the western clouds signal the day's end, the time when the goddess Nut will swallow the sun for another day and give birth to it again at dawn. What an image. There is nothing unsophisticated about a belief system that includes a woman whose every night includes surviving the consumption of a nuclear fireball.

My cat, Odin, follows a ritual as well. After I've neglected him for longer than a single day, he implores me with a very loud and insistent voice to pick him up and snuggle him like a feline basketball against my chest. This will go on for a couple of days. If I fail to comply, as now when I am writing to you, he leaps up on my standing desk and smacks at my fingers (stop that, Odin!) until I abandon my foolish human pursuits, give him his pets, hold him close enough to feel his soft fur and purr vibrations against my cheek.

Slow knowledge, slow food, slow life. I'm in, with the proviso that we can still dance to Gloria Gaynor, Donna Summer and Grace Jones.

Love,
Medea

P.S. I took a holiday card out to one of our neighborhood servicepeople just now. Never underestimate delivery people. They see everything. On the subject of the Renaissance Palm Tree across the street, he agreed that the tree has to stay, and said of the owner, "Doesn't he know there are two trees, on each corner of the lot? He should leave them for symmetry!" Then, the punch line: "I told that guy 'what the hell are you doing, cutting its top off like that?! It looks like a dick!'"

*December 21, 2021 cold, storm fronts approaching*

Dear Medea,
Happy Solstice to you, to the kitties, your men, and the wee birds who bring you joy.

I find myself bringing this solstice half year task to a close with a soul tiring brain fog that no amount of sunshine can remedy. I have tasked myself to find some help with grieving and, as if manifesting were always immediate, up popped a segment of 9 episodes of grief counseling on my Calm app. We shouldn't be surprised that any need like this can now be assuaged at the touch of a screen. The real trick, of course, will be whether I follow through, make progress, and learn why it is that grief can be so heart rending, and on a schedule that no one can reverse.

At the same time, I threw caution to the wind and ordered a pair of expensive Italian loafers which came, hopefully not prophetically, and are going right back to Italy where they came from and can find some skinny footed Italian woman to appreciate them. Remember the 70s when we all wore Birkenstocks and then one day woke up and realized we had wide peasant feet and roughed up toes and if we ever wanted a pretty pedicure again we'd better stop? Kind of like that.

Speaking of apps and omens, as I was sitting reading, my phone suddenly blared like a German police car and I was completely confused as to why. By the time I figured it out, the earthquake happened. No time to "duck and cover," no damage either. Next time there's a claxon on my phone, I'll know why, but it still probably won't be time enough to throw myself under the baby grand. As for omens, I figure there was one. Before the earthquake the ravens were on the grass outside the window not 4 feet from my perch and they were pecking madly at the ground, throwing up leaf matter and dirt and grass and occasionally stopping to look at me and hop closer as if to say, "hey lady!" When the earthquake struck, they flew off, work done. Their idea of a warning was far more effective, or would have been had I realized it was an omen instead of some random errant behavior. There is nothing random in this universe, of that I am convinced. The real question is how to bring all Gaia's creatures to a similar understanding that to survive these times, we must link hands, branches, fronds, hooves, paws, and claws and breath. Breathe together.

Love,
Jane


*21 December 2021 Solstice in the Northern Hemisphere. 42 degrees. Rain. All week. Bring it.*

Dear Jane,
Here we are, in reverence and awe, watching Gaia usher in another changing season. If we lived on side-spinning Uranus, half of the planet would bake, the other would freeze. Always. Our personal weather preferences aside, I doubt either of us would rocket off for either hemisphere of Uranus no matter how evil the misogynists on Earth become.

I indulged in a bit of materialistic binging for my family today. The last time I visited this shopping center at Christmas, the sidewalks thronged with bodies, and the line to visit Santa wound round Macy's. People were stacked twenty deep at the present-wrapping station. Parking required persistence, an eagle eye and combat-ready reflexes. This visit, the atmosphere was less circus and more anxious energy. Everyone wore masks and gave others wide berth. The parking lot's numbers resembled any random Wednesday in April. And still. Only a fraction of the cashiers needed were on hand. At Macy's, I was searching for a garment bag on the third floor. Not a clerk in sight.

We have both mentioned how Covid sort of suited us as we are pretty content hanging out with our birds and trees and deer. For my part, though, semi-frequent interaction with new people stimulates my little pea brain. One man who helped me with a gift for Bruce wound up teaching Dylan how to pack a suit to save it from wrinkling. He told the story of his British mum, who urged him to be "a little bit froggy! And learn to dance, because ladies love to dance!" We found we both love Miami, his birthplace, and Salsa dancing and speaking languages other than English—he speaks seven. I needed this.

My kitties entertain me, and Bruce is very smart. The birds wow me with their melodies, ballets and occasional fracases. And their appetites. The palm tree across the street reduced me to tears; first, tears of woe, when it lost its head, then tears of joy, as it regenerated, refusing to die. I feel a connection to these things that share our earth. It's humbling to look at, say, a lemon seed and realize that lemon seed came from a lemon on a tree that started from another lemon seed. Origin stories! I love to spend a moment at dinnertime and examine my plate.

Who planted the arugula? Who harvested it? Where was the garden? How often did it rain there? Whose hands put the greens into the box that some other someone drove to a warehouse and then to my grocery store, where yet another unloaded it and stocked it in the produce section? Where did the clay originate that found its way to a pottery factory? Who made the plate? Where did she learn to throw clay? Why did she paint dots on the plate and in the pattern that she chose? Is it any wonder that Bruce prefers to watch something featuring cartoon violence during dinner?

Tonight, we humbly close the curtains on the shortest day/longest night of the year. Winter brings this gift of the stormy weather we know will reanimate the forests and fill the reservoirs. What will become of the masked doe? Do Tinker and Burt have another clutch to give? Can Tweed contain himself and leave the fox alone? Will my sparrows eat themselves into a carb coma? How long before the black squirrel discovers that its super power is not invisibility? Is there any chance the pair of woodpeckers will build a nest together? What about the Mourning Doves for whom we mounted the protected nest platform? Will the Phoenix Palm's tenacity impress the homeowner enough for him to let it be?

And, Dear Jane, as we close our correspondence for the month of December, I can't help but wonder what surprises 2022 will bring.

Love,
Medea

# January 2022

*1 January 2022 Bright, sunny, clear. 37 this morning, 52 this afternoon. An auspicious start.*

Dear Jane,

Happy New Year! After the past six weeks of way too much revelry, I'd vote for moving New Year's Eve to the first of June.

As a Southerner in my soul, today is a day to prepare and serve black-eyed peas, greens and corn bread to ensure good fortune in the coming year. The greens, naturally, symbolize wealth. The black-eyed peas, some say because they swell as they simmer, some say because the "eye" stands for clear vision, represent the promise of luck or prosperity. The corn bread represents gold. Tradition includes cooking the beans low and slow, with ham hocks or hog jowls, because pigs root forward, like progress. No pork in our house, so I substituted a smoked turkey wing; although chickens and turkeys purportedly root backward, I figure a wing represents aspiration, heights, and I've never seen a bird fly backward, except during a hurricane, so I'm calling it a reasonable equivalent. And my grocery store's collard stash was emptied by the time I shopped last night, so our greens are not technically "greens," as in collard, mustard or turnip (or dandelion, which should count) but spring green chard and forest green kale.

The fact that the patrons of this store in Northern California are buying collards and fresh black-eyed peas, which did not exist in the produce section when I moved here thirty-two years ago, swells my heart with affection: for my Nana, who taught me to love the spotted legume, for my mom, who carried on the tradition after she moved to Florida with my dad, for the West Africans who brought the black-eyed pea to the states, under the worst possible conditions and for the most inhumane of reasons, for those who honor the tradition both here and afar. We'll say a blessing in gratitude for them all. And, naturally, for the peas.

I learned of a Greek New Year's tradition from Dylan's special friend. She makes a "1234" cake, which sounds much like the pound cake that my Little Grammy made, using one pound of butter, two cups of sugar, three cups of flour and four eggs. Inside the loaf, her mother hides a large, well-wrapped coin. She who selects the slice with the coin is assured good luck during the year. Sort of like the baby Jesus inside the Mardi Gras King Cake. We find comfort in ritual.

Wishing you a year ahead filled with good health, adventure, an eclipse or two, baby birds and fawns, clear, clean air, ample rain, and with any luck, bears.

Love,
Medea

P.S. Do you make New Year's Resolutions?

*January 1, 2022 cold—well, everything's relative, so not really so cold*

Dear Medea,

Happy New Year. When I start to think closely about calendars instead of creating stability, the diversity and obstinacy of the various dogmas gives me an uncomfortable looseness, a sense of chaos rather than order. The idea that January is a fiction, as was Christmas, and this state of suspension we are currently in kind of makes a mockery of time passing, of counting weeks, months, and now years that we have been held under the pressing thumb of invisible germs, or would I call them viri? Viruses? Ignoring all of that as mere details of life as it trudges on, our little world came clobbering to a new calendrical page with a broken refrigerator on a holiday. A fridge, I might add, that was filled to brimming with various leftovers and riches for a New Year's Day feast—yes, of a ham, and black-eyed peas. We're living out of boxes in the garage, and grateful for the unusually cold temperatures keeping most things chilled. It is amazing to note that my fridge mostly contains condiments: jams and butters, soy and fish sauce, BBQ sauces we hated (why still keep them?), Pomegranate sauce for Fesenjan, and Harissa and sambal and green curry paste. There are capers, and sun-dried tomatoes, pickles, and six kinds of mustard, a Costco size mayonnaise and ketchup and these are just the things I can recall right this minute. Of course, there is also a bottle of Champagne, and oh my, we deserve it.

I suppose I do make resolutions. I'd call them more a sense of ordering or reordering in some cases, a list of things I really would like to do this year (as opposed to things I need or have to do). At the top of the list is to read my Druid friend, Pascal's, new books which just arrived before Christmas. This seems reasonable enough except that they are in French. I can read French fairly well if I have a dictionary at hand so it will be slow going, but worth it. Pascal lives in Brittany on the coast where there are many cairns, stone avenues, and monuments all rich with the mythology and the energy of the ancient ones. He is a shaman and a Druid and a traditional Breton musician.

Next on my list is to study the genetic genealogy workbooks that I bought a year ago and then set aside, perhaps when we started this project, or perhaps the books just got submerged under a pile of other books I should or want to read. George Saunders deserves another look. And now you've given me the Barry Lopez I haven't read, and then there's a new book by Jon Turk the National Geographic adventurer I met through a friend and who must have been right in front of me in line when the angels handed out Fearlessness and he took my portion. If I can wade into my reading list, then I'd also like to pick up my knitting needles and start a new project with some gorgeous yarn dyed by some amazing and inventive young people who are carrying the craft of knitting into new and wide-open places.

In fact, that's a good place to stop for now. Time to pop the cork and raise a glass to a new year.

Love,
Jane


*2 January 2022*
*37 brisk, blue degrees here, almost 60 at the coast!*

Dear Jane,
Your friend Pascal Lamour is a prolific guy—I looked him up. His Breton music transports me to his France, which includes the coastal town of St. Malo, which is a choppy ferry ride from St. Helier, where I lived on that small sailboat with the alleged Pringle's can inventor. I can imagine returning there today and seeing the cairns that eluded me when I was a punky twenty-four-year-old, to feel the cobblestones underfoot, to listen for sounds of a moody Celtic harp. I'm listening to Arany Zoltán's Celtic music now. Suddenly, I yearn for a hot cup of cider, a shot of Calvados, and a dance with a dark-eyed stranger. Let me know how you find the book—reading it in its original French may be a bit of a challenge, but a fine way to pass January, your dismal month.

A new tiny visited the front porch feeder today. It wears an eye band that makes it look like a miniature flying raccoon, or Adam Ant. It's the smallest bird to visit yet, this Pygmy Nuthatch. To spy on the front birds requires stealth, since the feeder is so close to the front door. Assuming it returns tomorrow, I'll confirm the identity. Two Oak Titmice tag team on that feeder, keeping the chickadees on their toes. The bird bath out front froze overnight. Is Woodstock the only bird who ice skates? I'll let you know.

We drove over to the beach early, hoping to beat the inevitable traffic that comes on a sunny day after the rains. The curved-beaked whimbrels and Snowy Plovers, cormorants and pelicans, and a few families of ravens joined some gray and white sea gulls to meander with us from Poplar Beach south toward the Ritz

Carlton. This beach, a beach that I love because, well, it's a beach, looks almost nothing like my beach at Casey Key. It's walled to the east by high cliffs that the sea is hell-bent on reclaiming. The waves wash up a few rocks, a shard or two of sea glass, not the shell and (increasingly rare) shark's tooth treasures from the Gulf. Bruce reminds me that the Pacific drops far deeper off the shore. Florida was once underwater. So that's fair. Still, it's hard to believe that this Pacific is the same ocean that swirls around both Fakarava and Komsomolets.

A childhood friend who lives above Denver phoned tonight. One of her cherished friends lost her home in the nearby fires. Today, a foot of snow covers the embers of the thousand homes and business lost. No loss of life, pet or otherwise, but still, a punch to the gut. What would you do if fire consumed your home? I fantasize that I'd be sanguine. Assuming I'd evacuated the cats and all the kids' childhood pictures. And Bruce, of course. Then, thinking further, what about my teddy bear, whom I've had since I was born and have carried across oceans? The autographed copy of Julia Child's *Mastering the Art of French Cooking*? The vinyl copy of *Rapper's Delight* I bought as soon as it dropped in 1979? The Fiorucci jeans I've worn since 1980? Love letters? Where, really, do memories live? As you look around, is anything that you live with and care about irreplaceable?

Love,
Medea

P.S. Flocks of Red-winged Blackbirds at Poplar Beach blanketed the split-rail fences and the dusty fields. They remind me of the guy you never notice because he always wears blue jeans and a gray t-shirt and then one day he shows up wearing a golden and scarlet boa with a black velvet cape. Fabulous!

*January 3, 2022 cold—but everything's relative*

Dear Medea,
The horrifying accounts of the Colorado fires serve as an unwelcome reminder that this season of rain and cold is temporary and terror is a constant. What more could it take to convince absolutely anyone of the peril we all face? The Pacific coast news is about the King tides and how they can show us what the rising sea levels will look like. The news shows a cute young couple walking on The Embarcadero, she with her paper Starbucks coffee, tripping carefully around the widening ponded water on her sidewalk. How could anything bad happen to two people having so much fun? Will it help for all of us to stay focused? We are actually doomed, are we not? Should we do what little we can, and then move on

to whatever salves work? Is anyone seriously giving up alcohol for "dry January" when the world is hurtling and twisting to get us the hell off her back? Not I.

I see the ASPCA ads and despair as I know you do. And I give. Here's some good news, I sold 17 copies of my dog shaman book in December, so some folks somewhere care about their pets.

I hope the bird bath has thawed for your tinies. It wasn't cold enough here to freeze the water bowl, but it has been cold enough that I rummaged around the closet and brought down an assortment of jackets and coats including the one I bought for the trip to the Arctic. Inside the pockets I found a pair of wool gloves. Excellent idea. I do love sleeping in a cold room with lots of covers and the window open just a crack, just enough for fresh air.

The ravens are ravenous these days. Are they preparing for nest building? I couldn't say. They have started showing up for three meals a day. Morning also finds the little gray jays hurrying to snatch up what they can before the ravens make them leave. Tinker is nearly as big as Burt and only sometimes can I tell them apart. She has a longer body and different posture, but with the cold they both seem to hunker down into their feathers a bit more.

The deer herd is now at six. Either one young buck has been taken, or he's off on his own doing what bucks do when they aren't in rut. What would that be? Eat, I suppose. Like the rest, but alone. The females are pregnant. Sometimes I stare at the matriarch, and I swear I can see her belly shift and pop. Their schedule brings them to us at dusk to snip and chew their way across the clover and grasses. While they would move if Tweed ran toward them, they are remarkably calm and seem to realize he is no bother to them. As for us humans, they ignore us.

Have I mentioned how much I hate January?

Love,
Jane


*4 January 2022 54 degrees, a silver sliver of a moon, rain turning to scattered puffy clouds.*

Dear Jane,
The rain conspires to trap my brain in cotton wool, my fingers fiddling through cat fur or leftovers that must be tossed rather than writing to you. Thankfully, the sun came out this afternoon. With the sun, a pair of Anna's Hummingbirds set up a perch on a bougainvillea branch outside my front window. The mini-birds were so close that I could see their noodly white tongues darting out of their needle beaks. I hope they are sussing out the garden for their spring nest.

Those tiny cups woven inside sheltering branches fascinate me—how can eggs so miniscule produce the bird with the fastest wing beat in the world?

I've given up dissuading the two black squirrels from the feeders. (I've named them Stephen, since their antics remind me of Stephen Colbert. I've also named the gray squirrel "Abigail," for no particular reason.) In the interest of encouraging them all away from the bird feeders, I bought a massive, crushed-corn cylinder that the label claims equals twenty-five ears of "corn that squirrels love." After taking many photos of hummingbirds in the bougainvillea, I returned to the corn site, expecting to see squirrels at the banquet. Nope. Only a single Stephen, hanging by his toes, supping on suet.

Discouraged by the unruly squirrels, I asked Dylan to walk with me at the reservoir. We got a late start, almost 3:40, and it was so worth it. After all of the rain that has blessed this place, the running streams and waterfalls offered a soothing soundtrack. It's been at least four years since I've heard that sound at this trail. We talked about VR and AI, whether reality is as we experience it or whether it's manufactured in a Matrix sort of way by a weirdo (Psycho? Sadist? Comedian?) puppeteer, whether it's better to live by routine, whether a person can ever be defined by her job.

We covered a lot of territory in six miles. As the ideas flowered, we spotted a towhee high in a crippled oak tree. Then, the frogs. First, a single croak, then a chorus of croaks. We followed three resin-colored salamanders that looked like you could pinch off their tails and chew them like gummy worms. I've never seen a salamander on this trail. As dusk fell, a family of eight turkeys waddled out for a feed. We passed five different herds of mule deer. When the crescent moon rose, it carried clouds the color of shrimp, and all of that splendor reflected in the reservoir. By the time we reached the entrance, the air hummed with glee frogs belting out a synchronized song; in your mind, you could see them, the squat, speckled rana aurora, holding their hymnals, miniature golden halos circling their heads.

This is the same trail that I walked with Bruce and my parents in May, 1991, to encourage Max to just be born already. It's familiar. It's foreign. Every single time. Hallelujah.

Love,
Medea

Dear Medea,

What gets me out of bed every morning is my dog, Tweed. Often feeling somewhere between desperate and puny, I think that without Tweed's anxious, cheerful, energetic very Border Collie face nudging the bedclothes or, if necessary, jumping up on the bed and straddling me until I have no choice but to shift, well, without that the world would have narrowed beyond restoration. Thanks for missing me while I had a tough downturn. This ME/CFS monster is really quite straight forward, push at one's peril. Poor Long Covid folks have no idea the siege they are facing.

Now, back to birds and beasts both tiny and huge. I love the two Stephens and of course their Abigail. What is it that makes the black squirrel seem sinister but the gray squirrel not at all? I'm sure, given time, they will figure out all the treats you have to offer and then ask for more. We don't see many squirrels here but occasionally there is a ruckus between jays and squirrels, and very rarely I see something smaller and chipmunky. We don't have cats any more here, they being the first course of choice for bobcats and mountain lions, but when we did, we would find evidence. The leftovers of dismemberment and a meal well taken. I heard a new to me bird call this morning. I'll have to check with Cornell but in the end, I thought perhaps it was a particularly loud quail on alert rather than a new member of the society. Tweed and I were outside playing ball and at one point I followed him into the woods a little ways where there is a tiny clearing surrounded by brush veiled in brown pine needles and branches fallen. The deer use this passage from the yard back into the woods to their secret spots. I came across a line of enormous chanterelle mushrooms, far gone from picking, and then some white mushrooms with nubs all over that I have no name for and haven't seen before. We don't usually hunt mushrooms though if I find a chanterelle in time, I will pick it. There are several places on our land where they can be found in abundance.

And that, for today, will have to be enough. There may be something of a metaphor going on with those chanterelles and my current state of puniness.

Love,
Jane

*6 January 2022 51 degrees and gray, then dense fog. After so many dry non-winters, I'd forgotten that 95% humidity in January feels like relief.*

Dear Jane,

Well, it's been a year since the storming of the Capitol Building. Has much changed? A 107% increase in death threats to congresspeople! In the realm of international gun deaths, we're number one! Our leaders' approval ratings gasp for air! And don't forget those record-breaking Gulf of Mexico oil drilling leases!

A Medium writer from Sri Lanka published a three-part "you're in hell and you don't even realize it" series in September-October 2020 that I've just read in full this afternoon. To spare you the gories, he compares the situation here to the fall of his country from the time he was "zero years old" to his current age, mid-thirties, to what is happening here now. The point of the piece, as I read it, is that we're living in the midst of the revolution, and because most of us live in relative safety, play our Scrabble, dance at our raves, shop for cheese and bread, and are spared the daily explosions in front of our homes, or our moms stepping on land mines, or our boyfriend's heads being bashed in by crazy people, we don't really see it. Well, we SEE it, but maybe we don't feel it as acutely as we desperately must.

But, all is not lost.

There's a parallel in Thay's *Zen and the Art of Saving the Planet* that bears considering. Those of us who see the danger in the increasing frequency of wildfire, of tornadoes in December, of disappearing shorelines, know we created this shit storm enviro-mess. Our generation. We heard the cries of Rachel Carson and Barry Lopez and Aldo Leopold and we cheered their brilliance and even banned DDT. We passed some laws, some good, solid laws, to keep the air clean and the water clear. Imagine where we'd be today without those. And while we were thinking and trusting that the popular tide shifted along with these advances, another force brewed, one steeped in amassing personal wealth at any cost. I could descend into the historical weeds here, but will instead simply say that we have been alerted. Again.

And yet, all is not lost.

We, the global "we," gave our children life, requiring them to navigate not only the political climate but the actual climate. They deserve a shot.

What shall we do to save the world on this fine day?

Love,
Medea

*January 8, 2022 sunshine. Cold. Everything is relative, still.*

Dear Medea,

Tiny steps. Everything requires tiny steps. And that's not just a personal appraisal. What's that line, "the revolution will be televised'? Or will not? Is the insidious truth that the change we fear is happening under our very noses as we politely disagree. How did we get to this place? By putting our trust and faith and federal funding in the hands of elected officials who all, to a man, only wanted power and don't care a fig for our needs never mind those of the global community. After watching some punditry about the anniversary of January 6th I want to know why they aren't all in prison for treason? All of them. We can't overcome this just by voting. I don't have an answer to your question, but I think what I will do is make a donation to Stacey Abrams' efforts to protect voting rights.

It's so much easier to watch the natural world. The creatures don't need our help and don't want our interference. Our bird feeding gestures are frosting to the cake of their real world. Neither of us lives in snow or hard freeze where the birds of winter really do suffer. In some ways, we are leaving a small gratuity to the wild world for allowing us in every day to watch, listen, and learn. I'm so grateful for that focus. And for sharing it with you.

Twice since just before Christmas, the earthquake app on my phone has announced an impending quake. This last time we were having dinner and I heard a male voice announce "Earthquake! Take cover and prepare for shaking." Or something to that effect. You know what? We didn't move. We just looked at each other and shrugged. I said, again, shall we get under the piano? Gene said, in his best engineer voice, "I'm not sure that would help." He seemed disinclined to do anything except possibly get the damn app off my phone. It reminded me of when we were first married and living in Illinois. He would never retreat to the basement during tornado warnings. There is something in the life philosophy here. Is it his masculine nature? A fatalistic attitude? A Scorpionic (I made that up) refusal to be told what to do, particularly by an automated voice on a phone app? And why didn't I get under the piano? Or at least make a move to. Obviously by the time I got Tweed and made it under, it would be over. A discussion ensued about how much my deep soaking bath tub weighed, perched as it is right above our heads; and then another thread to the poor construction of our little two-story Victorian and new cracks in the ceiling. It all seemed futile to react energetically over. When and how the house will fall down around us seems already to be ordained, it's just a secret from us.

Love,
Jane

*8 January 2022 52, gray. The weather app promises sun, which Dylan and his sweetie found in abundance in Marin, where they've repaired for nature bathing.*

Dear Jane,

Your earthquake vignette reminds me of so many disaster movies, from *Don't Look Up* to *Deep Impact,* where the comet hits and the characters simply hold their loved ones and let nature have her way. I suppose you could crawl with Tweed under the piano. What if it gives? And bathtubs do fall through ceilings. Did you see *The Day After Tomorrow,* where a tsunami roars through Manhattan and pandemonium ensues as everyone tries to outrun the water? In 2004 when that movie was released, did anyone believe that humans could best a tsunami by taking shelter inside the New York Public Library? Or just pile on more coats to avoid freezing to death as the ice age suddenly descends? What about food, for crying out loud?

Gene may be Scorpionic, but he has a point. Joanna Macy talks about how we've mucked up the planet so violently, that now the best course is just to appreciate that we have been offered a chance to live, however briefly, on this miraculous blue planet. Death is certain, but not its time. To share this space with you, as well as with our furred and feathered friends is a privilege.

Did I say that I find the black squirrels to be sinister? I do find their play and movements to be hilarious, especially their hanging from their hind paws off the side of the feeder, or freezing in place to trick me into not seeing them. The gray squirrel, Abigail, isn't that clever; but she may learn. The ravens, I assume, lifted the corn cylinder out of its basket and tossed it onto the ground, where neither the Stephens nor Abigail has discovered it. But a murder of crows has its eye on something on the smorgasbord; each morning for the past three, at least twenty of them gather in the neighbor's pines on the other side of the fence and mutter, loudly, about how to chase away the tinies and lay claim to the feeders. At least that's what I'd be discussing with my mates if I were a crow. By 9am, they're off on another adventure. As I've learned reading Bernd Heinrich's *Ravens in Winter,* those corvids rarely gather in groups larger than six; but the reason for writing this book, per the author, is because he stumbled upon a group that appeared to be calling other, presumably "stranger," ravens to join the feast after they found a moose carcass. This kind of largesse surprised Heinrich, so he devoted four winter seasons to studying these birds in this Maine wood to learn whether this behavior was an anomaly or endured over time beyond customary ornithologic observation. I'll let you know.

Bruce just called me out to check on the ravens, six of them in our front pine, squawking over some perceived indignity or threat, or plotting a feeder attack. The paperwhites and hyacinths have poked their heads above ground for the first time in a year. Wild arugula is growing in the pot where daisies used to live—cross that off the grocery list. I collected enough lemons—Meyer, pink and Villafranca, a sub-species of Eureka—for a generous, refreshing batch of lemonade, which sounds incongruous given the temperature, but when nature provides, l graciously accept. I'm slowly, by moments, learning to love January.

Love,
Medea


*January 9, 2022 cold. Sunshine*

Dear Medea,
All day the set of three deer have been very present. At one point when they were out of sight, I took Tweed outside and was struck by how perfectly beautiful and varied the carpet of clover and grasses and moss truly is in the front yard. This never has happened before so something about deprivation and then abundance has triggered a season of plenty. It's no wonder the deer love to stay. And, as for wild groceries, there's miner's lettuce and fiddle head ferns and a few other things I can't name, but I do recall being told are edible.

In my early days of noticing the ravens, I had a major interaction with them which I wrote about in a poem. Early one morning just past dawn they gathered on the grass beneath my window. Seven or eight of them, making a huge ruckus. All sitting on the ground, hopping now and then, arguing with loud voices. Then one, as if nominated for the chore, came flying right at my window. I thought for sure he was going to crash into the screen, instead he veered toward the sky at the last minute and landed on the roof edge right above me. "I get it," I said. "I'm not paying attention. I will try to do better."

I read someplace that crows can't soar, and ravens can and that's one way to decide which you are seeing. We don't have crows here on the coast but there are crows inland in Anderson valley. I have no idea why 20 miles would stop them. If you figure that out, let me know.

Movies that imitate disasters bother me. Disasters that imitate movies are even worse. Today's disaster was the horrifying fire in the Bronx. I'd like to know if we can ever again have a single day without regrets and horrible news?

I didn't mean that you thought the black squirrels were sinister, I was just saying that I think they look sinister. For some reason, this brought to mind my grandmother's fur coat, with the actual body of some animal, mink? Good grief.

I guess we have come a long way in the past 100 years after all. Do you have a recollection of opening your grandmother's closet and what that smelled like?

Love,
Jane


*10 January 2022 52 sunny degrees*

Dear Jane,
I recall ladies wearing fur stoles with the snout of the critter meeting its tail, sort of a biting clasp. They also wore those pillbox hats with nets. And gloves. Stockings. While the current trend of wearing pajama-equivalents everywhere swings the pendulum too far in one direction, I'm grateful that I can run errands without having to wear my pearls. My grandmother's closets...hmmm. I'm not sure I ever saw the inside of my dad's mom's closet. We visited rarely, and her Northeastern sensibilities may not have tolerated my snooping around in her bedroom. My mom's mom, though, was all open heart, Southern hospitality.

I've told you about spending hot North Carolina summers with mom's parents while mom and dad adventure-trekked around the globe; Nana's closet, which she shared with Poppa, was dark and small. I'd love to remember a cedar or lavender scent, but it was more likely the smell of detergent and summer breeze—Poppa liked to hang the clothes on the line in the back yard to dry. Nana kept a Mahogony coat rack in the dining room, which commanded almost an entire corner and where she kept a church dress or two, a couple of her cosmetologist's smocks and her winter coat. I'd assume they absorbed the smell of the Winstons they smoked, the comforting kitchen aromas of the pot roast, green beans and fatback that wafted through their house, and the acrid odors of hairspray and weekly permanent solution from Nana's beauty parlor. What did your grandma's closet smell like? Is the fur you're thinking about a fox?

The ravens are on a tear outside right now—it's 1:30, and they've been at it all day. Aside from their larger body size, the raven's wings point at the tips, and their tails splay out in a wedge, rather than the squared-off fan of a crow. I read that about the soaring as well; Cornell tells me that while crows can soar, they rarely do, flapping their wings silently unlike the swishing sound the raven makes in flight, where it can do a somersault, which is something I long to see. And ravens have longer necks, and weigh twice as much as a crow. Still, telling the two apart takes practice, as with just about everything worth doing. That's our corvid lesson for today.

How many disaster movies does Hollywood have to make before people realize these are cautionary tales? I read an essay by George Monbiot yesterday in *The Guardian*, this one about how *Don't Look Up* captures the head-banging fury he has faced as an ecology-oriented journalist for the past nearly forty years. He talks about the humiliation of breaking into tears on national television during an interview on *Good Morning Britain* in November. The ditzy host, a Cate Blanchette look-alike, asked him whether he really thought that Insulate Britain (a group of climate activists that advocates for insulating all buildings to lower reliance on artificial methods of heating and cooling) was overreacting to the whole global warming situation when its members occupied the motorways during the morning commute. Monbiot lost it. This is what the creators of *Don't Look Up* realize; people who see the tipping point looming face a public that is largely more concerned with being late for a hair appointment than doing the hard work to ensure the studio isn't underwater in a decade.

On a positive note, and we need those, the Monarch Butterflies returned to Northern California this week, their numbers exploding from just 2000 last year *to over 150,000 this year. Hooray* for milkweed and the people who plant it. *Hooray* for the tenacity of wildlife.

Love,
Medea


*January 11, 2022 sun. cool. Quiet.*

Dear Medea,
My father's mother was a southern sort of socialite who dressed in style, smoked cigarettes from a silver case, and carved radishes into rosebuds. She was born in southern Illinois in a small and poor town to a family with pretenses if not money. She attended finishing school at a college now incorporated into Vanderbilt in Nashville, TN where she perfected her drawl. The class photos and yearbooks are a slice of life. I probably never saw the inside of her closet, or maybe even her bedroom. But she was kind, and generous in her way. According to my parents, neither she nor my grandfather were good parents but they threw great parties. My mother's mother—that was different. Her closet had a lightbulb pull chain light and smelled of musty wool and leather shoes. She was such a skilled knitter that she knit dresses for herself, sweaters, soakers, and rompers for all her grandchildren. She designed the lake house the family built, and taught me everything I know about genealogy. I know the sensation of pressing my face into her fur jacket, the prickly in one direction and smooth in the other brown fur that smelled of her perfume–the kind that came in a thin glass vial that you broke the end off and used it up all at once–and the scent of clothing not washable very often, and sensible shoes polished with paste and brush. Both

of my grandmothers died at about the same time and yet I knew one so much differently than the other. My mother once said that after my father's mother died, she felt her ghost as a cold breeze surrounding the chaise longue she used to sit on. My cousin Jim says my mother's mother, Dorothy, used to come and look at his cookbook—her copy of *The Joy of Cooking*—at night and they would find the book open, sitting on the couch in the morning. The grandmothers always referred to that book as "Mrs. Rombauer" which made me think they knew her, but of course they didn't. Or maybe they did. Stranger things have happened, and it was a smaller world then. This makes me wonder, if it were a smaller world still, would we be making such a mess of it?

The deer have been so close by last night and today that they have occasionally been standing right outside the windows. I wonder if they sense an alien presence. When I first saw them this morning, they were trotting across the yard headed from the creekside wood to the inside forest. Not for the first time, I'm wondering if that creek has a name. Certainly, lesser bodies of flowing water have had names. I'll have to ask one of the old timer residents.

I saw a piece on the news about the butterfly official count in Monterey. It was great to see good news and amazing to see the butterflies all congregating together. Apparently, that's called a kaleidoscope of butterflies.

Love,
Jane


*11 January 2022 From 62 and sunny to 56 and high clouds, all in a couple of hours. Reminds me of summer.*

Dear Jane,
Mothers remain mothers long after we shed our mortal skins. I still hear both my Nanas; dad's mom, Anna, cautioning me, between puffs on her Parliament, to bloom where I'm planted, and mom's mom, Mary, giggling into her tapered, red-polished fingers over some naughty gossip whispered by one of her hairdressing clients, whom she called "the ladies." Anna raised four boys. Mary raised one, and my mom. I've leaned on their experience while navigating the uncharted waters of being a mom to my male children, since I had not the slightest idea what boys want. Turns out that kids tell you who they are and what they need.

We are lucky that these formidable women left us with multi-sensory memories. Your grandmother Dorothy visited cousin Jim (is this Jim related to Uncle Jim who talks in bird?) and from the spirit world and offered meal planning suggestions via recipes from *The Joy of Cooking*? You have to love that.

Will our grands say the same about us one day? You'll have to check in with Quinn. I'm still waiting for my kids to get married.

Think about our planet now and when our grandmothers roamed. When putting your feet on the furniture earned you a switch to the thigh. When talking back showed disrespect. When canning tomatoes in the summer meant spaghetti sauce in February. If our earth were smaller, would more of us show consideration to others? Plan ahead? Think beyond the end of our own noses?

My dad used to warn me about committing "decision by indecision." We procrastinate at our peril. My contribution to Gaia today is planting kale, lettuce, celery and cauliflower. If the slugs don't feast first, if we avoid a freak freeze, if no one leaves the gate open so the deer wander in, I'll start the harvest with romaine in about four weeks. Caesar salad for Valentine's Day!

What's up with your deer? And what species of alien? It's not hunting season, is it? They're smart to huddle close to your house. The name of the creek might be as mundane as "Elk Creek"; the creek that runs from the end of my street toward the Bay is called "San Mateo Creek." In contrast, "squirrel" derives from the Greek, *skia oura*, or "shadow tail." I hope you find your creek a fitting name. How about "Trophy Pot Creek" from the Greek *strofí poto*, or "curving drink?" The deer might approve.

Love,
Medea


*January 12, 2022 sun. warm. Dry. Frowny face.*

Dear Medea,
There is an Elk Creek already. Our land is part of an old ranch, and before that was a seasonal camp for the coast Pomo. They would come to collect, grind, soak and process acorns into flour. The grove of oaks was nicely situated close to the stream which offers rushing water half the year. Acorns taste terrible and have to have the tannins leached through soaking in water, then dried, of course. I didn't know any of this when we built our house. At least not about the Pomo having first rights to this land I live on. That speaks to the sloppy job done by the environmental and historical impact reports more than anything else. If I had been aware, I would have situated our house away from the oak grove. I did already know about the acorn processing and the seasonal food gathering of California Native Americans. I began to put two and two together here when we started finding tools, mostly grinding stones called manos and smaller stones for smashing and crushing. These, once we are allowed to do such things, will get

the attention of appropriate Pomo history collectors. They don't have monetary value, but they are historically significant as evidence of original land use.

I'll ask my neighbor to remind me of the name of the ranch family. Perhaps that should be the name of the creek. There is a small strip of houses on the coast side of highway 1 to the west of us which is called "Little Geyserville." I have no idea why except that often people from Sonoma came to the coast during the heat of summer. Logic would say that someone from Geyserville built a house. Another question to ask a long-time resident to explain. There has been a mini water war with the west residents and those along the creek, claims of ownership which are not in fact lawful but which in typical male fashion, when declared loud and often enough make people acquiesce. At least outwardly. There is a lot of water stealing going on all over the county. Once we were coming west from a trip away late at night and passed a water truck, hose in the Navarro River, sucking out water. Not potable, of course, but who knows who the intended buyer was? Maybe just thirsty vineyards.

Back to grandmothers, a much sweeter topic. I loved my grandparents. All four of them were wonderful to me. I lost my grandmothers far too young; I was only eleven when Dorothy died, and thirteen when Glad died. Both of cancer. My grandfathers did their best to compensate and my connection to them all is strong. I love that Dorothy returned to thumb through her cookbook. Yes, this is Jim, son of Uncle Jim. We are double cousins and therefore, from a DNA standpoint, we are siblings, born six months apart and inseparable as children. For a while we were all raised together in my grandfather's red brick apartment building. Once when my aunt had us out in the front grass playing, a drunk wandered by from the bar down the block and gave her $5 for the orphanage.

Back to the present, I just noticed a bobcat in the yard. Gorgeous coloring with a bronze gorget shaped marking, and beautifully spotted. He was sitting still watching the gopher holes, no doubt, but then eventually strutted off, retreating into the wood near where the rabbits hutch. Gulp. I took a few photos. I'll send you one. This one seemed smaller than the one I saw last fall, but still far bigger than a house cat and the muscled power in the legs alone made that wildness clear. The tail, short, did have the white tip like the last time, so it could be the same creature. I'll have to look bobcat up in the animal totem book again. Tweed was inside and did not notice the visitor.

County rates of infection since Christmas have skyrocketed. New mandates for protective gear and avoiding social gatherings just dropped.

Love,
Jane

*12 January 2022 64 and sunny, then overcast but still warm enough to till soil
and bait slugs. No rain in the forecast. Drat.*

Dear Jane,

Covid rates everywhere look like Omicron caught the world flat-footed. The
*NYTimes* map that shows Covid hot spots is the angriest shade of purple I've
seen since March, 2020.

Where will you take the Pomo tools once it's safe to do so? I know your
sensibilities and that you'd never have sited your home in a way that showed
disrespect to a people or to their ancestors. The history of land ownership is so
fraught with nefarious deals. The subtitle of Simon Winchester's book, *Land*,
reads "How the Hunger for Ownership Shaped the Modern World." And left the
indigenous and renters to make do.

I'm sorry to learn that you lost Dorothy and Glad so early in your life;
maybe your relationship with the grandads would have played out differently
otherwise. My grandpa who was Mary's husband used to love to take my sister
and me to Rose's, a precursor to Target, which smelled of popcorn and burned
a billion watts of fluorescent lights. Poppa would buy us some kind of present,
a pale blue UNC sweatshirt or a paint-by-number kit (even then, I was partial
to birds) and he'd let us roam free while he watched out for us through his inch
thick glasses. As a "thank you," we'd help him hang the washing or stir the beans,
or just sit on the front porch and count the rail cars as they passed. He never flew
on a plane or traveled north of Virginia or west of U.S. 395, yet he could read
the weather and (correctly) intuit the veracity of anyone using his superhuman
perception. I loved Poppa Isphording too, (William, but he went by "Bill") just
didn't know him as well. Poppa Sasser must have absorbed the wisdom of the
ages through the red clay that splattered our shorts and caked our shoes. He was
so smart. Formal education only gets you so far.

January invited me outdoors to rummage in the garden this afternoon. I'll
fill you in on the details tomorrow; it did feel like coming home to press my
fingers around the seedlings, feel the warm soil and smell the promise of new
life.

Love,
Medea

*January 13, 2022 sun. cold. Dry. Just ask my sinuses*

Dear Medea,
I love your description of your red dirt childhood! I don't know that world at all but some things about being a child under the quilt of grandparent's love doesn't change no matter the geography. I do remember counting cars on the long, long freight trains out on the Illinois prairie where I was born, the smell and feel of my grandfather's Packard with a back seat big enough to hide in. I was never happier than when I was snuggled in with my cousin Jim and we were on our way someplace with my grandfather, Howard. But back to Virginia and the south of your childhood, it occurs to me to wonder about your ancestry. Did your people come to the South long ago? I do have family from 18th c. Virginia on my father's side–that southern belle grandmother. It would be fun to compare.

After reading about the migratory patterns of hummingbirds and butterflies and your own life I started wondering, is this country just too big? Should we be like Europe, broken into regional/ethic areas cohabitating as some economic trading partner? Has the desire for tribal stability facilitated this nasty racial divide we now face?

Love,
Jane


*13 January 2022 61 and overcast, misty over the western hills. The newly-sprouted daffodils, however, decided to come out and dance anyway.*

Dear Jane,
As tempted as I am to lead with my ire toward SCOTUS for failing to follow science and enforce the vaccine mandates, one, I'm not surprised, and two, vegetables are more interesting than those alleged jurists, so vegetables win.

Since the raised vegetable beds attract any number of varmints, I decided this year to plant in a more studied way; maybe I'll learn something. One kale seedling and two romaines will try their luck in the former tomato pot outside the sliding glass door near the kitchen, where all plants have remained undisturbed. Two cauliflowers and six celery plants found homes in the sunniest raised bed. As I tilled the existing soil and added some fresh, several earthworms came up to say "hi'—a good omen. For extra caution, I sunk a bowl of beer in the center, and draped netting over the top between bamboo poles. Unlike years past, when that netting knotted and snagged, I was ready with slow, deliberate unfurling and focused securing to the nubs on the poles. I finished dressing the entire bed without a single scream of frustration.

The next raised bed over needs much work. I'd pushed a couple of eyed potatoes into this bed last August, and they sprouted runners of tiny spuds. Those will roast up nicely! This bin I also use for lemon thyme, oregano, sage and chives. The chives looked spent, until I cut away some of last year's herb, and to my immense delight I found two small chive seedlings pushing through the soil, looking much like unopened elfin umbrellas. This is my second most favorite thing about being in the garden; discovering what survives year over year, and what has slept through the fall and early winter and demands renaissance. Last year, so many tomato plants and one "hat pepper" plant simply regenerated from last year's fallen crop that had nested in the dirt.

The pineapple sage with its magenta blossoms is a space hog that, so it may have to relocate to another part of the garden so I can add the rest of the romaine in this part-shade location. A little irrigation repair and mint removal to the third, shadiest bed and the spinach will live there. Then, we wait for Mother to work her magic and voilà!

While I will continue to plant my veggies, tend to the critters and limit the use of my car, the earth is still headed toward a tipping point. Thay says we can mindfully do what we're aware needs doing and since the impermanence is nature's state anyway, just accept it. This comforts me. As writers, we use our words to gently sway the unbelievers. Enter Bill McKibben. I learned today that he started a group called "Third Act" that he expects will mobilize people who have ended their first or second careers to join together and agitate for serious, large-scale action. I'm intrigued.

Love,
Medea


*January 14, 2022 cold. Sun. dry.*

Dear Medea,
Yesterday Tweed woke up feeling poorly. I wasn't able to pin down a problem and then solve it. Instead I managed to get myself worked up and worried. Around mid-day I called my vet, and they called me back (hooray for my amazing vet) and gave me the end of day emergency slot. I couldn't figure out if Tweed had had a seizure (he has epilepsy) or if something else traumatic had happened. But even the idea of playing ball didn't grab his attention. I was scared. It was time he had an exam and blood work anyway, so I didn't feel too badly about jumping the "wait and see" gun and driving up to the vet. I still don't know what was wrong, but we have meds, and blood tests will come back this morning; and after a good night, Tweed seems fairly normal. I'm telling you this because

the bigger problem now and in general, is that my emotional reserves are zero when it comes to Tweed–well, maybe when it comes to everything, how can I tell? I feel like a cartoon character, digging in, dust flying, as I'm pulled faster and faster toward the edge of the cliff. Today, all the tension of yesterday has settled in my neck. We do our best, and too often we are reminded that we are not in control even of the smallest things when it comes to the really important stuff. What would Buddha say? With no family and no attachments, would the monks just shrug and smile as death comes for everyone? How does that work? I don't think it does. If the pandemic has brought us anything at all, it should be a revised awareness of what is important, and what is inevitable.

Meanwhile. Yesterday's treat was that a new or at least revised herd of nine deer trotted up the driveway and made themselves at home in the front yard. I admit, the yard is at its finest right now, offering what surely must be a luscious treat to these herbivores. We noticed the coats of these guys were winter brown, thick and dark, and there did seem to be some competition going on. I wondered if the little group we usually have was being overrun by a gang of bucks. They did look bigger, and bolder. Some of them bedded down, chewing their cud, while others were less at ease and now and then in competition for space. I'll be interested to see if they come back today.

Have you read John McPhee's long essay about following Bill McKibben around? You would enjoy it. That man, McPhee, has a gift. Wouldn't it have been something to be in a class of his? The scary thing about McKibben and others of his ilk is that they always seem to be oddballs, and oddballs aren't reliable. Look at Elon Musk, or Richard Branson. There's something a little skewed right from the start. As leaders or narrators, we cannot trust them. McKibben is a character too though keeping well in the path of good. The McPhee book profiles another crazy person who wanted to build up southern wild areas and make them golf courses and did so. According to McPhee, listening to these guys tell the story their way can be so persuasive, that the truth, the global good, easily gets lost. The chilling part is that McPhee wrote this book a long time ago. I wonder how he would amend it today?

Your garden sounds wonderful. Caesar salad being my favorite. It makes me wonder, am I far enough north of you that my growing seasons and timing are completely different? How does a garden grow in summer without water and in a drought, versus in winter when the temperature is cool, but the ground is sodden and everything is green? My Midwest brain doesn't compute any of that correctly. But I suspect it is time to get some seeds ordered, nag Gene to build the raised beds he promised, and make a plan. If we have a plan, we can't possible die before we've started, right? Take that Covid!

Love,
Jane


*15 January 2022 Sunny and low 60s. Coral-colored skies at dawn and dusk. The calendar claims it's January. I'm not so sure.*

Dear Jane,

Don't know how I missed your letter from the 13th when you asked about my family and how they came to the South—Mom's family, anyway. Honestly, I just assumed they'd always been there. No one, at least that I've heard, knows any different. There was the talk about our having both Indigenous (Lumbee) and African American folks in the lineage. Since everyone was either a farmer or other laborer, I fantasize that if it's true, the couplings were both consensual and loving. Until my schedule opens up (until I open it up...) and offers limitless hours for online research, I'll have to wonder.

You've taken the time to dig deeply into your genealogy and created bonds that go back so many generations, back to the "old country." Do you find that knowing these forbears informs how you see yourself beyond the Celtic? Do you think if you found out that you were Kazhak it would make a difference? Sometimes when I feel powerfully drawn to something, like clogging, for instance, or a certain shade of iridescent green, or minaudieres, that one or more of my ancestors must have shown an affinity for these things. Maybe it's a way for them to connect, to tug on the thread of my sweater and insist that I open my eyes and see more than just what's right in front of me.

Tweed's health issue concerns me. I'm crossing fingers for a positive outcome. I don't interpret Buddha's cautions around non-attachment to mean that feeling grief for a sick or dying Tweed would be best replaced with an accepting shrug. A broken heart reflects the suffering all of us feel at such times. Perhaps what Buddha might suggest is accepting the suffering as part of life, embracing it gently, like a fragile butterfly, and, after acknowledging and nurturing that sorrow, accepting that loss is the flip side of life. If we can take one lesson from this damned pandemic, it must be that we take nothing in life for granted, not a brilliant, sunlit moment, not a cuddle with Tweed, not a woodpecker's treble clef squeak.

Thank you for this suggestion about McPhee/McKibben. Since Bill is urging all soldiers in his volunteer army to use courtesy to convince, he rings my Southern bells. I'll look up that essay.

Yesterday the garden and the birds held my undivided attention. After planting the test seedlings on Friday, I fixed the irrigation lines and amended the soil in each bed before earthing the rest of the plants. The birds kept me company: Four hummingbirds buzzed my head while playing flying torpedo. Two less-frequent visitors, a Ruby-crowned Kinglet and a Yellow-throated Warbler jousted with the regulars at the feeders. I chased one of the Stephens out of the seed cake feeder and around the yard, waving the corn cob I'd bought for him as enticement. He laughed at me and dashed up the pine tree.

With two hours of sunlight yet to spare and plenty more space in the bins, I dashed down to Golden Nursery for tarragon and whatever else looked delicious. I came back with red chard and watercress, French thyme and garlic chives, broccoli and heirloom lettuces with speckles and flouncy edges. And climbing green peas, one of my most favorite things to add to risotto, pasta, salads, or just to shell and pop right into my mouth. In the time it took to drive there and back and shop, some dastardly varmint (I heard wing beats as I approached the beds) had already nibbled on the tender shoots of spinach and romaine. I set about stuffing those seedlings into the prepped soil. By the time I released the earthworms and secured the final anti-varmint net, the colors of the sky had shifted from ruddy carrot to aubergine to charcoal. My agri-ancestors winked their approval.

Love,
Medea

P.S. Last night, I experienced two different dreams about overpowering waves that washed out the coastal roads and roared over the tops of buildings as I tried to make my way to the beach. This morning, the National Weather Service issued a tsunami warning for the entire West Coast. What will tonight bring?

*January 15, 2022 a Saturday in case anyone is wondering, cold, sun*

Dear Medea,
Your dreams were lucid and prescient, my friend! There's a witch in your subconscious clamoring to get out and lead us. Phones and computers lighting up shortly after 7am this morning to "advise" (as opposed to "warn') us of a tsunami in the Pacific which should be a contradiction in terms but isn't. The automated female on the audio alert did a remarkable job of not fucking up "Hunga Tonga-Hunga Ha'apai" which is going to bother spell checker for months. The what now? I had to look it up. Have you been to the Pacific Islands? Surely you have. I haven't. In fact, I haven't had any urge to travel there though

Hawaii was required en route at some point. There must have been a siren alert this morning as well but with windows closed all I had was a nagging sense of hearing some sort of ruckus and vaguely thought, "tsunami?". Of course, the predicted 1–3 ft swell is nothing for our coastline which regularly sees seas of 15–20 ft during storms. The advisory went on to say that people should not go to the beach to watch.

That was the morning's excitement. I was really glad I was already up; I would have resented being vaulted into elevated heart rate mode from a sound sleep. What's the tally? 2 Duck and Covers and 1 Tsunami in 7 days? A bit excessive?

I thought you did DNA testing. No? As for how I'd react if I found a new tribe threaded through my DNA, I'd love it. In fact, I've been rather fascinated lately with the history and ancestry of Finland after finding a tiny amount of distinct Finn DNA. Not at all Scandinavian, apparently, and quite more Siberian/Russian steppes. Maybe that's why I love to knit! Wild swim! Sit by a roaring fire! I find solace in my Celtic past, it makes the face I see in the mirror make sense, the response I have to the land itself is a deep knowing–something that came before the statistics, something that fed a need and longing I felt all my life. At the time I first felt that recognition I didn't know I was deeply Celt– I wished I was, but didn't know the ancestry. And yet the feeling, when I first visited Ireland, I stepped off the plane in the dark on a wet morning before dawn and started to cry with joy. And while my Celtic roots range across the ancient lands: Scots, Welsh, Breton, German they are felt most deeply for me in Ireland, perhaps because the Irish have tended their story with the liveliest care, I'm not sure. As DNA results become more refined, more threads are sure to appear, and I welcome all of them and hope someday that tiny percentage currently left "undefined" gets a new marker to some far-off land.

Now I'm watching some deer, five so far, meander around the corner of the house. One of them sees me in the window, so I waved at her, and she's gone back to eating, satisfied that I'm not armed or hungry. I don't think I would be happy if every time I took a step my neck had to jerk forward and then back again. Why is that their lot? There must be a word for that movement. Believe it or not, I just took a moment to look it up. My first try ended with the usual hunter advice postings for killers, but I tried a second time and came up with a lovely Google response for animal magic. Deer looking at you signals unconditional love, acceptance, and heart energy. Isn't that sweet? I do think the deer accept me, but I don't know about the love part.

Tweed has recovered from his event of Tuesday. His lab work doesn't indicate anything in particular, and we have given up trying to figure out what happened. I'm just glad he is all right. We can step back from the precipice again. If I had lots of money, I would create a mobile concierge vet van equipped with ultrasound, x-rays, portable surgical unit –all mod cons–and pay for a fine vet team to drive around the countryside helping small local vets like mine with sophisticated emergencies. Large animal vets must do this. Of course, right now there is a terrible shortage of veterinary docs and techs just as there is a shortage of human docs. Such a shame. Everyone wants to stare at a computer screen and play a game—no one is cuddling the four-legged furry ones anymore. At least not until it's too late to fall in love with *All Creatures Great and Small*, which, by the way, I hear is coming back very soon!

Love,
Jane

*18 January 2022 Sunny to the east, cloudy (or overcast or Tonga volcano ash?) to the west. 55 degrees.*

Dear Jane,
On many of the Pacific Islands I've humbly visited and not-so-secretly yearn to live someday, the dearth of veterinarians yields scores of feral animals, mostly dogs. When we bicycled around Fakarava a few years ago, we were warned to cycle past the hounds, fast. They were uniformly what I call "brown dogs," the color of tawny sand, with square heads and middling snouts and of medium builds. Lanky, probably from scavenging for their suppers.

On Hiva Oa I asked a local woman about vet care. She told me that the vet arrives by boat once every few months. People line up with their pets, hoping to score an appointment. But there were rumblings that a vet was going to move to the Marquesas Islands chain, so perhaps their pets would receive more consistent care. I wonder whether my cats' vet, the adorable Dr. G., would know how to treat a cow or a donkey? Is it like being a person doc, where you sort of know remember that the gall bladder rests in the upper-right quadrant of the trunk of the body, and that if someone presents with pain, nausea and jaundice that gall stones may be to blame? Or are the medical needs of cows and cats so vastly different that this uber-vet will muddle through the best she can, often learning on the fly and hoping the internet is functioning?

With the threat of a DT Redux in 2024, the remote waters of Fakarava hold tremendous appeal. Nothing much to do but dive with the sharks, kayak, bike around the pups, maybe go to services at the shell church in Tetamanu Village. As tempting as it may be to dream of a life so removed, I'd become one of those snowbirds that I love to hate. And I'd miss the kids.

When I see the deer at the reservoir next time, I'll remember that their big brown eyes look at me with love and acceptance. Their head bob as I understand it is an effort to confound predators into thinking the deer is unaware of the predator's presence. We think we humans are not so vulnerable as the deer as we go about our daily lives, then Michelle Go is pushed from behind into the path of a subway train. We finished watching *The Last Duel* last night. Men historically behave barbarically. Maybe this thin veneer of civilization we were tricked into accepting as part of the Enlightenment has worn itself down to the coarse, fragile particleboard beneath. Or maybe some people are just selfish, evil, and predatory.

An asteroid is doing the tango with the earth now, passing within twelve miles of our surface. The people of Tonga can't communicate with the rest of the world; even the ham radio waves are not penetrating. This week's rollout of 5G cell service in the US threatens to upend air traffic control from coast to coast. Who sang "the world is in an uproar, and I see no end in sight"? The Atlanta Rhythm Section. 1972. I would say that at least we don't live in the fourteenth century when women were chattel and rape was just part of the quotidian landscape. But that would ignore women's plight on at least half the planet.

Wandering into the darkness, but not dwelling there, is like acknowledging that stabbing pain in your back then making peace with it. Media is the opiate of the masses in our era. Zuck and Bezos and the Murdochs performing the Vulcan mind meld on the willing, poorly educated public.

Look up.

Love,
Medea

P.S. Apologies for this downer. I'm working on my taxes today and I lack any confidence that these funds will be distributed by intelligent, insightful minds to worthwhile causes and souls.


*January 18, 2022 cloud building, cool*

Dear Medea,
I wish I could talk you up from your downer, but I'm afraid I'm pretty much down there with you. I'm horrified to even contemplate that shoving someone into the path of an oncoming train is the next "thing," and I guess partly thanks to some recent snide remarks by Stephen Colbert, surely meant as comedic jabs but really, New Yorkers, are you proud to be so mean spirited? All tourists should avoid New York city. Is that where we are now? And no matter who you are, watch your back?

As for dogs, and cats, and feral life in general, there's a tradition around the world of a sort of acceptance of wild dogs and cats. Italian cats. Peruvian dogs.

It's heartbreaking. When I lived in Iran, there were wild dogs who roamed in packs and howled at night. Dogs were not pets to the Iranian population and there was no quarter given. Oddly, I don't remember seeing cats. If we can't find enough vets to work here in the US, then I'm pretty sure we won't find help for those poor strays.

It might help all of us if we were globally subjected to a black out, or ash out as the case may be, if only in the sense of losing our connections for, say, a month. A reboot. Time to think, formulate a new answer, a new political stance, a new acceptance of the "other," a new god? Sure, why not? We could continue with this…pen and paper style. I wonder how my fingers would respond to gripping a pen for an hour? Speaking of the 14th c., except for indoor plumbing, not much has changed. Not really. I read a headline in the NYTs that said there is a new kind of male supremacy at play. "Oh no," I thought, and did not read on. Can we really have had our moment, made our case, spent our penny on the numbers and statistics, and only been allowed a year of asking for what we should have as birth rights? As women and equals?

The weather reports are confused. The clouds form and shift but do not provide our due, which is rain, lest you forget. Nothing I've read says ash is going to be a problem, but then, I wondered, if it were, would anyone tell us? At this point, are we full up with bad news and not able to manage another single thing?

Here's a few things: my neighbor brought me eggs; the hens are laying again. The fox shit on the palette and it's looking like he doesn't feel well. The ravens had a set to after lunch. I'm not sure why, but the squawking and ruckus went on for five minutes. I wasn't able to tell whether they were having a marital dispute or chasing off an invader not invited to the table. Tweed is feeling more normal but played a lackluster game of ball, losing two. We're down to one left.

Give your kitties a cuddle and feel stronger tomorrow. We have battles yet to fight.

Love,
Jane

P.S. *All Creatures Great and Small* has returned. What joy!
P.P.S. Also: in the yard, 6 deer back for an evening graze. And the squabble with the ravens was half dozen buzzards descending on their meal! Oh no!

*January 20, 2022 sun. cold. Dry.*

Dear Medea,

For the most part, I have learned over the years not to despair at the ridiculous struggle and disappointment that so easily derails thinking that writing, my writing, is anything but a pastime. I learned not to bother submitting pieces unsolicited, submitting to "contests" which are really just ways some mags and presses get enough revenue to keep going; I don't read Amazon reviews, and I rarely even mention my trade to new acquaintances. All that said, it's tax time and boy howdy is that ever a reckoning. Bad enough that it comes in dreaded January, but really, does Amazon have to be so damned efficient at this too? Perfectly scored 1099s at your computer doorstep. Gee thanks. I guess I should be glad to know that my memoir, long long out of print but still available as an eBook, and my one and only novel written in 2012 (back when we were young and innocent and had no idea what was coming), anyway, I should be glad to know these two books have actually sold at all, and at a buck each royalty, $35. is a pile of gold! What stats! (My ego insists I add that these are just eBooks and there were paper books sold etc. etc.). No one, and I mean no one, should be a writer unless they have skin of Teflon and an ego the size of that damn building in the Persian Gulf because this is a time consuming and bruising struggle. And that's just the personal side of it, never mind the rigged hierarchy, the books written by ghost writers (how ego bashing would that be?!), crap, trash, and garbage books that eat up trees and litter the front table of bookstores across the country because… because why? Publishing is the pharmaceutical industry of the mind.

There. I feel better now. Thanks for listening. All that said, the best thing ever is to have even one complete stranger take the time to tell me that they read a poem I wrote and loved it. "It made me cry." That's the best! The feeling of substantiation, of true existential meaning, that even one unsolicited reader brings to the writer–it's the nun to the God, the ecstatic bride to the beloved, the birth of a child longed for to the mother. This recognition is why we write.

There is more ink about Orwell lately. Somehow, I touched a chord with a friend in England who has been sending me Orwell bios and pictures. Talk about writing literally for nothing. Poor man. Did you know his name was Eric? Eric Blair. If he hadn't adopted a nom de plume, we'd be saying Blairian instead. His poor wife died during surgery. Speculation has it that she had terminal uterine cancer, but it was said at the time that she died during surgery with no mention of her "female troubles." In fact, the biographer I read thought it likely Orwell didn't know his wife had uterine cancer. What? Here we go. Another oblivious male writer, consumed with his own thoughts. And yet, it does appear his wife, Eileen, had a social life before and during their short marriage, and was pursued rather aggressively. She wrote in her journal or letters, I can't remember which, that there was a constant stream of dates for coffee and drinks several times a day. Living life at full tilt. Orwell himself died of TB. He didn't seem to flail himself through life, not the way, say, Dylan Thomas did through the bottom of a bottle and yet at high speed. But the death toll on writers who weren't to know their own fame, who lived in poverty and in particularly poor health, and who I would struggle to pin acts of graciousness or charity to without spending some serious time thinking—how do we think about what we read, when we read, say, *1984*, or even *Jane Eyre*, or *Pride and Prejudice*? Who can read Dylan Thomas's absolutely perfect villanelle "Do Not Go Gentle Into that Good Night" without crying? And yet, we are still absolutely intent on war, on killing each other at the slightest disagreement. No pile of broken whisky bottles or dead poets is going to change that. And so, my friend, why do we write? Who are we going to convince?

Sorry. I know you weren't expecting this. Surely, we can blame the full moon this week on our moods. Full moon in Cancer. We are simply too tender, all of us, for this good night.

Love,
Jane

P.S. I'm sure you are shaken and yet relieved to have delivered your Dylan to SFO two days ago for his return flight to NY instead of today with an armed standoff, bullets, and death. It is a desperate world. Be safe.
P.P.S. What's the tiny bird who flutters when she flies and looks just like an oak leaf falling from the tree? Maybe Cornell Labs has an app for bird flight spotting?


*20 January 2022 Sunny and clear, haze over the western hills, 55 degrees. Where is our rain?*

Dear Jane,
Now that I know about the bullets at the airport, yes, I'm relieved that Dylan is returned safely to the land of "murder in the metro" from the land of "shoving the elderly and weak to the sidewalks for fun." Is Mercury in retrograde, joining with the full moon to wreak chaos across the globe?

We all sort of experienced our black out in the form of the first Covid lockdown, almost two years ago. Remember when the news was all-virus, all the time? People learned to use less toilet paper and bake sourdough. Neighbors peeked in on their elders, delivered supplies. Parents introduced their kids to the great outdoors. Skies cleared, birds reclaimed center stage, dolphins swam in the

Hudson. Essays filled column after column speaking to the great awakening of our love affair with nature, with simplicity, with civility and care for one another.

That didn't last long.

Bruce and I were talking about competition among nations and between people of different "tribes." He maintains that each country is going to destroy the planet in the quest to establish its supremacy, and that, biologically, we're programed to fight for dominion against those who represent the "other." I suggested that as humans, who ostensibly differentiate from lizards by virtue of our brains, our responsibility to the earth and to one another is to acknowledge, and then ignore, our base biology. As thinking, rational beings, with the gift of free will, it's our duty to find healthier and more inclusively productive solutions. It's so clear to me.

His answer? "That will never happen while men are in charge."

Right. Let's exhaust all the graphite in Mozambique (thank you, Elon!) so Tesla can produce more batteries. Let's dredge the bottom of the South China Sea before we even study what marvels may lurk there in furtherance of our quest for nickel for our AI devices. Let's redraw congressional districts so that red voters always win (and red candidates keep their seats.) While we're at it, we can take an entire segment of the population—women, gay folks, musicians, Uighurs, you pick!—and strip them of their agency, hence their threat to our authority. What then? We all gaze out on our vassals, patting our fat bellies, smoking chaat, grabbing pussy? How positively medieval.

In addition to your good egg news, a flamingo sighting in the 10,000 Islands section of the Everglades marks the first confirmed visit by this once ubiquitous bird in decades. After the plume poaching fiasco of the late 1800s, (RIP Guy Bradley, game warden, friend to birds, who lost his life to poachers in 1905) the flamingos and other avian victims that survived fled to Mexico and parts of the Caribbean. Who could blame them? If this flamingo survives and tells her friends, we could see a resurgence of this indigenous bird. Also, a massive pod of more than one thousand once nearly-extinct fin whales is frolicking and blowing spume thirty feet high near Coronation Island in the Southern Ocean. (Don't tell the whalers.) These silvery leviathans measure twenty-seven meters long. Hunting men often protest that the hunted creature threatens the hunter's own food sources. But fin whales are krill eaters. So, really, the hunters are just dicks.

As far as writing, why do we torment ourselves, alone with our thoughts, flogging our ego, spilling our ink? "I write entirely to find out what I'm thinking, what I'm looking at, what I see and what it means. What I want and what I fear." That's Joan Didion's story. Flannery O'Connor wrote to "discover what I know." For me, it's writing *through* more than writing *down*, so all of these resonate with me. Tossing a lasso around an idea and the notions it generates helps me to articulate in a way that helps clarify, illuminate and even expand on it coherently. As you found, when that poem or essay or story attains a universality that resonates with even one other soul, it's worth the agony inherent in killing all those darlings.

The largely, at least heretofore, male-dominated publishing industry, Amazon, ghost written books (*The Art of the Deal*, for example), books that incite fear and spread falsehoods, the fake "Dummies" books, which look like the real thing down to the triangle-headed mascot, 450 versions of The Bible (Really? Can't you guys agree on just one?), every diet book except the one that tells you to watch what you eat *and* exercise, false hopes spread by Tony Robbins and his acolytes—yes, that's a lot of trees sacrificed for nothing. But as you said, big business, whether it's pharma, "not for profit" hospital systems, big box stores, big oil—I could go on, but don't want to waste the paper—rests firmly in control of everything. Except our free will.

Love,
Medea

P.S. I was stricken to learn today that the FL legislature is mulling over a bill that would put sea grass restoration in the hands of private enterprise. As I wade through the mucky language, it appears that in return for fouling ever more wetlands and spoiling increasing acreage with development, the developers could outsource their natural resource abatement requirement to private companies that would then be permitted to use submerged public land to plant sea grass. (Which would then be off-limits to its rightful owners, the taxpayers of Florida.)

Sea grass is disappearing rapidly, not only because of unwise development but because sales of spring water to pumper-bottlers, as I mentioned last year. Sea grass is one of the least sexy aquatic species. But it feeds manatees, which are now starving in droves, and it protects coastlines from storm surge. This bill also permits a similar usurpation of coral reef and oyster bed habitats. It already passed in two committees.

P.P.S. The tiny fluttering bird you saw could be a Ruby-crowned Kinglet or a bushtit? There is very little in my immediate library about flight patterns. The Sibley Guide describes the Common Redpoll's flight pattern as "bounding" or "rollercoaster" but we'd have to travel to Canada to see that one.

*January 21, 2022 sun. mild. Where oh where is rain?*

Dear Medea,

Lovely of your Bruce to recognize the perils of leaving men in charge. What puzzles me is why women let that happen. From the start, surely it was obvious who really had the power? Why did we let it go?

I'm going to say here and only the once that for me, Amazon is not the bad guy when it comes to publishing. Amazon made it possible for anyone to find their audience. No one else. Did you know Barnes and Noble sells table space? Those books on the table at the front cost thousands of dollars. NYT will only review books by the big five old style publishers. Any self-published book can get major "eyes" thanks to Amazon's policy. They do not distinguish indie, self-published, or major corporate work. They allow individual authors who wish to, to set their own wholesale terms. Who else does that? And they are getting better and better at policing frauds, like that guy who bought thousands of dollars' worth of his own book with money he solicited for his charity to build schools in Afghanistan. It worked for him, but he's ruined now, and it won't work for the next chancer. Repugnant levels of wealth to a very few aside, the publishing and selling of books at Amazon is as good as it gets for us small fry. Without Amazon, you and I would literally not be doing what we're doing.

The news for flamingos is very fine to hear. Florida, in general, needs your help though. I wish you could run for office, but then you'd have to move there.

Today Tinker hopped over to Tweed's rubber ball, pecked at it to make it roll, pecked again, rolled more, and then picked it up in her beak! I think it was too heavy, she put it down almost right away but in the manner of "throwing" the ball. Or maybe not.

Last night we heard Great Horned Owls. I could listen to them all night.

Tinker is outside *cawing*, she doesn't usually do that, so I'd best go see what she's up to.

Love,
Jane


*January 22, 2022 should be a lucky number day? Very warm. Sun. Earthquake weather for sure*

Dear Medea,

I hope you survived the high winds last night and are basking in warm sunshine today. Since we have it, someone should enjoy it. As weird as it is to have summer sun in January, and wildfires to boot, maybe we should just accept that from now on every day is a mystery, and as long as there is no immediate tragedy, we should just go with it?

Mercury is retrograde. The astrologer I follow explains helpfully that mercury is retrograde about 1/3 of every year so we should quit complaining about it and just accept that 1 out of 3 times something breaks, there's an easy explanation or culprit. Today, the light bulbs I ordered (from China) arrived and not only were not the wattage I ordered but were 220v! It will be a hassle to return them and the aggravation up another notch about the crap we buy that needs returning, or repairing, or has a "life" that makes one wonder whether any of this modern progress we enjoy actually exists. If you can buy a thing made in China and get it here for less than $5, then maybe that's exactly what it's worth and the effort and pollution and human toil are really out of line. I try to think of all these things when I'm "shopping" (meaning when I'm on my computer since I don't live anywhere near a "store") but some things have no options, or even opportunity for alternative lifestyle choices. Like lightbulbs. What happened to going to the hardware store and paying your electric bill and getting free lightbulbs? I remember that!

I don't follow numerology, but 1/22/2022 should be a sure bet, no? As I recall, you add them up = 11, and then add the 1+1 and Bob's Yer Uncle, you have 2! Place your bets, mesdames et messieurs.

All the creatures here are well. The house just gasped and cracked, but I've decided to ignore it. Wildfires in Big Sur, and a little one in Sonoma, 100 mph winds overnight inland and dead calm here. It is quite clear that we are on a speedway to chaos, just like my recurring nightmare: driving blind and backwards down the winding road along the cliff's edge. If only everyone would open their eyes.

I suppose we/I should snap out of it. I will make an effort for next time.

Love,
Jane


*22 January 2022 After morning chill and wind, it's sunny, a warm-feeling 63 in those rays, and only a hint of breeze as the clock chimes 4.*

Dear Jane,
Yesterday was lost to the vegetable garden. Or won—actually, I prefer that. Since the birds and squirrels decided to feast on all of the seedlings, I set out to both replant and to cage the beds. Organizing the bird netting is an exercise in mindful cutting, wrapping, securing, re-wrapping, lifting, weighting (to ensure that no hungry beasts furrow underneath.) I used all of the PVC pipes that

serve as forms to hold the netting aloft. I tried bending bamboo sticks from the front forest, but it's not supple enough and works better as a homemade trellis. Anyway, after all of the political furor of the past couple of weeks, digging in the dirt, building veggie cages and feeling the sun all felt constructive, positive. And in a few weeks' time, we feast.

I know you love Amazon for the way it treats writers. I respect that. Lulu and some of the other houses are not as well-known or easy for the prospective reader to navigate, so your point about reaching a wide audience is well taken.

As far as China and lightbulbs are concerned, I listened to a staggering lecture after I posted on Friday about the rise of China's dominance in the shipping and commerce market. While almost every aspect of this lecture made want to stop consuming everything that I don't make myself, the statistic that blew my mind is that shipping, for all its polluting and roiling of the seas, has become so cheap that you it would cost you more to drive certain items from LA to SF than it does to ship them from China. Is it any wonder that Wal-Mart, Target, Costco and, yes, Amazon is so full of cheap junk?

Our house is falling apart one system at a time. Plumbing. Roof. Alarm. Bruce's eight-year-old computer gave it up this morning. The last OS he could find on disc is Windows 7. I suggested decoupling from tech. He was not amused. After twenty-three years in this house (on the first of February) it's reasonable to expect entropy. Rats chew wires. Sunshine bakes shingles. Hair sheds into bathroom drains. I think this is why my parents sold our house the second my sister left for college. Still, we cherish the garden. The space. We're fortunate and free to plant pink flamingos all over the yard and hang windchimes and bird feeders from the eaves if we want to. And we do. More good news: the shingles we'll be using for our second new roof will be crafted with pride in California.

In the past two days, we lost Meat Loaf, Louie Anderson, and Thich Nhat Hanh (aka Thay). When I was little, I remember my dad sitting in stunned silence when he learned that Alan Ladd had died. Peter Lorre died that same year, 1964. My dad would have been thirty-three then, a father of two little girls, kicking ass and taking names as an up-and-coming young lawyer in our small town. And his matinee idols were starting to disappear. I remember feeling his sadness, but it was harder to relate to losing these movie stars that honestly were not Captain Kangaroo or Gilligan, so, *meh*. When Alex Trebek died in 2020, I stood crying in the kitchen when *Jeopardy!* aired its first tribute to this poised, diligent, Renaissance man. Dylan walked in, saw me in tears, and said "Mom, I didn't know you cared so much about Alex Trebek," with a softness that made me even weepier. Goodbyes and unexpected acts of compassion both knock me sideways.

Thay would tell us that he's still here. Here with Alex and Tom Petty and Robert Palmer and Betty White. And our grandparents. Our beloved pets. As each birthday passes, as our turn to be "still here" inches closer, what I really want to do is go diving and see that "new" coral reef in Tahiti. Covid is starting to really piss me off.

Love,
Medea


*January 23, 2022 Sun.*

Dear Medea,
There is something funny about how we respond when a famous person dies. On the one hand, we should think "well that's too bad" or "she had an amazing life" (that'd be your Betty White) and then go on with our own little lives and yet sometimes someone dies and we are really knocked sideways as you say. I remember long ago, I was newly married and overwhelmed, it was Christmas eve and I heard that some young actor had killed himself. I liked the actor, but the starkness of his death is probably what hit me hard. I remember going into the bathroom and balling like a toddler. Surely his death was merely a trigger for a much-needed cortisol cleansing moment of pure grief? I also remember Natalie Wood's death; I think because it was a drowning and I have this feeling I must have drowned in a past life. Once we were driving across a bridge in Seattle at night and I looked out across the water and had this terrible weightless, airless sensation and felt something beyond an awareness of fear, something more.

It is also strange when one's peers die and it seems reasonable. Like they had long and full lives. Wait! There's much still to do! Poor Betty White, she made the most of her long life and yet she had to endure it without the love of her life. How unfair is that?! I thank her for standing up for the little furry ones, and I hope she and her love are reunited and sharing a nice bottle of something yummy with bubbles. My grandfather died at 100.6 and always said the weirdest thing was that all his friends had died long long before. Do you hope for a great age? I don't, but I do have a goal of 83. There's a great old tune my family all sang about a grandmother who dies at 83 and leaves her grandson an armchair stuffed with money. I think that would be a fine thing to do. My other grandfather, the lawyer, used to sing it and make up extra verses all about reading the will and legal battles.

Love,
Jane

*23 January 2022 Summer weather returns to Northern California. 68, sunny, still.*

Dear Jane,

My floribunda thinks it's April. This lush pair of bushes flank a utility building in the back yard. During winter months, the sculpture of gnarled branches invites the tinies in to rest. For the past twenty-three years, always at the end of March or early April, the plants explode with thousands of pale-yellow blossoms that perfume the air with sweet spice. It's not even February and both of them have popped out a good hundred-plus flowers. How will this early display affect the usual and much anticipated rose parade in the Spring?

My dad could not understand why I was headed outside to finish planting spinach and lettuce—I guess that's not something he grew up with in Pennsylvania, winter greens—but our mild climate nurtures these so in they go. One of the ravens stood above me in the pine tree and watched me place the last of the seedlings and cover them, thoroughly, hopefully, with the anti-critter net. His squawking sounded scolding and angry to me, so I reflexively ducked when he flew over my head; take nothing for granted, especially when its beak could peck out my eyeballs.

Someone else is interested in reading both *Ravens in Winter* and *Zen and the Art of Saving the Planet*. Usually my library books automatically renew, but not these two. I understand the *Planet* book's draw; it's a new release and Thay just passed. But the *Ravens* book was written in 1984. Do you think this portends a shift in consciousness, an interest in learning about and preserving our natural world? It occurs to me that, if we are going to join the voices of those who loudly proclaim the balls-up we humans are making with our gluttonous choices, the entire approach toward consuming has to change. The message around buying for the sake of "growing the economy," which everyone accepts as gospel, must shift to "the right to grow the economy must stop where and when life—all forms of life—is threatened."

Is it Pollyannaish to think this is possible? I read Part I of a three-part investigative journalism piece in the *Tampa Tribune* written in conjunction with the National Hurricane Center that lays bare the threat from storm surge from "simple" tropical storms given the predicted rise sea level between now and 2050. Reading the comments from residents whose homes flooded, molded, and, in some instances, became uninhabitable, it seems that a few have given up and moved away while others rebuild optimistically. (Except the poor guy who was electrocuted when he walked into the three inches of water on his laundry room floor.) The modeling shows various scenarios, none of them promising. But if you look at the photos of the neighborhoods, acres and acres of house upon house lining streets and waterways that arguably should never have been built or certainly not with this level of density. Neither realtors nor owners have an obligation to disclose past incidences of flooding when a home changes hands in Florida. It shatters me that a place I love is so corrupt! These two journalists, Langston Taylor and Zachary Sampson, are doing Gaia's work. Is anyone in Tallahassee listening?

I don't have a preferred expiration date, just hoping the celebration of my life goes on for as long as the living still love me!

Love,
Medea


*January 24, 2022 Sun. need I elaborate?*

Dear Medea,
To be fair, I should say that I looked up into the very blue sky just now and there are beautiful "mare's tails" clouds. I remember from sailing that this means wind up there. From here it looks like half of the sky is some white-haired goddess tossing her head, long hair flying. Sounds better than "wind."

It is very strange how desperately people manage to ignore the reality of the danger in their midst– be it rising sea levels, or drought/fire, or pandemic viral load, it seems like most people find someone to believe who tells them what they want to hear, and after that they cover their ears and shout la-la-la. And the more opinionated and prone to ridiculing the pundit, the more people would like to believe. Bill Maher lately is nearly unwatchable as he criticizes what he calls "snowflakes," the generations who want to be protected from everything including thinking, while at the same time he is tired of covid and wants it to be over so he's decided we should all just go back to whatever we were doing. Funny how men in particular become more and more conservative as they age, while women go the other way. I wonder how often that ends in divorce?

Is reducing consumption and focusing on the problem going to make a difference at this late date or are we doomed? I think we should try, for the babies, and because it is the right behavior. But in my heart, I think it's too late. As a species we are "snowflakes" and have probably never been told the truth. We make up gods and dogma, we theorize, and when we can't figure something out by science, we make fun of it, hoping that our scorn will make it stop.

Love,
Jane

P.S. Where's your dad from in Pennsylvania? Gene is from Oil City. North of Pittsburg when oil was so thick in the creek it used to burst into flames.

P.P.S. I want for someone reading this, say ten years down the road, to say "Bill Maher, who's he?" Not from ill will, really, just because no one should be so meanspirited and narrowminded and get away with it.

*25 January 2022 High 50s, morning gloom, afternoon sun and chill breeze.*

Dear Jane,

Eighty-three. How did you arrive at this age as your time to move on? My friend Chris spent her forties certain she would not reach fifty. My parents defy death both through their ages and their insistence on attending one or two parties a week, Covid be damned. The feeling of melding with the breeze, erasing the boundary between body and surroundings may serve as a prequel, so I don't really think about my expiration date. It's coming. I will no longer be physically with those I love. I may miss the sound of the wings of the nuthatches, the feeling of sand on my bare feet, the scent of a snow-white gardenia. I hope that the living will walk with me whenever they find themselves on the beach.

I don't remember whether I told you this years ago, but the week before my cancer diagnosis, I was driving past the hospital, I looked up at the lights in the "penthouse" patient rooms where I would soon spend four bloody, morphine-giddy post-op days, and thought "damn, I sure could use a vacation that no one could fault me for taking." Since then, I don't call down the evil eye.

Won't that tickle Quinn if you stuff your chair full of $10s? Take that, IRS.

It's one of the strangest things, one I've discussed with my kids, that death lives alongside us, whether your centenarian grandad, Amy Winehouse, our beloved white Tonkinese with the crossed green eyes who sat upright on his fanny like a fat old man and charmed even the most ardent cat-hater. And still, every death hits us like an undetected meteor hurtling through space and crashing into our roofs. When someone mentions to me that they'd "really love to write a book" the correct response is supposed to be "well, sit down and write it!" But that doesn't seem to inspire the same motivation as saying, "If you get hit by a car tomorrow, you won't be in any shape to write a book, so you'd better get on with it." Guaranteed that Natalie Wood never expected to drown that night. Which is usually how it happens.

Will the mare's tails return tomorrow? That's a far more apt descriptor than "wispy." I also like "mermaid tresses" for those ribbon clouds. Do you think Bill Maher gazes at clouds, finds dragons or hippos in the fluff? Given his usually sour attitude, I'm thinking not. We saw him live in SF maybe twenty-five years ago, and part of his act (was it an act?) was talking about how horrible children are and why would anyone have children and people who have children must have no imagination or just be lazy because if they were smart and motivated, they'd have jobs. I did not leave a tip.

Here in my botanical garden, though, we celebrate the green mind and its ability to see reality. That reality includes a surfeit of pop weeds, which occupy a place in Gaia's tapestry that, like yellow jackets, I've yet to appreciate. While I plucked them from the front yard, my adoring neighbor passed by and effused about the garden: "We just love walking by here and seeing what's in bloom." All we do is offer a place for the plants to perform, occasionally offering food, a haircut. Nature does the rest.

Yesterday, I watched an Anna's flick its barbed tongue at a stalk of fuchsia and collect small specks of spent blossom, intended for a nest, I hope. The finch couple will soon start collecting twigs and bits of dry grass to build a fresh nest in the eaves above the dining room. We've seen two hawks soaring above the house, one a small Cooper's and the second a massive Red-tail. Did they notice the extended family of gophers that has built tunnels under our yard, front and back?

Love,
Medea

P.S. It turns out that House Sparrows are not native, and one can shoot them without reprisal. Not that one should.
P.P.S. Daddy is from Philly, but Bruce is from Pittsburgh!
P.P.P.S. At the bookstore today, I spotted my jazz book in the "Local Interest" rack. Would it have been too bold to hand it to the lady who was browsing the shelf and offer to autograph it for her? An analog social media move, for sure.


*January 26, 2022 sun. dry. Cold.*

Dear Medea,
Tinker and Burt are spending more and more time preening. They stand at the peak of the garage roof several times a day and groom each other, cooing and chuckling, perfectly happy. If I'm sitting in the window which is a three sided very large space, Tinker has taken to perching on the porch rail closest to the window with glass and about 4 feet between us. She's a lovely bird with deep blue-black feathers that in some light show a dark reddish brown. If you painted a raven black, you would be doing nature a disservice.

In prepping dinner, I spatchcocked a chicken and removed the wings–we don't eat them, and they always seem a little desperate– so I took the wings outside and the ravens immediately saw I had something good in hand. I put one on the palette and the other one a bit away in the grass so that each one could get theirs without any kerfuffle. They grabbed them and flew off toward their roosting spot, I assume. It occurred to me I should warn my neighbor not to panic, the chicken wings came from the grocery store and not her hen coop.

Spring cleaning season seems to have started early. We were inspired here to finish the clearing out project started in December. The trouble though is that neither of us has short term memory facilities strong enough to remember where we now have put stuff. A discussion ensued about the vast empty hallways in my brain where facts used to be. Now, occasionally, a "little gray cell" will open a door to echoing space and roll slowing off into the void. Will it remember that I moved all the dog leashes and collars and toys to the other cabinet? (Border Collies disdain toys, by the way. Except balls which are a sad substitute for a sheep.) This leads me to respond about my goal of living to 83. Surely 83 will be fine? Why prolong the losses? The best of intentions (for control freaks like me) will probably not make one whit of difference in the end, the literal end, but we can and should make a plan. Mine is to stuff money and jewelry into my grandmother's wing back chair and then maybe even have the chance to watch from the great beyond. 83 is the target because that's the age of the grandmother in the song…'oh my grandmother she, at the age of 83, took sick and then she died…" Everyone in our family knows the lyrics just as well as they know that the old armchair was my grandmother's. She didn't stuff it with money, but she did cut the legs down by 4 inches and it's probably the only chair I've ever had that I could sit in comfortably.

Now that you tell me again, I remember that Bruce hails from Pittsburgh.

Love,
Jane


*26 January 2022 Impenetrable, icy fog, 45 degrees, lifting near noon. Sunny and hikeable by 2.*

Dear Jane,
AllTrails is my newest tool for discovering new hiking spots. Dylan and his sweetie found the Little Yosemite hike in Sunol on AllTrails; it's a close enough drive for a half-day trip. He also found the Coyote Hills hike on this app. Today, craving sun and action, I opened the app and a trail that sits four miles from my house popped up. This trail sits in the center of multiple housing developments, and it's as verdant and oak-studded as many of the hikes we drive much further to access. A sign at the entrance cautions that mountain lions live in these hills and canyons.

Part of me ached to see a mountain lion, the part that loves kitties, especially wild and elusive ones. I spotted no lions, though. Only mountain bikers.

I hiked in a mile or so to the park's namesake Waterdog Lake, where two small ducks bathed on the shore. The park is lousy with flying iridescent emeralds—it sounded like a beehive with all the hummingbirds buzzing about. Stepping deliberately, taking note of the scree, the mud, the bike tire tracks, the bright blue sky above, I only screamed two times, when two different mountain bikers rode up behind me, catching me in concentration. Each one greeted me with a huge, muddy smile. They ranged in age from late teens to old dudes, which is a definition whose number edges out farther and farther with each of my passing birthdays.

How is it that this park/lake/trail network sits so close to my house and yet I've just become aware of it? (Thinking that I was a lone female on a new trail and no one knew my whereabouts, I sent a picture of the lake to Dylan. He replied, "Oh, I love that place. Used to bike there with my friends all the time.") Not only have I completely missed this park, but my kid rode these trails and I didn't know where he was! Henry Beston nails it in *The Outermost House* when he writes, "...the world today is sick to its thin blood for lack of elemental things...for the dear earth underfoot...The longer I stayed, the more eager was I to know this coast and to share its mysterious and elemental life." He wrote those words in 1927.

Thank you, AllTrails, for reacquainting me with my mysterious and elemental surroundings.

Love,
Medea


*January 27, 2022 sun. cold. To be fair, I do love the slant of the light.*

Dear Medea,
I forgot to reply about your experience passing the hospital. Surely you knew deep in your subconscious that you were sick, I hate that word, were going to have cancer, or already had cancer. I must have had a similar moment when I waffled about and then postponed my annual mammogram until after my 60th birthday trip to the Arctic with Diane. Everything would change. Everything did change. Ignorance is bliss and sometimes that's not a bad thing at all. I'm glad we both survived. Mortality is a battle we will lose, but let's make it a timely thing, fought with fierce grace.

Our warm weather and any hope of rainfall in January have both evaporated and left you with that terrible fog–ugh, I remember that from living in the Sierra foothills, the cold fog that blanketed the central valley. Here the sun prevails but the mare's tails are gone, not a cloud in the sky. We have had sneaker wave warnings and while right now the ocean is quiet, there have been times over the past few days when the waves crashed, and the windows rattled. Sometimes it seemed a huge ocean cast tree must have landed on the beach, such was the thump and roar. I wonder what it would be like to see that happen. We walk on the beach after a storm and there are whole trees, huge logs cast ashore. How is that possible?

Your trail app sounds wonderful! I use a tracking app with Gene called Life360. When he's out riding it's almost always with friends and they are careful with each other so there's not too much to worry about, but I find I can't do without the app now. It's impressive that the map shows all the funny little trails, by name, that these guys themselves have built. "Purple Skirt" "Boiler" "Easy Out" (because it's not really) "TV" "Ride Thru Tree," the forest is their playground. Most of the trails are a bit far for hikers, but I think the bikers are careful about people on foot and there are even occasional equestrians. If you are out hiking often, you might want to download the app for yourself and Bruce, just in case. People have fallen off the trail and been injured. My friend Kristi was hiking and saw a mountain lion. She detoured and made it home safely. Gene's run into bears a few times and other riders have had mountain lion encounters. It's a good idea not to hike alone, and bring a hiking staff. Keep your 6th sense on high. That tingling feeling has purpose.

I'll watch from here.

Love,
Jane


*January 28, 2022 cold (all things are relative, it's only in the high 40s) red sky at dawn*

Dear Medea,

That old saw about "red sky in the morning'…I've always wondered how that can be true for both west coast and east coast? If our weather always comes from the west, and it does, what does it matter that the rising sun in the east makes the sky red through the eastern clouds? You're the sailor, do tell. Shouldn't it be flipped? And yet if the sky is red at night, it does not portend bad weather, it just signals poor air quality. Buzz kill perhaps, but true, no?

Now, for more important things, I completely neglected to respond to you about seeing your book on the shelves at the bookstore. Excellent! And isn't that a wonderful feeling? My local bookshop does carry books by local authors, and they are usually relegated to a corner of the shop just before the calendars and wrapping paper section, but I was thrilled to find my novel given a slot on the front table for a while which was such a treat! And my poetry collection was given full frontal space on the poetry shelf which is A–Z ordered. I know how good it feels and I'm so happy you got that boost. I think there are plenty of authors who would sneak around bookshops shuffling their books into better positions. I would never presume.

I had tea with Kristi yesterday and she identified that fluttery bird I was talking about earlier this week, the one that flew like a leaf falling from the oak tree. It is a Northern Flicker. There were several in the yard. When they fly, they have a dipping flight pattern (apologies to Sibley for the vocabulary gaffs) which must help keep them safe. When they fly their wings part to expose a white patch on their rear ends which is rather an unfortunate target. Kristi says that the Pomo traditionally love to use the gorgeous orange feathers of the flicker for their dance costumes. It must take a lot of birds, which makes me sad. I have four orange flicker feathers on my altar which Kristi gave me on my birthday. As for using bird feathers, did you know that it is illegal to take feathers? Only Native Americans and shamans for ceremonial rites can take bird feathers. Most feathers we see are turkey feathers that have been dyed. I have some owl feathers that an acquaintance gave me when I created my shaman's kit. She was an expert on owls and had an owl rescue place at her home. She invited me to her house once and showed me her deep freeze which was full of owls who had died, sometimes on the roads. She had bags of feathers and gave me a bundle. Taking feathers from birds that shed them, or have died seems fine, but I balk at the idea of culling birds for feathers, or any other thing furred, finned or feathered. Is it wrong to oppose traditional Native whale hunts? What if whales are gods of the universe and we will only evolve if we stop allowing them to be killed? This conversation could easily lead me to join you as a vegetarian. Sigh. Back to birds, the unfortunate wee things, in Peru people caught hummingbirds and tied a string to one leg and gave them to children to play with, like a live kite. Hopefully not anymore, but I fear we are back to George Santayana's wisdom, my favorite quote: "the spectacle of other men's follies continually awakens in me the suspicion that I, too, am surely fooled."

Love,
Jane

*28 January 2022 Day two with no heat and 40-degree mornings. Even the cats'*
*fur is frigid. Sun is out now, 63 here, but 70 in Santa Cruz. The beach is calling.*

Dear Jane,

You are very likely right when you say I somehow knew I was already sick when
I yearned to disappear into that hospital. You visited me there as an owl or an
eagle, as I recall. Your calm, wise, knowing presence offered great comfort.
Thanks again.

Bird feathers, whale meat, "dominion" over the creatures of the earth. If the
Pomo are allowed to kill wild birds to use feathers in rituals, can Catholics kill,
I don't know, elephants to cull their tusks and tails for the communion table?
Another slippery slope, in my opinion. One of the most heinous acts against birds
in my recent memory is of kids and youth in certain African and Middle Eastern
nations capturing small birds and crushing them between their fists because they
know that Americans find that so reprehensible. The intent was to shock us into
sending aid. The argument, twisted, bordering on seriously fucked up, is that
these people are so desperate for food that they will do anything to get our fiscal
attention. They've given up, I assume, expecting their own leaders to commit
resources to clean water, roads, the general attributes of a safe, stable community.

Do you know the publication *Aeon*? It's sort of like *Medium*. Based in
Australia and serves up thought-provoking, Orion and Emergence-like essays
and videos. Anyway, I bit on a headline that reads, "Why You Should Eat Meat,"
and the subtitle goes on, "Not eating meat is wrong. If you care about animals,
the right thing to do is breed them, kill them, and eat them." The writer, one
Nick Zangwill, lays out a piece worthy of *The Onion*, reciting head-scratching
ideas like eating meat is beneficial to animals, vegetarians are bad for animal life,
wild animals lead lives of insufferable torment (citing Tennyson, of course) and
that sheep, cows and chickens owe us their lives because we domesticated them.
After reading this, I thought maybe *Aeon* is not the publication for me, until
I read the comments, those that the editors didn't remove for failure to meet
community standards. Many were written by other *Aeon* writers, who found
this essay to fall beyond the high standards reserved for a place where lofty ideas
and philosophy are vigorously propounded and thoughtfully debated. It serves
us as thinking people to listen to other voices; that's not my truck with this
piece. Rather, it seems Zangwill had a stick in the form of his essay writing and
a beehive of animal loving vegetarians, and his goal was to poke the hive and
see what happened.

Thanks to Kristi for identifying the Northern Flicker! Sibley tells me they
(and the elusive, to me, Cedar Waxwing) live in abundance here, too. The wafting
flight pattern differs from the nuthatches and chickadees that it would stand
out; I'll keep watching. An uncharacteristically large Hairy Woodpecker stalked

the feeders this morning—not one of the usual visitors, this one had a narrow, creamy surfboard marking on its black back, and a white dickey with black flecks, a wide, anvil-shaped head and long pointed beak. It tried jumping around the different feeders for a nosh, but purchase upon the tiny suet feeders eluded him. Watching as twenty-inch-long ravens stand stalk still at the top of a wind-blown cedar, or as the nuthatches hang upside down while they nibble on the seed, the gymnastic prowess of birds seemed a given to me—but this woodpecker bears watching more closely. Is it sick, or afraid, or just uncoordinated?

After I finished Heinrich's *Ravens in Winter*, I've learned the mystery of the gathering of ravens at a carcass that's been "opened" and ready for feasting: a juvenile will call to alert other juveniles to the food as a way to prove his swagger and thus his desirability to a prospective mate. Did you ever hear Tinker or Burt utter a call that sounds like a baby raven begging for food? This is the sound that Heinrich describes, the loud, pitiful, hankering call for sustenance from a chick for a parent that an older juvenile raven repurposes as a loud, clanging dinner bell, a cry meant to invite his single buddies to feast and, in the process, find true love. Heinrich spent four white, frosty winters studying this phenomenon, bringing light to our inchoate observations. His work amplifies my own appreciation; I'll be listening for that plaintive cry.

Love,
Medea

P.S. The Santayana quote resonates...


*January 31, 2022 Wind. Cold. Sun.*

Dear Medea,
Yes! I love *Aeon* magazine and subscribe to all its forms. Most recently I even wrote a fan letter (honestly, maybe the second one in my entire life) to a philosopher from Finland who wrote an outstanding piece last week, Harri Macklin. He wrote about the phenomenology of art. It was a prescient piece because I was just having a conversation with friends about whether we can or should enjoy art by someone we know to be despicable (Nazi, pedophile, misogynist). In my philosophy studies, I would have counted myself a phenomenologist, so the article particularly resonated with me. Briefly, I would say that we are subjective sentient beings and cannot divorce our cumulative knowing from our aesthetics. The beauty of today's online world is that not only was I able to send Mr. Macklin an email, but he answered me! Back to your point, I saw the article about eating meat, but couldn't bring myself to read it.

The ravens have such an extensive language, I'm not sure I've heard the sound you describe, but I have witnessed them calling each other to come and see, come and eat, come and help me tear the roof off this house etc... When Tinker and Burt are grooming each other, it is clear they are communicating more than just, say, purring like a cat. They seem to say, "oh yeah, there, right there." Or "enough! You're driving me nuts!" The other day after I gave them each a raw chicken wing, I did let my neighbor Jane know that they hadn't murdered any of her hens. She laughed; and said she thought soon they would be remodeling their nest by removing the stuffing from her porch cushions like they do every year.

Love,
Jane


*31 January 2022 Cold, gray suburb of love. 54 degrees.*

Dear Jane,
February and Chinese New Year dawn in a few hours. Your month of torment draws to a close. How do you feel about this looming short month where we gather to celebrate groundhogs, departed presidents, hearts, athletes (amateur and pro), movies, Hoodie Hoo? It's the launch of our family's winter birthday season, too, starting with my cousin, her two sons, my nephew, mom, my beloved friend of over 40 years, Peter, who is a leap baby and as his birthday draws nigh, Dylan's blasts in with both barrels; if Dylan had been born 23 hours earlier, he'd also be a leap baby. As I write this, it feels like December all over again!

Our deceased heater will go to its great reward on Wednesday. When domestic systems fail, the ghosts of pioneer women past stand beside me, quietly whispering, "You have no idea." When I'm just about ready to grab my hair shirt, I look over at Odin, pressing the most of himself that he can against the lone 12"x 6" space heater, I realize that not even a cat covered from ear tip to tail tip in his mink-colored winter fur readily tolerates this degree of chill. My said friend Peter lives on the beach in Guatemala. He's warming my heart with daily photos of his opulent palm grove overlooking the western shore. He installed a bird bath this morning, very likely in recognition of another great February holiday, *Feed the Birds* Day, coming up on the third, in case you need to prepare a feast. Bruce reminds me that every day is feed the birds day here, so we're good.

I witnessed a bevy of swans rise into a wedge on the way to the Delta yesterday. It seems that swans intimidate the geese that invade each winter, to the dismay of those who object the Canada Goose's copious waste, so our Island adopted three mating pairs a few years ago and those three pairs since produced forty-four offspring. The skeins of geese that once flew above the San Joaquin near Stockton must now be detouring around the river and flying directly to Foster City.

My fingers are too frozen to write more today, so I'll sign off, in humility and awe for all who live and thrive in Bozeman and Caribou and Minsk, and in solidarity with my slacker feline housemates.

Love,
Medea

P.S. Sometimes it's better not to know whether an artist is a criminal or deviant, as long as no funds are exchanged. Writing a fan letter must be a welcome gesture, right? Mr. Macklinn replied. Endorphins, meet Jane.

*February 1, 2022 Cold. Sun. Wind.*

Dear Medea,

You're right. It's "feed the birds" day every day here as well. February 3, this year, is also Imbolc, the pagan Celtic celebration that preceded Candlemas and celebrates the coming of the sun on what we call a "cross quarter" day, balancing Lammas Day on August 1st and coincidentally marking our half year in this adventure in letter writing. Reason to celebrate! It is also St. Brigid's Day, the patron saint of smiths and poetry and, of course, a pagan Goddess of the same. Weaving the classic Irish "cross" from dried hay and then hanging it on the threshold is one way to celebrate.

I'm sorry you're freezing, and I mean that sincerely since it really is cold! And now the dreadful wind. As the Chinese say, "wind is the root of evil." I hope you get your furnace soon.

I don't have any current living people with birthdays this month, but it was my mother's on Valentine's Day, so I always think of that event as belonging to her. It seems to me that birthdays do come in clusters in families and among friends. Astrologically that makes some sense if we think about attraction.

It's been a day of nostalgia here. Or at least remembering since I would normally ascribe a positive vein to the word "nostalgia." My dear friend, Barbara, and I have kept all of the letters we've written since we were teens. Recently, we swapped them back and she started reading hers to me over again. This brought up things she wanted to explore about why she said this or that, so she asked me to send letters from a particular period. I made the mistake of reading one of mine and then felt as though I couldn't send them away without reading all of them myself. These 20 odd letters were from the first two years of my marriage. Difficult times, and yet, reading them over wasn't as embarrassing as I would have guessed. And poof: the day was over.

Love,
Jane

*2.2.22 Cold and sunny, winding like mad. Look at all of those 2s!*

Dear Jane,

I'm curious about how your nostalgia unfolded. Did you feel your younger self reading, or is your current self curled up with a less mature version of you? Could you feel any physical effects from remembering these difficult times? Will we feel embarrassed or proud or perplexed when we re-read these letters in ten years' time? Where do you keep all of those letters? Would you have felt violated if, gods forbid, the letters succumbed to fire or flood?

My friend Mary and I wrote letters when email was first born. Every day, long and probing letters, sometimes hilarious, sometimes tortuous. She and my felonious ex-boyfriend (he who swindled multiple childless couples out of hundreds of thousands and served time at Lompoc) worked as trust officers at the same bank. Max was also just being born. I was grappling with living here in NorCal with no support system and a colicky infant. She smoked like an illegal chimney on a spare the air day and weighed in at a good 325 pounds. Smart as a fox, she threw away her college scholarship for love, and gave birth to a sprite named Joy. By the time Max was three, her beloved husband, George, had died from the effects of the Agent Orange he inhaled while serving in Viet Nam. Before Joy was able to find a mate and make Mary a grandma, Mary was also gone. She lives on in our correspondence and the memory of everyone she touched.

Our new furnace arrived today! The kitties reclaimed their posts on the bookended heater vents. My puffy coat is back in the closet, where it belongs. Fingers survived with no lingering effects from near-frostbite. Wind is indeed the root of all evil, especially when it blows cold.

This is the year of the Tiger. Tibetan new year arrives in one month. It turns out that Dylan and my mom are both Rats (and Pisceans), my dad and Max are both Goats.

I'm a Dog. Bruce is an Ox. The idealist and the pragmatist. Whether you think of astrology as sense or nonsense, this description fits us like a pair of bespoke gloves.

Love,
Medea


*February 2, 2022 sun.*

Dear Medea,

It really is a strange experience to read letters I wrote fifty years ago and realize my "style," such as it may be, hasn't really changed much. I'm still trying to explain myself, and perhaps please the reader at the same time. I hope it's working because it does seem to be the real me! I was hesitant to start reading the old ones but because I was sending about thirty of them back to my friend, I thought I'd better in case they get lost. A while ago we combined the hoard and I had them, and then we decided to reclaim our own and swapped. My friend has been reading hers and then burning most of them. Now that she has a little granddaughter, I worry that she will regret destroying letters that might someday help to introduce her to this unexpected joy of a child. But it's not my decision. We did shift to email in the late 90s and many of those letters are lost. Now and then we talk about printing and binding them, but they are too honest, too raw, and far too personal to be lying about in book form. Beyond saying that, my lips are sealed.

I am a Rat. Happy year of the Tiger. I don't know much about Chinese astrology, but I did read once that Rats should never marry Horses. So, guess what Gene is? Yeah.

I'm glad you are warm and cozy once again.

Love,
Jane


*3 February 2022 High fifties and ample opportunities for both sun and cloud appreciation today.*

Dear Jane,
For the first time in two months, I ventured up to SF to walk with a friend. The sun set shimmers on the ripples of the Bay. Crissy Field is returning to its wild state, thanks to funding from the Haas family, so natural erosion in occasional spots along the shore sculpt winding grooves in the sand that connect with brackish water pools where water birds have moved in. We saw showy Snowy Egrets, their long necks extended to stretch and to feed. A family of rufous killdeer with dual black necklace feathers skittered along the shore, chattering true to their other name, the Noisy Plover. A few Great Blue Herons patrolled the skies, ever vigilant. The City when she sparkles beckons all comers to stroll, to breathe in her sharp, briny scent, to share her bright sky and feel her soft breeze.

Love,
Medea

*February 4, 2022 sun. warmer. A shift but still that clear blue sky.*

Dear Medea,

Your bird count reminded me I wanted to mention that I saw a white egret fishing off a snag in the Navarro River the other day, it was such a beauty, and a fairly still day so that one could easily imagine how nice the view into the water's depths was for her.

Here, yesterday, Imbolc, I was treated to the whole herd of nine deer spending the afternoon in the yard. It is rare that the twins and their mother join the others, or rare that I see them together at any rate, and it was sweet to see them. The twins still sticking close and occasionally walking within sniff or touch of each other. Mother always on alert. All but one of the herd look very healthy. What I take to be the senior member and leader has some frazzled look to her fur, perhaps not mange but ticks? Hard to tell. She may also be pregnant as, I think, is at least one other and perhaps all the adult females are. Time will tell. Tweed sat in the window with me and saw the deer grazing but didn't make a sound or move to go outside.

Tweed does well enough, but I am not completely content with his health. I'm considering buying a portable ultrasound device. Living here on the coast with access to diagnostic tools such as ultrasound is a problem, another of many problems of remote living. I sent a message to my vet asking if I bought one would he use it and teach me. And speaking of veterinarians, I'm listening to the audio book version of "All Things Bright and Beautiful" book 2 of James Herriot's story. I was entertained and amazed to hear him recount his accidental discovery of the use of an induced coma–the result of his giving a euthanasia level dose of Nembutal to a ewe only to come back two days later and find the ewe totally recovered. Subsequently, Herriot uses the plan deliberately on a dog dying from a gastro issue with success. Of course, Herriot (Alf Wight) doesn't use the words "induced coma" exactly, but he is claiming discovering it, perhaps only for himself? I'll have to ask my vet. I'm curious how often that's used for animals. It's certainly commonplace for accident victims with multiple injuries or severe trauma. I love the books and am happy to see the reissue of the tv series. Reading the books again I am struck at times by the snobbish attitude toward the farmers; Herriot making fun of their backward habits and manner of living to a degree we probably would feel was wrong these days. We're all so politically correct.

Love,
Jane

*6 February 2022 Warm and clear, a "pruning in a sundress" kind of day. With a tip of my bonnet to Mark Twain, the warmest summer I ever spent was winter in Northern California.*

Dear Jane,

Your friend may regret burning her letters. Her granddaughter may have no interest in reading them. Is curiosity inherited? We've been writing to one another for over ten years and your style remains smart and wicked and sharp-eyed. The letters won't see daylight, you say, which is your prerogative. But if a stranger read them, what might she learn about life—yours and her own?

The Navarro River flows through the Anderson Valley to the Pacific and extends only twenty-eight miles; you're lucky to sit ringside and watch the water and salmon run, and the egrets hunt. I did not know the dark history of this river, that it was called "Bloody Run" after the 49ers forcibly marched the Pomo up the Eel to a different reservation. The water carried evidence of the gold miners' brutality. I read today that over half of Gen Xers and Millennials surveyed did not know that six million Jews were murdered in the Holocaust. Ten percent of them believe that the Jews *caused* the Holocaust. Do California's schools teach about Bloody Run? Is history still a required subject in schools?

Max and I eased Windsong out of her slip on Friday for post-service engine trial. She started right up, as though she'd been trapped at the dock for longer than any healthy boat should be. She rocked us gently on a flat calm sea for the two hours we sailed to Belvedere's jagged coastline and back. Our only company on the water was an occasional, empty, Blue and Gold or Red and White fleet ferry, a well-fed sea lion snoozing on a green can buoy, and a pair of dolphins, swimming and breathing in tandem. After so many years sailing the SF Bay and hearing lucky friends' tales of dolphin sightings, this was our first. We could smell their fishy exhalations and see their spume dissipate in the balmy afternoon air, as though the dolphins were welcoming Windsong back to her proper place in the world.

James Herriot's stories kept us spellbound when the kids were small. A life filled with gratitude from the pets, farm animals, and their humans. If your vet advises you to buy the ultrasound for Tweed, what will you hope (not) to find? Our neighbor Paul popped by with his new thirteen-month-old puppy, Misha, who is a Samoyed rescue. This bounding bundle of fur was found chained to a balcony in Merced, her coat so matted that she's shaved almost to the skin. Her eyes sparkle with relief. She jumps for joy, happy for head and belly rubs despite her recent past confinement, possibly worse treatment than I dare to imagine now that she's safe and adored. All dogs should be this fortunate, this loved.

Love,
Medea


*February 7, 2022 cold, sun*

Dear Medea,
Today's weather reflects the core of the difference between where I am, 75 miles north of San Francisco and half a mile from the Pacific, and where you are nestled on the east-facing hillside protected by the coast range. I wonder how much and how fast our different climates will converge. Pretty damn fast, it seems so far. In fact, I think the shift is accelerating to a degree that most people aren't aware. You kind of have to be in it, in the fire zone, in the flood plain, in the heat, the mud, the dust, the dying forest ravaged by pine beetles, logged with oblivion and the objective by greed. There isn't time for a new forest of redwoods to grow up and enfold us in her moist embrace. This makes me anxious and terribly sad.

I'm so happy to hear that Windsong is back! And what a treat to see dolphins. I have to confess I didn't know about the old nickname for the Navarro River, but it doesn't surprise me. Logging has a dark past and a darker present since doing something when you don't know better is slightly easier to forgive than deliberately creating destruction.

I haven't heard back from my vet. In the meantime, Tweed is stable but while I watch this minute, he's in the yard possibly eating deer poop. Not on my watch.

My heart breaks and then fills at the thought of that poor puppy. Bless the person who rescued that dog. We know there must be many others waiting for the same.

Love,
Jane


*8 February 2022 61 and clear, just enough breeze to chill the air.*

Dear Jane,
Dogs and their culinary preferences baffle me. Is there a constellation of vitamins in poo that sends dogs to this "dish"? Say what you will about cats; I've never known any of them to resort to mining their litter box for an afternoon treat. Thankfully Tweed is stable, and, I hope, pain-free.

The Town of Woodside had its municipal wrist slapped by the AG for its attempt to circumvent the ADU law by declaring itself a mountain lion refuge. Sacramento is screaming "build build build!" and, meanwhile, we're back to pre-December reservoir levels with the accompanying calls to "conserve conserve conserve!" You're ninety miles north and modestly chillier, but ravaged by drought and fire and thirsty tourists. The evidence of weather convergence between our historically divergent climates appears in our pages. We will be long gone before forests naturally regenerate and lands are responsibly managed to mitigate these continual conflagrations. You aren't wrong to feel anxious and sad.

On a more intimate note, I watched two Sharp-shinned Hawks, all feathers and screams, tumble over each other in flight, much like stunt pilots who move too close in mid-air and scare the spectators. One repaired to the interior apex of a tall pine. The other disappeared, only to swoosh past my shoulder after I'd walked another quarter of a mile. This bird lighted on a fence post where I could swoon over its ruddy breast brushed with creamy waves, and sooty charcoal wings and legs the color of a Meyer lemon. Its head is small for a hawk, but not as dramatically small as the mourning dove's head, whose tiny head almost seems like an afterthought compared to the girth of its body. While documenting the sighting in Merlin, I read that the Sharp-shinned Hawk catches its food on the wing (is that what I was witnessing?!) and "often stalks feeders in search of prey." I remember seeing a very animated Sharp-shinned Hawk in the pine tree at the front of my house a few months ago. Was it...? Thankfully, the ravens shooed it away, though from my tinies' standpoint, that's probably not much of an improvement.

I spent yesterday pruning and shaping citrus trees, chasing rolling fruit, weeding, and wrestling bamboo. Today, a bushel of lemons awaits the juicer, destined for ice cube trays and the freezer. Though November–April marks the season for grapefruit harvesting, my tree missed the memo.

Love,
Medea


*February 8, 2022 warm. Sun. the sound of chainsaws and chippers echoes the hillside*

Dear Medea,
Gene's cousin, Scott, has died from covid. Long Covid. #900k+1. It has been a somber morning as I write a letter to his family and read some of my poetry. Is it a good thing that I write so much about death? Sometimes it helps people. I was reading a poem I wrote for Scott. When my collection *Outskirts* launched, I offered to write a poem for anyone who bought two copies. Scott was the

only one who responded. I wrote the poem "Blow" for him. It's mostly a poem about climate change, but it's also about death. Scott was a UConn professor of archaeology and one of my few friends with whom I had academic interests in common. He was outspoken, fun, and smart. We emailed often. I will miss him. Here's the poem:

### Blow

Within a triplicate crisis–
man versus god versus nature–
the thin margin of chaos
brings a penultimate debate:
if death is the final issue,
then this squandering of nature's soil,
this chaotic crumbling of a loving earth,
is just a long-forgotten skeleton
blown eastwards by a harridan wind:
chalk bones and ashes, skeletal misery,
faint memory, no remains. We stand
at the tower's gabled edge
and there is no longer
any worthy god.

Meanwhile, speaking of climates, we are having a summer day in February which I am reminding myself is often the case, a few days midwinter of sun and warmth. Thing is, there's no end in sight to this endless blue sky. The weather did provide the perfect opportunity for Chris and family to launch his sailboat in Noyo Harbor on her maiden dunking. She floats! They motored out beyond the mole and over the small swell the inlet creates (on a good day. On a bad day it tips over even the bravest of crafts). As they crested the wave, Quinn turned to his dad and said, "This is the most fun I've ever had!" I nearly cried when Chris told me. A ten-year-old boy who has free access to a gaming computer and virtual reality goggles finds fun in the real world of water and boats. Saints be praised. I knew they were going to launch but didn't know they would go out of the harbor first time. I told Chris I was glad he didn't tell me that beforehand. He said they only went a few hundred yards past the buoy. But I'm a mother, and we worry. Do we not?

As for hawks cartwheeling in the air. Were they mating? I believe that's how they do it. Ravens as well. Tinker and Burt are spending a lot of time love-birding: preening and cooing. They seem to be starting to collect stuff, leaf matter and bits and bobs. I haven't seen them take up any bundles of sticks yet this year. But surely, they will be revamping soon as per CA mandates for new housing.

Love,
Jane


*10 February 2022 Hazy blue sunny sky. It's already 70 degrees at 10 am.*

Dear Jane,
Please know that my heart is with you and Gene as you mourn Scott's death. The world is reopening while lives remain upended by this virus. Your poem may unintentionally have foreshadowed the past two years as well. The "thin margin of chaos," standing on the edge, man fighting against nature, when we know that nature always wins. I'm so sorry that your friend will no longer be writing to you and sharing your academic and other curiosities.

Noyo Harbor looks relatively forgiving, until you nose your boat into the Pacific. Nearby shores, in any case, if the swells swamp your craft. Even if all three of them can swim, hypothermia sets in fast. We never stop thinking like moms. Every time there is a random shooting anywhere in Brooklyn or in Midtown, or a fatal crash in the South Bay, my first mind immediately assumes one of my kids must be bleeding on a sidewalk or wrapped around a tree. Thankfully, that doesn't last; Dylan often reminds me that Brooklyn is a city of three million souls. The statistics weigh in favor of his safety. Quinn is captivated by the boat, being on the water, seeing his surroundings from a different perspective; he inherited the water bug from you and your ancestors through Chris. Michri too, or she'd be waving from the shore. In this tech-saturated world, this boat and its possibilities to enrich Quinn's life marks another small victory for the young and the wild.

The inherent love of water, the endless sea, meandering rivers, mysterious lakes must be a character trait. It seems to run in families. There is a difference between "character" and "personality," the first, immutable, the second more pliable. I think about how being on the Bay during a howling gale may suit my mermaid character, but pisses off my preference for gentle, warm breezes. Over time, while I still don't love being on the Bay when it's blowing like stink (as they say) that part of my personality that would rail against the elements has learned better. You can't force a person to love your choices, but you can smile and nod politely when they attempt to dump their dismay on you. The unfortunate remain trapped in too-tight personalities throughout their lives.

I'd intended to go to SF to wash my grimy boat, intended to take the Great Highway since it's one of the last safe streets, free of carjackings and random gunfire. Until last night, when a guy was shot in his front yard and the shooter hopped in his truck and drove down this sacred street where he seems to have shot himself and died. Guns may not kill people, but they sure as hell make it easy to get away with murder.

Love,
Medea


*February 11, 2022 sun. low 50s overnight. Shift to offshore light breeze might mean a more normal day, but then, what is normal?*

Dear Medea,
Ah motherhood. It is true, every emergency is given free rein to spark terror in our imaginations. And even with all the concentration at our command we are not in control of even our own outcomes, never mind those of our children. If only there were a worry-switch to turn off. I can't imagine having young children in today's world.

Tinker and Burt have been keeping close by. Yesterday I watched as they scavenged the yard and seemed to be assessing the quality of various bits and pieces of leaf matter. Will this do for nesting flooring? Can we redo our walls this color? Still not at the point of collecting sticks like last year, and maybe they won't need to. Perhaps a sprucing up (sprucing! Aren't words funny?) is all that's needed and major construction a thing of the past. I wish I knew where the nest is. Two noticeable things about how the birds look, first, Burt's feathers are fluffy and ragged but not unhealthy looking. They look like he just got out of bed and hadn't brushed his hair, and second, Tinker's "hood" seems more pronounced. Maybe it's my imagination, but the cap of shiny black that makes a raven look like a monk from the Italian Inquisition is a bit raised and defined.

Our frustrated new neighbors returned from their Coastal Commission hearing with the news that the Native Plant Society, without once visiting the building site, have made an objection that the new house would be a threat to the native Bishop pines. First of all (and you can imagine me shouting now) Bishop pines are not native this far north, secondly, they are all dying of beetle infestation and other physical results of drought, and all one needs to do is drive from Elk to Fort Bragg to see that the bull pine are dying and as long as there is drought there will be no hope for these trees or the oaks or the fir or, sadly, the redwoods. The building site has a lovely view of the ocean, but as for trees anyone should consider special or healthy enough to stop removing a few, no. They are dying. The objections are simply to further frustrate anyone, anywhere, from doing anything. Don't get me wrong, laws protecting against cutting timber, especially redwood forests, are extremely important, now more than

270

ever. But in this particular case, it's misplaced. This "society," if they had their way, would probably want to prevent us from removing dying pines as a fire prevention measure. As I look out my window, I can see at least a dozen trees which would burn like a 4th of July display and are clearly ready to be removed so that younger, healthier species can find the space and water needed to thrive. Will the native plant police stop me? Someone with some brains should be managing this crisis. Who would that be?

Tinker is on the porch rail asking to speak with me. Must dash.

Love,
Jane


*12 February 2022 74 and hazy but only at the edges of the sky, like a heavenly tonsure. Ha!*

Dear Jane,
Those Native Plant people need some botany lessons. And manners.

Though it's six weeks too soon, Spring is sprung, and the birds are out there pairing up like it's Homecoming Week. The absolutely most phenomenal sighting of this entire week happened at the Marina in SF on Thursday. As I scrubbed Windsong (in shorts! And bare feet!) a gunmetal band of ten Great Blue Herons wailed and reeled overhead. I've never seen more than one, maybe two, within a few feet of one another. Never more. Never ten. It honestly felt like a holy moment. As I rested my head on the boom to observe, a couple dispersed to the southwest, one flew due east, two glided onto the rooftop of a house on Marina Blvd and five made tracks for the cypress trees that populate a very tiny green area next to the Bay. As if in solemn procession, each one lighted at the top of its discrete tree, looking like feathered candlesticks at the top of their domains. I learned that they nest near the Palace of Fine Arts across the street every year. I'm usually with my mom in Florida for her birthday, far from the city, so have missed this cavalcade. We had a Snowy Egret rookery at my Delta haven for years, before the eucalyptus (not native!) disappeared, eliminating the nesting spots. Other trees have grown in to replace the eucalyptus, but the egrets have moved on to other nesting grounds.

Speaking of coupling, Max stopped by to show me his wedding suit today. It is custom-tailored and he paid the supplement so it could be sewn in the US and not in a sweatshop in Asia. Good man. Honestly, I think if that darned way-back machine would ever operate, I might suggest that they elope. The planning for a wedding with limited access and facilities is hard enough. Coordinating all of that and remaining centered requires meditation, communication, forbearance. An unshakable sense of humor. The occasional tequila shot.

Where will Tinker and Burt site their nest?! It's so exciting, Jane. I can't find the hummingbird nest, if there is one, either. The falcon cam at UC Berkeley shows Grinnell and Annie huffing and singing during their mating dance this week. The pair has a view over the entire Bay from their UC digs. Not bad.

Love,
Medea


*February 13, 2022 sun. a tiny tease of puffy clouds came to nothing. 60s.*

Dear Medea,
Let the mating and nesting begin! Yesterday was such an interesting day. No ravens came to breakfast. Not a sign of them anywhere. Then Burt came to lunch looking frazzled, his feathers more fluffy but somehow also bedraggled. He perched on the garage roof as he usually does and called a medium sized *waaahk waaahk*, all the while looking around him, looking for Tinker. I went out and put food on the sawhorse and Burt didn't care. He wasn't going to eat without her. (The Gray Jays, on the other hand, were happy to chow down in peace). I walked around the house and didn't see or hear any raven. Burt flew away and left me sitting in the window, wondering. Is it time? Is she nesting? By 4 o'clock I was convinced, or I would have been, if Burt hadn't shown up again alone *waaahk waahking* in a soft voice. "Soft" "plaintive" these are words of an anthropomorphizing birdwatcher surely, and yet, the ravens have an elaborate language, startling in its ability to convey meaning and surely feeling. Burt was either enticing Tinker away from her business, or he'd lost her. Which was it? I stood at the kitchen window and wondered. Burt sat in the big tree where our Wi-Fi receiver lives and called to her. He flew into the woods towards where the nest is, or at least the one from last year which I can only assume is still in use and available and started to cluck and bobble the way the ravens do when they are mating. Pause. More chortle. Pause. He flew back towards the house and back to the tree. Perhaps a better view of all approaches? At last! Tinker. A quick fly by, landing in the tree nearest the pallet. Why not the garage? I hurried out to refill the feed. I'm not sure she even waited to eat. Maybe she just came to reassure Burt, or ask him to get take-out, then she was off again.

This morning, on schedule, they both came. I was so glad to see them I nearly ran outside. Tinker looks tired and worn, her feathers are ruffled, and she's clearly been busy. Is she laying eggs, is she plucking feathers for her nest? Hell if I know. She ate. She left. No discussion.

Is there a wedding back up plan if something new happens? Will you provide pretty face masks to all participants? Tests and vaccines required? Keep that tequila bottle handy, you're gonna need it. Is Windsong involved in the ceremony? Where will you sleep? Where will they sleep?! Pace yourself.

In other wildlife news, my new neighbor Audrey saw her first bobcat -casually walking right by her window in the middle of the day-cheeky bugger. She's thrilled. We're all thrilled. Well, all except next door Jane who loves them but would love them more if they'd stop killing hens and stealing eggs. Probably the bobcat is the female of the pair I've seen here, speculating that the female is smaller than the male, that is, I haven't seen them together.

And in the wee hours, before dawn, but just, there was the scream of fox, three times, in the silence, very close.

Love,
Jane


*Valentine's Day, 2022 Winter whooshed back with a vengeance. Gray. Cold. Windy. Fine mist but no rain. Dry, day 38.*

Dear Jane,
You could apply for a Raven Cam from Cornell. Either Tinker and Burt are birds yearning to be on film or your observation faculties surmount those of the average mortal. Possibly both. Where was Tinker all that time? When they produce tiny ravenettes, do you know how long before they fledge? We owe respect to these beautiful and noble birds, and if following their every move provides entertainment, that's a sign of honor.

Observation here is different, probably because I am a baby bird nerd. Though discerning between raven and crow is as simple as watching the flight pattern and tail formations, identifying different actual birds is a talent I've yet to master. A murder of crows took over my neighbor's tree today, making such a ruckus that I could hear it with the vacuum running. As far as I know, I'm the only one on the block with feeders and the feeders attract the tinies, including a new pair of soft gray bushtits, with tails as long as pine needles and heads so compact it's a marvel that it accommodates two eyes, a beak and a brain.

Along with all of the bird love, the flowers profuse. More daffodils perked up overnight. Forsythia burst from dull gray-green spines to tendrils of buttery yellow that waft over the ground. Some of the pale pink plum blossoms have begun to scatter, so that it looks like it's snowing fuchsia petals up and down the street. The spectacle of this February flower rain never fails to tear me away from whatever mundane task I might have been pursuing to stare in wonder like a kid who stumbles upon her very first sand dollar on a familiar silver beach.

Oh! The wedding. So much to tell, so much to say. Who will stay aboard Windsong? He or she must either be very tolerant so as not to feel the gaps between the four cushions that pass for a "bed" once the salon's dining table is lowered, or so short as to not find a five-foot V-berth a bother. As for masks, haven't your heard?! Covid is over! Seriously, everyone must provide a vax card. The wedding and all attendant festivities take place entirely outdoors. Weather does what weather will, and I've alerted all Floridians to coat-up. Don't talk to me about April showers.

It's Valentine's Day. Here's to all of the people who may find this day melancholy: the new widow, who is conditioned to wait for the basket of gardenias that will never arrive again, the angsty teen who has yet to discover that she's a superhero trapped in a town that will rue the day it dismissed her power, the married man who waits up in vain for his beautiful beloved to come home from her night out and wonders whether, perhaps, he proposed to the wrong woman.

And here is to love, which demands a level of humility and vulnerability and sacrifice that breaks your heart over and over and over. And that is worth every single tear.

Love, and Happy Valentine's to you and to Gene, to Tweed, and to Tinker and Burt, Medea

*February 17, 2022 sun. cold. California cold which really doesn't count*

Dear Medea,
Forgive my neglect, I will try to catch you up. We'll just skip past Valentine's Day, or maybe not. It was almost a non-event except for the foul mood from 50% of us and refusal to partake. Taking the high road, I made chocolate pot de crème with organic cacao and muscovado brown sugar, sea salt and cream. Kill them with kindness? It doesn't really matter. Valentine's is for people who still have sex. Breast cancer disabused us of that notion long ago. I did spare a bit of quiet time to wish my mother a happy birthday, she would have been 100 which is something, but breast cancer foiled that goal as well. Some theme.

On to the wildlife. Surely, I was wrong about raven doings. The routine has returned to normal. It makes me wonder if Tinker was injured during her absence. She did look ruffled. The way they fly through the trees, it wouldn't surprise me. Burt did us all proud by calling and calling, cajoling her back. After several days of interaction, I don't see anything new except that there might be more attentive watching for threats from Burt. He stands on the roof peak and watches in all directions while Tinker catches up, or while she eats, and she always starts to eat first.

Yesterday, we walked the property line and looked at the state of the forest. We have ten acres, not a great amount but there is wild land on one side and parcels of equal size on the others, so the forest seems bigger. Sadly, the ten acres to the west has been completely infested by pine beetles, at least forty large dead trees still standing. Makes me itch to think about the beetle mania going on under the bark. These bull pines are not pretty when they are mature trees, they tend to look rangy and fall over with regular and annoying habit. Our problem is that removing them is almost impossible. Cut the dead trees down, and then what? The logs and slash are as big a fire hazard as the dead tree was upstanding. The bull pines crowd the fir trees which all, thankfully, look pretty healthy and when given half a chance branch out into full and lovely trees reminiscent of parkland. We crashed through the brush, mostly water willow, rock rose, and giant ferns, and noticed that the wetlands are at least wet, though not the small ponds they should be this time of year. Here and there we came across matted grasses where wild animals, probably the deer, have been bedding down. In an hour's walk poking around, I saw only one deer at a distance in the field to the west. After we got home and put the kettle on for a cup of tea, we looked out the window and the herd of 8 were munching the yard grass.

It is too cool here for daffodils yet, but I did see blooming wild iris on the walk, and the tea tree and hypericum in the garden are blooming so we have a little bit of color against the lush green grass.

You're very kind about my bird knowledge but the truth is, I know next to nothing. This is an experiment in observation. When I'm tempted to Google raven behavior, I stop myself. I don't want to know this by book. I want Tinker to teach me.

Love,
Jane

P.S. It's supposed to be good luck for it to rain on a wedding day.


*17 February 2022 Mid-60s, hazy to the west, clear up above. Not a breath of wind.*

Dear Jane,
Happy belated birthday to your mom, a warm reminder that love endures.

If it's any universal consolation, I know of women who remain sexually adventurous after breast cancer. And others whose mates would never think to slip off her top during foreplay, finding the now-damaged or nipple-less or insensate chest area akin to Chernobyl. Which, I suppose, is why the enlightened say that we make love first with our minds.

Your beetle-infested trees pose a conundrum. My neighbor's infested tree fell on her other neighbor's house, taking out half the garage roof. Without structures to damage, maybe the best course is to do nothing while the bugs slowly munch on the pines until they've picked it clean. The vultures of the forest fill their bellies, the birds find branches for nests and roosts, maybe nibble on the beetles, and nature takes its course. Being pine-specific, the beetles pose no danger to the fir trees, right? Before my tree guy cut my infested pine, I watched woodpeckers and nuthatches peck its bark, hunting for beetles and other insects. A full-on ecosystem that might have fallen on a passing car, injuring my beloved mailman, or a neighbor walking her dog. Your bull pines may fall over, but they'll decompose. This might be one instance where looking down at the ferns and puddles and leafy deer beds outweighs looking up.

After being trapped indoors deciding which glassware to rent for the wedding, gnashing teeth over taxes, writing committee reports, and devising menus for my cooking weekend for the work crew on the Island, Max and I will spend the next two days sailing Windsong to the Island. She's at her best up there (am I projecting?) offering a crash pad for wedding guests and a sanctuary from the crowd for any who wish to disappear in the quiet lull of a sailboat on the water.

This will mark the first time we've taken her out in February, a consequence of climate change and the upcoming nuptials. It will also mark Max's and my seventeenth year sailing up together, typically just the two of us. He was thirteen when we sailed up alone the first time. Bruce said "you'll never make it," and you could hear an uncharacteristic tremor of terror in my dad's voice. Naysayers make lousy cheerleaders. That first trip was not without its moments, like when Max stood at the mast just after we'd cleared the harbor and announced that he'd never hoisted our mainsail, or when a twenty-five-knot gust nearly blew us into a wrecked barge, or when we flawlessly navigated a tricky short cut called False River. After an eleven-hour cruise, we arrived at the dock, sweating, smiling and puffed full of confidence. My friend, Peter, insists that these are the moments a man remembers most when he thinks of his mom in later years. I'll write from the Island with observations, maybe a Sandhill Crane sighting, and with very little wind in the forecast, no reports of near-misses. Watch for a red sky tonight; it portends a high-pressure system and stable air coming from the west. Crimson sky in the morning? That's a sign that the air is pregnant with moisture, so rain is imminent, which, as much as we wish for more rain, I'd appreciate it waiting until after Sunday.

Love,
Medea


*18 February 2022 Chilly and clear but promising 68 by the afternoon.*

Dear Jane,
This will be a quick post—Max and I had to abort our Delta voyage so will take Windsong out for a sprint on the Bay instead, give her and her sails some exercise.

Do you remember the issue with something gnawing on my seedlings in the vegetable garden? A culprit sweeping in from above? Worms? Talented squirrels? I'm still not sure but was distressed to find a Golden-crowned Sparrow cowering and tangled in the netting. I cut it loose immediately upon finding it but noticed a white substance that looked like froth around its beak. The poor thing struggled to breathe. It let me lift it and stroke its pillowy tawny and black-specked feathers. It weighs less than a rose. I placed it into a box where I'd laid some soft green leaves and a few bits of kale, which it seems to have loved nibbling. I set it in what I hope is a protected spot inside the bamboo grove. My guess is that a raptor had seized it but dropped it and injured its neck. The vet would not see the bird. The SPCA had closed for the day. I can't bring myself to go and check on it, yet, but I'm not expecting a miracle.

What should I have done? This is the ugly side of loving the tinies. Should I have wrung its neck? Would that have been the compassionate move?

I have so much still to learn about interbeing.

Love,
Medea


*February 19, 2022 chilly. Sun. Light breeze.*

Dear Medea,
Poor little thing. Either it will live, or it will be there waiting for burial when you return, or something will carry it off as the cycle continues. Maybe take up the netting? Something I think about a lot is the process of any action–if this, then this, then that–it might be unfair of me, but I have the feeling women are better at this than men and mothers are better at it than any other group. We're charged with that processual logic when we give birth and keep it, guess what? Forever!

When Tinker disappeared the other day, I suddenly realized a new depth to my commitment to the ravens. Now we have a relationship, an intimacy. They watch me constantly, curious, and hungry of course. But is it only that? Only greed? Or do they care for me as well. If Gene goes to the garage, even if he ventures to try to feed them, they don't seem to care. There is a relationship. I have responsibilities to them. Not the same as those I have to my son, my grandson, my daughter in law or my husband. For all of them there is a constant logic going on during all hours of the day, even sleeping I am calculating risk, it's obvious from my dreaming. I sometimes think that if everyone had a sense of each other that was not only sympathetic but also empathetic, first, everything would grind to a halt; but then some brightening, some glint of calculation would begin and we'd look around, looking beyond our little intimate group and we'd evolve. Just think, if the whole world evolved in one day! We might survive! As long as this kind of calculated compassionate logic is the sole provenance of a few moms, we're not going to spot every humpback whale that gets trapped in a crab net, or rescue every tiny sparrow from above or below, or protect the vulnerable from invisible pandemics because that's what's humane.

Love,
Jane

*21 February 2022 Cold, blustery, inhospitable but for the sunshine.*

Dear Jane,
It's mostly moms, you're right, I think. And we both know men with this sensitivity to the world and its vulnerable creatures. Peter, who posts a thousand photos each time the turtle babies crash through their shells and sand burrows and flap flap flap from beach to sea. Bill, who reveres Jane Goodall as though she were a saint, which she surely is, and who mourns every finned hammerhead as though it were his first born. My dad, who can't help himself from sending awwww-inspiring photos of a mama dog nuzzling an orphaned kitten or a gorilla kissing a duckling. The world needs more of these, too.

The sparrow lay stiff and cold in the box on Sunday. No one at SPCA until tomorrow, so I watch its relatives with their lemony foreheads closely for signs of infection. Birds may not contract rabies but other diseases threaten. This theory, of course, absolves me of responsibility for netting my crops in an attempt to avoid the produce aisle for a few weeks. I consider myself a more enlightened being than the Florida rancher who said there are "plenty more panthers" so as to justify the killing of the one who attacked her herd. But, in the end, I'm just another delinquent party-crasher, meddling with nature's way.

I thought about Tinker today as I braved the gale to fill the feeders. She's not tame, technically, yet she shows signs of...domesticity? She prefers you to Gene, food be damned. If you asked that raven lady in England, she would likely agree that you and Tinker are bound. My tinies appreciate their suet and seed squares. The juncos and chickadees and woodpeckers scatter when they hear me approaching; not the nuthatches. We lack the intimacy you share with Tinker. Still, if all of them or half of them disappeared for even a day, I'd be on the phone with the Audubon Society, hoping for an explanation that didn't include my own culpability.

This world you envision, driven by sympathy and empathy over base survival and greed; it may commercially grind to a halt, but so what? You have a forest. I have vegetables. People moved by our irrefutable connection, one to the other, would share. The act of simply pausing to listen to the wind ruffle the palms outside opens space in the mind. It gives us momentary freedom from the dipshit monologues that trap us in busy-ness. Would such a protracted pause (assuming the opportunists have been put into one of the penis rockets and blasted off to Planet Oblivion) offer anything but a mutually respectful, shared appreciation for every being from the most microscopic slime to the king of the sea? Covid's "Great Pause" nudged open the window onto our collective consciousness. May its hinge stick until everyone taps in.

Love,
Medea


*February 22, 2022 yikes it's cold.*

Dear Medea,
Forgive the brevity. The best of intentions were to continue the high falutin" conversation about how we might or might not evolve (you're right, the covid experience indicates it takes only a tiny nudge to send all of humanity right over the brink leaving their generosity wrapped in a dirty T-shirt), but sadly, rather than snuggle up warm inside, I convinced Gene that we should at least look for the stack of foam water pipe insulation tubes we thought we had somewhere and make a pretense of maintenance. We did. We found half dozen unused foam tubes and after horsing around for a few minutes we (meaning he) dug in and got busy. With four buildings to assess for outdoor pipes plus the well head house itself and the storage tank…you can see where this is going. Being as it was my idea, and therefore my fault it was supposed to be a hard freeze, I carried the tubes and the duct tape and said encouraging things while I froze my ass off. Wet feet, stiff back, oh boy are we getting too old for this. Hours not worth

counting later and extra foam tubes put safely back where we found them, our pipes are out of danger.

Love,
Jane


*22222. 10. Where is the numerology expert? 49 degrees with Maxfield Parrish clouds and, blessedly, rain.*

Dear Jane,
The DeYoung will feature an exhibit by 20th century painter Alice Neel starting in March. Her portraits, not "portraits" like Little Blue Boy, but representations of people, with freakishly large, kind eyes and frizzy curls and wrinkled tee shirts lacked commercial appeal during most of her life. And yet, she persevered. At age eighty, Alice Neel painted a brave, badass self-portrait, nude. With her paunchy belly and saggy boobs, her white wisps of thinning hair, her translucent "presbydermis," her slumping shoulders and gnarled fingers holding a brush and a rag, she sits, a "so what?" look on her face. From her blue and white-striped throne, stripped to her essence, she looks every bit the Monarch.

Alice Neel reminds me of our house, constructed in 1978, where we've lived since 1999. Most of its alterations date from either seventeen, twenty-three or thirty-three years ago. Does my house notice its riven Poly pebble, pushed skyward by the jade plant we brought from our first rental? The blood spattered on the door jamb in the powder room, a signature from the time a bungee cord split my eyebrow wide open right before—really, right, as in an hour before—our Thanksgiving dinner guests would burst through the door? The dulling of her coat of buttery yellows and crimson reds? At night, she groans in protest, she creaks, like an arthritic old woman.

Alice Neel would tell my house to strut that blood and fade, and to rock the history of her sheltering, to keep doing what she's doing.

Love,
Medea


*February 23, 2022 Sun. Cold. Low of 32.*

Dear Medea,
Statistically, I think it is assumed that people will move house on average about every seven years–some sort of ancillary itch. But like you, we have been in this

house for 24 years this July and keeping up with the unfortunate facts of a scarce work force, poor quality initial construction in some rather shocking places coupled with too many buildings and too much stuff, well, the only upside is that Gene has plenty to do and not a moment to spare to despair over retiring. On the downside he is too clever for his own good and finds almost 100% of the time that he has to do it all himself. Our house also has blood spatter–a prospective buyer with the foresight to bring an ultraviolet light like on the crime shows would no doubt turn and run screaming. The blood being mostly shed by poor Tweed having nose bleeds of a shocking quality and quantity during a particularly difficult period of his life. Poor thing. He's ok now. I'm just glad we put in hardwood floors.

I know vaguely of Alice Neel's "come on and look at me, I dare ya" artistic style. I admire her bravery and forthright skill. I can barely bring myself to look in a mirror.

We did not have a hard freeze, not here. My guess is that some areas inland did see frozen pastures and vineyards–does it matter if the vines are dormant now anyway? Tinker and Burt are right on time for meals the past few days, and while sometimes one or the other arrives first, I'm guessing they are not sitting on eggs. I hope that's the case, because it's perilously cold. This morning, there was fox scat on the sawhorse, and bobcat scat on the pallet. I might have to think about a new place, higher up, to feed them.

Speaking of mirrors, have you ever noticed that there are good mirrors and bad mirrors? "Mirror mirror on the wall..." I wonder if that tale has another side. I have a lovely gentle soul of a mirror in my bathroom, but the one by the front door, which happens to be a 19th c. antique and so can be forgiven for its spitefulness, but I seriously wish it would stop catching me sideways and showing my hag at a bad angle. It's not there for me to fluff my hair or check my lipstick, after all, it's just there to keep the money and luck from rolling down the stairs and right out the door. Buddha, a three-footer in wood on the landing of the staircase, has a "yippee, touchdown" pose and seems an unlikely character to care about either my happiness, or my fortunes.

Love,
Jane


*25 February 2022 Not just cold. Damned cold.*

Dear Jane,
Despite the inhospitable temperatures, the sun beckoned us out for a late-afternoon walk. The finches and titmice belted out duets all along our path

from home, around the perimeter of the college and back. Lovingly, ironically, called "Harvard on the Hill," its amenities impress: an entire building dedicated to instruction in "Emerging Technologies." Its own planetarium. The finest gym in the county. An Olympic-sized pool, football field and track, baseball field and bleachers, softball field and bleachers. A performing arts venue, a jazz radio station and speakers that announce the hour to all of San Mateo and environs between 8 am and sunset. The College of San Mateo had a public television station until the district trustees sold it in 2018. It trains firefighters. It paved over a horticultural teaching garden to add yet another parking lot, this one with EV charging stations that we suspect might be free to those who can figure out the code. The college boasts a Bay view that extends from downtown SF to the north, and down past the San Mateo Bridge to the south. For the past two years, we've had the place largely to ourselves and groups of dog lovers who congregate, "no dogs allowed" signs be damned, to exercise their pups.

I'm lucky to have such an expanse, no longer overrun with students, within walking distance. Do the taxpayers know this exists?

In Florida, the kind of disclosures that might require you to alert a prospective buyer that the abundant blood had nothing to do with Santeria have handily been waved away with a haughty sniff by legislators (possibly? probably?) bought and paid for by the real estate lobby. You could make a fortune selling those UV lights to prospective buyers of Miami-Dade homes. I'm happy to learn that Tweed's nose is healed.

Where will you place Tinker and Burt's food? Thankfully, these ravens can fly. It occurs to me that perhaps the Golden-crowned Sparrows have frightened the nuthatches to distant feeders. Or to fend for themselves. I've not spied one of those tinies at the feeders in ten days. Perhaps there is a migration? It's almost March and no sign of a Cedar Waxwing. After the February spring, winter roared back to claim God knows what animal or vegetable. Max is concerned for his blossoming plants, since after weeks of mid-70s balm, he and his darling awaken each morning to an arctic chill so bitter he has to put on socks before he gets out of bed or his toes freeze.

So, the mirror thing? It's not just me? In my bathroom mirror, I usually recognize myself. It depends on the light. In the powder room, I flinch at the reflection, wondering who this slack-skinned broad is who followed me in there. In the rear-view mirror of my car, especially when the sun shines and the convertible top is down, voilà. There I am.

Love,
Medea

P.S. The Florida's Senate President and aspiring Commissioner of Ag (who also happens to be an industrial egg producer) is in the process, through SB2508 and the bill's sponsor, his buddy Ben Albritton, of ensuring that control of the Everglades water continues to flow to Big Sugar. Those soul-less, spineless, gutless bureaucrats. And the annual, suffocating sugar cane burn? That's been happening, with its attendant stench and smoke, since I was a kid. C'mon Karma. Do your thing.

*February 26, 2022 cloudy, just beginning to sprinkle or is it my dirty window?*

Dear Medea,
All the gods and goddesses, ancestors, ancient ones, Elders and Grandmothers, please gather and cast your cloak over Ukraine.

WTF. All this saddens every human being who has a heart beyond the limits of our explanation for the sensation: fatigue, fear for those in danger, anger, and a rising and inexplicable incredulity at the audacity of Russian leaders. How can we help the Ukrainian people in this moment?

In my backyard, I am excited to share that Tinker has been on the grass searching for small and soft twigs, but Burt has outdone himself and just flew onto the garage peak with a foot long twisty twig in his beak. He fiddled with it and after about four shifts around he had it the way he needed it to take off and fly. He landed again in a tree nearby, adjusted the branch again, and then flew into the trees in the direction of their nest. Yippee! The nest refurbishing has begun!

We are supposed to have light rain, not in great quantity, but the weather radar is promising in its greenness. At some point the true skeptics will start to tell us nothing that could come would make any difference, but hey, if just putting away my rain jackets worked, who's to say when we should give up and descend into weather gloom?

I know you're throwing a birthday party for your Dylan tonight. I hope it feels like a pre-pandemic event and it's filled with joy and fun. We all need that.

Love,
Jane

*28 February 2022 Warm and sunny enough to walk in a skirt.*

Dear Jane,
Putin commits acts of unprovoked aggression, and the world responds with revulsion. From Disney to Shell, Taiwan to Finland, humanity is discouraged and

disgusted by a "small, feral-eyed man" (thanks, Mitt Romney). I join you in your plea for all the powers, terrestrial and beyond, to protect the people of Ukraine.

Throwing a party in the midst of chaos half a world away is in part a Hail Mary and in part a Fuck You. Max and I prepared paella. I juiced Meyer lemons from my tree and transformed the juice into a lemon chiffon pie. Life goes on, the tantrums of addled dictators be damned. So many of us cowered after 9/11. We were so afraid. Within days, that fear morphed into fury. "If we stay locked in our homes, dear, they win," said my wise friend Rita, who survived WWII's German shellings of her English town with a stiff upper lip.

You wait for rain. Burt bends twigs. Stephen the squirrel ravages the latest seed square. Dylan will welcome another year; I almost wrote "unless Putin decides to go nuclear," but why tempt fate? Every year since the kids were small, I write a list for them on their birthdays, "X things I Love About You" in which "X" equals the age they will turn. Corny? Maybe. Still, it gives me a chance to reflect on all of the moments, quiet, boisterous, weird, delicious, that we've shared since their last birthdays. I've considered that maybe they felt these lists were an annoyance to read, another demand on their packed schedules. They may pitch them, or put them under the pillow, or just remember, during dark times when the world feels cruel, that there are at least X number of things that someone loves about them.

The White-throated Sparrow's song rang out loud on our walk this evening. The finches, too; they sit in the trees at the college, at the tip of the tops, and belt out their sweet trills. A concert accompanied by the woodpeckers' percussive taps. The pittosporum blooms blasted out their sweet, spicy, heady fragrance, as they do around Dylan's birthday. The scent could be jasmine, could be gardenia. It's the alchemy of beauty and calm. May the renaissance of Spring come soon to Ukraine.

Love,
Medea

# March 2022

*March 1, 2022 mild, a change in barometer. It would be going too far to say possible rain*

Dear Medea,

What a sweet and lovely idea to send those letters to your boys. I would hope and expect that they have kept every one of them, and some day in a few decades they will share them with their own children and continue the tradition.

There is a sense of holding space for the people of Ukraine, and for the pawns of Russia's demented leaders, that keeps Ukraine on my mind and more on my television than normal. I am still searching for meaningful ways to help. What brave and fierce people they are, a true tribe of warriors deeply born of their homeland.

The efforts locally to support the Pomo outcry to regain their rightful lands, or at least to have say over how they are used, increases with talks, walks, and social media events. We're anxious to help. But there must be something I can do. We can do. Sure would be an amazing full circle from my ten-year-old self's letter of complaint to President Eisenhower about the dreadful treatment of Native Americans by the Dept. of the Interior. I was a fanatic radical. I did get a reply, a form letter and a big envelope of gov't bullshit. I still have the letter.

Yesterday's excitement was an aerial battle between Tinker and the Red Tailed Hawk (who, by the way, visits daily to hunt in the front yard and probably deserves a name of his own). I think the hawk discovered the dog kibble and might have made a dip down onto the sawhorse for a look see. In any case, Tinker chased him off, squawking like a fish wife.

Love,
Jane


*1 March 2022 Cloudy, 66 degrees, humid. Please, let it rain.*

Dear Jane,

Today is Mardi Gras, a great excuse to dance in the streets, catch garishly colored beads, bare one's breasts, drink copiously-cupped cocktails, and eat King Cake, taking care not to break a tooth on the plastic baby Jesus. People sure are weird. Tomorrow, things (for the observant) get real; the cross of ashes on the forehead a reminder of our impermanence as the priest whispers, "You are dust, and to dust you shall return."

As I write, two chickadees are courting in the rhododendron outside my window. They chirp and flutter, like teenagers in love, wheeling around the branches, up into the sky, back down into the leaves. Odin is losing his mind, pacing the length of the sill, back and forth, head riveted to the commotion just out of reach of his fang and claw; though he's never tasted a wild bird, his actions indicate he knows the little lovebirds would make a tasty snack. Instead, he's getting a fistful of Friskies Party Mix, Beachside Crunch flavor.

What is our responsibility to Ukraine and her people? Perhaps holding space and finding others whose voices have been silenced are two of the more constructive things. When a world leader assaults a sovereign nation, aiming at civilian targets, how do the sane respond, knowing that leader lacks anything anyone might recognize as a conscience? Sanctions against Putin and the oligarchs seem like a slow, irritating burn, like boiling a frog alive. Will it raise his ire just enough to press the red button?

For my own sanity, I must turn to birdsong and cloud animals, watching for spring green to emerge on the tips and skins of the maple and gingko trees, breathing in the scented air of Spring, guiding the mind away from thoughts unthinkable. Knowing that the Berkeley falcons are sitting on a new clutch of eggs, that you have a new hawk (could you name him "Olek" in honor of Zelensky?) bearing witness to another spin of the earth round the sun for my son: each affirmation of life shifts the mind from hopeless to optimistic.

One way or another, this, too, shall pass.

Love,
Medea


*March 2, 2022 sun, mild, humidity! Such a blessing*

Dear Medea,

It's a funny sort of day with the glorious weather springing that sense of new beginnings and growth, I can almost feel the earth shifting as the bulbs push up toward a sun and sky they've never seen. And yet, I woke up this morning feeling a sense of endings as well as beginnings. For a while now, I've been in the limbo of change that the wise person gives space to in order that the change not be a bad thing but be yet another step on this great ladder that is a life. There's an Irish song I love, sung in the dusky throated alto of Dolores Keane (who I passed on the street once in Dublin), I can't remember the title right now, but the best line is "lost the friends that needed losing, found others along the way."

286

We do evolve, in our own little meaningless ways, and it's only right that the artifacts of a life come and go, shift and age, the way a closet needs cleaning. My spiritual center is also finding new depths and some of the trappings are finding a place at the back of the altar box, while others emerge. This is a good shift, nothing for concern, but it is a refinement that is preoccupying my quiet mind. Is it bad to whittle down the list of intimate friends to just a handful? The advantage of a non-existent Christmas card list aside, as we age do we need quantity over quality simply because of the mortal attrition? It seems out of my control anyway, but it is something to think about. At extreme moments, who do you call, my friend? Who will you call?

Zelensky is the perfect hawk, isn't he? Is Olek his nickname? The UN speech Zelensky made and the interpreter's voice breaking with emotion brought me to tears as well. I was heartened to see that Biden did well in his speech last night also. As my friend Richard said this morning, only Putin could have brought the EU, UN, NATO, and the US together in a common goal even if that was exactly not what he wanted.

Funny you mentioned the "red button." Someone on CNN mentioned the Cuban Missile Crisis and got the sitting president wrong. It was Kennedy, of course. I was a high school student in Beirut at boarding school. We were told to pack a bag and be ready to catch a charter flight to Cyprus. Overnight, the crisis was cooled, and we went back to the usual. But it's a vivid memory, feeling suddenly completely loose from any sense of safety—a rare thing in boarding school in the first place. We would have flown to Cyprus without our parents even having notice of intent or consent. Crazy ass world.

Here's a fun thing to do. The London Times has a free live podcast of the day's radio shows (Times Radio). Check out the morning drive show with Stig Abel for a fascinating take on events from the British perspective—and if you listen around 9 pm it will be morning. Germany's army is a shambles, who knew that?

How will this end?

Love,
Jane


*3 March 2022 Rain so welcome that the frigid air must be ignored.*

Dear Jane,
Today, my friend Jim would have turned sixty-nine. His sister texted a raft of photos, early Jim, middle-aged Jim, Jim's creations, like the five-foot tall double-action Ferris wheel that he bought at Opie Taylor's Toy Store, press clippings

from Jim's entrepreneur days. Whatever his current form, he remains a force of nature for those of us who knew and loved him.

A pair of Western Jays showed up at the feeders. Are they a couple? Both appear male, according to the Sibley images. Maybe part of an extended family, searching for food for their mates. The tinies give them space, unremarkable given that the jays' beaks measure about the same length as the diameter of a Dark-eyed Junco's head. These two have such intense blue feathers that I first mistook them for Western Bluebirds. Just when you think the same sparrows and chickadees are the only birds interested in my feeders, up pops a blue jay.

How many friends do we *need* as the years unfold? We both have nurtured some of the same friendships for decades. I don't actively recruit new friends; days are already full with work and play, filling the feeders, stocking the larder socializing with my familiars. Then, out of nowhere, I'll interact with someone. We click. It's not like I *need* a new friend, just like I don't *need* another pair of orange socks. But the spice is irresistible.

The existential threat of war and a planet overrun with humans sucking dry all the wells must influence our personal evolutions. We nourish our birds who nourish our souls and cook a nice meal for the men we love. While we make small gestures to save water and beleaguered Ukrainians, men smear the skies with the carbon stain of their private jets and mega-yachts and carpet bomb apartment buildings and orphanages. All of those parka-clad families clutching their babies and pets, flooding into train stations and subways, those are you and me and yours and mine in a parallel place and time.

If you believe that the thoughts you think emanate into the universe, and sometimes they stick, then the foibles of oligarchs, despots, and stupid people may, eventually, with enough concentrated, compassionate brainpower, fade into obscurity. In the interim, the U.S., France, Spain and Britain might consider opening the doors of the appropriated penthouses and gangplanks of the seized yachts to those two million refugees.

Love,
Medea

P.S. Olek is a diminutive of Zelensky's middle name, Oleksandrovych.


*March 5, 2022 overcast. Cold.*

Dear Medea,
Our own friendship is testament to the ways people can connect and maintain lively affection and interests for sure! Who would have thought, considering

what each of us was going through at the time a decade ago that we could nourish anything beyond our own broken bodies! And here we are, with a multitude of words between us, and not even a voice in our head to match the words to. It will be a weird and wonderful day when we finally meet in person!

The prize for Ukrainian resistance against a Russian invader this week goes to the woman who yelled at a soldier driving a military vehicle, translated as, "Nearly every other woman in this town is a witch, and we curse you all that tomorrow your penises will not stand!" Excellent curse. I'm on board for that. To see the video, find Stephen Colbert for Wednesday of this week. As for us, what comes next? This old school approach to a civilized war is so embarrassingly outdated, I cringe every time someone in our government mentions "war crimes." Isn't war a crime? Isn't all death, intentional death, a crime worth fighting against? A bully doesn't back down unless he's beaten thus. How do we make compatible our desire to be free of warfare and our requirement as a democracy to protect those who cannot protect themselves? War has no space for the honorable.

Blue Jays are dominators at the feeder and will try to keep your tinies away. Eventually, there will be more jays, fewer other birds, and the jays will shout at each other and make a racket. I wouldn't encourage them, but that said, it may be too late. Not that there is much you could do. It's rather like Russia.

We had serious wind, gale warning, yesterday which kept the birds hunkered down for the most part although Tinker and Burt did both show up for food twice, holding onto the roof edge for dear life, their purple black feathers ruffling like the boa of a 20s flapper. The male contingent of the deer herd all gathered before the wind came to feed on the grass by the house. After a while they seemed alert to an intruder, and as I watched they formed into a circle facing out, the two most easterly deer began to stamp their hooves. I went out to the porch and heard them make a cough/hissing noise at the intruder. Three deer were on the driveway, perhaps females, I couldn't tell, but clearly not welcome to the main body. Thus is life. It made me sad, but there is no changing that mechanism. Perhaps there is good reason. Males being dangerous as they are. Eventually the seven moved on, and the others had a chance at the good grass before night came.

Did I already say that the hawthorn is budding? The sucker branches need clipping, also for the Japanese maples. I noticed the hawthorn is rather unstable in her roots. I'm worried the gophers are winning underground. If the fragile hawthorn trying to recreate life in the cycle again is threatened by the willful gnawing of destruction unseen, is that a good enough metaphor for the state of global politics? How do we rid ourselves of the pest without blowing up the tree?

Love,
Jane


*8 March 2022 It's summer again, 74 degrees, sunny, clear.*

Dear Jane,
Do you remember that George W. called Putin, "Pootie-Poot"? Here we are, thirteen years later, and that same bare-chested pony rider is ripping it up in Ukraine. One hundred and fifty baby and toddler orphans shipped to Poland. Children who lack human touch suffer mightily with attachment disorders and alienation psychoses for the better part of their lives. News footage shows soldiers holding and cuddling these apple-cheeked innocents. For how long? When will the deluge of unescorted tinies overwhelm the Polish safety net? Is there a dusty scintilla of compassion buried inside what remains of Pootie-Poot's heart?

I spent the weekend cooking for an intrepid group of construction volunteers at the Island. Morning temperatures topped out at thirty-five degrees. The kitchen is outdoors. Coffee and early morning sustenance must be served by 6:45. The pale, golden light rising in the east, silhouettes of palm and mulberry trees near the docks with the quiet, steady river coursing onward. You know how this place feeds me. This weekend, the Northern Flicker joined the Mourning Doves in a midday chorus of Morse code calls and throaty coos. When I activated Merlin's Song ID, the app went nuts, recording American Robin! House Finch! Canada Goose! Great Blue Heron! The streaming sound of scores of songs prints like someone's really scary EKG.

The jays were gone when I returned home. Stephen decimated the woodpecker seed block, but not before a Hairy with a perilously pick-like beak had its fill. Don't tell Bruce, but on Friday I saw a rat clambering up a branch toward the feeder that he gave me for Christmas. Since the feeders are currently empty, they'll remain thus until day breaks. No sense tempting rat fate.

How will you rescue the Hawthorn from the gophers? Mature trees are like Alice Neel. Maybe you needn't worry about chawed roots. And don't ravens enjoy a wee nibble of gopher from time to time? Where are Tinker and Burt?

My neighbor informed me that a security camera spotted a mountain lion, twice, near our homes. Where does that kitty live? Does she have cubs? I think of your deer. And our neighbors' ankle-biter puppies. I remember the alligators that lived peacefully in the canals near my childhood home until developers' interminable tract house arrays co-opted the nubby reptiles' feeding grounds. The gators had to eat something.

Wildlife corridors. Humanitarian corridors.

O you men of small and flaccid penis, honor for the innocents a pathway to survival.

Love,
Medea

P.S. Those Ukrainian witches might be candidates for a Nobel Peace Prize. I'd vote for that.

*March 10, 2022 calm, sun. warmish but cooling off with sundown*

Dear Medea,
So much to catch up on, sorry about my vertiginous absence. While sitting still the past few days, watching out the window and trying not to shift my eyes too fast, I've been treated to more visits from the herd of nine deer–pretty sure six of them were young adult males joined by the mother and juvenile and another female. The lead adult male seemed to want the does and the young one to move away, they did allow them a bit of the lush grass. The condition of the mother and young one doesn't look great. Perhaps she's just shedding a winter coat or picking at ticks a lot. The young one seems to have labored breathing. There's no way to know.

At the same time that I'm feeling puny, Tweed is also ailing. His problem may be directly related to the deer. I saw him eat a little bit of deer poop, those little raisins of excrement that cascade from their backsides. Why Tweed thinks this is a good thing to eat is beyond me. But he came inside, went back out and ate some grass, came back in and puked on the Persian rugs. Sigh. Deduct another $500 from the value of the Isfahan. Maybe, in order to maintain the pair, I should see if Tweed would like to puke on the other one. It's ok. He can do what he needs to. I love him more than carpets.

Yesterday, or maybe the day before, I was standing at the kitchen sink and here wanders a small female bobcat. "Small" here means bigger than a domestic kitty but not as big as the male we saw recently. She was completely unconcerned that she was right next to the house, and she wandered down the brick walk and around the fence of the garden and out into the yard. Good girl! Catch those gophers! I was glad Tweed was inside.

Tinker has been away all day today. Is it finally time? Burt has been by and collected gullets-full of kibble, hopefully sharing. He must know where she is and what she's up to because he doesn't call or search the area. He just shows up, collects the food, and leaves.

It sounds like your island chef duties had rewards. These things, mundane or otherwise, are important for our own mental health. I told Tweed today that we'd be in a sorry mess if we were in Ukraine. It doesn't take much imagination to feel incredibly vulnerable. On that note, I have seen two fighter jets today flying the coastline, or maybe the same one coming and going, those curved snout nosed, rather sinister looking planes that mean business. It is rare to see them here, so far from a military airstrip.

I hope your neighbor is cautious about her puppies. Are they really puppies? What kind? There have been a lot of sightings up here as well, though there always are. Someone saw a mountain lion capture and kill her pet cat. It's really not a good idea to have small pets who go outside at night. Or sheep. Or goats. Out walking at night? Take a flashlight and look for eyes in the darkness.

Love,
Jane


*11 March 2022 Clear, bright, a whisper of wind, high 60s.*

Dear Jane,
It's a relief to read your post and learn that your vertiginous trap has sprung you. Welcome back!

The benefit of simply stopping, forced or voluntary, invites moments like yours with the deer. The stillness in your house must have wafted outside, inviting the herd to muster peaceably. Without groomers, how do the girls keep their fur clean, shiny and tick-free? The deer that wander at the reservoir seem more kempt than they should, given they spend their days navigating scrub and bramble and coyotes. I hope that your deer are molting or bothering ticks rather than suffering some loathsome disease. Maybe noshing on the spring blooms will fatten them up, add some sheen to their coats.

My neighbor who told me of the puma has no puppies, but the preponderance of neighborhood dogs means that any lapse in locking up a pet at night may result in the same kind of harsh witnessing of lion eating cat. That's hard to stomach, and why my spoiled feline boys spend their days and nights inside. You can't blame a puma for hunting.

As for Tinker and Burt, though, it sounds like you're going to be a raven-grandma! I saw two scarlet-throated finches scuttling about this afternoon with bits of twig in their beaks. I can't see exactly where they are building a nest, but it looks like it is on top of a palm frond a meter from the family room window and just beneath the rain gutter. That's not wise. Opportunistic animals will find any eggs or babies. A raccoon once swiped three dove nestlings by hanging from our gutters and swinging into the nest, ill-situated right beneath the eave. Watching the parents search in vain for the babies left a scar on my heart.

I walked around downtown Los Altos this morning while the repair shop put new tires on my car. Los Altos reminds me of Venice or Los Gatos or any intimate small town with few if any chain stores. Two gray-haired couples sat with their matching white retrievers sipping coffee and reminiscing about a cruise they'd taken together—one of the wives created a photo memory book they thumbed through, reliving the Captain's Dinner and Portofino and younger days. A toddler tugged on his mom's hand, "Look mommy! Light!" and she smiled and said, "Yes, baby! I saw the light!" I saw it, too, as I walked past the shuttered beauty salon and with a strand of lavender lights twinkling on a white branch standing in the corner. A different tiny boy insisted his dad lean over a planter to witness a lone, brown coffee cup sleeve, set askew against dark green foliage, one thing not like the others.

Delight. Wouldn't the world's mood improve if everyone could spend a periodic day with a child, heart wide open, and sally forth into the world bewitched and enchanted by tea lights and random bits of refuse?

Fighter jets overhead, spewing carbon and terror. The world's children deserve so much better.

Love,
Medea


*March 11, 2022 overcast, light fog, a shift in weather is coming*

Dear Medea,
The ravens seem unconcerned about the little Gray Jays who crash their party and gobble as much kibble as possible before being pushed off. Is it because they hail from the same family? Does Tinker think, ah those tiny cousins, aren't they cute? Or are the tinies risking their necks every morning for a quick and easy breakfast? Tinker was back yesterday. For the second time, one of them has left something mysterious in the water bowl (and no, that's not a riff on Cold Comfort Farm's famous woodshed). The item might be akin to an owl pellet, and since the water bowl is under the garage roofline where Tinker perches, I'm assuming it's something she vomits up, something stuck in her craw. Is she commenting on the food? Or unwell? Or imitating Tweed? Or here's an idea, is she trying to explain to me why Tweed is sick? In any case, I have to keep cleaning out the water bowl lest Tweed ingest the disgusting mass–which "melts"

in the water over time (overnight, in this case). I've decided to move the bowl rather than just empty it since I know so many visitors drink from it; and keep Tweed to drinking indoor water.

After a hectic and fraught two days of trying to diagnose and then cure Tweed of his stomach ills without bending over too often I think we are both on the mend here. As usual, the response I get from my vet is far better than from our own medical system. Speaking of animals, after donating to a couple of charity organizations doing work in Ukraine including World Central Kitchen, I've been worrying about the dogs and cats left behind and wondering where to donate to their care. If you come across anything, do let me know. Some footage on CNN showed a group of people searching for humans left behind and one person went into the apartment block and shouted, "is there anyone here?" No human voice replied but there was plenty of barking from outside the building. They drove away.

Love,
Jane


*13 March 2022 What looked like thunderclouds to the West this morning gave way to diaphanous clouds by midday. Warm in the sun. Not so nice in the shade, 61 degrees.*

Dear Jane,
The image of the three Ukrainian family members shot by Russian soldiers played on TV with an audio recording of a yelping dog. Reading an account from the grieving husband and father, he said his family had their pup in a carrier as they tried to flee. Was the dog injured? Did someone rescue it or show it mercy? Just across the Polish border sits a no-kill shelter. The next time I hear the name, I will send it to you. What will become of this suddenly-alone man?

That water bowl sounds like a science experiment. If Tinker is mimicking Tweed, you might consider adding an anti-emetic to all of the critter food? In any case, you're wise to move that bowl.

On my walk today, I followed a meditation from Thay. "As I breathe in, I am the sun, the moon, the stars." Nothing dies. Nothing is born. We are the mountains and the ocean and stardust. Some grieving people do not wish to hear this. Maybe it's not true, and maybe, like Bruce's dad told him when he was a little boy, "You die and then you rot in the ground." But the sunset tonight held a certain hue, a pale saffron, that reminded me of the color of William Hurt's hair the first time I saw him in a film. William Hurt, and actor I revered, died today. Nothing is born. Nothing dies. It only changes form.

Active birds abounded today—three different blue jay pairs in different parts of the neighborhood. A Townsend's Warbler and a California Towhee and the usual suspects at the feeders, including the raven that remains to reveal whether it's hungry or hunting. Black lizards sunning on low stone fences. Lavender and white Tulip Magnolia burst their buds. Spring springs the week after we spring forward. Tigger would feel right at home.

Love,
Medea

*March 14, 2022 sun gave way to overcast. Rain is promised.*

Dear Medea,
Yesterday was the birthday of a friend who was critically important to me the past two decades but who has drifted away- much to my regret. In trying to decide how to deal with the loss, I pulled a tarot card. The Lovers, 2 of Cups, more than just for couples, it is the card of deep and meaningful relationships and the honoring of them. So, I sent her a birthday greeting, and instead of walking past the day, felt the loss keenly but cherish the memories. It is always important to cherish the connections, however they might evolve or change. Dismissal would be too easy and unworthy.

I love your meditation walk with purpose. At night when the moon is up and I'm outside with Tweed, I greet the moon and take a moment to touch hand to heart. Last night I added to my usual, "Grandmother Moon, hold me gently" with "never mind me, grandmother, hold the people of Ukraine." The moon was curiously on her side, as if cocking her head in wonder. Probably wondering how man can be so incredibly inhumane. Will no one "rid us" of this prick?

Tinker and Burt were nowhere in sight yesterday and I wondered if they were sitting at last, but this morning right on schedule (Daylight Savings Time) so once again I can't explain. Probably some building process kept them busy. "Here honey, hold this twig for me while I weave in this hay, and some stuffing," "No no, use the dog hair!" Both the bobcat and the fox visited during the night and left their usual editorial comment. "You people are shit!" Yes. We are.

I'm going to break my rule about not watching TV during the day and sit still to watch President Zelenskyy speak to Congress. Maybe I won't be able to sit still, being me, so winding yarn from skeins into balls seems like a good idea.

I feel like if it starts to rain, I might just burst into tears. For joy, sure, but also to release this horrible grief developing. Grief that I can't allow to fill in with detail. Grief that won't abate by making donations to charities, or reading every scrap written in the news, or talking about/wondering about why men behave so badly and have done so since before man started keeping track. Is this the beginning of the end? The moon is waxing gibbous now and has no name, but Thursday when she is full perhaps instead of calling her "the moon of sore eyes" she can be "the moon of no more war."

Love,
Jane


*15 March 2022. Rain, glorious if sparse, with nacre-colored cotton candy clouds giving way to mermaid tails and sun.*

Dear Jane,
This weekend will offer rain for grieving. Grandmother Moon must be listening as the cries come louder and stronger and from ever more quarters. Ukraine, her land and her people suffer, as did Crimea, Syria, Georgia at the same evil hands just a few years before. American Presidents shake fists and threaten "severe punishment," whatever that means, while we wring our hands and wonder whether any person of character exists in a leadership position with enough courage to definitively shut the door on Putin's maniacal, inhumane aggression. Grandmother Moon?

Your estranged friend surely felt the depth of your nostalgia for a relationship that's lost its ardor. I've wondered how it can be that a person who means so much to us can slowly drift away in the absence of a seismic event. Priorities shift. People move away or along. It always thrills me when I hear from someone from my past; the connecting thread may wear thin, but the underlying fiber maintains its integrity.

Tap dance class started again yesterday after two tap-less years. We were twelve eager souls performing the shuffle and flap across the dance floor at the Senior Center in San Bruno. I had never actually been inside a Senior Center; this one buzzes like an active hive. Signup posters show that the St. Patrick's Day bash is fully subscribed, as is the museum field trip and this week's movie night. Groups of ladies in one room hunch over green-felt tables playing Mah-Jongg. Three different people stand at the door filming snippets of our step-ball-changes. Two teenaged boys wipe spilled coffee from our dance floor lest someone break a hip. Our teacher, a trim, blue-eyed woman named Rosalie collects $5 from each budding Ginger Rogers (and one Fred Astaire named Raul) in a Country Crock margarine tub. She brings a boom box and we practice our steps to snappy, tappy tunes like *Straighten Up and Fly Right* and *Sing Sing Sing*. For an hour, even masked, it feels something like "normal."

After tap, I tackled the bamboo forest and the sun-singed palm fronds. Though gloves make sense, I can't feel the life in the plants with them on. So, I now realize why certain peoples use bamboo shards driven into fingernail beds as torture. And why digging a hole in the ground, studding its bottom with stubs of bamboo cane, and covering it with tree branches makes a lethally effective trap. On a lighter note, the neat, even folds in palm fronds must have inspired the first pleated skirt, *non*? Perhaps even the accordion's bellows?

Wedding watch: Nineteen days and counting. We will survive. Hey. Hey.

Love,
Medea

P.S. My birds are also acting weird in the backwash left after springing forward. P.P.S. Costco stocked tomato plants today! I bought two Early Girls and a Red Cherry. They will go into the beds Friday, after the plants have acclimated. And I confess to considering loading up on water, beans and canned goods. For the bunker.

*March 16, 2022 sun. cool. Light breeze.*

Dear Medea,
We didn't get much rainfall accumulation, but we are grateful for whatever comes. What did fall, came during the night and I lay awake for a long time, the window open at my head, just listening to the quiet sounds. The ocean, for once, keeping her mouth shut. This morning the ocean was back to crashing, spitting, and throwing things–mostly large trees–onshore. The weather forecast sneaker waves but didn't know about the 7.3 earthquake in Japan. At what point will we have just had enough?

I haven't been able to think of anything better to do to help Ukraine, so I made another donation to World Central Kitchen, but my sentiments echo yours exactly. We must, really must, have a better, stronger response to this horror or it will never end. Time to write our senators.

No sign of Tinker and Burt today so far. The deer have circled the house, munching as they went, and moved right along just before Tweed's usual time outside. Lots of wildflowers for them to eat, and two beautiful calla lilies in the garden which are volunteers and safely away from the deer.

There is no taste so fine as a home-grown ripe tomato, except a homegrown ripe tomato with bacon. And mayo. And iceberg lettuce.

Tap dancing! For inspiration, I highly recommend you find the Irish twins who dance on Instagram. Oh my. But good for you, in general, to do something wholly for yourself. I love it when women find activities for themselves in which they cannot be approached or interrupted until they have finished. Read a book? No. Nap? No. Take a bath? Heavens no. Tap dance? Hell yes.

Love,
Jane


*16 March 2022 High 60s and sunny today, a breath of crisp air.*

Dear Jane,
That you hear the ocean every day, whether she whispers, moans, shrieks or howls, somehow eases my lack of daily access. My coastal friend Peter who shares his world through frequent photos, offers me catharsis from yearning for the sea. Instead of lamenting that I'm not where you are, I'm full of love and gratitude that you two share your beaches with me.

I walked at the reservoir today and the sable-colored deer who breached the fence were munching on bright green grass. The bullfrogs croaked their creaky songs, still, which I believe we can seize as a water-positive sign. A man with a crazy long camera lens caught the hawk whose screech I'd heard at the end of an old oak branch. "It posed for me!," he said. My friend Candace told the photographer that she hates it when the crows divebomb the hawks. "It's nature," he said. It's also "nature" when the ravens attack the tinies, which I've not seen, but suspect, since now I have two lurking about the feeders. And I think of Tinker and Burt, who might attack tinies, but since they are part of the family now, I trust that they will not.

Do you have any faith in our elected officials? I'll write a letter. I'll call or tweet or post a picture of myself wrapped in blue and yellow. But I am afraid that if any of those pleas arrive without a check for the reelection campaign, the words, images, intentions evaporate like summer rain in Scottsdale. To describe many of our elected officials as "venal" only, barely, captures the seamy undercurrent that motivates their votes, their behavior. They'll vote to support Ukraine until a dark pool operative offers to fund a bridge or a public pool or a quiet trip to a private island on a mega yacht. Then watch how quickly the rhetoric turns.

Ending on a positive note, which we must, it appears that the weather for the wedding (W -18 and counting) will be sunny and 83 degrees! Maybe only some of us will appreciate that.

Love,
Medea

*March 17, 2022 Sun. cool. St. Patrick's Day*

Dear Medea,

Erin go Bragh! As my neighbor and I observed today when she stopped to bring me fresh eggs, we're Irish all the time so we don't need to wear green. We shared our memories of a trip we took to Ireland almost 20 yrs. ago now. Sailing in Bantry Bay with two Irish men just starting up a business entertaining tourists. We were their first customers. A beautiful day on the water, a stop at an island for a hike and a pint, then back to dock. When we returned to their house, the missus was not happy. I think she thought they were out with two young American women and got herself worked up over it. We hardly fit the bill.

Back to now, if we must, "venal" is the right word to describe our political representatives. They do not represent us, of course, just their wallets. That said, the news seems to be pushing closer to a "no fly zone" and I have trouble curbing my itch to promote war. War is always obscene, but what else to do? How many dead children do we figure is the limit before we say "enough'? Yesterday, CNN's female anchor shed tears on air while interviewing a father who lost his family. Her mascara was running. As a woman with children of her own, she, like many of us, must be physically sick at what is happening. I know I am. I know you are.

I saw that the weather is going to get quite warm. 83! I guess that's better than windy and fog. For a wedding anyway.

Tinker and Burt are keeping odd hours but they are showing up. I think also there is another pair, or at least another individual raven scouting out the situation. It will take some time to sort that out since I don't see all three together. It could just be that my own erratic behavior has them baffled. Setting the clocks forward has us all confused.

Love,
Jane


*18 March 2022 Sunny, mid-60s, zephyr moving aside for pearly poofs of possibly pregnant rainclouds. Please.*

Dear Jane,

I love your St. Patrick's Day memory. Jealousy can drive people batty. I hope the gents found success with their tourist venture. Growing up as a redhead, everyone assumed I'm Irish, so adopting this holiday came easy, until I met a German-Italian couple who threw a locally legendary St. Patrick's Day party every year; he lovingly brined the corned beef (or was it pickled? How does one corn a beef?) and assiduously boiled the cabbage to bits. Clearly, this meal is a feast, judging by the eager plate-piling and lip-smacking of the other guests. I happily skipped the meal and twirled to the tunes of the fiddlers instead.

We can't fix this war thing, Jane. We can't even fix the homeless situation close to home or put brakes on the corporate gaming interests (I'm talking to you, DraftKings) that are trying to subvert the agreement we made with the Chumash and other tribes. Gavin is loudly supporting Caltrans in its efforts to remove rows of tents and shopping carts and tarps and stolen bikes from the rights-of-way along the I-80 corridor. Commuters veer around whatever detritus from the camps tumbles onto the freeway. How long has this been going on? But 2022 is an election year. "Cynicism" is the prickly badge of the observant.

"Joy" is another, rapturous badge of the observant. Euphoria. Glee. A fully-formed miniature being with iridescent feathers, a sticky, forked tongue and the ability to throat sing like a Tuvaluan, perched on a thin, silver branch of a nearly-budding gingko tree captured my attention today. Children deserve more than the messy world we're leaving them. But they still have hummingbirds.

W -15 and counting. Rehearsal dinner in two weeks' time.

Love,
Medea


*March 19, 2022 Rain.*

Dear Medea,
"Tis a fine soft day." As we'd say in Ireland. Meaning rain. No gale, no wind, just a beautiful mist of rain. A Mendocino facial kind of day. Stand outside and look up. Everything looks better. The madrone tree has been flowering for a couple of weeks but today the rain gives a shine to the leaves and definition to the pale yellow flower pods, drops of water slip along the surface and resist letting go. The madrone is not a pretty tree in this state. She lost many of her leaves (every year, I say, "is she dying?" and have to be reminded that this is what happens to these trees. They never go dormant, they just wander through the seasons doing this or that, sometimes their leaves covered in rust, sometimes falling off.) This tree's purpose in life, though she doesn't know it, is to shield my bedroom from the summer western afternoon sun. Without her, my room would cook. Keeping her meant doing battle with the builders of our house who were all in favor of cutting every possible tree that might get in their way. This madrone is one of a kind, she has no mates nearby, and must have landed here in the kindly digestive system of some bird from Humboldt County. In the beginning she needed heavy pruning, and awkward as she was initially, now she is a perfectly balanced tree standing as an anchor on the northwest corner of the

house. When the wind blows, her outermost branches brush lightly against the edges of the house.

Your red hair is surely Scandinavian. That red gene pool is not native Irish in an ancient sense though it is associated with the Irish now. We have marauding Vikings to thank for the red hair, who raped and pillaged their way across the north of Briton onto Ireland and down the Irish sea between the coasts taking women and livestock, and land, for their own. A friend of mine says I must have links back to the Viking kings who ruled over Dublin in the 10th century. This meander has only diverted my worry brain for a few minutes because Viking raiders leads me back to the here and now and the terrible anger, frustration, and sadness I feel, we all feel at the Russian invaders of Ukraine. How long can we hold our breath before this is over? I ordered iodine, by the way.

As we head into our wedding countdown break, I'd like to give you some fantastic advice for the next few weeks. Let me think, so here goes: be yourself. Love your family as only you know how. Everything else will be fine. Hydrate.

Love,
Jane


*19 March 2022 Rain and chill. 55 degrees.*

Dear Jane,
Chris will take care of the madrone when he becomes the steward of your land, right? She's integral. Coming across a madrone with its rust-colored skin perks up an otherwise green, gray and dun hiking trail. Those shiny emerald leaves and white berries must shimmer in the late afternoon sun and the *shhusshing* of the branches against the windowpane offer a gentle lullaby. *Arbutus menziesii.* I'm surprised to learn that although the tree is native to the Pacific Northwest coast it's not found in Ireland as the climates are so similar. I'm sure you've read Horace's quip that "idle men delight to lie under this tree." Does Gene own a hammock?

It pains me to think some people draw parallels between Vikings and Putin. I've been proud of my Viking heritage, based upon the more egalitarian aspects of that society, the tradition of seafaring, the call to wander—flâneurs, albeit with sometimes nefarious methods. Are the Vikings worse or better than, say, Genghis Khan? Atilla the Hun? The Portuguese conquering Indigenous tribes in Brazil? The Spanish slicing the hands off the Lucayan and Aztec, demanding directions to El Dorado? The U.S. government "resettling" natives from New York to California, Lenape to Pomo, and laying waste to their ancestral lands? It's our collective sin, all committed in the name of discovery, expansion, progress. Putin's war strikes me as fundamentally different than these other conquests.

We're supposed to be global citizens who learn from the past. The Vikings lacked humanity in raping and pillaging the towns in their path, no question. Still, they sought to answer questions about the limits of the land and sea, to open trading routes, to expand the "known" world. As far as I can discern, Putin's megalomaniacal goal begins and ends with self-aggrandizement.

We made it through another winter, Jane. The arrival of the sparrows, the fly-bys from the jays, the mystery visits from the ravens and the insistent presence of the Stephens served to lift me from my usual dismay over cold, short days. Rain kept the grasses green and the bullfrogs boisterous. Clusters of yellow-eyed Narcissus scented the air. Cerise plum blossoms fluttered in tinted relief against oystery skies. I welcome perceptibly later sunsets. Our correspondence. The kids' personal and professional triumphs. Lettuce, kale, chives and cauliflower growing taller and tastier by the day. The return of tap dancing! Though Summer will always be my first and favorite love, I've awakened enough to find enchantment in Winter's quiet rhythms.

My first baby takes his husband vows two weeks from today.

Love,
Medea


*March 20, 2022 cold last day of winter or first day of spring? Mother N doesn't care, she blows when she wishes.*

Dear Medea,
The coast has developed a serious hatred of abalone divers. It's good that there is no season these days for diving. The parking lots and sides of the roads were jammed with whole families and gangs of divers, often taking illegal numbers or smaller than legal size abalone. They rent vacation houses and ruin them—there to work and process the abalone, not vacation. Abalone poachers trashed the kitchen of our friends—a beautiful house overlooking the ocean—they apparently boiled abalone and boiled the fish water over onto the stove to the extent it never came clean and had to be replaced to get rid of the smell. Shells and detritus all over the house and deck. It's not unusual. The poachers are environmental bandits decimating another species.

We spent most of yesterday replacing the pool filters. In the freezing and windy cold! But the chore is done, and the pool hopefully looks sparkling this morning—haven't ventured down yet. It's quite cold here and still windy. Not the day for swimming but we shall see.

Yesterday we had just sat down to dinner when 5 turkeys showed up in the yard. Two massive males and 3 females, all with beautiful plumage but good lord they are not beautiful birds. Glad they had their munch and then moved on.

Happy Spring.

Love,
Jane


*20 March 2022 Happy Spring! It's sunny here, but not warm.*

Dear Jane,
Turkeys have such magnificent rainbow feathers, but those snoods and wattles and warts; the head belongs on a less resplendent bird. We always seem them staggering around at Filoli and often at the reservoir. Only the one sighting on our street, so far. You really do live in a natural wonderland, complete with rugged coast and crashing surf. It's not the South Pacific, but we can drive to it from our house. That's a plus.

Congratulations on replacing your filters. A sparkly pool is an inviting pool.

Poachers (and too many politicians) behave so badly. Did you know that Jane Fonda has a PAC that's seeking to unseat pols who pander to oil and gas and coal interests? It has around $17 million in the bank now, vs the $139 million the dirty fuels industry throws at Washington. There are people who still remember her as Hanoi Jane who would oppose her cause just to right that perceived, fifty-year-old, wrong. Revenge may be a dish best served cold, but Resentment is a crippling task-mistress.

Love,
Medea


*March 23, 2022 sun. warm. Pool temp: 74°F. That really is too cold.*

Dear Medea,
You won't believe this, but I sat outside in the sun in my bathing suit. Didn't last long. Too damn hot. But I thought of you. It's really warm here. Creepy warm. Earthquake weather.

I was just on Amazon buying a few things: pepper spray, iodine pills, and digestive cookies. Oh. and bubble bath. unscented, of course. I add my own essential oils. I think Amazon might have a melt down over that combo.

Chani Nicholas's astrology for the week is dire. This week is akin to the week in March two years ago when we went into lockdown. I hope she's wrong. Biden is predicting a cyber-attack, so I downloaded a copy of our letters and backed up my computer.

I might need a nap after too much sunshine.

Love,
Jane


*24 March 2022*

Dear Jane,
That is too cold. Only with a wet suit and then only if there are hammerheads. I hope Tweed loved your walk.

I was thinking today about Kilroy and Zorro and how driven some people are to leave their mark on the world. Does anyone understand those references today? Is Banksy the new Zorro?

I bought myself a Valentine's Day present called *How to Know the Birds* by Ted Floyd. This afternoon, I (finally) carried it with me to my orange swing and opened at random to Entry Twelve, "Age-Related Plumage Variation." The bird under consideration is the White-crowned Sparrow. I learned that the plumage difference we notice in these birds is not due to sex, but to age; the white crowns develop only after their second year. Thereafter, all birds wear the crown.

Love,
Medea


*March 24, 2022 sun. cold. Well, for here, you know what I mean. I admit, were we in Chicago we'd be sitting in the sun, happy as Windy City clams.*

Dear Medea,
I read your email and thought, Valentine's Ooooo a chance to buy myself something! When is it? and then realized, oh yeah. Last month. Well, if you can, I can.

Zorro comes up a lot lately in various places which is weird. From Russian army symbols to movie heroes.

Waiting for a Tsunami Warning Test this morning. So far, all alerts are working. Always nice to know. I'll give Wordle a try now you've explained it. Seems everyone is doing it.

Swimming in cold water is good for the body but not particularly soothing at the time, that's for sure.

love,
Jane

P.S. Never heard the siren part of the warning test, the f-ing tree chippers and chain saws eternally running next door drown out everything. It's so annoying. P.P.S. I think I have the gist of Wordle. Got today's in 4 tries and 20 wasted minutes. My father used to do crosswords, the hard ones. Eventually he started copying them to a blank form without the filled in spots to make it harder. The whole exercise was lost on me but he was addicted. Also addicted to gin martinis by the way. Probably Wordle is great for memory and vocabul

    a
    R
    y
(Tweed did that, and I decided it was apt).


*25 March 2022*

Dear Jane,

The harbor phoned early this am to tell me that my boat was sinking. I dashed up and started pumping water with help from the friendly staff and the bilge pump. Three inches of dirt and sludge. Much nastiness. Sets of drenched sheets and towels and a case of fizzy water that somehow lost all of the fluid from the cans while remaining sealed. It is so disgusting. I am waiting now for one of the harbor helpers to bring an adaptor to plug in my brand-new power cord after the existing and almost-new cord seems to have arced for a mysterious reason and taken the power outlet with it. Or do those two things happen in tandem? I'm not an electrician, clearly. Anyway, after we situate the new cord (with its borrowed adaptor—who knows when the City will get around to the repair?) we shall see whether the power is ample to reset and restart the pump. Otherwise, I will come up tomorrow morning with a big straw.

Many herons and some very curious ravens have kept me company. It's a good thing we've sprung forward since it will be a while before I am finished here.

Wordle in four! Kudos, Jane!

Love
Medea

*March 25, 2022 sun. cool. No swim today. Pool temp 72'F*

Dear Medea,

I had an eventful night as well. Tweed with an upset tummy again. Poor guy. Complicated by a scary moment in the dark on our trek outside for a nighttime wee. He saw something and took off, forgetting he was on lead, ripped the lead out of my hand and was running full tilt down the driveway with the retractable lead (florescent) bouncing behind him. He must have thought he was being chased. It wasn't funny at the time, but in recalling, it was rather a cartoon moment as he came back toward me with this yellow thing clattering behind and disappeared into the woods. I ran to get the tracker and see where he was only to find it had used up all the battery and was dead. That's when I panicked, imagining him hung up on a tree stump or stuck somehow. Gene and I headed for the barn (last known sighting) and then found him, the nylon web lead broken off, the yellow reflector handle gone. Took some serious force to break that. Tweed won't talk about it.

So we got inside and ready for bed but Tweed had other ideas. Maybe the trauma of his frightening night caught up with him. We spent the next 4 hours up and down, in and out, throwing up and barking—Tweed, that is. I may be barking mad but haven't actually barked in years. It's only been three weeks since the last time and he hasn't even finished the meds! I'm thinking it's not external, but some gut issue. In this case, triggered by stress?

Did you see the speech Zelensky made asking everyone to march and rally in support of Ukraine? I went to sleep last night trying to figure out if I have any yellow and blue fabric for a flag. Maybe I'll buy one. Yesterday I donated money to a charity called Viva! in the UK who are on the ground in Poland and Ukraine rescuing dogs and cats. They assert that all of the donation goes directly to the effort, unlike Peta who won't even commit that all the $ would go to Ukraine animal efforts. Could end up paying for some protestor's fake blood or protest placards.

Good luck today. Don't forget to take photos of everything for insurance. And contact them asap. If something shows up down the road you want your ducks in a row. And floating.

Love,
Jane

*26 March 2022 Sun*

Dear Jane,

I have not contacted the insurance company yet. Perhaps the fates are sending a gentle suggestion to divest and simplify our lives.

Dylan left NYC this morning for his cross-country drive. He will arrive back home just in time to declare Max and his bride officially wed. Have you ever driven alone across country? I love the change of scenery, culture, accent— but you miss most of that if you stay on the interstate, which he'll have to do given the very short window between today and his command performance.

The finches that built their nest on the palm frond outside my family room window must have hatched babies. They chatter all morning and evening. It's melodic, hypnotic. I can't see them; I just listen.

Love,
Medea


*March 26, 2022 warmish. Sun. potential for fog.*

Dear Medea,

Here we are having emerged from this week of horrors with red eye fatigue (me) and chilblains (you) but oh my things could be so much worse, and are, for so many. My frustration increases with every scanning of the news. Deciding to make donations to various charities every few days is helping my worry-brain. But it's all so seriously not enough. Is it ok to admit that I'm all for going to war in this situation? Nothing else will stop a bully.

Meanwhile. Tweed had another bad night. I finally had a chance to sleep at 4 am, but only intermittently. He seems in decent spirits which is a plus but between eating grass and throwing up, he's what I might call on the back end, stable.

Pretty sure I will crash shortly but at the moment I've finished ordering seeds and seed potatoes from the catalog and assembled the raised bed frame. I might actually get seeds started next week if things around her calm down. I'm anxious to see what next week's astrology looks like.

I'm hoping your boat is clean and dry, but I'm worried it will be a long and difficult effort. You're going to need a serious manicure before the wedding. I hope your men-folk can take over some of the effort. Surely this can't be helping your back.

Not to neglect the birds, the ravens are visiting for food solo. I hope that means they are nesting now. At one point today, Tinker was in the front yard trying to get my attention. I had the feeling if I opened the front door, she'd march right in. Speaking of front porch action, a woman in Fort Bragg filmed her front porch and caught a mountain lion casually walk up to her front door! And this was in a neighborhood in town! From the image, it looked like a young animal. Still. Surprise!

Love,
Jane


*29 March 2022*

Dear Jane,
You are the first person to whom I'm relaying this story. It feels like a natural progression of our writing and our own observations, feelings, revelations. Dylan, as you know, is driving from Brooklyn to SF via Indianapolis, Kansas City, Denver and, and, last night, Moab. We were chatting as he was traversing the Eisenhower Tunnel. When he emerged on the other end, I heard "Holy ****" and of course my first thought was that a sleep-deprived trucker veered into his lane before regaining his consciousness, barely avoiding a fiery, bloody head-on collision. No. It was the view. The scene as you exit the tunnel apparently rivals Yosemite's reveal of El Capitan and Half-Dome at the Eastern end of the Wawona Tunnel. Worthy of a string of admiring expletives.

The three hundred mile drive on to Utah, across and through the Rockies and its various white and green landscapes unveiled majesties at around every bend. After he arrived in Moab, he beelined for Canyonlands National Park with just three hours until sunset. We hoped he'd at least squeeze in the "Big Four"— the Grand Arch, Upheaval Dome, Delicate Arch and view of the Green River.

When he reached the vista overlook for the Green River, he said he literally couldn't speak it was so magnificent, beautiful, indescribable, as breathtaking as anything he's ever seen. He talked about that feeling you and I know well, of dwelling in the world, integrating with waves and redwoods, the bristlecone pines, the ruddy cliff-faces that have millennia worth of tales to share.

I sense that he felt the ultimate humility born of that lightning bolt moment when you realize your place in the universe of all things, animate and inanimate is infinitesimally small.

Love,
Medea

# April 2022

*April 1, 2022 pollen level "extremely high" sun, cold, windy*

Dear Medea,

Ah, springtime in northern California. Pass the tissues. The dog's water bowl outside has a skim of bright yellow pollen.

Thank goodness for Dylan and his ability to see, to really see, that where he has been and where he should go have meaning and purpose and the world is up one for his coming to this point.

Tweed is recovering. I figured out how to help him on my own. That's where we are. If you're sick. Heal thyself.

Tinker is minding the nest and has been sending Burt to collect take-away.

Love,
Jane


*April 3, 2022 Sun. Cold. Wind. Pollen "extremely high"—like I didn't know that*

Dear Medea,

I've had you on my mind the past two days, imagining you in various stages of wedding mama effort and bliss. Hopefully mostly bliss. Now it's Sunday morning and you are still on the island, like the Captain and MaryAnn, I hope the crew is feted and tired but happy. The newlyweds are off someplace special and the details of the various corners of the wedding weekend will be repeated and enjoyed for years to come. Good grief you must be tired.

Today is apparently National Tweed Day. Who knew? He is doing well on my supplement diet composed mostly of ox bile and digestive aids. We've caught up on lost sleep.

Burt continues to support Tinker with trips to the feeder. The nesting tree is to the south and across the little creek that has no name, high up. Yesterday there was a serious screeching and kerfuffle that brought me outside searching the sky. I'm not sure it was Burt or if Tinker was lured from her nest but a hawk was menacing them, that's for sure. Burt, let's assume, was having none of it and with a lot of loud and harassing caws he pecked and dove and hassled the hawk away. This morning, though, I hear a hawk whistle high up in that warning way they do, so I'm afraid they will have a time of it protecting the eggs/chicks (no idea which).

Cold as it is, it is still time to plant the vegetable garden. So that's what I'll be about while I wait for you to return to habit. My friend, Baba is planting a Ukraine garden: blue and yellow pansies and violas.

Love,
Jane

P.S. Kim finished the artwork for our book jacket. She's an amazing talent!


*6 April 2022 Sunny, light breeze, 86, holding steady for the next two days.*

Dear Jane,
The other side of the wedding feels like victory. Bearing witness as Max and Haley answered "Yup!" and "Yes, sir!" to Dylan's "Do you take each other to have and hold forever" erased any lingering traces of frazzle from months and days spent organizing ferry schedules, choosing canapés and champagnes, wrangling RSVPs from the indecisive, following the directions of the dapper wedding producer, and playing musical chairs with the seating charts.

Phew. I'm still humming. The word most used to describe the event, as sometimes hackneyed as it can seem, is "authentic." Everyone behaved, including the smiley, squirmy eight-month-old, the garrulous five-year-old, the two dauntless 90-year-olds. Guests who drew the short ferry straw were obliged to arrive two hours before the ceremony; they entertained themselves by walking the perimeter of the Island, visiting the Lighthouse and climbing to its tower. Old friends reconnected. New friends shared Max and/or Haley origin stories. It was a lovefest all around. The bride glowed. The groom beamed. An ebullient future groom caught Haley's bouquet, eliciting a kiss from his boyfriend and cheers from the crowd. After dinner and wedding cake, the DJ urged us to our feet. We all danced together, including the little ones and the fearless ones, a tangle of limbs and laughter, singing along with "September" and "Uptown Funk." Max and Haley will continue to build their life from this solid foundation of love, kinship, patience and, possibly most importantly, fun.

"Authentic" fits perfectly.

Tweed healed himself as Tinker and Burt defend their nest from intruders, which means they'll soon have Tinkies if they don't already! I noticed Eurasian Collared Dove nests in three different Island trees. Two owls are roosting near the West Dock. I spied a few white egrets and the sentinel Great Blue Heron, but, alas, not their nests, which I hope only means the nests are well-camouflaged. The coming weeks will reveal all.

Have you seen *The Power of the Dog*? I'd have made a terrible, or very hungry, prairie wife.

Love,
Medea

P.S. *The Power of the Dog* is ostensibly about toxic masculinity but the message I received conveyed our inability to accept ourselves as we are.


*April 8, 2022 windy, cool, very high pollen*

Dear Medea,
Yesterday was a scorching day where the temperatures hit 80 and my breasts responded by inflating to possibly twice their size which obviously resulted in my own temperature and temper to flare. It was nasty. After concentrating enough to make a salad niçoise and put ice in my white wine we watched a stage of the Tour of the Basque country and tried not to think doomful thoughts. 80 degrees in April? Evening cooled things off and with a cool shower I managed to roll myself into bed without screaming or shedding tears. But really. Sometimes this is unendurable; still, I reflected deeply while I was falling asleep about the true grit of Ukraine's grandmothers and felt mollified if not embarrassed to be so puny.

I'm so happy that your Max and Haley's wedding went off without a hitch! That is excellent. Are your parents back home in Venice? I saw that yesterday there was severe weather in their area.

As for Tinker and Burt. Tinker is clearly on the nest and is not coming for food. Instead, I can hear her occasionally squawking at him to go pick up the take-away order and not to stop at the bar on the way home. Burt comes several times a day looking as disheveled as a middle schooler on a Saturday morning. I remember last year when the parents brought the Tinies and introduced them to me, to the food stand, and the water bowl and three of them tried to get into the water at the same time. I can't wait! To that end I checked my camera and am charging up the batteries which were dead, of course. Why is it that a camera so easily turns itself on? I can't seem to put it down without accidentally triggering the on switch. As for the four legged and furred, little madam bobcat has made herself so at home that yesterday I was standing at the kitchen sink mid-day, looked out, and there she was, not ten feet away sitting in the sun having a bath. She had picked the only patch of dirt in a grassy area where she blended into the colors so perfectly– a bit of black stick, several shades of brown to tan, a white stone– that at first, I didn't see her. After a short bath she headed along the house and surveyed the landscape looking for mice, gophers, and other small morsels for dinner. I wish her luck.

The deer are coming regularly in the evening, the herd of six seem to be five pregnant females and one juvenile female who I hope isn't pregnant but could be, given the nature of things in nature. The most obviously pregnant of the group has bits of fur falling out, perhaps she's pulling it to make a nest for hiding the fawn? I'm not sure, and apparently, she smells of something significant because the other females come up to sniff her and she chases them away like it's none of their business who had her. Her coat is brown-gray, darker than the others but I see that all of them except the young one are developing darker coats. The juvenile remains very pale tan. I hope that's a sign of her virgin status.

I have seen *The Power of the Dog* and I liked it. I usually do like Jane Campion films and expected it to be a little weird, as it was. It wasn't *The Piano* but we get the drift of her work. It certainly is a good point to make that there has been homosexuality in life since humans first decided on partnering so why shouldn't there be stories made about it in the canon of the West? What was telling was the sad spectacle of the iconic western actor who let his phobia out decrying the movie. Now he will have to sit on the naughty steps alongside Mel Gibson. Sam Elliot, in case you missed it. As for westerns in general, I do love them. Best one? *McCabe and Mrs. Miller*. A Peckinpah masterpiece.

The headline, saved for the end, of the week is that the Hermit Thrushes are singing their amazing songs, an incentive in themselves to get up early and stand outside. Please find the Irish tune *The Jug of Punch* online and give it a listen and then compare it to Cornell Labs.

Love,
Jane


*8 April 2022 Sun and low 80s shifting to filmy clouds, wind, 59. Thank you, Yves Chouinard, for my puffy parka that looks so fetching atop a sleeveless sundress.*

Dear Jane,
*The Jug of Punch.* How can you beat the Clancy Brothers version? Though Altan's lilting arrangement is worth a listen. Altan's feels more like a dream, less like a pub song sing-a-long. Cornell Lab can scarce compare to a little Irish bird singing *tou ra lou ra lou.*

I'd not heard about Sam Elliot. It sounds like his reaction is best left to the dustbin. Anyway. I'm glad that you liked the movie, and *The Piano.* Harvey Keitel won me over with his performance, brutal as it was, and though it may elicit a different sort of debate in the current climate.

Thank you for the lovely words about the wedding. The texts and letters and wishes continue to pour in. We're still high.

I can't believe your temps reached breast-billowing highs. No such luck here, though it won't be long before the weather people begin wringing hands and declaring heat advisories. Speaking of heat, the *NYT* ran a piece today about the proliferation of AirBnBs in Joshua Tree. The article naturally lit all of my fuses. But what really floored me were the comments. Readers expressed strong opposition to short-term rentals, corporate ownership of real property and tolerance of owning multiple homes. Meanwhile, governments insist that every town has a housing crisis. Who's running the zoo?

Apparently, Joshua Tree, the town, is not a town, per se, but an unincorporated part of the county whose elected "representative" has announced absolutely her fealty to the real estate pros who wine and dine her. Other comments from across the nation and world speak about loss of housing stock, affordable included, to corporate owners, foreign owners, multiple-property owners while communities disintegrate, and elected folk just can't say "no" to thirty pieces of silver. Lo. Oh. And speaking of lack of leadership, there is no water in CA, especially in the desert. But we knew that.

You're in full Spring nesting/breeding season there—we are too, but it's more subtle. The finches that have nested in the most unlikely palm frond visited multiple times today. The hummingbirds that built nests in the Podocarpus in February spend the day slurping nectar from orange candelabra agave blossoms. The Stephens? Do they have a little squirrel den someplace? They're ravenous, and the season of rebirth inspires tolerance at the bird feeders. I so want to meet your bobcat and your deer. And the Ravens. Well, and you, of course.

Love,
Medea


*April 9, 2022 windy, cool, unpleasant. Gale warning. Am I never satisfied?*

Dear Medea,
I saw the Joshua Tree piece as well. Firstly, that general area is a shameful dump of "witches' purses" (plastic garbage bags stuck in the brush) and bottles and cans. The wealthy people of Palm Springs should be ashamed of themselves to allow their wider environment to look like that. I've been twice to a shabby retreat center in Joshua Tree for 4-day sessions with the Q'ero in shaman training. Not my favorite thing but also not in my control. Dry. Oh, so dry. It's so clearly one of those places that has attracted renegades and old hippies and people with nothing but two old airstreams to rub together. The suburban sprawl of

LA encroaches with wind farms and housing developments. Why anyone would want to holiday there is beyond me. Rattlesnakes, wind, garbage, and yes, an occasional cactus.

It will be a fine thing when we can meet in person. I'm already a little bit nervous. What, for example, did Diane mean when she obliquely said, "You have to meet Medea in person."?!

We're back to March winds in April, hoping the Wind doesn't blow the promised rain off. Before I learned about March on the coast, I thought Gale Warnings only came with rain, but not so. The wind is for the trees. The pollen billows off the pines, the dead leaf material, stragglings of usnea, pinecones, twigs and branches fly through the air. There was some question last night out for a quick pee break for Tweed, whether it was such a good idea walking under 150-foot trees. Surely not.

Also, last night, three of the four deer came into the yard and made themselves at home, munching and settling down for a rest. The female I described yesterday was not with them. Is she giving birth? Time will tell. I have never before been so constrained to live in the present and, I confess, I am guilty of too often living in some "pluperfect" future, a doll's house of all things in their rightful places. As much as I write to predict, I am bound by my ignorance and ready to be surprised.

I forgot to ask if *Windsong* made it to the Island, and if so, is she staying on?

Love,
Jane


*9 April 2022 Warm, mid-70s, sunny. Spring!*

Dear Jane,

Russia's—Putin's—Ukraine desecration is nothing short of amoral. Bruce has a theory, posited after we watched one-and-a-half episodes of "Servant of the People:" is this attack some kind of small penis, Trumpian revenge for Pootie-Poot's portrayal in the Netflix series? Anything is possible.

A companion piece to the wretched Joshua Tree piece appeared in the *Florida Phoenix* today. In addition to wreaking havoc in the single-family home market, private equity and investment bankers are buying up the final frontier of affordable housing, the mobile home park. When PE/IB swoop in, lot rents suddenly double, sometimes triple. Many of the residents may own their structure but cannot fund a trebling of monthly fees. The goal, of course, is to force the residents out and repurpose the ground as "luxury condo development." That phrase should be stricken from the lexicon.

314

My grandmother lived in a mobile home. On her social security, it allowed her autonomy, dignity, and a small plot of ground to tend. It also offered community and rides into town for doctor visits and trips to Publix. What will happen to people like Nana if this trend continues?

We just never know what comes next, do we? You try to live the pluperfect existence, and then, gales. Putin. Space tourists blasting past the stratosphere. Those PG&E tree cutter guys. The Stephens, who try their damnedest to pass for sparrows. Have I mentioned that the palm across the street has nearly recovered all of its fronds? Anything is possible.

Windsong remains trapped in SF. I'll spring her during the next heat wave.

Love,
Medea

P.S. I know how you loathe the heat and dry, but the spectacle of the Joshua Tree in silhouette against a fiery desert sky as the sun sinks low and the evening breeze builds erases any perception of ugliness.


*10 April 2022 Gale force winds blowing cold—no good.*

Dear Jane,
In the face of this wind cyclone, I marvel at the intelligence of the animals. The finches that built their nest in the most perilous, in my mind, spot imaginable— the elbow of the palm frond resting up under the eave—earn an "A" for their Darwinian survival skills. The rocker out front is bashing itself to pieces against the porch stone. Bruce's ham radio antenna threatens to cave in the garage roof. My Day-Glo orange porch swing is twerking with itself in the back yard. And that tiny, fragile nest? It's still, quiet, secure.

Love,
Medea


*April 12, 2022 calm, cool. Very light breeze.*

Dear Medea,
The wind is evil. It has finally passed here. Last evening at dusk a huge cumulus cloud formed in the ocean and flew past dumping five minutes of strong rain, a bit of hail (more inland), and a final gust of wind. We're grateful for the rain in any amount and form. We are living that dystopian climate description of

violence in earth, wind, and fire. It's a scary thing to contemplate. Tomorrow you should also have a respite, but I did see on Windy that your gale was stronger than ours. And that is strange.

Burt has been dutifully braving the gale force wind to collect food for his brood (I love how that rhymes). He arrives flustered, perches on the garage peak and hangs on while the wind ruffles his feathers to the point one wonders whether they will straighten out so that he can fly. The deer have been collecting, they don't seem bothered by the wind, heads down, tails flicking. So far, Gene won't need to mow the front yard. This morning the turkeys did their bit. Are there really that many bugs or are they eating deer poop? I don't know. If they were it might explain their greasy looking feathers. Tweed is afraid of them. We noticed Tweed is also afraid of Gene's eBike which makes a gentle whirring noise. And yet, Tweed runs circles around the tractor without any qualms at all.

I made another donation to World Central Kitchens after reading a tweet in which they were feeding cats and making sure they were safe in their bombed-out building (with video, not for the faint of heart). There must be tens of thousands of abandoned cats and dogs in Ukraine. Another dreadful and dystopian consideration. Will they become feral and desperate? How do we make those in charge of NATO, including our own government, take bigger steps to intervene in this tragedy? We simply must not stand idly by hoping Putin will reverse course.

I hope your bird friends survived the wind. They don't always. Even sea gulls know to hunker down on the beach, backs to the wind, but it doesn't always work out. Nests, chicks, eggs, and birds are blown to their ends often enough. If Wind were a god, he would be as evil and indiscriminate as some other gods we know.

Love,
Jane


*12 April 2022 50 degrees and sunny, with thunder mountain clouds advancing from the west. The wind nearly blew me over as I collected the garbage cans.*

Dear Jane,
The nest still sits snug against the eave. With the windspeed waning, it has averted at least that potential natural disaster. Do squirrels eat bird eggs? One of the Stephens hung upside down to access one of the feeders, his spring breeding manhood busting out of his tummy fur. I've never actually seen squirrel privates in Full Monty until this morning. I felt a visceral trepidation, that this critter is emboldened, possibly a little bit dangerous, if not inclined to attack me directly

then to make a move on the smaller birds or their eggs. It's funny how primal we can feel when confronted with nature in the raw.

Thank you for letting me know about World Central Kitchen and its efforts to feed the animals left behind in Putin's war. Streets and shells of buildings teeming with pets abandoned by desperate Ukrainians seeking an escape from soldiers and bombs presents an unbearable dystopian image, rivaled only by footage of orphaned or unaccompanied children gazing blankly at an aid worker or clinging for life to an older sibling's backpack. I read yesterday that hundreds of these kids were swept up into cars at the Polish border and whisked off to God-knows-where to meet Devil-knows-what fate. Bruce, ever the optimist, postulates that the kids are chained in foreign basements, destined for lives as domestic servants, or far, far worse. Let's chalk that possibility up to a very dark worldview, shall we? If not for people like José Andrés and the thousands of nameless and faceless who feed the frightened, maintaining an optimistic outlook for the future of humanity would feel as tenuous as the future of polar bears on arctic ice floes.

The big excitement here this morning came when the headline blared, "Shooting on Subway in Brooklyn Injures 10." Brooklyn covers sixty-nine and a half square miles of land. Statistically, the odds of Dylan (back in Brooklyn for the final two weeks at his current job) being one of the ten is close to zero. Moms don't really give a damn about odds, though, do we? I phoned him immediately. Though it was after 9am, he sounded groggy. And safe. What would you do if you were standing on a subway car and a guy pulled out a gas mask from his backpack? It's a danger sign—but where do you go on a train packed with morning commuters and kids headed to school? Say what you may about the environmental superiority of mass transit, but as long as there are violent, crazy, opportunistic murderers, and Covid, riding on the subway is like playing Russian roulette.

After such a gloomy letter, I'd wanted to end on a light note. Scrolling the latest *NYT* headlines turned up this bright light: The eastern islands of the Weddell Sea in the Antarctic, still brimming with ice and krill, support 3.8 million breeding pairs of Adélies Penguins. It's better than nothing.

Love,
Medea

P.S. Do humans really need krill pills, taking stock from these penguins' only food source? So many battles to fight, Jane...

*April 13, 2022 overcast, rain coming, yes, I said rain! The rest of the week. Goddess let it be so.*

Dear Medea,

I'm having trouble cataloging stresses and reflexes into proper response levels. Maybe that's what everyone is dealing with and is leading to subway shooters and road rage and airplane rage and crazy fuck oligarchs and rampaging raping Russian soldiers. It's all just too much. I'm not too much of a doomscroller or calamity howler but as a woman and a mother and wife and sentient being it's quite impossible not to viscerally freak out at the idea of Ukrainian children fleeing their country with only their names and addresses written on their backs in Sharpie. I have seen, though, reporting that the people at the border helping with the evacuations are trying to be very very careful vetting people who show up to "help" and warning evacuees to be careful. Will that protect everything? Probably not, but it's not a free for all.

Meanwhile, my animal welfare buttons have been pushed as the village folk are trying to help a lost German Shephard dog seen wandering up the road from town. Several attempts have been made to befriend him, as yet unsuccessful. Good, kind, caring people are working on the problem. I'm holding my breath for good news.

Not to end on an ugly note, but rodent genitalia is rather gross. The image I have of Stephen hanging upside-down Full Monty does bring a chuckle though.

It has just started to rain lightly. My joy at the rain is tempered by worry for the lost dog. It's cold and going to be colder tonight.

Love,
Jane


*14 April 2022 57 and rain. Thank the stars it held off until after the wedding. Skies, you may open wide and let it pour.*

Dear Jane,

Apologies for the squirrel image; it may seem juvenile and unbecoming a mature, learned adult. But. Seeing Stephen like that really caught me off-guard, like I'd walked into the wrong bedroom in a Vegas hotel. Yikes.

A prettier sight, and one that may displace that other, is the male junco feeding his nestmate seed fragments, tenderly depositing them from the tip of his beak into hers, waiting, open and ready to commit, for the season, at least. Another primal moment for me, this display of care and concern for the mother of his tinies. Forget, please, that she is perfectly capable of snatching her own food from the confines of the feeder; his chivalry reminds me that being tough and self-sufficient has its place but allowing others to spoil us sometimes feels right, welcome, luxurious even.

A more Instagram-able sight confronted me at the checkout line at Safeway this morning. This Safeway fails to pipe any decent (read: danceable) music at all through the aisles. The woman behind me in the check-out line righted that wrong. As she approached, I could hear a bass beat, and "Get down..." She put her Easter Peeps on the conveyor, three boxes, one magenta, one purple, one yellow. She turned up the volume. The device (o would that it were a Walkman!) belted out "Boogie Oogie Oogie." She shook her groove thing, oblivious or perhaps totally aware that the guys behind her and the cashier were smirking. She wore her hair in a lavender crew cut, army green pants, a flowered t-shirt and a fanny pack. She did the Freak under an imaginary disco ball, sprays of colored light sparkling in a halo around her. Instead of bombs and lost children and crazy fucking presidents, we took a little trip back in time, to the relative safety and sanity of 1978. Thank you, Disco Lady.

Whose dog is this German Shepherd? Did someone abandon it? Was it frightened by thunder or chainsaws or shotgun blasts and ran for cover? The good Samaritans must prevail. The Times ran a gut-busting photo of a young man in a heavy overcoat and beanie standing in the rubble of yet another Russian fuckover clutching his gray and white long-haired cat. Will he be able to carry himself and his cat to safety? Will the cat bolt when it hears another cluster bomb explode? Will the boy risk his life to search for his friend? Why is Putin such an irredeemable dick?

The birds that visit the small conical feeder are active this afternoon. House Sparrows mostly, a junco, the massive jay that invariably swings the spiral feeder so forcefully that it unlatches from the hook and disappears inside the foliage below. They all are keeping quiet counsel, or maybe their songs are muffled by the gray gloom that hangs over the garden, over the neighbors' gardens, over the western hills. You would love my world today. Here comes the rain, again.

Love,
Medea


*April 14, 2022 light rain all day.*

Dear Medea,
The rain was so welcome and so unusual that I responded like a bear and felt like crawling into bed and sleeping all day. As it was, the day was small and soft and more attuned to reading and thinking than any overt actions. It didn't stop Burt

from showing up on time for breakfast looking only a little wet. The Jays, Gray and Blue, wait for feeding time as well. And there is a small bird in the trees who signals a beautiful clear trilling when the food arrives, but I can't tell which bird is making such music. Surely not the Blue, complainer that he is.

Good news! The German Shepherd has been reunited with her family. Word is that she traveled a fair distance from the ridge top and was gone for several days. Maybe that's why I'm so tired today. It was so emotional and brought back sad memories and feelings of helplessness. I don't know the story of how she went missing or why. It's such a small community that probably the word will come out.

Love,
Jane


*15 April 2022 Warm in the sun, 63 degrees, breezy. A good Good Friday and launch to Passover week.*

Dear Jane,
A one-day rain break sent me outdoors to survey the garden work that awaits early next week, before the blessed rain starts again. Numerous globes of sage and purple artichokes weigh down their stalks. An early strawberry begged to be plucked and eaten. The lettuces are near the end of their producing lives. Celery is sprouting leaves, as is the cauliflower. The chives asked to be snipped and added to cheddar biscuits. I can do that. Last week, I marveled at how last June's massive pruning still seemed to be holding. After these recent rains, forget it: the grasses and hosta and euphorbia exploded across the front lawn. The bottlebrush trees sent scads of spears skyward with their red and pink pillows of bloom. White and purple irises popped up in few the bare spots. It's lush and exquisite and will demand attention sooner than I thought.

A few lavender rhododendron flowers have poked their heads out from the green, and maroon and gold alstroemeria blanket the beds in the back. Somehow, I missed the appearance of the coral roses; they are almost ready for deadheading. Probably as a result of a too-severe haircut last summer, my bromeliads skipped their vermillion-throat display in September—but I just noticed that at least the few on the back hill are glowing brilliant red in the afternoon sunlight. Yay!

A quartet of Golden-crowned Sparrows arrived for the early-bird special at the feeder. With their dark bandit masks and bright yellow mohawks, they look like punk pre-teens trying to look tough. It's adorable.

Dylan is officially between gigs as of 5pm today, headed for his self-styled, albeit brief, sabbatical at 5am tomorrow. I'm jealous, impressed, elated; he's visiting three countries I've never seen. The best kinds of lessons we can learn from our kids.

Love,
Medea


*April 17, 2022 Happy Easter Bunny. Sun, mild. Ham's in the oven.*

Dear Medea,
Your garden's profusion sounds absolutely heavenly (in keeping with the day). We have very few "planted" things because deer would only eat them, but they eschew rhododendron, rosemary, tea tree, bottle brush, and lavender so we have that outside the little fenced area. I noticed small bees at the hawthorn blossoms this morning and wanted to sit outside under the tree for a bit and try to recall all the words to Lake Isle of Innisfree, but sadly, various annoying chores interrupted the reverie. Another day, perhaps, and a cheat sheet for the poem.

Yesterday Tweed and I went out in the evening to be greeted by a hellish screeching that made Tweed race toward the sound barking and yet looking a bit nervous. Whatever it was, it took off into the woods between the house and barn and Tweed backed up and reconsidered his approach. I was able to call him back. It could have been a very noisy fox, they can sound alarming, or it could have been a mountain lion. I have heard them sound that way here before. I wasn't taking any chances and retreated back to the house.

Traveling vicariously through adult children can be wonderful and sometimes challenging. They older they get, the easier it is. I guess I missed the punchline of Dylan leaving his job? Will he move west now, then?

Love,
Jane


*17 April 2022 Cold and bright, 55 degrees. A day to ponder resurrection.*

Dear Jane,
Tweed reminds me of high school bravado. Race toward the ruckus! Oh! There may be blood! Retreat! Retreat! You've raised one smart dog. When you know what the critter is, I hope you'll let me know. Every time you mention the foxes, I think of those that the Aldea Mar developers killed off. I read today in the

*Times* about a fifty-two-year-old software engineer, a holdover tenant in a 128-unit Borden Dairy building-turned-apartment complex on the Upper East Side that its new owners intend to raze and replace with eleven units, prices starting at $8.5 million. The developers offered him $30k to leave quietly. The Aldea Mar developers just killed the holdovers and built new condos next door to my childhood home.

Foxes. Tenants. All expendable in the eternal quest for more. What would Jesus have to say about that?

You always have the best poem references. I remember the words to "Flander's Fields" and "The Road Not Taken." "The Owl and the Pussycat." Oh. And e.e. cummings' "The Germ": "Do you, my poppet, feel infirm? You probably contain a germ." A Covid poem if ever there was one. It's a motley amalgamation of remembered verse. But set the poem to music, and it sticks. "Desiderata" comes to mind. And "Romeo and Juliet" by Dire Straits. Well, and pretty much anything that comes on the radio, much to Bruce's chagrin when we take a road trip. Did I tell you that I snagged two Early Bird tickets to Outside Lands, resurrecting our annual music festival tradition?

Sedge, from what genesis I know not, threatened to insinuate itself, into not only multiple, varied spots in the ground, but into the container gardens as well. So many of our plants self-propagate. Everywhere. It's a beautiful example of nature's way. But the sedge. It's spiky and insistent. It does not respect boundaries. So, I took my spade and big fork and wrassled those suckers out of the soil. To atone, I planted tomatoes, two Early Girls and one Sweet One hundred. A Dark-eyed Junco and a finch conducted a song contest, which kept me entertained.

How did I miss mentioning that Dylan is moving back, for an unknowable period, to the Bay Area? I am forever grateful that his time in New York makes this city now familiar, endlessly mysterious, eternally approachable. And he visited a flamingo sanctuary in Bonaire today. That's my boy.

Love,
Medea


*April 18, 2022 overcast, light breeze. Rain coming, yes please.*

Dear Medea,
The headline here is that my neighbor, Jane–not to be confused with my own alter ego–reported in this morning with sad news that a bear visited two nights ago and tore the walls off her chicken coop and killed all her hens. Sigh. I'm so sorry about this. Such a reminder of the line between domestic and wild. This also explains Tweed tearing off again last evening in the falling light, nose

to the ground, after something, and then suddenly there were a series of loud "coughing" huffing sounds that alarmed me to a panic. Tweed appeared out of breath shortly after, luckily. I'd assumed the noises were Tweed coughing, though hardly likely since he was pretty far away at the bottom of the property toward the bridge, and Jane's. I love that we have a bear, and I'd love to see it from afar, but the bear is a good reminder that there is more wild here than we allow caution to, and it's not their fault, it's our human encroachment.

This morning there was some medium size scat belonging to a carnivore of some sort—probably smaller than Tweed and bigger than the fox-bobcat?—sitting on the driveway. How do I know it's a carnivore? It's black with old blood even though freshly laid.

I think a little exposure to NYC for Dylan is a good thing, but I'm happy he is coming back to the family environs. We all need family close now. It's tempting to become inured to danger and temper and charge through life like a pissed off New Yorker, but do we really want that energy in our own kin? Especially as a persona, not a natural archetype. I'm always baffled by being proud of that. How far down the road of thick skinned did they get for that to be a good thing? It's like all the patterns of ethnic animosity that layered one over the other over years of immigrant settlement is thrown into a collective pot of "we're just all really pissed off." And yet, are they? If they are, then do something about that, and if they aren't then why make that the thing they agree on? I don't get it.

As for poems, your collection is impressive. So eclectic! How do you get through "In Flanders Field" without sobbing? I do love the folk song taken from that though, and if I need a good cry, it's the perfect prompt. As I've mentioned before, Dylan Thomas' "Do Not Go Gentle into That Good Night" also makes me desolately sad and even though it should be a pretty easy poem to memorize, it's almost impossible for me to do so. You're right about songs, though, I have some really awful lyrics from my youth rattling around in valuable brain real estate.

Love,
Jane


*18 April 2022 Sunny giving way to angry granite clouds that now spill thin veils of rain—the scent more pronounced than the* pit-a-pat.

Dear Jane,
My seventh-grade teacher assigned *Flanders* as a memorization project. Had we studied WWI yet? Perhaps, but only in passing. And the poet, John McCrae, served in that war, and died in 1918. In the face of the catastrophe in Ukraine, the poem offers a grim reminder of the sacrifices every soldier, every citizen

faces during a war. I wonder whether any current seventh-grade teachers have read this poem, or asked students to consider its depth? "If ye break faith with us who die/We shall not sleep..." Nor should we.

A question about luring wild animals to our yards: could your friend, Jane, face misdemeanor charges for keeping hens in an easily-breachable pen, taunting bears and coyotes, bobcats and hungry feral dogs? As we've learned, thanks to Gene's (annoying, but honest) friend, feeding or enticing the wild ones in our state of residence is a misdemeanor. This includes leaving peanuts for the Stephens, kibble for Tinker and Burt, suet cakes for the chickadees and Dark-eyed Juncos and woodpeckers and ravens and and and. Could this be the infraction that finally brings down Amazon, selling all manner of bird feed and hen pens to CA residents? What about the beloved owner of the wild bird store where we locals flock to find feed and feeders? Could she face fines, or worse?

My cynical self says that when stealing under a thousand bucks' worth of chicken and frozen pizza and beer from Safeway remains non-prosecutable, we remain above reproach. And, as you point out, the birds/bears/coyotes/deer are simply treading where they've trodden for eons—it's we who impose upon their territory. So, your honor, I maintain that rather than committing an infraction in feeding these animals, we right a wrongheaded wrong conceived in the cold stone halls of the legislature, where certain interest groups deposit large sums of money in return for permission to despoil pristine landscapes, therein displacing the rightful residents thereof.

Your verdict?

Love,
Medea


*April 19, 2022 overcast becoming rain. Yes, please. Elk.*

Dear Medea,
My verdict? Feed. And not guilty. Obviously, we are careful and mindful of our place in the grand scheme of this synchronous world we occupy. If that makes us special, then I feel sorry for the need to make these laws of obvious behavior. Don't feed chocolate to dogs, don't put rat poison out for rats, don't give bubblegum to a bear, don't leave aluminum foil smeared with pork chop and BBQ sauce out by the grill overnight (or the Thanksgiving dinner turkey out on the porch either—I know someone who did that and found a bear eating it and I confess to being guilty of putting the leftovers in the trunk of the car, but at least it was in the garage.) This is a plea for processual logic. Can't we each just agree to think every now and then? I think it's the least we can do. Without

hurting any racial group, I think I can say "the animals were here first." I'm quite certain the ravens think of me as their property, not vice versa.

The report from next door is that the bear (we are assuming she is female, I have no idea why) returned to the destroyed coop last night and rummaged around some more. Farther down the lane, Marilyn says she (the bear) tipped over her compost bin, and another neighbor across the street from me to the north also reported a rummaging bear over the weekend. Tweed and I were outside this morning, I was potting seeds, and suddenly Tweed was gone. The tracker showed me he was down at the bridge and headed for the chicken coop. He ignored my calls, the rascal. I finally had to get in the car, in my pjs, by the way, and drive down to where he was. He saw me and ran into the bushes—guilty as charged. Back in the car and home, a little bit chagrined, he has been attentive ever since. Thank you Findster for making a tracker app that works perfectly every time!

The official tally for the past few days is fox, bobcat, mountain lion, bear. (Saw the first two and heard the second.) And this afternoon, for bird entertainment, I saw a lone Canada Goose flying north, cackling up a racket. I suppose this means summer is inevitable. I hope you're happy.

Love,
Jane

*19 April 2022 Rain at dawn. Sun, blue sky, wispy clouds, low 60s from mid-morning, on. More rain to come. Mayflowers assured.*

Dear Jane,
Tweed's rascally nature makes him sound like a cat. So curious about the hen pen that he can't contain himself. That bear is a night-ranger, right? May Tweed remember his shame and stay close to you henceforth. If that bear is female, she probably has cubs...

Big wildlife news here: the raven figured out how to access the suet feeder! Is this the same raven that thudded in obvious frustration from branch to branch in search of one that would hold it close enough to peck into the food? I confess that this raven looks like the other raven. Nevertheless, it located a branch substantial enough to sustain it for a few minutes—and it must have been hungry, because every other time I've spied the raven at the bird tree, it flies away empty-beaked. As for the tree itself, it's showing signs of some sort of distress, with wilted leaves lacking in chlorophyll. Did I injure the tree by attracting all these birds? I hope that's not nature's way.

Thanks for absolving us of animal endangerment. Unlike any candidate who comes to mind at the moment, your reelection to the nature judiciary is assured.

We finished watching "Servant of the People" last night; not because we are disinterested in subsequent seasons, but because Zelensky was elected to office before a second season could launch. Story lines dangle, apparently forever. I can't help but wonder where those actors are now; after twenty-three episodes, I'm invested in them, concerned for their safety—especially the children.

Love,
Medea

*21 April 2022 63, sunny, shaving cream clouds approaching. More rain!*

Dear Jane,
The rain last night sounded like my favorite Florida storms, especially the patter on the palm fronds just outside my window. The promised hail has yet to arrive, but Bruce parked his car in the garage, just in case.

Tomorrow, we celebrate Earth Day, fifty-two years after its launch. Fifty-one years after Marvin Gaye lamented the sorry state of the planet in "Mercy Mercy Me." Forty-nine years after the O'Jays pondered the evil of greed in "For the Love of Money." Just sayin'.

I know that Tweed is not feeling up to snuff. Ingested deer poop and intestinal tracts make for strange, uncomfortable bedfellows. Thinking of you both, of our dear Gaia, of the brave people of Ukraine.

Love,
Medea

*April 22, 2022 Sunshine.*

Dear Medea,
Forgive my absence but sleepless nights and sick dogs don't inspire flowing prose. I think we have passed the crisis once again and are on the mend. We were just outside for a walk and a bit of ball and Tweed did pretty well. I heard a racket of ravens to the north (so not the direction of Tinker's nest) and then saw a hawk pursued by an angry raven high in the sky, pecking and scolding and now and then reversing order. I hope her eggs weren't disturbed, and all is well. Beautiful sight, that hawk. Made the raven look small. Speaking of ravens,

Jane next door says the eggs haven't hatched. She says when they do they make a huge ruckus, so she'll let me know.

Pause: Burt just flew by the window, low, arcing to take the corner. We were just outside; don't know why he didn't arrive then.

Last night when I fed the ravens, they both came! Very briefly. Burt came back but Tinker came only for a moment to eat and then disappeared. It was nice to see her. Reassuring. Perhaps after watching the hawk and raven duke it out in the sky, it'd be best if Tinker stayed home and feathered her nest.

I heard an interview on NPR with Robin Wall Kimmerer. She sounded so fragile and yet so wise. I know I've read *Braiding Sweetgrass* but I think I want to read it again. I read it before I worked deeper into my own animism. There will be much to relearn and cherish and it's a chance to step respectfully closer to the wisdom of the Native American ethos that deserves so much attention right now. That energy is rising.

Love,
Jane


*April 22, 2022 Sunshine, rain, sunshine, rain.*

Dear Jane,
Such a relief to know that Tweed is on the mend. These loved ones test our capacity for faith and resilience. Loki has been sneezing. Bruce thinks he has Covid. But then Bruce, love him as I do, thinks everything that sneezes has Covid.

We're watching parallel birds. And we saw a crow attack a Turkey Vulture four times its size, full on, in mid-flight. Suicide mission? I suspect s/he defended a nest. Or maybe just feeling feisty? We also heard a hawk, then saw the hawk, flying its solo spiral up, then down, then up, catching the drafts as they wafted through the sky.

The Gamble Garden in Palo Alto offered tours of its own grounds and five local, old Palo Alto gardens as a spring launch. My friend Betty and I roamed the gravel paths, marveling at the snow-white dogwood and variegated euphorbia, cabbages so massive that each one could easily produce cole slaw for a hundred people. Or kimchee. The rain fell in soft veils, followed by longer stretches of bright blue sky. How many succulent varieties exist? It seems that every time I visit a garden, another introduces itself. The garden store sells a tomato plant whose fruit wears a purple crown and a yellow tummy. Don't you want to taste that tomato?

I'm glad you spent time with Robin Wall Kimmerer. *Braiding Sweetgrass* sits beside my bed, waiting for a long, uninterrupted spell of time. Her essays remind that when we listen to the land and respond to its needs, the results are mutually beneficial.

Love,
Medea

*April 23, 2022 sun. dewy. Grass green and new mown.*

Dear Medea,
In reporting the story of the hawk and raven high in the sky yesterday, I started thinking about how much bigger the "hawk" was, and I'm going to conclude here that it was an eagle. Not far-fetched since we have had eagle sightings and there was an eagle's nest at the bottom of our road ½ mile from here. It was so much bigger than the raven, it seems likely. Yesterday had another treat in store, with a late afternoon visit from missy fox who appeared from the bushes and skittered her way toward the feeding station as if she knew exactly where she was going, wary though she was. No food to find so she peed on it instead. I haven't seen a fox in that way, usually they are high tailing it out of sight, but she was unaware of my watching, and it was fun to see her markings, so very like the bobcat in many ways, except for the bushy gray tail. She's careful but bold. It doesn't escape me that I should move the raven's feeding to higher ground. Too many four-legged friends are finding it.

Tinker and Burt both came to visit this morning at the same time. Is this a sign that the eggs have hatched? Tinker ate and left quickly after having a drink from the water bowl. I hope all is well. She looked fine, though thinner.

Tomorrow is raised bed planting day. The weather is due to be fine for such things. No seedlings showing in my windowsill pots yet. I've never planted anything from seed directly sown outdoors. Wish me luck.

Love,
Jane

*24 April 2022 70 and still, shorts weather, mostly.*

Dear Jane,
Your furred visitors sure have interesting manners. They excrete on all of your offerings. After watching the Stephens and the single gray squirrel for nearly a year, I've yet to see them soil the suet. What does it all mean?

The idea of an eagle excites all of my noble bird synapses. Even though we "rescued" them from the brink of extinction—I remember fretting over that as a young person—the eagle remains one of those remarkable sightings. So, hooray for your eagle, but only as long as it spares Tinker and Burt and their as-yet-to-be seen young.

On my walk today, the bird chatter in a certain one-block area sounded like a rowdy soccer crowd; highly unusual. With Merlin's sound ID activated, the verdicts for likely crooners poured in: Lesser goldfinch, House Finch, Dark-eyed Junco, Spotted Towhee, Anna's Hummingbird, Black-capped Chickadee, Bewick's Wren, Brown-headed Cowbird, Oak Titmouse. Phew. All of those birds in such a tiny space. I heard them all, singing in near-unison, but the only visible two were the wren and the goldfinch—not that I'm complaining, as the goldfinch's bright lemon chest looked as regal as a peacock against the deep red of the bottlebrush from which it fed. Merlin also identified a Cedar Waxwing. I've shared my admiration for this elusive (to me) bird with you. I stared into the branches of every oak, birch, cedar, even palm. But, alas, no waxwing sighting. Still, I felt buoyed to hear so many different birds, on a day when no other sound ruptured the air.

And this is news to dance to: the palm-formerly-known-as-headless I've re-christened as "Lazarus." It's not quite as showy as its lot-mate, but its fronds have graduated from stubs to fans. Take that, thwarted tree killers.

Love,
Medea


*April 25, 2022 chilly, high clouds*

Dear Medea,
What joy to hear so many varied birds! And thanks for reminding me to use Cornell labs when I'm outside! Yesterday's avian treat was to see an osprey rise up from the high tree cover to the west, surely rising out of the river mouth or the ocean itself and as he gained altitude, I could see a captive wriggling in his talons. A fish! Poor thing, it wriggled but to no avail, it was caught. A fine dinner for some nestlings. No sign of ravens here all day until evening when Burt came by briefly. I think they are keeping close to the nest, perhaps there are hatchlings but definitely there is danger as I have seen both the hawk—in the front yard hunting—and the eagle high is the sky again. What a threatening world it is.

I'm happy, and exhausted, to report that Tweed is back to normal, or his normal because there isn't really any such thing as normal, right? We are all who we are and none of us is the same. A bit of Monday morning philosophy.

What will the week bring? Taking my phone and Cornell labs outside to get some inspiration.

Love,
Jane


*26 April 2022 Brisk, breezy, milky sky. A good day to huddle with the cats.*

Dear Jane,
All of life faces such peril, and exhibits reassuring resilience. In a popularity contest between the ravens, the ospreys and the eagles, how could you choose? The nestlings, though, would always win in my polls. They deserve a chance to soar.

Tweed is back to normal. That's welcome news. Too many of my familiars are ailing from everything from a "bad cold" to skin cancer. The body does heal itself, usually, partially. Except when it decides to rebel.

In the Marina yesterday, a wedge of gray-brown pelicans passed overhead, perhaps headed out beyond the Golden Gate to where the fishing boats gather. The blue herons, so abundant a couple of months ago, must be guarding their nests. A lone, emerald-headed mallard squawked and honked as it waddled along the dock; I wondered whether it lost its way since I've never seen a mallard at the harbor, but plenty of them on the lake at the Palace of Fine Arts across Marina Boulevard. Maybe even ducks need a change of scenery sometimes.

Dylan just landed in Iceland. The second of three countries on his itinerary I've never toured.

Love,
Medea


*April 27, 2022 cold. Sunny. Wind.*

Dear Medea,
Tinker and Burt came yesterday for food, and again this morning. I'm sure this is significant, but of what? I took my phone outside in the morning with Cornell Labs turned on and had fun with the results: Hairy Woodpecker, Steller's Jay, Wilson's Warbler, American Robin, Hermit Thrush, Dark-eyed Junco, and Pacific Wren. I love this app!

Wait. Dylan is in Iceland now? What happened to Guatemala? Costa Rica? Is he traveling alone?

Love,
Jane


*28 April 2022 Still cold, windy, unfit for humans. Only five degrees difference between the temperature here and in Reykjavik!*

Dear Jane,

Yes, Dylan is circumnavigating solo around Iceland. The photos he's sending show a stark landscape, no trees but much texture. Waterfalls everywhere. A geyser. Slate gray, stormy sky melting in to the stony ground, with remnants of winter's snowfall, and pops of spring's pale green vegetation. Even the sea water looks like granite. While it's not the candy colors of the Caribbean that I'm prone to prefer, there is a quiet, contemplative quality to the monochromatic scenery. I hope he's taking notes.

Two nuthatches have returned to the feeders! I'd missed their tiny little bullet bodies, their nubby little heads, the white stripe along their eyes, and the way they dangle from the wire food cage. They share the stage with two different woodpeckers, a Hairy and a Nutall's, the latter wearing a full red cap. Even though the woodpeckers have become regulars, I get a tingle each time I spot one. The Nutall's pried a large chunk of food from the square and carried it in its dart-beak up to a dead pine tree on my neighbor's property and I watched it stuff the morsel into a cavity inside the wood.

Have you heard of Dr. Doug Tallamy and his "Homegrown National Park" movement? There are warriors out there, Jane. Dr. Tallamy is a professor of entomology at U. Delaware. After he bought a ten-acre parcel carved from a former farm in Pennsylvania, he began searching for caterpillars. He found none. He set one of his students on a caterpillar quest and she discovered that the preference for lawns (and concrete) and an emphasis on exotic over native plants have wreaked havoc on the caterpillar population. Of course, that tumbles down to the butterfly population, the bird population—the whole biosphere. So, he and his wife began planting their property with natives. He now counts over one thousand different species of resident caterpillars. His quest with HNP is to eliminate half of the forty million acres of lawn space across America, and in so doing, inviting the caterpillars (and butterflies and birds) back into our lives.

Listening to the very passionate doctor speak about his project, I learned that 90% of caterpillars eat only one kind of plant. Did you know that? Plants (apparently notoriously...my science ignorance showing again) excrete noxious-tasting substances to ward off those who would feast on its leaves. BUT! Certain plants remain tasty to certain caterpillars and those bugs eat, live, reproduce and cocoon, all within the bounds of this one type of plant. Looking around my own yard, I realize the only caterpillar I've ever seen is an inchworm. And the inchworm becomes a moth, which I've rarely seen. Either I'm not examining my plants carefully enough, or my plants do not attract caterpillars. Or, the birds pluck the bugs off the leaves before I notice. Another fun fact: the protein and carotenoid content of a caterpillar is off the charts, and the malleability so squishy it is the preferred nestling food for chickadees—the parent just shoves that green sucker down its baby's throat. Anyway, I registered as a "Homegrown National Park" and will add a suggested native plant, the San Bruno Mountain Golden Aster to my garden; unfortunately, Bruce is wildly allergic to the monarch-loving milkweed we used to grow.

It looks like we're headed for a rumble with Russia. Retreat into the Merlin app sounds like the best antidote for those of us who watch in horror from the sidelines.

Love,
Medea


*April 28, 2022 Sun, cool. A little less wind. Yet typical of May.*

Dear Medea,
Yesterday, I watched Tinker forage for food without my help. She spent half an hour hopping around the yard, often darting this way and that and eating whatever she caught. I have no idea what, but perhaps moths or small flying bugs? So, take that, critics! These birds are fine and dandy. As for caterpillars, I often see the beautiful orange furry ones which I've assumed create Monarch butterflies, but can that be true? I'm afraid I slept through science class. We also have inch worms, seems like all oaks do. Any moth was once a caterpillar. Planting for them, as for bees, and birds, is a very proper thing and enhanced by planting native species. Observation has taught us that the things that will grow and be happy are the natives: the rhododendrons, the ferns, the pines and firs. Makes sense.

Today (drum roll please) I went to the grocery store for the first time in two years. Put on my big girl panties and ventured out. It was great! I really enjoyed being inspired by spotting something I hadn't thought of cooking or eating. Talked to the wine buyer about rosé wines and bought a few to try. Planned a spur of the moment Mother's Day meal for myself. It was a turning point in my process of the pandemic, I think, in keeping with the solar eclipse coming on Saturday which, apparently, is a positive moment of opportunity to shift. Are you ready?

Let's hope Russia is ready. A shift for the positive is long overdue. I loved seeing teenagers on the news at school in Polish schools, smiling and looking like happy teens, welcomed by their classmates.

I've never been to Iceland, but it is a compelling landscape with a mythology that is wonderful and amazingly linked to the land. The roots might be Viking, but the land made and holds the fairies in the landscape in a real way, alive each day. It's a fine thing.

Love,
Jane


*29 April 2022 Sunny, 67, which, lacking wind, feels pretty toasty.*

Dear Jane,
Your expedition to the market is welcome news! It's a big step, and reaped many benefits for you—what will you prepare for Mother's Day? We used to make eggs benedict; the boys' proficiency in making intact poached eggs rivals that of any Michelin-starred chef. Perhaps I'll put a bug in Max's ear; Dylan will be in LA, enroute to Guatemala.

You'll find it amusing that, rather than the assiduous note-taking I'd hoped for, Dylan is living in the moment. Yesterday, he sent eighteen photos, more chromatic this time as the sun was shining. Glaciers, coastline, something that looks like an underwater cave, and a few black cylinders that remind me of Devil's Postpile near Mammoth. "Looks beautiful! Where are you?" I texted. "I don't actually know. A glacier. Haha," he replied. He's not mentioned a fairy sighting. Yet. Though they've no doubt had a look at him.

Two eclipses this year, but not for us, it appears. Tomorrow's eclipse favors the Southern Ocean and parts of South America. Imagine being an ancient mariner and watching the sun disappear while you're surrounded by nothing but ocean and horizon and a crew of restless sailors. Yikes. On October 25th, 86% of Russia sunlight will be snuffed out by the moon. Sending a plea to the universe that Ukraine is safely out of the dark wrought by the Bear by then.

I'm dashing to the Delta to toil for the weekend. Highs expected in the upper 70s. Hallelujah.

Love,
Medea

P.S. Tinker could be the symbol for female resilience after childbirth. She's an inspiration.

*May 2022*

*May 1, 2022 Happy Beltaine. Sun. cool. Light breeze.*

Dear Medea,

As my mother's perpetual calendar noted, "hooray hooray, it's the first of May, outdoor fucking begins today." I hope there are appropriately pagan relationships blooming this day inside as well as out.

I'm still trying to figure out the logic in Dylan's itinerary, but who am I to judge, even if I was a travel agent for a while. Definitely all in favor of lapping up the world as much as possible, fearlessly, openly, and with a big heart.

As for me, my gallivanting days are over but the memories simmer. After my foray to the greater local world on Thursday I received all sorts of dire emails from friends and family suggesting I get boosted for the second time before I do that again. OK. Point taken. Tomorrow, Gene and I will get our second boosts. The Covids, as Bob Roll calls them, are going to chase us all until it's over.

On the safe home front, Tinker and Burt are coming together for food at least once a day and I'm seeing Tinker out and about at other times as well. I am assuming this means the chicks are hatched. Once yesterday she was here and then suddenly took off squawking with righteous indignation back to the nest, hopefully in time. Last night when Tweed and I went out just before dark, we discovered 5 tortilla chips by the water bowl. Awwww. A gift! We'd seen Burt with something in his mouth earlier in the day and wondered what it was. It was such a touching moment that I made Gene come outside and see for himself. He was duly weepy. I left the chips in place, not having a spare hand to collect them in any case. A middle of the night foray for Tweed showed that the chips were gone and in their place? A fox scat, floating in the water bowl. What a funny bunch.

This morning Tinker and Burt came for breakfast and when I walked to the platform Tinker cooed and murmured to me. Burt doesn't talk to me. It's lovely to be loved, isn't it?

Speaking of Bob Roll and cycling, the Giro d'Italia starts next Saturday! Yippee! It's so much fun to watch, to see Italy, to ignore politics…can't wait.

Hope you've had a good time on the island doing your chef duties.

Love,
Jane

*3 May 2022 Warm and sunny, a perfect day for recovering in the back yard.*

Dear Jane,

Somehow, the weekend away cooking for friends landed me back home with a raging fever. Not Covid—I've taken the tests—but something that kept me horizontal for twenty-four hours. I'm crawling back to life, slowly. The good news is that I spent some time in the back yard, just reading and listening, and remembered that sometimes all you have to do to find peace is to open the door and step outside.

We had an irrigation guy here this morning, Dom. He and I were talking about my tiny speck of lawn, which is more like a postage-stamp crabgrass party plaza for the gophers. He suggested I stop watering it. I told him the critters have taken it over anyway, so that's a fine idea. "Yeah! There are so many birds and squirrels back there I thought I was in a national forest!" He noticed! My heart warms thinking about what the leafy and furry things give to us all.

Did I tell you that Dylan has decided that Iceland (45 degrees, raining) is his favorite place in the world? And Max is so happy to be in New York for work, where the current forecast is 50 and drizzle, followed by cold and gray? My beloved sun shone for me here today so I could, with heaps of gratitude, take the ancient remedy for flu-like bugs: a right bake of the head and chest. I'll absorb another dose tomorrow.

No one (ahem, Bruce) fed the birds while I toiled, so the feeders hung, limp and lifeless, swinging idly in the wind. The bird tree, forlorn. The birds... curious or patient or nonplussed? The first critter to find the refreshed feeders, Stephen, took a cheek full before I politely shooed him back to the fence. The Nuttall's Woodpecker and the Hairy Woodpecker both carried bits back to their respective tree stashes. The Oak Titmouse arrived with its trilly, almost machine-gun song. I sat too close to the fuchsia and two of the hummingbirds tried to peck my eyes out. Or so it seemed. I moved my chair.

Love,
Medea

P.S. Roe. I am too sick at heart to talk about it yet.


*4 May 2022 Another clear blue super-sunshiny day, 72 degrees.*

Dear Jane,

I forgot to wish you a Happy Beltaine. May Day was such fun when I was little: festivities and pretty dresses. We sashayed around the Maypole with ribbons crossing. May Day in Florida offered one last chance for the heat sensitive to frolic outdoors before the humidity soared and the mosquitoes descended. You would have hated growing up in Florida. I somehow survived and loved it.

I just passed my third Covid test and am ostensibly Covid-free, but honestly my head feels like it's being pounded from within by tiny, evil fairies wielding sledge hammers. Staying awake requires Herculean effort. Bruce said my nighttime coughing sounded like a TB ward. In the past fifteen minutes, I've seen two emails from people who were exposed to Covid at their first in-person meetings since lockdown. This virus is not finished with us yet.

Dylan saw an Arctic fox on a hike yesterday. A cute and snuggly little ball of cloud-white fur nestled in a bed of tundra, against a snow-streaked slate gray mountain backdrop. I forgot to ask if he's heard the Iceland band that was selected to compete in Eurovision in Italy this year. It's acoustic. Systur, three singing sisters and their drummer brother, presenting *Með Hækkandi Sól*, which apparently means, "We're so over winter, let's welcome the sun." Art imitating life. I'd not heard of Eurovision until *Eurovision Song Contest: The Story of Fire Saga*, Will Ferrell's movie, came out last year, but the spectacle is older than I am and it made both ABBA and Celine Dion household names. What is the likelihood of a quartet of Icelandic acoustic siblings winning Eurovision? We'll know on the 10th of May!

The bug is winning, so I'll close for today. Thinking of you, and Tweed, with love and care.

Love,
Medea


*May 6, 2022 overcast, light rain overnight*

Dear Medea,
It's Friday but my brain thinks it's Saturday and I'm having trouble reorienting. Already wished my neighbor happy birthday (it's tomorrow) and wondered why the pharmacy called on a Saturday, and started the rhubarb sauce for Mother's Day pie. I feel all a jumble.

Tweed has recovered once again. He's had his quarterly trim and bath which means my back hurts and there's a shopping bag of hair to dispose of. In the right time of year, I put that out for the birds, but this is not that time. Tweed will see the vet Monday who will appreciate the rear-end clipping and clean up.

I'm concerned to hear the details of your plague. It does sound like covid, but I don't know—is it possible to have flaming symptoms and negative test? Our county is in a high-status flare up with double the number of cases. So much for my newfound freedom, eh? Glad we got our second boosters, as repulsive as the experience was. I seem to need to remind myself several times a day that I could be so many other places, people, and situations which are so dreadful and frightening that I should just fucking shut up with any and all complaining. Life is grand. I'm also spitting mad about Roe, and we probably don't need to talk further, being of identical minds. I bent my own rules and posted a comment on a NYT opinion column. Roxanne Gay's, she always talks the talk and walks the walk.

Yesterday was the day to remember the millions of indigenous women who are missing (as in dead, or really missing, as in disappeared) because of abuse and we are asked to say their names and so here I present Khadija Britton, missing, presumed murdered by her ex-boyfriend. May she be at peace. In her photos she is a lovely girl, full of sparkle. Her family, her tribe, will never forget her, will never stop searching for her. In northern California, indigenous women and girls aren't warned about the possibility of sexual abuses and harm, they are warned of the inevitability of a life of actual abuse. Khadija Britton, missing.

Love,
Jane


*7 May 2022 59, sunny, so brisk as to freeze bone marrow, at least the marrow in my bones.*

Dear Jane,
A light for Khadija Britton, who shares your maiden name, and the fate of an unspeakable number of other Indigenous women. They deserve attention and protection. I watched a gut-wrenching movie called *Wind River* during lockdown about a Native American girl named Natalie who lives on a reservation in the frozen West, and escapes four drunken oil men who imprisoned and raped her by fleeing their trailer, barefoot, in a snowstorm. You can imagine how that ended for her. Her father's grief is so powerful as to feel like separate character in the film.

Perhaps all of the insanity at home and abroad is causing your disorientation. And the shot. Heaven knows that if we are listening to anything but the sound of the wind and the waves and the birds, the chaos disrupts our natural rhythms. What will Putin pull on the 9th? Is Biden still breathing? Covid mocks the ignorance of the anti-vaxxers. PG&E threatens "massive power outages" for summer, while Gavin promises massive housing construction. I'm dizzy.

On the nature front, I caved and bought a squirrel baffle, which is a sort of squirrel-deterring umbrella top that sits above the feeder. Stephen and his gray girlfriend are eating my birds out of their rightful rations. The raven, who jumps four feet vertically to grab a morsel, should be the stormtrooper here. His beak gleams like an obsidian arrow, and must be equally sharp and serious. The Steller's Jay, with its proud crest always at attention could also impose some bird order. But they don't. I looked for squirrel food at the hardware store where I found the baffle, but perhaps ACE is corporate and must hew to the CA anti-wild animal feeding law—there was not a corn cob to be had. However, it did offer a full wall of agents for killing every rodent in the garden.

We're a pair at the moment, Jane.

Happy Mother's Day to you, my friend. Savor every bite of your rhubarb pie and hug that sweet Tweed for me. Max is taking me out for an afternoon of big fun.

Love,
Medea

P.S. Dr. Joanne Stolen writes in *Summit Outside* that in Northwest Native American mythology the Steller's Jay "is the message of hope in disrepair and the will to live. The jay is willing to teach you fearlessness, adaptability and survival but you must be willing to follow its lead."

*May 8, 2022 Rain and lovely cumulus clouds pregnant with moisture*

Dear Medea,
Tinker and Burt are regularly on hand for feeding. They stand close together in the wind and rain and coo and chortle at me when I appear as fast as possible. We had some hail and I worried, but they seemed to be fine.

It's a day to rest and reflect and yet the energy is full of chaos and neglect. I'm not sure why I choose that word, but it's what seems right. Perhaps the day will unfold differently but I'm skeptical.

Love,
Jane

*8 May 2022 Cold, 54, unsettled sky, from robin's egg to stuffed with angry, scuttling thunderheads. It even rained.*

Dear Jane,
How was your Mother's Day? Max treated me to a luxurious afternoon of wine tasting under the oaks followed by a bona fide New Orleans dinner at The

Bywater, Bib-Gourmand approved. We had to start with Old Bay fries and suck-out-the-heads crawdads. Which no one did, since we're disinclined to eat the brains of others, but their little white bodies packed a flavor that conjured skiffs on the bayou, Great Blue Herons in the reeds, gators watching from the water's edge. All this atmosphere in a gingerbready little house with worn plank floors, a friendly bar, lots of Mardi Gras beads and a cozy dining porch on the northern periphery of Max's town. It's good to be Mom.

A new woodpecker flew in today. Another Hairy. Its spikey beak would puncture or at least deter Stephen if only the bird felt a sense of ownership over the feeder. It does not. Other grazers today included a pair of soft gray nuthatches, half a dozen House Sparrows and the ubiquitous team of Chestnut-backed Chickadees. I stood still as a rod in the shadows with my grown-up camera, hoping for a frame-worthy shot of the black and cream Hairy, who had other flighty plans. One of the hummingbird couples spun arcs over, around and above, stopping together on a high branch to discuss how to make sure I can never capture them in the same frame.

Something (probably a mouse) has died in the garden bed near the front door, mercifully far enough away from the veggie bins not to taint the tomatoes. It's too late for the cauliflower and broccoli, though; some complement of the winged and/or furred ones nibbled the florets off every stalk. Celery, mint and herbs hold no interest for them. It's time to reinforce the anti-avian netting. It's been suggested that feeding birds and planting a vegetable garden may create conflicts of interest. Who is the smarter earthling?

Far more valuable, noble and honest than almost every politician in office today are my dear college friend and her English husband, subjects of Her Majesty the Queen, who are fostering a Ukrainian mum and her nine-year-old son. Mum, an attorney, works remotely. Son is enrolled in the local primary school. Behold the Righteous, whom we must acknowledge and applaud.

Love,
Medea


*May 10, 2022 bright blue sky now and then an enormous cumulus cloud bounces down from the coast range and Trinity altitudes, clearing the air*

Dear Medea,
Yesterday's silence is due to a day spent piecing together the disastrous energy of the weekend (don't ask) and also shepherding Tweed to his vet appointment where we contrived to get $1k worth of blood work ordered and a plan to have x-rays and ultrasound checks next week. We are looking for clues at this point,

but the dreaded idea of cancer lurks in the background of every symptom, line of inquiry, and clutch of the heart. I am not ready for more grief, but I'm mindful that the stars align this week for a whopper of an eclipse. (Lunar super blood moon eclipse in Scorpio). Best to hold on tight. All that worry-ness laid on the table and exhausting, and yet Tweed is doing very well right now and seems perfectly normal. Gene likes to say that it isn't the thing we worry about that gets us in the end, it's the other.

Yesterday's treat was the first sounds of the baby ravens. Tinker and Burt came to the feed palette when we got home from our vet trek and talked and talked, then Tinker ate while Burt kept watch–this is how they proceed, ever vigilant. Tinker flew south to the nest and next I heard there was a huge commotion and the squawking of wee birdies raising a ruckus of major proportions. Hooray! Not only for the chicks, but for the fact that clearly, they and their nest survived the weekend wind and storm (and hail). Motherhood, it is a trial of survival.

I'm so happy to hear that your English friends have taken in some refugees. And wouldn't we as well if we lived anywhere that was possible for that? California is not exempt, of course, and there is a huge crisis at the Mexican border with Ukrainians added to the people trying to come across. And what is the hold up? Well-meaning relatives and friends trying to do the right thing and keep children safe and finding those very children removed from them to camps. I haven't heard much about this in the past few days, have you? I understand being careful about human trafficking, but there is a crisis here and we are not handling it well.

Love,
Jane


*11 May 2022 59 degrees. Blustery. Sunny, but what a waste. Does that sound whiny?*

Dear Jane,
I've deleted reference to Mitch McC. from yesterday's letter. Though he unfortunately exists in real life, and though we do have an obligation to report the unvarnished truth, these are our pages to reflect our realities. Right? Though I wouldn't mind creating an alternate universe as we spin toward the end of a year of letters. Imagine this: all living things coexist on a planet with ample space, inter-species mutual respect, peace, and an unsullied Home. Greed exists only in tales a parent shares with his child only then as an illustration of the face of evil. Those who wish to abide by certain strictures, mores, dogma, fairy tales confine that behavior to her own decisions, to his own life.

Are you in?

The best news ever is that Tinker and Burt hatched nestlings! And they survived the gales! Do you feel as though you have grandbirdies? Remote in space from you as I am, I share your awe at this creation from "our" ravens. Will the fledges remain, return to your safe, green, nurturing plot? (At times like these, I'd pay for a photo portal to accompany these letters.) Life marches on.

My friend, Peter, whom Dylan visited while he's tasting Guatemala, told me he's never seen me this nervous about anything before. Peter knows me best as a fancy-free friend. I'm not nervous about Dylan visiting Guatemala. But I'm a mother. Granted, Guatemala (like Oakland, like Chicago) hosts pockets of violence. Kidnapping shares the stage with hiking Volcan Atitlan in terms of sport, if one heeds the fearmongers. This is why, though Peter has owned his Shangri-la on the beach for nearly twenty years, Bruce has never agreed to visit. When my kids get on a plane, I ask for the universe to hold them safe and tight. There's an element of trust—in our fellow humans, in the order of things—that removes fear from the equation. Perhaps "cautious" is a more accurate word.

And you and I have new wish and a new word: "καλοταξιδο" (kalotaxido), meaning "'wishing it a good journey" as the book is finding its way to people's homes and hearts." This wish comes from my Greek artist friend Nikki. The verbal keys held by the ancients find their way to us, eventually.

Love,
Medea

P.S. The Lazarus Palm sprouts new orange frond pods almost every week. You try telling a sixty-year-old tree that, just because some idiot decided to chop off its head, it could not grow a new one!
P.P.S The Ukranians won Eurovision, with its Kalush Orchestra performing *Stefania*.


*May 12, 2022 overcast, cool.*

Dear Medea,
I'm in! I despair we may never educate humans in a wide enough plane to achieve harmony, I think we have to try. In fact, I think it's our only mandate (woman-date), we must evolve or die. There is no species we can do without–and I say this as a person with deep deep morbid fear of snakes. And yet, merging your two main themes from yesterday, how will we convince this huge portion of the population who have been pushed to extremes such that kidnap, and mayhem are lifestyle choices? If we had to have a pandemic with mortality statistics in the

millions, is it wrong to ask why the dead couldn't be the evil and worthless? This hole, this judgement, leaves us to ask about our gods. What are they for, exactly?

I've been feeling lately like I'm not funny. My apologies. There is still sweetness in the world but so often the worry overwhelms. And then I go outside, and Tinker and Burt are rubbing beaks and necks and cooing and if I coo to Tinker, she coos back and hops closer to the edge of the roofline to see me, cocking her head. Tweed does this as I walk by, watches me move about the living room with adoration money cannot buy. I'm his lifeline. He is mine.

Today I turned on the tap to rinse the oatmeal from the saucepan and the water ran black as ink. Fucking mercury retrograde.

Dylan will be fine. He will feel your worry across the thousands of miles, and he will learn a new set of travel savvy rules along the way, without paying a price. You envelop him in your care, and you have taught him well.

Love,
Jane


*13 May 2022 59, clear, sunny—Carmel Valley, for a change.*

Dear Jane,
Mercury in retrograde. Friday the 13th.. And yet! From my perch above a man-made lake, an "uncommon" Green Heron soars by, as if to remind and reinforce that life's richness is composed of these small moments, like your *coo* exchanges with Tinker and mutual adoration with Tweed.

We're in Carmel this weekend for the Quail Motorcycle Event. Those "biker scum" of yore who barreled through San Juan Bautista back in the 1960's, striking terror into the hearts of the locals, are now retired dentists with the time and means to travel to this verdant, pastoral resort for three days of iron and chrome horse worship. Keanu Reeves usually shows, but not this year. Rats. But we met a guy named Phil who is showing his taxi-yellow Dunstall Norton 810, which he bought new from Paul Dunstall Organization in 1972, and his wife, Linda, who spends her days deep inside Ancestry researching other people's lives. Only one "famous" person is registered this year, but I've never heard of him. About one hundred of the gray-haired knee-draggers took off at nine this morning for a hundred-and-fifty-mile backroad adventure. Those of us who chose to commune with the herons, the ducks and the bright red dragonflies will heave a sigh of relief when they roar back into the parking lot, unscathed.

When I think about the fuel burn/waste for such an event, I'm not comforted by the Bezos/Musk/Branson space tourism and each four-person craft's purported $CO_2$ burn, equal to fifty to one hundred times more than a single long-haul flight filled with three hundred passengers. A friend told me that the second Bezos Fun Flight burned 1800 gallons of fuel per second over its fourteen minutes in the air. I've not found a fact check for that figure, and Bezos has used a nitrogen/hydrogen fuel rather than fossil fuel. Still. Wretched excess keeps billionaires mischievous and often oligarch-y, while this hotel is asking guests to forego housekeeping because it can't find workers willing and able to make beds and clean toilets for $15 an hour. As you say, we must keep trying, rather than hurtling into blind despair.

As to why only the evil didn't succumb to Covid, or why yellow jackets could not be disappearing rather than bees? We reap what we sow, we humans. We'll turn our backs on Mother Nature until she's fed up with our disrespectful hooliganism. Then, she'll unleash cyclones, fires, droughts, plagues, famines. Just you wait.

Love,
Medea

P.S. The bullfrogs that live in the pond beneath our room kept us serenaded all night long—for some reason I don't understand, they stop croaking in unison, and resume at some possibly pre-arranged interval, also in unison. Our server last night had so much info about the bats and birds and frogs that I asked him whether he's a biologist. He is. Shouldn't he be able to live on a biologist's salary and not moonlight as a tequila and pie slinger? See "wretched excess," above...


*May 13, 2022 Friday the 13th. A mix of fog and mild sunshine.*

Dear Medea,
There's some sort of motorcycle gathering up this way every year about this time. Dreadful. Noise pollution roaring up and down the canyons, swerving out of their lanes in traffic and generally disturbing the peace. Seriously annoying. I hope your man returns satisfied and unscathed. This need for noise and speed has got to stop though. Starting with Bezos and Musk and Branson.

This morning I watched Tinker sip water from the copper firepit bowl repurposed to a bird bath and when, apparently, she had a full gullet she took off. Seconds later I heard the tinies causing a racket. Oh! She's giving them drinks! Of course, she would need to. Never occurred to me before though. Thinking myself a great wag, I asked Tinker today if the children were driving her "batty."

I'm so heartened to hear that Finland, and possibly Sweden, will be coming into the NATO fold. Take that Putin! Finland in particular is very vulnerable with such a long border with Russia. My .6% Finn ancestry blushes with pride.

Speaking of ancestry, that's a great career your new acquaintance has. I've thought of doing that myself. Sometimes I think of career opportunities and think "I could do that" and then remember with a start that I'm old now and don't need a career. It's a letdown, to be honest. I spent so many years wondering what to do, and since leaving the need behind have come up with a few things more lucrative than setting up a lemonade stand like Lucy selling bits of philosophy for 5 cents.

Love,
Jane


*16 May 2022 Another bright, bold, cold, blustery day in the suburbs of San Francisco*

Dear Jane,
You'd make a great genealogist, between your penchant for deep research and your interest in other people's pasts, fictional or otherwise. Is there a poem that you might usher forth about finding that perfect profession when the need is long gone? Yours always see light fully formed. One of your many talents that I admire deeply.

Tinker can hold enough water to hydrate her tinies. She's teaching me so much about ravens, birds, mystery, connection. Why it never occurred to me that birds would need to both feed and water their young I can't say. I've learned from birds that eating the eggshells of their offspring provides the parents with essential calcium. I've grudgingly accepted that cannibalism—of robins or blue jays or other nourishing familiars—in the service of their nestlings is justifiable avicide. That stunning insects like the blue-eyed darner, a dragonfly that may be a cousin of the red flier that lives above this pond, very likely wind up as food for the bats, kites, swallows and falcons that all call the Quail "home." Sometimes I wish that only gnarled, gray thistles would serve as food for all. Then, I remember that many of us feast first with our eyes; wizened weeds fail to nourish on multiple sensory planes.

The Wild Ones did make it back unscathed. And I totally botched the history of that ride: It took place on a scorching Fourth of July weekend in 1947. Hollister, not San Juan Bautista. No women or children fled to basements. It was a ride not unsimilar to this one, but Harper's Magazine got wind of the "invasion" and published its reporter, Frank Rooney's, version in January, 1951. He thought reporting about 4000 WWII vets and random others gathering on iron horses to blow off the vestiges of their memories of war would make far better copy if the bikers blazed into town, emptied pyramids of beer bottles, and then posed for provocative pictures. The event, according to Bruce and filmsite.org inspired the movie *The Wild One* with Marlon Brando and Lee Marvin. Director Lázló Benedek reimagined the uneventful event as a more audience-enticing biker gang war, and the film is credited with spawning real biker gangs like the Hell's Angels. Yes, motorcycles may be loud, annoying, disruptive. But the bikers in the Quail sphere would pitch in and help you polish Tinker's copper bowl.

You recommended a book called *Golden Hill* when I was in New York last fall. I borrowed it from the library two weeks ago finished it over the weekend. You were right. The rough images of Manhattan and Broad Way, with muddy, mucky winter streets juxtaposed with stone mansions of the immigrant fortune seekers, the compact town grid, the utter lack of monetary cohesion, held me in suspense, wondering what this mysterious Richard Smith's story would reveal. This was not Dylan's New York. But, in its redemption and grit and capacity for unending surprise, it's everyone's New York.

Love,
Medea


*18 May 2022 Hot hot hot, perfectly perfect for a six-miler along the sparkly reservoir.*

Dear Jane,
When you fall silent for a couple of days, I know that Tweed needs you. I'll make this brief.

In the midst of this latest Covid infection explosion, we will board a plane in the morning, packed tightly with one hundred fifty other passengers, bound for Orlando. Five hours of togetherness. Folly or resignation? I'll let you know three days after we land. This is supposed to be a pilgrimage to an uninhabited barrier island off the South Georgia coast. Hundreds of species of birds, mostly shore and water, live or migrate here during any given year. Several species of palm, palmetto and oak shade the grounds and house the critters. We're hoping for (respectfully distanced) sea turtle- and nestling-sightings. Seven miles of golden sand. I can't wait.

Love,
Medea

*May 19, 2022 gale force winds, sunshine, splinter dry. Red flag warnings.*

Dear Medea,
You're so brave! On a plane with passengers so crazy they try to open the cabin door while the plane's still rolling. Yikes! Travel was bad enough before, I would not have imagined I'd be able to say this only two years ago, but forget travel, I'm done. That said, you have fun! I hope the midges and mosquitoes leave you alone.

It has been a difficult week, but we have come out of the eclipse season with our lives intact and a plan. Tweed is doing very well; he always does in between episodes. But pancreatitis is terrible and I'm holding on to Tweed and to my resolve with all my reserves.

I have used genealogy as the inspiration for some poetry but haven't written about careers. Interesting idea. When I actually needed a career there was no such thing as genetic genealogy and almost no one paid for ancestry research. I think now that many people are searching for their biological families, that a real genealogist can do quite well. It's a fun hobby, solving mysteries.

I'm looking forward to your report from Florida.

Love,
Jane


*20 May 2022 90 degrees, breezy, birdy. Not a sound but the crack of the Boat-tailed Grackle and the whoosh of the wind.*

Dear Jane,
A triumph of love, determination and devoted veterinary medicine over pancreatitis for your faithful Tweed. I think Tweed might be energized by all of the bird calls and songs that prickle the air around me. This Island only an hour north of the bustle of Jacksonville has every distraction a healthy dog could imagine. Since you're sworn off travel, I'll send a video for you two to share.

The uneventful flight followed a southern route, a dusty, dry moonscape over New Mexico (with no evidence of fires save an all-too-familiar veil of gray to the north). Southern Arizona, also dusky and brittle, sprouted miles of solar farms since the last time I flew this route. It's not until the edge of East Texas that bits of green begin to show. From there to Orlando, serpentine waterways weave through wetlands and piney woods, and suddenly the landscape calls me home.

Love,
Medea

*22 May 2022 85, overcast, gentle wind dancing with the Spanish moss, and sending the biting insects inland. Little St. Simons Island (Georgia)*

Dear Jane,

A juvenile raccoon just toddled up to the birdfeeder near the porch where I'm writing to you. It looked startled, but not interested in banter, unlike the grackles that chatter among themselves, with me, with any of us who care to engage. They are like the "Miss Hospitalities" of this island. This feeder, a cylinder that must hold a pound of millet, was full when we arrived on Friday. Forty-eight hours later, it's down to dregs. Since it's on an anti-critter pole AND surrounded by a cage, the birds ate every scrap. Much talk amongst the naturalists and guests involves the ethics of bird feeders. I think it's time we put that debate safely to bed.

Staying in a place where the natural world provides all of the entertainment, I was reminded of this statistic: the average person today can name only ten wild plants but can readily identify over a thousand corporate logos.

Aside from the lull of the river and the *cheep* and flutter of the grackles, the *trill* of the cardinals, the *coo* of the doves and the slap of the human palm against mosquito, silence reigns like a benevolent professor, nudging the skeptical student to stop. To listen. To feel.

We walked the beach this morning, due south, past the twentieth loggerhead turtle nest discovered hours before by Mary the Turtle Tech. The pregnant loggerhead paddles her way up the beach from the sea, flipping first to the left, then to the right, in a helix search for the safest spot to deposit her eggs. Too far from the shore and the babies become egret or Ghost Crab food. Too close, and the tide may drown the lot of them. She scrapes out a light-bulb shaped nest in the sand where she deposits her leathery-shelled eggs. They will breathe and self-nourish here for fifty-five to sixty days, then barrel out of their hole, ocean-bound. The naturalists will move a nest if it's sited in a precarious place; mama never returns to check on her babies. These eggs won't face the threat of locals who consider the eggs a rare delicacy, one that they could not afford even if it were on sale at the local market. With the vigilance of the LSSI eco-squad and the utter, blessed darkness of the night sky, I'd say these littles stand a decent chance of hatching, climbing from their nest, scrabbling down across the sand and at least taking a baptismal swim. What happens next is up to the gods.

Love,
Medea

*May 22, 2022 another good bet day perhaps? Sun, light wind, cool*

Dear Medea,

I might have to cop to some activity specific agoraphobia. Not, as the Latin origins would suggest, am I afraid of wafting around the Acropolis market with my flimsy linen gown tangling in my rush basket, gathering olives, and artichokes, and a piece of lamb to cook for my master. I could manage that, the fullness of the Mediterranean Sea air, the bright blue sky. Have I ever told you about my very first déjà vu experience? We were arriving in Athens on our first visit to Greece in our first trip to Europe en route to purgatory on the Persian Gulf. Well, maybe not purgatory, but to a twelve-year-old it was enough to cause a whopping case of agoraphobia right there. Anyway, we're driving from the airport after a short flight from Rome into the city of Athens and I had the most urgent sensation that I'd been there before. Not from the ancient point of view, of course: I would have seen lots of photos of the ruins, read Baedeker from front to back (I still have it), but what I recognized was the road from the airport, and the signs and the smells and the sea air. It was a goosebumpy moment that I've never forgotten. I have since had other similar sensations but usually involving a situation rather than a place. Now, where was I? Oh, agoraphobia. I do find shopping exhausting, I would have to put department stores on my list, not because of crowds or people just that the whole experience makes me tired just to contemplate. I don't like grocery shopping, particularly if I run into people I know. The deadly small talk that has to peter out on its own or seem like rudeness. I'd put gas stations on the list. Maybe it's from watching The Birds and having a Hitchcockian memory of fire erupting. I'm not good with mechanicals and to this day am too chicken to use the stop on the nozzle so I can do something other than hold the damn thing. It appears I'm creating a list of commercial venues to avoid. Libraries. I hate libraries because they are always ten degrees too warm. In college I would become so tired and sleepy, nothing good would get done. And now, to the point of this: airplanes. I like airports, hotel lobbies, museums, concert halls, I like to watch people, wonder who they are and who they are meeting…but airplanes. No. It seems inconceivable that we should fly. I've flown many many miles, around the world twice and I lost count of the number of countries at 60. But the act of flying? I'm just not a fan. I don't panic, I know how to behave, sometimes I can even sleep. But I feel dirty and ruffled—as if my body has been separated from my spirit. That's jet lag, by the way. So, I'm really fine with saying no more flying. Unless, of course, one of us finds a windfall and buys a private jet.

Love,
Jane

*May 23, 2022 Sun, light wind, warmish. Happier garden*

Dear Medea,
While you are off grid in the wilds of Florida–which doesn't really seem likely or possible, but it is reassuring to know Florida isn't entirely ruined–I will carry on and eventually you will fill in.

The important news here is that for the last three days we have seen new behavior in the ravens. More and more they had been coming for food together which I took to mean that the chicks had hatched. Several times there was a battle in the sky as a predator hawk tried to attack the nest. Lately though, Tinker and Burt have come over at the same time and then perch, one on the garage roof as per usual, and the other in a tall tree which could possibly be *in sight of the nest*, no way for me to be sure. Then Tinker starts squawking *"whaak whaak whaak whaak,"* look around, repeat, *"whaak whaak whaak whaak."* I think she's trying to get the nestlings to start thinking about flying. Perhaps it's a complicated message about where that great tasting food comes from, maybe it's "mind yourselves, we're both over here." As usual, we will never know and/or time will tell. But the excitement, the prospect of seeing the tinies for the first time, is getting me out of bed in the morning with anticipation. Last year we experienced the same behavior and then one day the parents and all five babies showed up, lined up on the roof peak and took turns splashing about in the dog's water bowl. This year, knowing what's coming, I have arranged for a bigger bird bath. Now we wait. Will there be four babies to match the four squawks? Tune in tomorrow.

Love,
Jane


*23 May 2022 80 degrees and just overcast enough to lull the unwary into walking the beach without a hat. Little St. Simons Island (Georgia)*

Dear Jane,
Internet issues on Georgia's barrier islands left me writing in Word and trying to paste those letters into our shared document, then I connect to our correspondence and find that not only are you going to avoid all manner of public interaction, but that Tinker and Burt will bring tiny ravens to meet you any moment now! Given the hazards of even the most brief, most outdoor intercourse, I don't blame you. (See below.) Déjà vu strikes at the oddest moments, and of course you were on that road in another life. Do you think the librarians kept the libraries warm to lull us to sleep? My library in Venice, it being Florida,

always seemed far too cold. Though I loved this job, my first job, Mrs. Zook, the head librarian (who wore her silver hair in a tight bun, and, as I am picturing her now, always wore a cardigan) insisted on keeping the infernal a/c set to "icy." My preferred scut task was collecting the books from the curbside drop box just so my bones could thaw out.

Today Bruce's prediction came true. One of the guests tested positive for Covid and was voted off the island by management. As inevitable as hurricanes in September. Though Bruce feels vindicated, it's not in a "brotherhood of man" kind of way. Once again, we marvel at ignorance in the face of fact. We gathered outside at picnic tables for lunch. Our gang of four Covid Realists has its porch corner well-staked. We're told the other guests will dine indoors, but further separated. No ventilation. And now, Monkeypox courses through Alaska and Broward County, FL. What the hell is Monkeypox anyway? Mother Nature is just plain messing with us.

A pod of six Atlantic bottle-nosed dolphin meandered alongside our pontoon boat in the Hampton River this morning to everyone's delight. They "vocalize" through their nose, the Fran Dreshers of the sea, and the mom imprints her unique sound on her offspring at birth. If mom and calf become separated, they use this vocalization to find each other.

Bruce has advised that he's seen enough birds, thank you, and how can you really tell them apart anyway, much less remember all of those names? The skimmer looks like a tern, which looks like a more compact, less scavenging seagull. A black grackle could be a blackbird or a crow. All of those tiny ones are too small to differentiate. A heron is an egret is a bittern is a rail. This is exactly how I feel at the motorcycle and automobile concourses he adores. How can you tell a 1960 Porsche from a 1962? Who cares? They'll all wind up in the landfill anyway, or in Jay Leno's garage.

The armadillo squad is out in force today, nosing into garbage cans and holes in the ground. Are they ugly or cute? Or both? They migrated to Texas from South America and made their way to Florida then up to Georgia. Miniature armored cars marching across the Southern hemisphere to settle in the piney woods, snuffling their snouts into holes in the ground looking for treats. Despite their segmented rattails and body blanket, their squat, toaster shape, and their reputation as roadkill, their perseverance makes me want to give them a close cuddle.

An approaching storm cell changes the light from butter to ash in an instant. The rain calls the crickets and Leopard Frogs to rehearsal. The rain whispers, the oaks bow, the marsh imbibes. Someone filled the feeder.

Love,
Medea

*May 25, 2022 heat event: coastal temps 20 degrees above normal.*

Dear Medea,

Georgia! I don't know why but I thought Everglades. I guess because I didn't realize where you were going in the first place. Barrier islands make so much sense with the John McPhee book! I read the one where he goes to the islands with some guy who wants to buy them, or one of them, and completely messes it up. I think he succeeded in the end, no? A golf resort? Oddly, I don't think of barrier islands as having reptiles. Silly me. And not just human ones.

No news on raven babies. Last evening, I looked out the bathroom window and was treated to an up close with a furry woodpecker, that can't be right, oh, a Hairy Woodpecker. What a beautiful red head. He was on the hawthorn tree and except for the pane of glass, he was only a few feet away. I watched for so long, Gene asked if I was ok. Early this morning, sleepless and too hot, I was treated to a dawn chorus that I mostly miss on a normal day. The Hermit Thrush was the loudest voice but at least four other bird voices came from all directions, the farthest being a water bird from the river. I tried to get Cornell to work and failed, something I was doing wrong, surely, and in the end decided it was a distraction to try. I closed my eyes and let the thrush sing me back to sleep.

We have had our first fire. A tiny 36 acre fire far south of us but within the limit of the 50 mile radius of the warning text messages. It took three days for CalFire to put it out. Mostly the grass is still green, but it's going to seed and in a matter of days the landscape will be California brown. Inland temperatures today nearing triple digits.

I'm sorry to hear your nature vacation is hampered by covid, but also glad to hear there are precautions and miscreant campers are banished promptly. Monkeypox sounds like a fun one–I was uneasy that the CDC instantly started warning that it is highly sexually transmitted with an emphasis on gay men. Really? That sounds like conservative scare tactics. Lots of people enjoy sex lots of ways. Targeting gay men seems like 1980s behavior.

And lastly, not to be too much of a wet blanket to your fun, but I read once that armadillos carry leprosy. Probably don't tell Bruce. But also, no cuddling.

Love,
Jane

*26 May 2022 Low 80s, bare hint of breeze rustling the oak leaves, every shape and texture of cloud high against a gauzy blue sky.*

Dear Jane,

The armadillo would not be cuddled, try as I might to lure it to my lap. My new friend K and I agreed that these armadillos, smaller than the Texas brand, and a warm shade of brown, not granite gray, engender unusual endearment. Nature's peculiar way.

It's our last morning. I'm swaying in the porch swing, watching the light and the parade of Painted Buntings, who look like Chagall took to the blank birds with his palette fully loaded. The family of Northern Cardinals nibbles at millet, and the female's bright orange beak pops like fire against her olive feathers. A few of these brown doves that my mom insists are the only doves she knows poke around on the ground, looking for feeder spoils. Spanish moss dangles from the oaks like lacy kitchen curtains. The Boat-tailed Grackles are at it, singing their lungs out. A (Pileated?) woodpecker thwacks out a hidey hole on a tree nearby. Someone left the screen door ajar, so every few seconds I must smash a mosquito against my bare skin lest it add more lesions to my already bumpy body. A small price to pay for such a variety show.

In our six days here, I've seen two snakes, the Coach Whip that I thought was a rat snake, and a Diamond-backed Rattler, stretched across the beach road as I rode the bike back from the shore. Add those to the four gators K and I spotted while kayaking and the other that Bruce found taking a dip in the ocean, the possibly leprotic armadillos, possibly Hanta virus-carrying rats, abundant mosquitos that we're told are disease free, but who knows, and you have to wonder what kind of person chooses to visit an undeveloped barrier island. I'd return for the birds and the endless expanse of empty beach alone. When all of the turtles hatch, that will be an affirmation of hope to remember.

We have feeder wars going on now, the brutish glossy grackle intimidating the buntings and cardinals. Your Hermit Thrush might love the marshland here.

We have one last bird viewing this morning in a few minutes, so I'll close with this: the plural of titmouse is titmice, and a phoebe is pronounced like the woman's name because that's its call. Ask a naturalist and ye shall learn the truth.

Love,
Medea

*May 27, 2022 fog and cool, clearing to high fog and cool. Perfect.*

Dear Medea,

Snakes! Ugh. And poisonous at that! It's no accident that ancient cultures honored the reptiles in ways we cannot imagine–thinking of the bare breasted women holding wiggling serpents in the statues found on Crete. I have hope that the ravens know part of their job is to remove the snakes from my vicinity, even if they aren't poisonous. As for southern latitudes and disease, it does seem that very cold temperatures are necessary to our health, as another factor in climate change is that hard freezes will become rare and the plagues that are alive and well south of the Mason-Dixon Line will move north.

Within my own small arena, I am having a battle with that Red Breasted Sapsucker I mentioned last time, who seems bent on sapping the strength from my beloved hawthorn tree. Does he not know it's sacred? Does he not realize the energy and soul invested in the clootie ties that adorn the tree now and then? The tree is pouring sap, it seemed like in no time at all. This morning I cut strips of aluminum foil and hung them on the branches, just like the clooties. He ignored them and I was barely back in the house before he was at it again. Then I wrapped the trunk loosely in foil covering the wounds. That might have worked, and yet, all he did was move over to the Japanese maple. I admit, the hawthorn isn't thriving in the first place having almost fallen over three years ago when we actually had a lot of rain in January and the ground gave way. The Japanese maple looks pretty healthy except that in winter when the branches are leafless, the usnea moss is startling. Said not to attack a tree but live symbiotically, I don't know if I believe it. Seems like usnea, which, by the way, is good for kidney/ bladder issues and apparently rare some places–not here, climbs on like the grim reaper signally imminent demise. Still, the maple does live and at the moment is a brilliant lizard shade of ripe green. Sapsuckers are the vampires of the woodpecker family.

I cleaned out my fridge and sorted out a dozen eggs from my daughter in law that were a bit past their use by date. I did the float test to make sure they weren't "bad," and then gave the ravens six of them. It was great watching them pick up an egg and fly off to the nest. I noticed when they came back after the first one their beaks were still half open. Was it a struggle to open wide enough and so they returned for more without bothering to shut? Then last night, Tinker came by and sat on the garage roof and cooed to me. I cooed back. In that moment, all was well.

We have Phoebes here. Something makes them special.

Love,
Jane

Dear Jane,

Sapsucker Woods is the name of the forest adjacent to the Cornell Lab of Ornithology. I wonder why the lab selected a vampire bird? The sprites of the green places respect your efforts to save your beloved hawthorn, even if the sapsuckers do not.

Here's the deal with armadillos. Once again, man interferes with the natural order of things. According to an LSSI Naturalist, a medical lab at a university in Florida (he was unsure which) used armadillos to study leprosy back in the late last century. After the scientists finished the study, they released the remaining armored ones. Twenty-five percent of those carried leprosy, a percentage that apparently still wanders the earth with this nasty disease. So, no armadillo-cuddling for me.

My jazz singer friend Pat Yankee appears poised to join her late husband in the next realm. She is unable to walk or move, but did respond when her old bandmate Bob sang a few of her tunes to her when he and his wife visited her in the nursing home. I've mentioned to you that her dignity, the light of her near-lifelong fame has gone all but ignored by the staff at this facility in the year and a half she's been "incarcerated" there. We've exchanged our good-byes a few times, our mutual admiration, our love. The world, my world, is richer and my heart more compassionate because of Pat's presence in it.

Good luck with your trees. I'm heading to the Delta for the night, and my peripatetic youngest son returns to start his next chapter tomorrow.

Love,
Medea


*May 28, 2022 light rain, what a blessing!*

Dear Medea,

Are you sailing to the Delta? I'm guessing not. I hope the weather is amenable in whatever way is required–preferably not hot dry winds creating fire hazards.

I was all set to drive out to the mercantile and load up with more potting soil, but instead plan to curl up with a good book and admire the rain. I've just started Brian Sykes book *Once a Wolf* about the evolution of dogs but I'm not saying yet whether this is a "good" book or not, certainly it is a subject of interest to me, but he has a disclaimer in his intro that gave me pause (paws?) when he declared that he wasn't really a dog lover, having had a childhood scare. Having written books and understanding the arduous process involved, I'm a little baffled as to why he would write a book about dogs when he doesn't like them, even if genetics are his gig. I shall report back.

I am claiming at least temporary victory over the sapsucker. I saw the miscreant head off to another pine tree. Much better idea since that tree is definitely dying as are many of that species here. The beetles. The newest pest news is that there are termites on the pool house north end framing. Not overwhelmingly so, but enough that it's a problem we have to solve. I think we may have to adopt our carpenter and give him resident housing status before all the work that's piling up gets done.

Your friend Pat Yankee lived a full and creative life. Ending that vibrancy in a warehouse for the dying seems unfair. I wish her blessings on her journey.

Love,
Jane


*29 May 2022 79 and sunny in the Delta. 60s back here.*

Dear Jane,
After prepping breakfast for our hundred and twenty guests, my shift concluded, and speed bocce in full swing, I seized a quiet moment for myself and walked the Island's berm to see who might be singing or waging war; a pair of otters raised a ruckus last night but wore themselves out, apparently, as I could not find them. The little swifts who last year built their nests in the struts of the launch vessel decided, I suppose, that tending to a nest while underway threatened to drown the babies and themselves, so this year they've opted to nest among the adult life jackets that sit stored in racks above the seats. The Great Blue Herons starred in the Island bird show today. I watched one crouch into a football shape and tuck its head and neck low against its back. Its silvery feathers match the gray-green leaves on the trees along the levee, so it remained in stealth mode until it struck out its sword and stabbed its lunch. Three others flew above the tree line, close enough to give the impression of togetherness, so I'm curious about this trio. Perhaps the summer will reveal all.

And no, no sailing to the Delta. The kids are non-committal, understandably. I did spend time with a couple of avid, amiable sailing women over the weekend, so my family crew might find itself replaced.

So many people write dog books. One of my Stanford writing class friends wrote about the psychological bond between us and them; she is a professor of the Jungian school, so the bits of the book she completed during our time together taught me quite a lot about the human-canine link.

The bugs will rule the world one day, Jane. Gnawing, crawling, infesting or viral. Sea Island sprays pesticides to eradicate its mosquitos and green its golf courses, which poisons the water and fouls the air for the birds on LSSI, which does not spray, and we're still smearing hydrocortisone on our bites. Sea Island has a private jetport, too.

Love,
Medea

P.S. Thanks for sending blessings to Pat. She will receive them, wherever she is, with an open heart.


*May 30, 2022 Wind. Sun. Not pleasant*

Dear Medea,
Happy Memorial Day doesn't sound right, however, I have spared a moment to think about the devastation and futility of war in general, and the tragedy of those who lost, or are losing as we spend this day, their lives. My aunt Enid married her high school sweetheart who then went right off to WWII to be killed almost immediately in some major battle. I think the moment she heard he was dead shaped the way she approached life from that day forward: as if life were a series of kites in chaotic flight across the sky that she absolutely must at least try to catch. Reading my parents' letters to each other and home from Pacific navy life, I am struck by their innocence, their excitement, as if war were another party, another fraternity. Once my father experienced war firsthand at Okinawa, his tune changed. He too, grew up in a day, but unlike my aunt, he experienced life through a gin-soaked veil from then onward. Bless them all, every one. It would surely be better if this day were irrelevant, and yet, here we are, another enemy, justified, another senseless loss of life, a country battered while we watch.

Love,
Jane


*30 May 2022 Warm, then winding. Parka-over-sundress weather.*

Dear Jane,
A bow of respect and gratitude to your father, Aunt Enid's beloved, and all who sacrificed their lives for our freedom to speak freely, love without fear, assemble

in praise or in protest. My Uncle Bill. Bruce's father. Those who have never held the hand of a fellow soldier breathing his last, or read about such an unspeakable horror, are all too eager to kindle the flames of rage, ignorant of how it feels to drag half a human from the shell of building obliterated by the "enemy." And when the enemy is us? We would all be wise to hold this day in reverence, to really think about the nature of killing another person because he disagrees with our notion of freedom or equality, treaties or borders, "right" or "wrong," or any other human-made construct within which people choose to argue.

Love,
Medea


*May 31, 2022 sun, calm, dry*

Dear Medea,
I feel the approach of summer with a combination of hope and dread. If I narrow my eyes, squint at this strange world we find ourselves in, maybe the sharp edges that cut so deep will dull a bit. Like the carving knife on Thanksgiving Day, it seems always to get handed back for a sharpening. Gene's grandmother used to say, "you could ride to Pittsburg on this knife," well, I'm here to declare that a soft ride some place in peace and calm might be a great idea about now. Since that's not literally going to happen, I'm going to promise to "lighten up" and find the sprites and gentle spirits wherever they are hiding and invite them for a cup of tea, or, better yet, a fine crystal glass of something sparkling; and ask them to share a story we can tell and retell, build into our mythology some new promise, painting over the sheer awfulness of the past decade. Has it really been so long since things felt right? I think so. As we head toward our final weeks, may the important cream rise to the surface with the sun and give each day a sweet and gentle peace.

Love,
Jane


*31 May 2022 75 degrees, gentle breeze, clouds removed to other climes leaving only blue blue sky above.*

Dear Jane,
The things we've observed, obsessed over, hinted at and picked clean over these past ten months will fill a book. We've entered my favorite time of year, though

I'm not as attached to one season over another thanks to this period of reflection and exchange. The sun rose this morning at 5:49, and will set tonight at 8:24, offering its light for nearly fifteen sparkling hours as it will for another three weeks before we celebrate the year's longest day. The atmosphere shimmers with possibility in all these illuminated moments, extra time to walk among the ravens, to shake a fist at the Stephens and the latest bandit squirrel with its four white paws, whom I've dubbed "Boots." Extra light to repair the irrigation pipes that Boots, Abigail and the Stephens have chewed through, again, because I failed to offer a beverage with their meals.

The New Moon rose overnight, an incidental salute to Pat's passing at 6:30pm. She is reunited with her husband Lou, a pig farmer, mortgage broker, furniture wholesaler, bar owner, and their precious white rescue Lhaso Apso, aptly named "Jazz." Pat also joins her former bandmate, the legendary trombone player and composer Turk Murphy, who died on the same date in 1987. Turk's band is now reassembled; listen carefully, for the heavens will surely swing.

You and I revel in opposites; you the autumnal equinox, me the summer solstice, and the winter solstice as well, if only because it means the days will start to lengthen again. The past decade may pale in comparison to the next; we may enter an intractable war with Russia, China may fish out the seven seas, the ex-president whose name we dare not speak may find himself with his finger on the Big Red Button again.

Or. The Russian people may rise against. The Chinese people may shun seafood in protest. The American electorate may consider that differences among people pale against the humanity that unites us, and decide to elect a president with the power to unite and strengthen our republic. In the meantime, we listen to the ancient wisdom of the birds the trees. We count on Gene and Bruce to love and vex us. We cherish our kids, who remind us that motherhood is not for sissies.

My garden is calling.

Love,
Medea

*June 2022*

**2 June 2022 68 and breezy, here. Blue skies above.**

Dear Jane,

Many stats today: Queen Elizabeth celebrates seventy years on her throne; Day Two of Pride Month, with the famed and fluttering Pink Triangle lighting up the night sky; 233 mass shootings so far this year, in America; Day 100 of Putin's War. Hope and despair as the world turns ʼround.

My dad told me today that the Queen took her royal vows when he was stationed in Germany. They were nearly the same age; he was twenty, she was twenty-five, so he's felt a certain kinship with her and her reign. Adorable. Only a third of Brits wish to see Charles ascend; this one-third seems focused on his environmental stewardship, while the majority holds him in contempt for maintaining his mistress while fathering two sons with Diana. He would likely do well to pass on the King gig and settle on into his dotage.

The excitement in the garden involves the census and the tinies. We welcome this week a pointy-headed Steller's Jay, a blue and gray Scrub Jay, three different types of woodpeckers, at least three different nuthatch individuals, a total of twelve Black-capped Chickadees, two Oak Titmice, and several Dark-eyed Juncos. The ravens and jays swoop in when I'm not looking, dispersing the tinies and feasting on the corn cobs meant for the squirrels, who wonder why I'm trying to distract them with food meant for swine. Tell it to the jays, Stephen. Anyway, when I went out yesterday to refill the feeder, the tinies flocked to the bird tree, completely unfazed by a nearly six-foot tall person milling about. Have they come to trust me? Today, I tried extending a large square of food, of ample size that they could either land on its edge and take a nibble or slide on by and eat on the "fly." Four of the chickadees and two nuthatches approached in increments, an inch here, half a foot there, until I could have stroked their coverts from where I stood. To continue earning their trust, I crumbled some corners of the food square onto a few easily accessed surfaces and stood close while they, calmly, assuredly, took their shares and munched them on a branch within my arm's reach.

I feel like St. Francis.

Love,
Medea

*June 4, 2022 overcast, fog, mist a Perfect Day*

Dear Medea,

I have BIG news! The baby ravens have flown from their nest! At the raucous encouragement of proud parents, they made their flappy way over and through the trees to see for themselves where all this food has been coming from. I think there might be three, certainly there are two. They fly well but landing is a comic vaudeville act of flapping wings as they gain their sense of balance. They didn't dare come down to the plank where their food is but squawked and flapped around while Tinker and Burt described the process, showed them the way. We're so proud! Tinies they are not. At this point they are nearly as big as their parents. Because last year there were five, I wonder: is climate change affecting fertility? Did one of the hawk raids take a tiny? We'll never know. Or. Maybe only the bigger nestlings made the morning trek and there will be more to come. Sigh. I couldn't be more excited, but you're right, motherhood is not for the faint of heart.

St. Francis indeed. A saint to admire. If only he had been in charge instead of an outlier Hermit with strange ideas about love and care for all creatures.

I will leave it at that. This feels like the climax to this year for me and my natural world, though, of course, there is the denouement to come as the cycle completes and then…well, we will just have to wait and see. I have been reminded more than once in the past few days to live fully in the moment and think only within the given joy of it.

Love,
Jane


*4 June 2022 Humid and threatening rain, or promising rain. 64 feels like 74. I'll take it.*

Dear Jane,

Hooray for the Tinker and Burt babies! You've taken a photo or two? I feel like an auntie, in the marvelous way certain of my friends mean it: someone who cares for someone else's kin freely, lovingly. Congratulations. This may be a major highlight of our correspondence thus far. What size is a baby raven? Robin? Mid-sized crow? I noticed at the feeder this evening what must be fledging nuthatches. Yesterday only three came; today, there were six. One of the more confident birds nipped off some suet and fed it to two others perched on a higher branch, who carry the same slate gray feathers and white eyeshade but looked tentative and a tad smaller. Two others swooped in and nabbed beaks-full and flew off to the nearby pine trees, where newer chicks likely await their dinner.

How long until all of our babies will fend for themselves? Are the Stephens hiding a scurry of pink, bare-naked squirrel kits nearby and that fuels their voraciousness? I feel a debt of gratitude to you, to Covid, to Thay, to Barry Lopez and Aldo Leopold and Rachel Carson for walking with me to this place of reverence for all living things.

"The moment" is a grand place to live.

Love,
Medea

P.S. How did St. Francis feel about rats?


*June 6, 2022 Tweed's 10th birthday! Sun. breezy. Tolerable.*

Dear Medea,
The astrological mudslinging storm that drained me and made a mess of a perfectly decent weekend has deflated into a quiet and exhausted household, restored, perhaps, but leaving behind a sore jaw from grinding my teeth. Tell me, do you think choosing the brand new (used twice) $150 All Clad sauté pan as a bathroom sink drain catch was a good move? Me neither.

Meanwhile. Happy Birthday to sweet Tweed who seems to be enjoying the day and has been quite stable if I may say so without antagonizing the gods of blown pancreases. I ordered him one of those fluffy "anxiety" beds advertised everywhere I look. He deserves a comfy bed. Not that he doesn't already have the best Orvis has to offer, but he seems to sleep in it backwards which makes me wonder.

The second day that Tinker and Burt brought the fledglings for breakfast they were cavorting on the lawn, making lunges at the glass of the garage door, and chattering away. I opened the kitchen door to get them some food and Tweed ran out which scared the children off back to the nest from which they complained and cried for their parents. I suppose not a bad idea for them to see that the ground contains hazards. For Tweed, the ravens are playmates of sorts, and he has grown used to playing tag with them since he was a puppy. They will learn. I still haven't managed a confirmed head count but there are definitely four, and possible five fledglings. They are almost as big as Tinker and Burt which makes it even more confusing trying to count them. Seen together, they can be separated, but so far that hasn't happened in a total group. This afternoon two were on the roof of the house, and one with Tinker on the garage roof. Another in the trees, or maybe two. I recall from brief reading before we started this project, that they abandon the nest at some point and roost together as a group for a year or more. It is such a beautiful thing to witness, to feel their attention and affection. And, to feel yours as well. What a gift.

Love,
Jane

P.S. What with the plagues, I suspect St. Francis drew the line at rats. When I lived in Beirut there were rats the size of cats roaming the streets.


*6 June 2022 Crystal blue sky from here to the SF Marina, mid-60s, parka-weather. I'm told that Portola Valley is warm, high 70s, today. Tech titans know how to site a company.*

Dear Jane,
Happy Birthday to Tweed! I hope he figures out the proper end of his new bed. Loki still prefers the cardboard box and its "awning," but only between about noon and seven pm. Animals, like people, have their quirks.

The tinies still resist hand-feeding, which might be ultimately safer for them, everything being equal. But the nuthatches and chickadees pay me no mind at all, and approached food I placed just inches from my person this afternoon. Did you know that chickadees, and titmice, wear blue hosiery on their legs? It's not discernable from ten feet away. Being this close, I've been able to see the subtle differences between otherwise "brown/black/white" birds. One has lost the feathers around its beak. It's one of the braver chickadees and scarcely waits for me to remove my fingers before snatching a morsel better sized (in my mind, anyway) for a sparrow or robin. Two of them have what look like pin feathers around their eyes; they remind me of the Sisters of Perpetual Indulgence.

I can hear the raven issuing orders now, so I'm glad I stood guard while the tinies had dinner. It seems that the ravens love spent corn cobs; the cobs I've left for the squirrels somehow slip, or are beaked, off the peg and disappear. Who eats corn cobs? What would Tinker and Burt say about that?

Will you name their babies?

St. Francis, the Outlier of Love, who drew the line at rats. I like that.

Love,
Medea

P.S. In no universe is placing an All-Clad sauté pan under the leaky sink an acceptable solution. That's what the Baccarat decanter is for.

P.P.S. The Sisters of Perpetual Indulgence is a non-profit order of "queer and trans nuns" who "believe all people have a right to express their unique joy and beauty." Keeping it real since 1979. I think St. Francis would approve.


*June 7, 2022 Wedding Anniversary # 52. Yes, I said 52. Sunshine. Calm. Warm*

Dear Medea,

I think we should call ourselves the Sisters of Birdy Indulgence, surely? I know I run out at the ravens' every beck and call and lay out their repast. And so it seems do other folks since I have seen them with both "used" corn cobs and finished BBQ pork chops. This was last summer. I inquired of neighbor Jane if they came from her picnic, and she said no. Who knows how far they went to scavenge such treats, but the funny part was that they left them at my doorstep. Figuring, what, that cooked food was for humans? Or just as an "I love you."?

Last summer when there were five babies, we only named the smallest one, that's Tinker, and then as you will recall, I became uncertain about whether Tinker was the runt, or just a very harried mother! I still don't know the answer. Tinker looks robust now though. I haven't had a chance to really see the kids well, but I hope they will come around like the last brood.

I love that your tinies are so used to you. I bet they think you are a beautiful flowering tree and any minute they will be landing in your hair.

Necessary pleasantries and a nice meal are required. I will write more tomorrow.

Love,
Jane


*8 June 2022 67 and blustery, overcast.*

Dear Jane,

Happy fifty-two years of wedded...bliss, torment, adulation, tsouris, laughter, victory. What an accomplishment. I'm very happy for you and Gene, two determined, committed and very fortunate people.

The tinies, two sparrows and a single nuthatch, did snatch a morsel from my fingertips this morning. They wait for me now, at around four each afternoon—I can hear them starting to twitter—and when I walk out with the suet cake, they scurry to the bird tree, ruffling up feathers, belting out songs, auditioning for "first fed." How did you know that I envision myself as another tree when I'm standing still and watchful among them, offering nourishment and admiration?

Anthropomorphizing aside, you know the birds' behavior changes as exposure to us widens. Who will stay with you after this brood matures? I remember when you first noticed Tinker as a unique raven personality, curious about her age and identity. We've come to know her so well this year. What a gift.

You remember, I feel sure, the Lazarus tree? The Canary Island palm decapitated by new owners of the home near mine that defied its death sentence and sprouted fresh fronds over the past months? I don't know how to process what happened this morning. A metallic roar shattered the birdsong that typically lights my morning. I ran outside to find its source and saw a battalion of trucks and heavy equipment parked like enemy tanks along the street in front of the Lazarus tree. A gang of workers lifted saws and axes around its base.

"Where is your permit?" I asked. "That lady, she has it," said the super, gesturing toward the owner's house down the block. My eyes went to the treetop, which bore the wrath of the sawblades last year and the fronds remained intact. Whew. Then I followed the line of the tree from its crown toward the ground. Within just a couple of minutes, the tree killers had hacked a gash in Lazarus' lower quadrant, inflicting a mortal wound. I spat out a few choice words before choking on tears. The supervisor laughed at me, gestured to his crew to laugh at me. Bastards.

I am not ignorant of the fact that the land on which my home sits once belonged to the Steller's Jays and titmice, the raccoons and gophers and coyotes that still roam here, now cautious and wary, occasionally brutalized by car strikes or poison or traps. I'm not sure whether Indigenous people inhabited this plot, but do think about that as well. As a steward of this place, I feel an obligation to safeguard. The naturalist and storyteller Barry Lopez implored us to imagine a future where we all feel of a community, responsible for our human failings and living our lives in atonement for those shortcomings. In one of the essays in the posthumous collection of his essays called *Embrace Fearlessly the Burning World*, he writes,

"We will need to trust each other, because today it's as if every safe place has melted into the sameness of water. We are searching for the boats that we forgot to build."

How can I trust a neighbor who harbors no sense of stewardship? Must I forgive or fight? Hate or love? What serves the earth best? After last summer's carnage and the subsequent rebirth of Lazarus, I trusted that the tenacity of this tree would touch the owners the way it touched me, my family, our neighbors, all of whom marveled as first a few frond tips sought the sun, then a few more. Over the next weeks and months, for almost a year, Lazarus stretched its arms to the sky, a full bouquet of fronds almost completely replacing what had been taken. I thought the beauty, the strength, the majesty of this aged tree as it battled to stay alive and relevant would sway the owners. How could they ignore its demand to live?

The optimists among us believe that nature always wins. I still believe this. Yet, today I will sit quietly among the birds and beseech the universe to reveal to me exactly how the stump that was Lazarus will perceive this as victory.

Love,
Medea

P.S. The Sisters of Birdy Indulgence. I needed that giggle today.


*June 9, 2022 sun, dry, inversion point*

Dear Medea,
Like you, I thought the great palm tree had escaped death last year at this time when we started this project. Lazarus was our point of hope. Now, Lazarus will stand as the message, the messenger, of the heart of what we want to share and hopefully have shared in this year of letters: we are all creatures of equal value. No one has the right to destroy the way your neighbor has destroyed their environment in order to squat in their fancy new home. If they wanted to live on barren land, they should have looked elsewhere. It is a discouraging symbol of decline, of failure, that they felt so bold as to start again and take away that majestic tree. But you know what? They are forever noted here on the pages of this book as an example of how not to be a good steward.

Love,
Jane


*10 June 2022 So hot you can hear the tree sap crackle. Hot.*

Dear Jane,
Thank you for your kinship in this. Yesterday, as the stump grinders macerated what remained of Lazarus, it occurred to me, too, that she lives on in these pages, as do the sins of the landowners, for whom the word "steward" probably denotes a servant on a yacht, and nothing more. When I mentioned the incident to my mom, her first remark was, "Is the tree on your land?" But after gentle words about the trees not really "belonging" to anyone, she told me that a new neighbor immediately chopped down a flowering, innocent orchid tree

nurtured from a tiny pot by her former neighbor, and another newcomer who excised the business half of a banyan tree that I walked past on my way to school fifty years ago. "It's going to die," Mom said. "A slow and painful death," I added.

Two more tree lives commemorated here.

Love,
Medea


*June 11, 2022 warm, sun, still air.*

Dear Medea,
The Raven family are beginning to spread their wings a bit and come around to learn the ropes: pecking through the wood chips to look for bugs, flying low around the house looking for me, and sitting on tree branches with a good view of the kitchen. Six birds on the garage roof peak with much shuffling and waddling to form a decent line, nothing at all like can-can dancers at an audition. Well, maybe a little bit. Lots of squawking by Tinker and Burt to call them all to order for the next lesson in ravenhood. I'm pretty sure there are four young, but there could be a fifth that just isn't quite with the program. Sometimes Tinker acts as if she is still calling to one more baby. The "babies" are huge, nearly as big as the parents and far beyond being called "baby." Fully fledged they aren't fluffy fledglings either. Oh, how quickly they grow up. After all the anticipation! And yet, they are still scaredy-birds, learning the rules of the forest, who run back to the nest area at the slightest hint of danger and fully under the keen-eyed rule of their parents.

We have also seen a fawn with her mother, not a tiny, but still one with spots. There is a lot of activity here just now as we have work going on to repair molding and repaint all of the buildings. It is a summer long effort, probably, which will keep the deer at the edges of their usual places, deep in the forest, or out in the north meadow. Speaking of land use and preservation, I've recently learned that a while ago our neighbor, Kris Kristofferson, declared his several hundred-acre pasturelands as a Land Trust, changing the zoning from ag to wild land. This is fantastic news for all of us. Thank you, sir!

Tonight, you fly east and south. Safe travels, my friend. I'm spending the day reviewing and refreshing the Go Bags. Ah summer.

Love,
Jane

Dear Jane,

Thank you, Kris Kristofferson, for this gift of wild. After this week of carnage, good news works extra wonders.

The vision of Tinker, Burt and the four big, brave-ish tinies just tickles me. What a sight that must be: six black shadows perched on the crest of the roof, Tinker and Burt *hawhawing* instructions, Tweed cocking his head in wonder. And your seat is front and center: you followed a raven from ingenue teen, through a courtship and union, and on to her fully-formed and almost fledged family life. Broadway in your backyard.

It must be cooler up your way, as the deer here hide in the foliage down by the reservoir rather than roaming the streets in search of flowers to nibble. In the past two weeks, I've seen only one lone tawny doe rustling under a grove of oaks up on the ridge south of my house. The creek at the end of my street and down in the valley below looks more like wet dirt than quenching watercourse. We don't make it easy for the critters.

This time tomorrow will find me with my other friend Jane on the banks of the Caloosahatchee River, looking for snipes and Glossy Ibises, grateful for a friendship that has sustained us through the ups and downs of our marriages, the birth and growth of our babies, (and now her grandbabies), wildfires, hurricanes and blue-green algae and the three-thousand miles between us.

Thanks for your safe travel wishes, and reminder to pack the Go bags.

Love,
Medea

Dear Medea,

I hope your delayed flight didn't make you miss your connection and that you are snug in the bosom of your family and dear friend Jane. Isn't it true that so often it is these deep friendships which sustain us rather than the tangle of family where obligation and blood bind so tightly?

This morning the dawn chorus started with phoebes, I think, with Hermit Thrush more distant. Then the ravens got up and dressed and began to rattle around the forest calling out. Maybe they were playing tag or Hide and Seek? Eventually they started flying around the house, landing with a thud on the roof and generally making enough noise that only a devoted sleeper like myself could ignore–tempted as I was to actually look at them. When I did get up–

here's my routine—I turn on the electric kettle, pour my green juice drink, and grab the garage door keys. The rattle of keys is Tweed's cue to leap up and race to the door & out the door barking because he knows the ravens will be there, if not perched on the fence posts outside the door, then up on the garage roof, still close enough to play the game. It's all perfunctory though the baby ravens don't know that yet. There are two or sometimes three small ones who seem to be learning the drill faster and sometimes one will come with either Tinker or Burt and be waiting on the roof. Their food is in the garage, of course, which is why I occasionally see one of them flying up and hovering at the door window trying to see exactly what's what inside. Well stocked with bird table food, they are happy, and Tweed and I take a short stroll for his nature break before we go back indoors for morning tea. In all, Tweed alone requires at least three trips outside in the morning in short succession and no variation to the routine is tolerated. Then we will often have a longer ramble, or I will have a swim and Tweed will sit with me. Lately, because there is more activity than usual here, as I mentioned yesterday, I'm keeping my activity with Tweed closer to home to give the deer a bit of space. Like the ravens and their game of tag, Tweed gives them his attention, but it is half-hearted, just a trot toward them and a bark or two, sometimes just mutual recognition and no chase or vocals. It's good training for the young ones, not all predators are as benign, especially the human kind.

I was thinking this morning that summer bringing lazy days is just as much a state of mind as it is long days providing a sense of there being "no rush." I'm finding so much joy in Linda Hogan's *The Radiant Lives of Animals*—her calm voice and obvious kinship with the creatures around her make me feel that perhaps there is a legacy growing and renewing of understanding not only the past and the clear present, but also a future of grace and knowing.

Love,
Jane


*June 13, 2022 windy.*

Dear Medea,
Just briefly, all six raven family members gathered together last evening to learn how to toss wood chips in search of bugs. This morning all six gathered in the early hours to practice flying, and more importantly, landing in fierce winds, and this evening, all six were perched proudly on the garage roof ready for their "tea" (the weird British slang for the evening meal). Together it is obvious that the four children are about 3/4ths the size of their parents, and I must say, Burt is looking rather fat, if not paunchy, but that's for Tinker and him to figure out.

Hope you are enjoying Florida.

Love,
Jane


*14 June 2022 88 degrees and sunny, with puffy cotton clouds and light breeze.*

Dear Jane,
Florida has opened her arms to me once again, welcoming and warm. This is a trip with multiple purposes, so please forgive my failure to check in until now.

Of note is the differences in the meteorological definitions of "hot" between here and NorCal. Announcements and warnings of "extreme heat" commence in SF as soon as it looks like it might get a little bit toasty, and mercury approaches eighty-two or so. The weather forecaster yesterday displayed a chart that shows the local definitions of heat. Up to ninety degrees is called "very warm." Ninety to one hundred is "hot." A hundred to a hundred-ten we consider "very hot." Not until the thermometer hits one-ten is the purple level, "extreme heat" achieved. You'd hate it. My folks set their air conditioner at seventy-eight, which is a rare summer temperature, outdoors, where you live. This palmy paradise, where White Ibises with their curved pink beaks wander the town's sidewalks looking for insects and lizards as the sun rises, where I can walk the beach well after sunset, eighty-five-degree seawater lapping my shins, this is my definition of "home."

The raven family entertains far more effectively than, say, the January 6th hearings or the Depp-Heard trial. Those next-gen corvids, learning the art of the hunt, the game of chase, the benefits of accepting gifts from the kindly lady who lives under the eaves, they follow the ancient wisdom. Do you have an elementary school nearby? I read a series of interviews in the local paper with Floridian writers of children's books, and each one of them took their inspiration from some experience with birds or crocodiles or the local indigenous cultures. Back to basics, just in time for this next-gen of human young'uns. I'm thinking that a book about Tinker, Burt and their big tinies, featuring Tweed in a supporting role, illustrated by Kim would be worth sharing.

My friend Jane, with whom I spent a luxurious Sunday afternoon, shares her yard with a pair of Northern Cardinals, the cherry-red male and the tawny female with her showy orange beak, a kindred woodpecker, a couple of bronze, chatty mockingbirds, two blue jays with their Mondrian-esque tails, a family of grackles (plain, not Boat-tailed) and several curious, bold brown squirrels. We rocked on her patio sipping Sauvignon Blanc and watching the animals on perpetual parade. My dad scoffed when I told him we quickly passed two hours this way. "Who can spend two hours watching birds?" We ran out of wine or would have happily, gratefully, spent three.

The turtles have returned to the beach to lay eggs. I counted a dozen nests in a short span of sand at the public beach, and still more further south on Casperson's Beach. Casperson's was wild and vacant, our party place when I was in high school; it's now not only a turtle refuge but offers nature trails and dune-preserving walkways and rocky outcrops for exploring. Gators, surely, though they hid from me as I pedaled by in the late afternoon, clear of the harshest UV rays. The bright lights of the interloping high-rise condos that line the beach sent the turtles to nest elsewhere for years. But we're presumptuous if we think that nature will stand for our interference forever.

May Tweed continue to heal thus sparing you and Gene a trip to Davis.

Love,
Medea

P.S. I sucked in hard and rode my bike past the lot where my childhood home lived. I think I told you that it, and my mom's beloved fishtail palm, were razed last fall, leaving only gray sand and a " For Sale" sign. Price tag? $1,000,000. Someone clearly bit, but instead of replacing the house and yard, some crass developer split the lot and built two zero-lot-line, faux Tuscan boxes, one in dreck brown, the other in vampire gray. Not a frond or flower in sight.

*June 15, 2022 Sun. Wind.*

Dear Medea,
Having northern European skin and endured a few shocking episodes of heat stroke over my 73 years, including 6 long summers in 120 degree relentless sunshine in southern Iran, I'm not impressed by heat tolerance bravado, but I will agree that to some degree many people acclimatize, or have a preference right from the womb–think of the high Andes indigenous people who are born to the thin air and scamper up hill and down dale running circles around the outsiders. I guess there is a place for everyone, and everyone to their place. While I long to sit by a pebbled lake shore with a cool breeze rustling the maple trees, my feet in the water playing across the stones looking for treasures, you are happy as a clam in the sand, sun, and reptiles baking along the shoreline. It makes me hot to consider, but I'm happy you love it, and are able to be there! That's the main thing. As for San Francisco's heat warnings, I'm absolutely certain they stem from the tragic deaths last year of several different collections

of people who went out for a hike or a run, never to return. The warnings are important, and yet, still people will do stupid things.

This morning all six members of the raven family lined up on the roof peak ready for breakfast. Later, I was in the garden and heard an argument, or what I thought was an argument, and saw two ravens either mating or pretending/ learning to mate. Hey! I yelled! You can't do that with your sister! Or can you? Like cats on a fence, it's hard to tell if they are enjoying it or not, but the raven male certainly knew the moves.

Visiting the plot of land where your house used to be took courage, particularly since the sting of development is up near the top of the list of things that piss you off. I'm sorry you had that experience. Even without going there, I was struck with a pang of some sort of shock when I learned that my house in Iran had been bombed to rubble in the Iran/Iraq war. And I didn't like living there! Something my cousin Jim and I love to do is drive around places where our ancestors lived and find the addresses, farms, houses, churches where they were baptized or buried, especially graveyards, marking each one, finding a tether from ourselves to that past, whether distant or far. Your house is gone, but your place there lives on.

Love,
Jane


*15 June 2022 92, sun to the west, thunder and its storm approaching from the east.*

Dear Jane,
Bravado isn't quite what I was aiming for, simply a difference in, as you say, tolerance. People freeze to death. We pass out permanently from the heat. The Andean people's ability to breathe at altitude, in the cold, while tending to the quotidian necessaries of life places them high in my roster of respect. Variety is spice.

I took another long bike ride today, this time past the first two houses where my first family has lived. Both still stand, intact. I saw Mrs. Cade in my mind's eye, her soft face and grandmotherly smile, her simple calico dress and ample bosom peering out from her kitchen window, across the bleached shell driveway and into ours on Nassau Street where we'd wave to one another from our Spanish-stucco homes. Mrs. Steinke, who stood maybe five feet tall and wore a cap of curly silver hair, lived next door to us on Dawn Street. Her house and ours, cinder block construction with tar and gravel roofs with carports attached, look as they did fifty-five years ago. The oak tree in our back yard, where daddy hung a two-by-four from a rope for me to swing, has grown taller, spared the wrath of tree murderers. So, redemption today.

A storm is passing over as I write from my parent's swing, which is topped with a tin roof, so all of the raindrops are pattering, now drumming, and just a few landing on my knee. The temperature has dropped ten degrees. Rain smells like soil, and green. It smells heavy, and the air feels like you could grab a handful and stuff a pillow. Lightening cracks the sky in two. Just like I remember, these storms visit, unleash a heap of baggage, and pass over before you can change your plans.

Today's nature tally from a tour along the Legacy Trail includes one speedy, "threatened" Gopher Tortoise that escaped into is burrow before I could click a photo, one juvenile iguana, darkly buff with darker spots that made it invisible in the sand and scrub grass, one very hungry bunny, one Kangaroo Rat, many White and one Glossy black Ibis, one Pileated Woodpecker drilling into a palm trunk in front of my piano teacher, Mrs. Rayburn's, old house, two "vulnerable" Florida Scrub Jays and too many mockingbirds to count. I'll have to ask Bruce to check on the tinies.

The rain falls faster with plump drops and I just had to cover my ears from the lightening/thunder display. It's early still, though, and the beach never, ever, turns me away.

Love,
Medea

P.S. Forty-five minutes after it began to unleash, the storm yields to dappled sun.


*June 17, 2022 sun.*

Dear Medea,
Oh! I envy you your thunderstorms! I do love a good storm. On top of never having them here, we can't even wish for them, for fear of one actually materializing and starting hundreds of fires, which happened a few years back. I love the electric air, the way the earth smells when the big drops of rain start after a warm day, I love the noise, the light, everything about it. Enjoy!

With chainsaws and woodchippers raging on two sides, the deer are coming back to the yard in ones and twos, chased, I think, by the threat and noise. On one side, new neighbors are clearing for their house building. On the other side, the homeowner is having another strip of dead Bishop pines felled and chipped, victims of the dreadful beetles that are bringing down more pines than they are leaving standing. To a large degree this is part of the drought, which is part of climate change. One of the deer I saw today was the young small one from last year who always tagged along with the group. The poor thing is now on her own, having been run off by her mother. I know this because I saw it happen several times last week. I think the juvenile is struggling on her own and keeps finding the mother and trying to hang out with her again. But if the mother has a new fawn, she won't let the juvenile stay. Sometimes all this nature stuff makes me really sad.

In avian news, there was a commotion today when a hawk threatened the ravens. Tinker took off after it with lots to say about the affront. Sometime later all six showed up for a bathe in the copper firepit converted birdbath, three at a time, and clamoring for some easy food which I, of course, obliged.

Tweed is a little under the weather today, and I am trying not to overreact.

In extended family news, Chris took the family over to Clear Lake and launched the sailboat for their first overnights on real water. They are thrilled and having a beautiful time.

Love,
Jane


*17 June 2022 89 with a "feels like" of 103. Not to me, but that's the party line. Pale blue sky, puffy clouds, a hint of breeze.*

Dear Jane,
This will be brief, as the sun sets in just forty minutes or so, and that's a salutation I'll honor.

I understand your sentiment about the fawn. The sense of all things being right with the world that we get from observing, admiring, communing with our non-human friends shatters when a mama shuns its baby, or a daddy smothers its young. Oddly, it just feels disgusting and wretched when we read about humans torturing or popping off their children, not like a betrayal of trust, but more like an epiphany that humans exist who probably should not.

How is Tweed's pep today?

Do you remember the first time you slept aboard a boat? What tales will come from this trip to Clear Lake? What I remember most about sleeping on our runabout when I was a child is the dark, diamond sky, and the turbulent hush, like whispers of friends from long, long ago.

There are tiny chirping frog noises everywhere around my parent's house and particularly around the door to my room, which overlooks a small patio. Over the past days of my visit, without any attacks upon my person, it's easy to make peace with the frogs, my life-long rivals. Ranaphobia is so rare I guess that spell check changes it to Nanaphobia. How many people are afraid of their grandmas?

The sky is silver now as sunset approaches. Its white light silhouettes the tall fronds of the queen palms, changing their hue from forest to onyx. Jane visited again today and we talked about what it means to be able to extract meaning from the petal of a flower. Some find meaning in Miami raves or crashing the party of an influencer in Bel Air. And others look for the universe in the carnelian eye of a mature White Ibis.

The beach beckons.

Love,
Medea

P.S. A cloud lightning storm walked the beach with me and followed me home. Someone blasted fireworks off to the east, a sound that wishes it were thunder.

*18 June 2022 Another scorcher. Thunderstorms predicted for the next two hours, until 8 pm, so just enough time to run to the beach before sunset.*

Dear Jane,

The local newspaper reports that the brain-dead or possibly corrupt council members in Lee and Collier Counties approved something like 40,000 new housing units to be constructed over top of some of the last remaining panther byways and gasping wetland ecosystems. This, while toxic blue-green algae choke the waterways and knee-cap the fish guides from making a living. But wait! So many new tourists have shown up, eschewing Mickey and the sprawl of Tampa-St. Pete, that bed tax coffers brim with bucks, record-breaking bucks, bucks that will allow for more road building and parking meters and gun fights for towel spots on the public beaches in SW Florida.

If ever I sound cynical or negative, you just let me know.

Tomorrow is Father's Day. This will be the second year in a row I'm fortunate to spend all day with Daddy, doing whatever he wants to do. I might have to lure him down to the Avenue, where the swings await and the squirrels remember the guy who brings the peanuts.

Love,
Medea

*June 19, 2022 wind. Sun.*

Dear Medea,

Happy Juneteenth. I've been thinking about how good it is to have an official holiday that is a reminder to many of us just how truly awful things could be. What I can't figure out is why this day of remembrance has been a national secret from the very people who need to be reminded of what terrible brew of hatred some people are capable of? I think of myself as well informed and historically accurate, yet I never knew about this day's significance until Black Lives Matter made us all stop and listen.

Also, happy Father's Day to your dad who sounds like a real character and who clearly loves you as much as you love him. I'm about to call my cousin Jim for a short round of "who's dad was the more crap dad" and that will about do it for today.

I continue to be low in my spirits, depleted with anxiety for the natural world. There should be a word for that in the medical lexicon. I'll save additional details until I am on a more even keel.

The sound of lake water lapping against a wooden boat, or boat dock, or shoreline, is the best sound in the world. There's an app for that. It's the best I can do for myself. Many days I can hear the ocean, but it is unsettling in its power and not the least calming. As for sleeping aboard, I have only slept on a boat that was docked except for cruise ships which don't count. When my parents lived on Coronado Island and before they bought their Islander 32, they rented boats to try out. We visited and slept on board. In the middle of the night the onboard communications system came on blaring some sort of relay and I started out of my sleep, forgot there was a step off the couch platform and fell flat on my face. I managed to grope my way in the pitch dark toward the noise–having no idea where the comms unit was–and managed to find a light and the unit to switch down the volume which some wag had no doubt left on high volume on purpose. In the morning I had a bruised body. Because I get seasick, sleeping on any boat or ship doesn't have great appeal for me. If I'd had the chance, I'm not sure I would have taken it. I've done a lot of day sailing but need to stay on deck. It's weird to love the water and yet suffer so. The most seasick I ever felt on a sailboat was in San Francisco Bay. Ugh, that swell. And when they rigged the man ropes on the Arctic cruise for the crossing of the straits, I gulped down an extra pill and went to bed. No, sadly, I'm better off in a small craft on a small lake. If wishes were horses…

Enjoy your parents and tomorrow please explain why you fear grandmas?

Love,
Jane

*June 20, 2022 sun.*

Dear Medea,

Today's post is about ravens. I have learned some things in the past 24 hrs. First, that ravens have distinct voices. Of the four young birds, there are four different tones and calls. One raven seems to say *"whaa whaa"* instead of *"caw caw."* Another has a strange low distorted, throat clearing *"blah"* while the other two sound more ravenish and yet one is low and the other high. Will their voices change to more normal sounds?

Second, they have established routines. In the morning is bath time, and flying practice. Flying practice also comes in the evening. Last evening, they were doing close maneuvers not very high up, cartwheels and sharp turns, playing tag with each other. They looked just like a favorite painting of mine by Julie Higgins who has a passion for ravens far greater and more knowledgeable than mine.

Third, and this definitely eases my heart, the ravens are still being fed bits of regurgitated food by their parents. Not sure which young one was asking but Tinker was drinking from the bird bath and the young one came and opened her mouth extended upward, begging for food. Tinker obliged and then they both drank. So even if the runt gets aced out of the goods fresh on the feeding table, she will be fed. So far.

Preparations are in hand today, cleaning house and preparing my altar for the coming solstice which, to be exact, comes at 2:13am tomorrow. Special charms are being prepared, charms of protection against evil, and connection to the moon and the earth, water, and sky. For you, the pinnacle is at 5:13am, will you be up? Will it be light? I remember being in Ireland on one solstice, sitting on top of an ancient portal tomb in meditation as the light finally came dark around midnight and then reappeared at 4am. It really is a wonder, this universe, is it not?

Love,
Jane


*21 June 2022 Summer!! 95 degrees, light wind, sculptured clouds in bright white and dove gray.*

Dear Jane,

Thunder sounds like the amplified purr of the world's most content cat. It hugs those brave or ignorant enough to wander out into the maw of an approaching storm. This is what I love about thunderstorms. The sky to the west is clear and blue. The sky to the east looks like a boxer's black eye. Tiny cells of lightening flash in jagged horizontal lines through the marching clouds. Walking in the swash zone, the sand crackles. My beloved dad was struck by lightning, twice, in hardware store parking lots. What are the odds? Though it feels like it might be a risk to keep walking the beach with this cloud cell approaching, what's the worst? I keep walking, noticing that I'm sort of sneaking into the surf to make sure I'm lower than all the boogie boarders and end-of-day sunset fans who line the shore. Then, the sky cracks open. Pellets of rain the size of Concord grapes slap the sand. Instinct directs me to run for shelter, but this rain is warm. The breeze feels as familiar as a hug from my younger self. I meander to the parking lot, stopping for a moment to look back at the Gulf, my consistent, forgiving, welcoming friend. Now, the rain comes down in buckets. That is an archaic expression perfectly suited for this moment. I can't see the car, which I would usually not have driven, walking instead, but, weather. By the time I start the car, I can't see the parking lot. Windscreen wipers? Futile.

Heading home, with only fifteen minutes of rain to manage, water chokes the storm drains and cascades rooster tails against my tires. Ten minutes after I'm back and dry, the sun shines again.

How cool is that?

I saved, perhaps ephemerally, a killdeer sought by two evil crows. Now, the crows are evil. I visited a friend yesterday who told me that when her mate finds an invasive iguana on their land, he shoots it. This is right. Invasive species threaten local ecosystems. This is wrong. That iguana didn't ask to move here. Should a well-intentioned homeowner shoot an innocent iguana in the head with a pellet gun?

Since you're not a fan of summer, I will wish you a happy "only six months until winter solstice" instead. I was not awake to usher in my favorite season but took full advantage of a sun-drenched day by whispering a prayer to the gods of the land and sea asking for an awakening before we self-destruct. I feel your planetary anxiety. Driving down Casey Key Road last evening, where low-slung wood or cinder block homes used to disappear into native landscape but have over the past decade been razed and replaced with gaudy, pseudo-Italianate mega-mansions that would look ridiculous on ten acres of lawn, and on a fragile spit of barrier island look like the embarrassing testaments to too many super egos, I broke down sobbing. There should be a word to describe that abject grief. For the agony of the loss of habitat, scale, reason, restraint. For those who've lost the ability to feel the scent of the sea or taste the color orange. Try nature bathing in concrete and steel. Good luck with that.

Love,
Medea

P.S. I do not fear grandmas. Spell check, however, does not realize that "ranaphobia," fear of frogs, is real.


*22 June 2022 Sunny and bright, a cool 85 degrees this morning. In my element.*

Dear Jane,

Reading your raven observations is like watching "Mutual of Omaha's Wild Kingdom." I can keenly see Tinker and Burt vomiting up a nourishing treat for their tinies, the tilt and whirl of their flying lessons, their unique vocalizations. The connection to your place, to you, a safe spot to raise a brood, through you they've given me much delight over these past months.

Seasickness and SF Bay go hand in hand, unless the wind has settled. It's not a gentle body but a roiling, wet trap for the unprepared. Once we were sailing back from the Delta and were cold-cocked by twenty-five knot winds as we rounded Alcatraz. The seas must have reached five feet. We'd left the 85-degree island in the morning and arrived ten hours later after a gentle enough sail into the jaws of a very feisty Zephyrus. The boys were freaked out. One lost his lunch. All of us were battered and drenched by the waves. Bruce sent the boys below and we wrestled the helm and the lines, wanting so badly to get to port but so wet and cold that our limbs nearly froze. Just another summer day on the Bay!

You mentioned Juneteenth and I neglected to comment. The recognition is long overdue. To think that many people were unaware of their freed status for two years after the Emancipation Proclamation was signed reminds me, once again and as if any of us needed a reminder, of the power of commerce and riches to warp the mind and spirit beyond redemption.

Love,
Medea

P.S. Daddy thanks you for your Father's Day good wishes. How did your dad session with Jim go? Did your dad really routinely wear an ascot?!


*June 23, 2022 sun, cool, fog just offshore if I need her cloak.*

Dear Medea,

Haha! No, my dad didn't routinely wear an ascot. There was a period in the 60s where that was done, I believe Hugh Hefner started that trend in the US but surely it was very British, the smoking jacket and ascot. He did own a "morning suit" including top hat and tails, required dress for play acting the big image with similarly pretentious royals. Mostly Iranians of the Shah's ilk. There were many occasions for formal dress. Very ridiculous considering (e.g., it was an oil refinery at the end of the earth for god's sake). And a tux for evening wear. I'm sure he loved all that gear. Jim said we should call it a draw since they are both dead. But what's the fun in that? Besides, I win. Unfortunately.

Back to ravens. Because the construction/remodel work is now centered on the garage, I moved the bird "table" around to the front of the house, interested to watch and see how long it took them to readjust. 40 minutes. They just watched me at first from high up in a fir tree. I tipped the black rigid plastic horse trough over to use that as the food table and put it under the shade of the madrone tree so that everyone (meaning you, you rascal Blue Jays) could escape to the upper branches if need be. Then I moved the copper firepit/bird bath and filled it up. Put out food and walked around the house once just to let them know I was outside. By the time I got back into the house the jays were already taking advantage, and the ravens followed. Now, several days later, it's all figured out, and they seem happier with the new location, with the birdbath close to the food source, it's like an outdoor party in LA. Because my usual chair is only feet away in the bay window, we can enjoy each other more, and more closely.

Last night the wind shifted back to "normal," which means onshore, and brought back cool temps, and dew, and tentative fog. It took a while for the house to cool down but by bedtime I was ready for a nice cool sleep, windows wide open, and was treated with a lullaby of Great Horned Owls discussing society at large for a long while before I nodded off.

I don't know if you read it, but yesterday I saw an article in the NYT about SSAD—no, not SAD Seasonal Affected Disorder, but SUMMER SAD. Yep. That'd be me. I feel vindicated! I don't want to hear again about how terrible it is to have SAD and how that's my fault because I love winter's quiet light and long dark. Or at least I won't hear it without responding in kind. In any case, it is a relief to have an end to the last heat wave which did indeed make me sick and will take a few days to "get over."

I'm reading Jon Turk's fabulous book *Tracking Lions, Myth, and Wilderness in Samburu*. It is prescient and important– a story of one small group of African people wrapped in a serious discourse on human evolution and destruction.

Love,
Jane

*June 24, 2022*

Dear Medea,
Mark this day as dark, Roe v. Wade has been overturned by a corrupt Supreme Court. Who would have thought that this country would send itself so far into the Dark Ages of suppression and ignorance? What next?

Love,
Jane


*24 June 2022 90 and breezy in Venice, with more milky skies. Promised rain never materialized, so another sherbet sunset is squarely in my near future.*

Dear Jane,
June 24, the date which will live in worse than infamy, the date the Wretched Five declared that women must live as service animals. On the heels of letting every yahoo who couldn't pick a musket out of a lineup carry a gun in any public space, I'd say it's been a shit week for American jurists' and our citizenry. "Outrage" is one of those overused words that has lost its meaning. I'm searching for another. We need to coin it.

The thing I most wanted to tell you is about my beach walk last night. First, I could hear the waves calling me home. Second, a single patch of mango sky started as an angry crab, then morphed into Grace Jones' face with her carmine lips, and before the sun retired, a gray wolf drinking from the sea. Finally, after standing in the swash for who cares how long and marveling at the way the summer sea feels amniotic, I realized I was the only person left on the beach. No Summer SAD for me, but you are absolutely vindicated.

The birds who live with you have smarts we only now begin to understand. It takes humans three weeks to reorient after moving the location of a trash can, and the ravens figured it out in forty minutes. Hmmm.

At your gentle urging, my copy of Jon Turk's book sits on the nightstand, ready to crack tonight. We shall discuss. Mom and Dad have discovered a series of YouTube videos of Botswana wildlife set to music that they (blessedly, meditatively) play in the background on the weekend.

I'd mentioned our book to my parents' friends J and G. J brought an owl book for me to read. He then brought photos of an art exhibition in town with many images of herons and owls and chickadees, in photo, oil, ink. Birds, nature, bring out the universal in us.

I hear thunder. You know what that means. The wind has picked up. Temperature dropped. A StaPuff marshmallow cloud is flying toward the beach.

My sister came yesterday for a short visit, and we had sister things to take care of this morning, including monitoring an aerial battle between a Red-shouldered Hawk and a mockingbird and buying mom a new pair of shoes. So, no beach this morning. May the rain gods move through with haste.

I have to go back to CA in a couple of days so will close now and swing with mom and dad. Maybe we'll feel the kiss of raindrops.

Love,
Medea

P.S. I forgot to tell you that a tree frog jumped upon my thigh two nights ago, and would have been happy to stay awhile but for my own flailing and swatting, which sent it soaring into a nearby hibiscus bush. It left a slime that lingers still. But I didn't scream, and I didn't die, so perhaps ranaphobia is become ranaversion. Still. I'd prefer not to have tree frogs visit my thigh or any other part of my person.

*June 27, 2022 fog, cool. Perfect.*

Dear Medea,
My attention lately is taken up with counting ravens to make sure all six are getting proper nutrition, or, well, "my nutritive efforts." Usually, I can find five rather than all six. There is always an outlier. If five are lined up on the roof tops, there is another in the trees. A spotter? Who knows. The family are all about the same size and it's very hard to tell them apart except when Tinker and Burt are together. Then, Burt is looking ruffled, and Tinker is looking amorous and motherly all at the same time, nudging closer and closer, cooing to him, picking in his feathers to clean off some tiny bug. He's the portly gent to her tall, elegant vamp. Yesterday they were on the garage roof along with two of their young and Burt had hopped to the edge of the roof, where peak meets wall, and he perched there with one wing hanging off the edge. It reminded me of the way some birds will pretend to be injured and drag a wing in order to lure a predator away from the nest. I watched for a while and he stayed in place, and then, of course, flew off the minute I wasn't watching. Was he working on his balance? Practicing a dance move? Threatening to jump? Trying to explain that he's injured? Just another moment in our year long project of wondering.

Our lone deer is keeping close. Poor thing. But wise choice, to sleep in the tall grass near the house, graze in the dandelions, and then find shelter in the forest during the day. Yesterday, Tweed went out the door about six feet and froze, pointer style, and there in the grass was the soft questioning head of the deer, still bedded down for the night. Tweed didn't bark or move, just waited while she rose and moved off. Good dog. Even though I am informed that the deer herd will reunite, and that should happen fairly soon, I worry about a solo deer who has always struggled, and clearly seems to miss her place.

As for predators, the bobcat wandered into the yard, cool as a cat, master of her rodent universe.

You might not have seen that Mark Cavendish won the British National Road Race yesterday! Boring race until the end, but a joy to see him looking fit and winning, fair and square. Will he make the Tour team? No one knows yet. We'll see if there are parallels to draw between competitive sport and the natural world. I kind of doubt it.

Love,
Jane


*29 June 2022 Windy, clear, low to mid 60s. Obviously, I'm not in Florida anymore.*

Dear Jane,
Before I commiserate over the ignominious new Supremes, I'd like to offer a glimpse into the farewell that the critters in Venice offered on Monday. First, a Northern Cardinal, male, fiery red, followed me halfway round the yard while I helped mom look for a site to plant a Bottle Palm that has lived in the same pot for twenty years. No luck—my parents instilled the jungle approach to home gardens in me and their lush plot lacks space for a tree that, in the ground, will grow to ten feet with twelve-foot-long fronds. So, it will live in a larger pot with new soil where it may raise its arms and touch the sky. When I was a little girl, mom told me that seeing a red cardinal meant good luck, and urged me to wish on the powerful bird. What to wish for? Peace in Ukraine? Monkeypox upon the tyrants in D.C. and beyond? Renewed health for sea grass and corals? I settled on an era of tolerance. That cardinal has work to do.

After wishing, I rode to the beach for a "last walk." Several groups of four or seven Ruddy Turnstones disappeared into the sand until they staccato-walked to the wrack line in unison to peck for coquinas. A few javelin-beaked terns pecked at a small cluster of Laughing Gulls, who looked surprised by the attack. In the tall grass that borders the Deertown Creek next to Walter Farley's old house, a solitary Snowy Egret hunted for whatever small fish can actually live in that turbid water. I moved in closer to snap a picture, and noticed something prickly out of the corner of my right eye. A gator sunning at the water's edge. Oblivious tourists ambled by. I thought about warning parents of small kids, but maybe that's insulting to their intelligence, so I walked on and asked the cardinal to keep an eye on the gator. Every step on any day on this the same stretch of sand is a glimpse into a different world, I thought, and a group of teenage girls ran toward me shouting "Look! A manatee!" and damn if a huge cow wasn't swimming right offshore, lifting her head every few minutes to sip for air. She slowly waved her unmistakable paddle tail up, then down, expending just enough energy to propel her forward. In all of walks I've taken on this beach, probably many thousands, I've never seen a manatee.

The two ravens that sometimes visit my feeders *hawed* at me this morning until I peeked out the blinds to see them staring at me from the fence. Like Tinker and Burt, they ruffle their feathers and talk a bit more, then flew off to a nearby pine bough. Do they prefer a different food? Do they need fresh water? The blue Scrub Jay is content with whatever I offer: suet, nut squares, peanuts, corn. The nuthatch family has turned a blue-gray in the two weeks I've been gone. The wee ones have learned to access the feeders and no longer squawk for mom and dad to drop food into their upturned beaks. The juncos and lone titmouse turned up reliably. Noticeably absent are the chickadees. Did the pounding from the roofers frighten them off?

Your source for deer intel keeps me from fretting that this lone doe will remain in exile. The bobcat, though...

I'd not heard about Mark Cavendish. His impish eyes, big grin and thundering thighs drew me into his fan club when I first started watching the Tour de France in the early 00s. Crossing fingers he lands a spot. Parallels between competitive sport and the natural world? Have you ever watched a pair of lionesses take down a kudu?

Love,
Medea


*June 30, 2022 sun, breezy. Not hot.*

Dear Medea,
What a joy! Seeing a manatee for the first time after all these years? Now *that's* a sign. And what a treat for those teens. A learning moment.

I've been waking up writing here and falling asleep writing here and yet nothing on paper. My experience is that this is a sign I am neglecting my duty to the page, and yet when I try to bring back the words in my head, they have flown. I've resolved to stop whatever I'm doing and rush to the computer the very next time it happens. There is so much to say as we approach the final day, and yet, I do feel as though this isn't a novel with a plot and there has been, for the reader, a clear path all along the way of what we have intended to bring forth.

On the way home from the vet the other day, we spied the lone deer (at least I think it was her) with the fawn and mom, so I am hopeful that she has survived her isolation and been allowed to rejoin. Perhaps the others will come out of hiding soon as well.

The raven juveniles are as big as their parents and it's nearly impossible to tell them apart except during feeding, when there is a clear level of parental oversight and much directive vocalization: chew your food, get off the table, don't be such a pig (or whatever pejorative ravens use). I saw the runt beg from Tinker again and this time she refused. Either she was busy eating for herself, or hadn't eaten enough to reproduce (as in vomit) anything, who can tell?

Very excited about the Tour de France, yes. And think it's terrible that Cavendish isn't on the roster. Mercs' Belgian record have anything to do with it? Probably.

Love,
Jane


*30 June 2022 Sunny and 65 near the Bay, 59 and foggy here. Bay Area Summer.*

Dear Jane,
The chestnut chickadees returned to the bird tree this afternoon. Someone allows as how he may have forgotten to fuel the feeders regularly in my absence. So, it's not a premature late-summer flee to cooler and higher climes, just feeder operator error. Since they nest in tree cavities, with nests that measure just seven and a half centimeters, and they use mosses and animal fur in nest construction, I'll prowl the grounds after it stops winding to see whether I can find any of these cylindrical works of avian art.

If I don't grab a scrap of paper and write down the glimmers of observation, I mean to relay to you, forget it. Do you keep a small notebook at hand?

Here's something keen. My college friend, Nani, she who "fostered" the Ukrainians, was called back to the US by her younger brother for the heartbreaking task of seeing off their brother, who passed away peacefully in his sleep. She called from Rehoboth Beach, where their family spent summers when the kids were growing up. The plan was to scatter Douglass's ashes into the sea at sunrise, where he would join their mother and an older brother. Bagpipes, the wail of which Douglass loved and the celebrants would love to have procured, were discussed, but where do you find a bagpiper on twelve-hours' notice?

The family gathered at the shore and set out their chairs to watch the sun launch another day. An older man made his way down the shore with a duffel and a chair. He stopped near their group. He opened his bag and pulled out, yes, bagpipes. Nani's husband asked "did you arrange this?!" She had not. No one had arranged this. Nani and the older man exchanged greetings. She told him the nature of their business, explained they had talked about honoring Douglass with "Amazing Grace" at sunrise. "Do you know how to play 'Amazing Grace'?" she asked. Of course he did.

But that's not the whole story. The older man's name is Robert, which is the name of Nani's late dad and older brother. The man's wife, who showed up later, is Nancy, my friend's given name. Their daughter is Martha Ann, Nani's mother's name.

The Universe is badass.

*Birds of the World* must have intel on ravens. The chickadee babies only stay with their parents (who are monogamous, but occasionally divorce, which is an ornithological as well as legal term) for three weeks or so after they hatch, but remain in the vicinity of their nest. The raven kids must have more complex behaviors to learn. Keep your eyes peeled.

Love,
Medea

*July 1, 2022 8 days till my 74th birthday. Sun. breeze. Fog.*

Dear Medea,

Wow! What a story! The universe is indeed badass. And this time, in a wondrous way. Nothing so spectacular has happened here, maybe ever, since seeing a ghost or two doesn't compare to a bagpiper on a beach. But we did have a small bear encounter, small as in encounter, I didn't see the bear so no idea of the size, but she wanted to check my recycling, probably interested in counting up the empty wine bottles, and seriously bent two sides of the plastic lid until she finally got the lid off and tipped over the can. Finding nothing more palatable than empty dog food cans, she wandered off across the road to where the neighbors had put out their garbage for weekly pick up. I expect the bear has Wednesday nights marked on her calendar. She made a right mess of things with garbage all over the main road. That she is around, and hungry, bears remembering. (Sorry, couldn't resist).

The raven family is intact. I was able to get a firm head count finally. Their routine seems to have settled into three visits a day starting with breakfast at 8. An insistent clamor around my bedroom window–thumping onto the roof, sitting beneath the second story window, impatient, and maybe worried. Gene asked how my ravens were, and I said, first of all I'm their human, they aren't my ravens, and that would be obvious to a keen observer since this is all about their schedule not mine. Last night's dinner time ruckus included more sex on the roof peak. If you are looking stuff up maybe you can figure out if they are playing, learning, or actually copulating. And if any of the above is true, what age do they have to be to fertilize eggs and get the, ahem, ball rolling? It's far too soon for nesting. Speaking of nests, I have seen them all roosting in the very very tall tree to the south of my kitchen window. I do know that once they fledge the group takes to roosting instead of using the nest which probably needs serious refurbishing before it gets used again next year. And so the cycle goes. There are mysteries that remain: for example, where are Tinker's siblings from last year? There are raven families across the street, I know, well, actually there are ravens everywhere and for obvious reasons I now see (I refer you back to the rooftop sex).

It is true that, just in time, I feel the cycle pulling together, the circle closing, the loop bound in an infinite geometry– all those philosophical ideas of life and love and death, and the comforting recognition that life is not a straight line, it is a spiral of soft edges, true wonders, and bagpipers on the beach.

Love,
Jane


*2 July 2022 55–62 degrees today. Drizzly misting. Twenty-six knots of wind. O the horror. Seven days until your 74th, for which I'm grateful.*

Dear Jane,
Tomorrow, I shall set myself the task of learning when ravens mature enough to mate. Since my subscription to *Birds of the World* is fully paid for the next year, feel free to ask me anything at all about any bird. As for "my" birds, which Max reminds me are not mine because I can't tell them apart and I know that anyway, they feast on a sort of schedule. First nip comes shortly after I have my coffee, then midday, often coinciding with my replenishing the feeders, then a gorging in the late afternoon. The tinies today numbered at least twenty, nearly evenly-split between juncos, nuthatches and chickadees. The titmouse flitted in and out of the party, like an indecisive barfly. When the jay crashes the scene, most the tinies flee, but not the nuthatches, who must believe that they are eagles.

The most interesting animal to visit my garbage cans is a raccoon. You're so lucky. Who could blame a bear for investigating something that smells of Tweed food?

At your suggestion, I'm reading Jon's book, as well as another by Madeline Ostrander called *At Home on an Unruly Planet* about navigating the climate crisis. Reading the two in tandem, I'm again struck by the commitment to fixing the mess we've made while also asking myself, again, why we made the mess in the first place given the warnings that issued over six decades ago. One of the concepts mentioned in Ostrander's book is called "Solastalgia," the pain/grief of being estranged from home, and the intangible cost of climate change/development. This strikes me as exactly the word I've been looking for to describe how sick at heart I feel when I see things like new condos on top of wetlands or the death of the Lazarus tree, or entire towns and their kangaroos and wallabies wiped out by wildfire. And the paralyzing claustrophobia I feel for all of the women who will be forced to give birth against their will in the post-Dobbs world. And the infiltration of fear-driven fascists into our government and personal lives. It's a universal tool, this word.

Love,
Medea

*July 3, 2022 fog clearing to sun for a moment and then back to fog*

Dear Medea,

As for climate, we are having a fairly typical summer so far. May it continue. And yet, for all the dripping fog and cool days, the earth is dry as a bone and no amount of mist is going to fix that. The madrone tree lost all of the rusty and blackened leaves in the last big wind, leaving a sparce amount of young green leaves behind, not nearly what would be normal. It occurs to me to wonder if the proximity to the septic tank and field has something to do with it? After 25 years? Surely not?

Max is right. We are their servants, they are not our birds, benevolent and friendly as the relationship might be. But we mother them anyway, and I think that is the way of things in the universe. The poet Linda Hogan speaks about her relationship with the creatures around her in this way, and as a right relationship to have. My ravens are learning new things, and sometimes learning them right in front of me. The four kids spend time now in the front yard, pecking and collecting and playing tag. Fighting over twigs, leaves, and bits of duff. Are they pretending nest behaviors for later when they will build their own? Also, they are eating robustly three times a day. The jays run from the feeding station when they appear, but I noticed twice now that both jays and ravens run from mourning doves, of all things. Newcomers, the dove has only come late and rarely gets much to eat, but perhaps she will bring friends next time, and arrive on time.

I've almost finished Jon Turk's book. I'm inspired by his forthright advice to the world, and a life well lived from start to … well, we'll see what he does next!

Love,
Jane

P.S. Happy 4th of July. It's raining! I love Mother Nature's sense of humor. In an abundance of caution and to keep the stupid people from setting fires or blowing off their own hands, she brings much needed rain. It is completely silent outside, not even ocean's usual hum, as if something important might be about to happen and every creature, every bit of the natural world paused to listen.

*4 July 2022 Cool, misty fog giving way to sun and 74 degrees.*

Dear Jane,
Rain on the 4th to keep the firebugs from burning down the House. Brilliant. What incantation of Mother Nature's would keep a skinny teenager from gunning down

the crowd at an Independence Day parade? Honestly, it's not her responsibility to protect us from our own lunacy. She's got bigger landscapes to protect.

We celebrated freedom by communing with our garden. Bruce tackled spent bechornaria spikes, which the hummingbirds have sucked dry, and which sprouted simultaneously and make our front yard a maze of crimson and white spears. I tended the palms, cutting withered fronds and stacking them in the driveway. Were I more industrious, I'd build a thatched hut in the back yard—since I've let the lawn go, the dun-colored square cries out for a tiki bar. I worked without gloves today; after this chilly week I needed immersive gardening to lift my mood. Two Dark-eyed Juncos kept me company while I cut back and excised an invasive green bush that insists on covering the asparagus fern by the front door. Of course, hosta, flax and cordyline all needed trims since they've gone without since last June. The soil, leaves, cocoa mulch covered my hands and feet in delicious, earthy kisses. I uncovered a carmine allamanda that I'd planted last year but was obscured by a volunteer pittosporum. I fixed some irrigation lines that I accidently sliced with my aggressive pruning. Today felt like an honest day.

With all of the gardening, I neglected raven research. Another question I have about your brood is whether or how many of the kids will remain nearby after they're ready to leave Tinker and Burt? The nuthatches have their own comedic routines but not like the ravens. I noticed one of the fledglings today pester its parent for food, and the parent bird wiped its beak on the branch and flew to the feeder as if to say, "Remember what I showed you?"

I'll finish Jon Turk's book after I finish *At Home on an Unruly Planet*, and we can compare notes.

Love,
Medea


*July 5, 2022 overcast, fog rolling in and out, window washing day*

Dear Medea,
I'm sitting in the bay window watching the raven family at the feeding station. New behavior I haven't seen before. The four juveniles were eating away and then Burt jumped up and aggressively made them all get off, whether just by squawking and darting at them, or occasionally leaping at them with intent and pushing. One poor kid got toffed in the head. It did get them off, but they were right back up, so dad is perhaps not as scary as he thinks he is. It seemed as though the only exception was made for the smallest kid, who was tolerated at the other end of the table while Tinker was eating. In seeing them all together

and this close–8 feet or so through the window– I recognize that the adults have a far larger head with a pronounced cap of feathers, exactly like a Cathar monk but without the chin ties. And black, of course. Once the parents had eaten, the kids finished off the meal and they all took turns drinking water. As always, my heart goes out to the runt, though she's nearly as big as the others now, she does always seem to be last in line. And since it's not possible to tell the sex differences, what is wrong with me that I keep calling the runt "she'? No democracy in the wild.

What I read in the past (before I decided not to use books or the internet to learn about ravens) was that raven families stay together for a year or more. I don't really see evidence of that with Tinker and her family from last year, though as I said yesterday, there are at least two sets of ravens in adjacent properties so that could be the families. Once Tinker had her own brood, she would naturally earn her own territory.

A Tiki bar! Just the very thing you should have! You could decorate it with lawn art from 50s Florida—plastic alligators, flamingos, and have a thatch covered bar top serving cocktails in colored martini glasses complete with umbrellas. Coincidentally, so that you don't think I'm kidding, my cousin Kim– the artist responsible for our beautiful cover artwork–has built a pub in their backyard as a place to showcase her husband's model train, and, of course, to drink beer on tap.

Love,
Jane

*5 July 2022 Fog? Sun? Clouds? Humid? Dry? The only definable stat is the temperature, 71 degrees.*

Dear Jane,
According to *Birds of the World*, your family of ravens, and likely Tinker's former family as well, will stick to a territory measuring just over five kilometers. This small turf differs from, say, the Arctic, where those birds might rule over a hundred-plus kilometer territory. Your birds are also taking an extra daily meal. Most ravens only eat breakfast and dinner. Lucky ravens. The juveniles may only stay with Tinker and Burt for a few more weeks; but given the limited range for the coastal CA Corvus corax, you might find them hanging around indefinitely. Who knows? All of the raven relatives might roost together at night, a multi-generational slumber party.

The other birds allow the runt to eat, a good sign for "her" survival. Have you noticed any of them buzzing Tweed to peck at his tail? Apparently, this is a documented behavior, meant to test the fight in the dog (or cat). If one or more of them succeeds in nipping Tweed's tail, they'll aim for the nose next. Watch your back, and your front, Tweed.

A new bird visited the feeding tree today. While the nuthatches splashed and sipped water from the hose, this bronzy gray bird scratched in the mulch. It had a tail that extended about four inches from its body like a Scrub Jay, but a smaller bird and not blue. Delicate white spots framed the edges of its wings. Its beak was thinnish and pointy rather than blunt and thick like a grossbeak's, but its breast was the same olive color as its back. Merlin's suggestions failed to identify the mystery bird, and I combed Sibley's with no luck. Who is this newcomer?

I asked Bruce last night about a Tiki bar. He reminded me that every project we've undertaken in the twenty-three years we have lived here bears no design relation to any other, and perhaps it's time for cohesion. That's not fun. Besides, the three outside patio lights are Tiki faces. That's enough cohesion for me. And my orange porch swing would love to live next to a Tiki bar. It's worth pursuing. Max crafts beer, Haley brews mead, I infuse tequila with habanero peppers, and since Covid continues to send us outside for gatherings with friends, it's the logical next step. Plus, the back yard flamingos would feel right at home.

I forgot to tell you that berry season exploded in the back yard over the weekend. Harvesting sweet scarlet raspberries and succulent strawberries and juicy blackberries every morning for breakfast adds another reason to swoon for Summer. Figs, pears and apples have popped out on their branches and should be ready to be baked in pies in just a few weeks. Now, if we can muster a few more hot, hot days, the many clusters of green tomatoes will rejoice and redden up.

Love,
Medea

P.S. A bit of happy news: Federal Judge Jon Tigar today overruled 45s attempted gutting of the Endangered Species Act. Remember our outrage in 2019 when the Orange Oaf tacked on an economic price factor to protecting endangered and threatened species? After this multi-week run of deflating court decisions and brutal gun treachery, it's a welcome reminder that sanity still exists.

*July 8, 2022 sun, light cool breeze. Perfect.*

Dear Medea,
I'm sitting in the bay window and once again watching the behavior of the raven family. Burt is apparently a fan of corporal punishment as he occasionally

strikes one of the kids and once pushed one over on its side on the ground and jumped on it! I hope he isn't tormenting the runt but is rather teaching "sharing" or some other behavior required for survival. All eight of them are rather twitchy at the feeder as a result of Burt's imposing size and short temper. The ravens have blood red mouths which are a bit startling when opened wide. After almost an hour watching them, I think they are sharing, but with some serious stern and aggressive behavior from dad. It is a good plan for them to know how to forage for food, and I've been happy to see them practicing their own hunting gathering activities even if it's only instinct and mimicry and not life or death. Once the table was bare and Burt clearly had a full gullet of food, the four juveniles surrounded him, mouths open like little chicks begging for food. He didn't oblige but at least this showed me that they aren't afraid of him, and it's all part of a system.

The Steller's Jays sit in the madrone, waiting to clean up, and sometimes if the ravens don't find the food fast enough, the jays get it all. Speaking of jays, your mystery bird might be a Gray Jay? Cheeky little guys. "Camp Thief" is one nickname, I think.

Tweed used to play tag with a previous pair of ravens. They did dive at him but never close and were clearly playing and not attacking, thank goodness.

Birthdays, for me, are a conscious opportunity for shift. This year does feel like a major turning point–but, from what and to what, I'm not sure. It seems to me that spending the day in contemplation would have been far more fruitful than celebrations and parties all these years. It is only now coming clear that a birthday should be without compromise and perhaps spent in solitude. Of course, we have other plans! There are some things that I always do: pull a meditation card, do a full tarot reading, and decide what resolutions I made last year were kept and should keep on, versus those that I didn't keep. It's as important to find the new as it is to let go of the old rather than feel loss or regret. That damn journal keeping resolution is a great example. My excuse this time is that we have been filling pages with these letters. I'm so grateful for that.

Love,
Jane


*8 July 2022 71 breezy degrees under a bright blue sky. A fitting birthday's eve.*

Dear Jane,
Where is Tinker when Burt brutalizes the babies? Perhaps he appears more stern than his actions reveal because of his size? The babies have to learn to forage and fend for themselves, unless they remain in your generous sphere; still, they may fly

their five.one kilometers away to roost with the other new kids, and should they lose their way, survival skills matter. The nuthatch family exhibits only some of this behavior, and since their coloring and markings appear identical to me, it may be the mom or the dad who encourages the juveniles to help themselves to the feeder. Then again, the longest time I've spent sitting and watching them is fifteen minutes or so; your dedication to observation of the raven family reaps rewards.

At the reservoir yesterday, a possible family of four hawks shrieked and wailed from the tops of the oak trees. I heard them—*kip kip kip*—long before I saw them. Usually solitary, two of them, Red-shouldered I believe, sat on the branch of one tree, and a third flew around them to land on a different tree's branch. I stood and watched them howl in unison, as though the distress of living on this summer day with too many people out rollerblading and bicycling and walking past their home intruded unbearably. The fourth bird, too high in the foliage to see, joined their lamentations. The lone hawk stared down at me with its round, dark eyes, keening. Was it anxious or alarmed?

I remained a respectful distance away from them, and they continued their communal kipping long after I walked on. Half an hour later, a tremendous din from across the reservoir that sounded like bird murder left my blood cold. Was it rival families exacting mutual revenge for nest robbing or prey theft? Great Horned Owl intrusion? Dust up with a crow? I'll never know.

Gentler than the hawks were the numerous fawns trotting behind their mamas, a pair curled up together with only their snouts and giant ears visible among the flaxen grasses, another who seemed very interested in a human baby that its mom held aloft so the littles could admire one another. Thoughts of the coyotes and bobcats and mountain lions that would soon begin their hunt had no right to intrude, so I banished those thoughts to the bottom of the reservoir.

The mystery bird might be a Hermit Thrush or a Pipit; the Gray Jay's range doesn't extend this far south. I'll keep watching.

Having your way on your birthday matters. If you rise early enough to rest in solitude for a few hours and then cavort with your visiting friends, toss in a tarot reading, have some wine and a stroll with Tweed, your birthday will play well. Do you write down the goals or resolutions you set for the coming year? Together and after many false starts, we set our intention to write to each other about the unraveling wisdom we find in sitting with, listening to, hearing and heeding the ants and the birds, the trees and the bobcats, the winds and the stars. We've talked to ravens and chickadees (wouldn't Uncle Jim be proud!) We've reveled in grand moments and mourned senseless losses. As I celebrate with you from afar tomorrow, I thank you for taking this leap with me.

Happy Birthday, Jane.

Love,
Medea


*July 11, 2022 sun, mild.*

Dear Medea,
Thank you for the birthday wishes.

Rather appropriately, the raven ruckus continued over the weekend, though I had less time to observe, they made such a racket that we certainly had them in mind most of the days. Some sort of teenage power plays? Bad dad? Or the rightful progress of learning one's place in the world. Damned if I know. I'm not even sure I know my own place in this world after 74 years of trying to fit somehow, somewhere. I described my "happy place" to our friends on my birthday, with longing but also sadness at knowing I will never know that place again: the quiet lake, the water soft and lapping, the boat kissing the weathered wood of the dock as it waits. But I'm lucky to hold those sensations in my heart, having grown up with them as the beginning of my settlement with the natural world.

A fox displayed his opinion of the raven food table by shitting all over it last night. It was time to hose it off and clean up the bird bath anyway, so that was my first morning task. Once I set out food, the ravens immediately flocked to it, leaving almost nothing for the blue jays for once. And they seemed to cooperate as well.

Your bird might be a Hermit Thrush. That would explain the rusty feathers. A bigger bird than the Gray Jay. We have a lot of those here. I love the song of the thrush, which has mostly stopped, but perhaps you've heard them and can identify that way?

Tweed continues to be stable so far as I can tell. My friend Ken Green–whose beautiful photograph is the cover of my last poetry book– had to let his lovely dog go today. The sadness, even when the dog has had a long and full life, the sadness is unbearable. It stops me in the progress of my day and will take time to place those memories back, tucked in the heart here and there. In the end, we are the accumulation of these jabs of memory, and hopefully not too many bald regrets. That's not a cheery birthday declaration, but I think I'm past the onward and upward sentiments of cheery birthdays. There will always be joy and laughter, of course, but anyone at an age who thinks life is just a bowl of cherries has surely not been living.

Love,
Jane


*11 July 2022 80, blue skies, breeze, just right for digging in the dirt.*

Dear Jane,
How do we continue to adopt and adore our four-legged friends knowing we'll surely outlive them? I feel for Ken, and for you, and for the heartache that overwhelms you both. Sometimes, we're right to wallow in our sorrow, to conjure the sensation of soft fur against our cheek, the clumsy puppy body tripping over the stairs, the thump of the tail against the porch boards, all too real and as ephemeral as the clouds. Save the stiff upper lip for another day.

Best intentions to sail to the Delta on Saturday fell prey to rusty sparkplugs. The story of poor Windsong's life. We've ordered another tune up kit. It was a cold, gray morning anyway. Bruce's fury at the state of the engine quickly gave way to relief when it became clear he'd avoid spending the day slogging up the river for twelve hours in light wind and an iffy engine. Windsong deserves owners who appreciate her mahogany interior and analog accoutrements, who don't mind bending in half to fold into bunks built for children and short, skinny people. I suppose it's time to consider letting her move on and bring joy to another family.

The day's plans now upside down, I spent your birthday on the back patio, reading.

Jon Turk talks about our ancestors taking time from hunting and gathering to draw pictures of buffalo with ochre on dim cave walls. He argues that rather than frittering time away, this brought beauty and wonder to the daily grind, and spurred imagination and higher thinking. I've written that I'd spend any day basking in the green and spice of a field of jasmine and find that as if not more enriching than wandering the halls of the Louvre. But that's not entirely accurate. Walking the beach and finding a shell that once housed a hermit crab while a trickle of perspiration rolls down my back connects all of the interbeing dots. During those nature baths, when I can no longer feel my own skin but instead the mingling of my molecules with those of the surf, the sand, the space around me, it is in this silent communion that I become a daughter of the Big Bang. It's visceral, primal, a sense of melding with the creator and all of her handiwork. Standing, staring in wonder at the Venus de Milo or the Mona Lisa, excites neural pathways that generate questions, stories. I wonder about the original block of marble, the first chisel tap. Was Alexandros tempted to kiss her lips after he finished carving them? (The first time I saw David, my knees buckled, and my heart fluttered. I'm sure I blushed.) What went through Lisa or Isabella's mind as Leonardo sketched her inscrutable smile? Why is Mona Lisa the most widely-recognized, highly-valued painting on earth? Would Leonardo admire or revile Elon Musk?

Also today, I sang a requiem for our ornamental plum, which we found toppled over in front of our bedroom this morning. The tree declared the advent of Spring each year that we've lived here, its dark pink blossoms sending the sweet scent into the house and across the garden. It had begun to develop pale green scallops of fungus and algae in the past few years, its branches producing fewer and fewer flowers. It eked out more than its projected twenty years of life, and it enriched us, as well as the birds that used it as a reconnaissance platform to identify tasty, tender new vegetables to devour before they were ready to harvest for the dinner table. A life well lived.

The possible Hermit Thrush is gone again, but if it returns, I'll check Merlin for a song ID. Your fox is kind of an ingrate. Is your place in the world with the ravens or at the lake? Can it be both? I keep thinking about Thay and his thirty-year yearning for his homeland while in exile, until he realized that if you stop fighting yourself, every place that you find yourself can be "home." Madeline Ostrander differentiates between the home you possess and the home that carries meaning. When you put it that way, possession sounds obscene.

Love,
Medea


*July 13, 2022 overcast, cool. Historically typical weather*

Dear Medea,
You wrote such a beautiful description of being at one with Nature, with the universe. Those moments of not being "other," of being in sync instead of out of sync, are perhaps what people who seek God are wanting? If only they could realize that the symbiosis you describe– molecules merging and smoothing your body into the wider body of the world–that's what we should all be after. It isn't about climbing the mountain faster than anyone else but never looking up from your own feet. It is exactly as you say–dive into the depths and let your "self" go, let "self" be devoured by the great sea of the universe. I needed that reminder. To look up from my feet in the daily grind and breathe. It isn't enough to just watch. Thank you, Medea. You inspire me. However much I have managed to put myself with the furred and the feathered of my own realm, there is more to

be felt, more to be given over, shed, merged. I will do my best. And isn't this the point of our year's work?

Love,
Jane


*13 July 2022 Mid-70s, windy today, 64 and still this evening. Also typical, if that still exists.*

Dear Jane,
After working all day, not for a paycheck but scrubbing floors and scouring toilets, a light breeze and the last amber rays of sunshine beckon me outside for a much-needed dose of quiet. We've given each other much inspiration during this year of correspondence, as have our furred and feathered families. Some lessons are arriving on my mind and heart's doorstep later in my life than I might have wished, but not too late. Never too late.

Love,
Medea


*July 14, 2022 sun. cool. Light onshore breeze. Textbook coastal day.*

Dear Medea,
OK, back to nature. Bunnies! The bunnies are back! As I watched five of the ravens pluck around the yard, in the distance so a bunny hopped. I had a moment of panic. Do I startle the ravens and make them fly away? Will they see the bunny and find him dinner menu material? Help! The human dilemma up close and personal. Watch and learn from nature, sometimes unavoidably interfere by moving their furniture (cutting trees, mowing grass, building houses), shrug and walk on? Or am I truly able to be a part of the natural world? This for me is the point of the past year. It isn't as easy as it might seem. And it is sometimes joyful and sometimes a horrifying journey. I'm not tough enough for the horrifying part; now and then even the joy is more than I can bear.

Love,
Jane

*14 juillet 2022 69 and sunny, very little breeze, which gives my world a "feels like" temp that feels like real summer. Happy Bastille Day.*

Dear Jane,

Your day was "protect the bunnies" day. Or was it "support the ravens" day? Here, it was Blue Jay Palooza. A pair of Steller's Jays with raised crests like one massive Liberty Spike, then another pair of Scrub Jays, who left a respectful distance between the two couples' visits, and who picked up kernels of corn and a stray peanut or two, swiping each side on a branch of the bird tree. Wiping off dirt? Cooties? Bits of the tinies they brought to the party? I'm with you, Jane. The bloody tooth and claw, real as it is, isn't something I wish to watch. And Gaia's irreducible, ever-changing magnificence reduces me to tears.

Love,
Medea


*July 15, 2022 sun. cool. Onshore breeze.*

Dear Medea,

Yesterday the wind blew fiercely all afternoon and bent the strongest of my sugar pea stems over past the breaking point. I felt like that scene in "Room with a View" where the mother is struggling to protect her beloved roses and failing. A metaphor for motherhood?

In exciting raven news, the juveniles found one of Tweed's orange rubber balls and were playing with it! At first, they were curious, was it food? Was it hard? It surely wasn't fun when they pecked at it. Then one of them hopped at the ball and made it move. Ah ha! Hop…ball rolling. A second raven stops the ball with his beck. Then the other pushes it again and it rolls. They did this for a few minutes, occasionally talking over what the deal was. It was so funny to watch!

This morning while walking with Tweed, I found a fitting from Gene's socket wrench lying in plain view on the driveway. Shiny and bright, I could not have missed it before, and think the ravens found it and moved it to a place it would be noticed by us. It reminded me of years ago when ravens brought our dog Fionn's lost tags and left them on the driveway for us.

And after that excitement, today the ravens are off schedule and have not appeared for "breakfast" for the first time in a year.

What next?

Love,
Jane

*15 July 2022 65 with a light breeze and cloudless sky at 7pm.*

Dear Jane,

Bent pea shoots and endangered roses. If sailing is a metaphor for life, or football, or gardening, then certainly protecting the fragile is a metaphor for motherhood. Our kids are stronger and more intuitive than we realize, but that epiphany alights long after we've exhausted ourselves trying to "save" them.

Raven Soccer! Elk United. I'm thinking black feathered uniforms. Is Tweed the referee? Or Tinker? Gene? I love this visual, Jane. Odin, though not a bird, loves it when I shell peas. He demands his own pea-ball to bat across the counter (yes, he's allowed on the counter) and it appears the he is left-pawed. I'll bat the pea to him. He'll bat it back. Should the pea hit the floor, the fun begins. Is there a Zamboni equivalent for a wood floor? He needs one; even though I'd just mopped the floor, these cats shed. Roomba. Of course. He does occasionally bite into the pea. Though he's tasted many peas, he continues to hope it will taste better this time. Kind of like dating.

Today I planted peppers and tarragon, yellow squash and Thai basil. Six of twelve seedlings of salad greens I bought yesterday, because last time I planted greens, the birds/squirrels/rats finished off the tender shoots before I woke up. The frame and screen configuration I crafted this time may work. Or it may not. I'll let you know tomorrow. I harvested six clusters of mature spring onions, five destined to share. Cleaning these clusters reminded me how far removed we are from the business of food when we stroll grocery store aisles and admire grit-free produce. Thank you to all of the people who pick bits of rock and ant parts and mud from the roots of the scallions we slice over top of the cheddar cheese on our chili.

As it stands, after many hours (seven) toiling in the garden, my fingers are gnarled, my nose has dirt at its tip, my ankles are sunburned (don't tell my dermatologist) and herbs and veggies wiggle roots into new, enriched, soil. I hope the home I've offered feels rich and nourishing. Today was a good day, Jane.

Love,
Medea


*July 16, 2022 sun.*

Dear Medea,

Eating raw peas hoping for a better flavor as a metaphor for dating! I love it. Thanks for the chuckle. We had a cat who loved to eat peas. And cantaloupe. The peas were cooked though.

As I was wondering what, if anything, I had to write about today, I looked up and outside the window were two does and their fawns! I haven't had much to say about the deer for months, they having decamped to the inner scrap of forest to hide, give birth, and nurture. There has also been a lot of activity outside around here which I'm sure disturbs their usual inclination to graze on the prolific dandelions in the yard (at least I can grow something!). Today, they are on their way across the open space of dead grass and dandelions from the safety of the woods and toward the stream which will be a trickle, but good enough for a drink. The fawns, one for each mother, were skittish but well trained, eating their way across the yard briskly, jumping now and then and keeping a pace with their mothers. Within minutes they had moved into the high tan weeds and then the shade and disappeared. I watched for a while, and saw the flicker of an ear, now and then, and knew they were resting–safe in their camouflage, tan spotted bodies with darkened fur almost identical in color to the dry earth. Isn't Mother Nature clever?

Love,
Jane


*18 July 2022 80, sunny, cloudless, a bare flutter of breeze.*

Dear Jane,
Your deer disappear into the brush as my juncos seem invisible under the bird tree. Not until they hop or scratch the ground can I see them against the cocoa mulch. Two that visited this morning showed white outer tail feathers, which they had only displayed before in flight (I'd thought these were leucistic but, no!) Mother Nature is indeed clever. But sometimes the genes goof, as when a red or brown bird instead sprouts pink or white feathers. The chance that one of the fawns in your paradise is born albino is one in 100,000. How can leucistic and albino critters blend in?

The garden continues to vex and charm, calm and pique. The Thai basil I planted to replace the chomped plant, this one double-netted with the netting staked, was also attacked and consumed. A young man who helped me with my suffering trees said that his uncle always tells him that any creature that eats his plants is part of our same ecosystem, so you can't get mad about it. Not that I'm mad, but it would be nice to grow some basil outside. If you have any thoughts on bullet-proofing basil, please do share. (I moved the sweet basil plant indoors after "someone" ate half of it. There are limits.) So far, the spinach is completely gone, but the red lettuces and arugula remain intact. Somewhere in the trees or under the hedge there is a very strong visitor flexing its Popeye muscles.

Today, the Times published an interview with "pioneering economist" Herman Daly, who won the alt-Nobel in economics (the Right Livelihood Award) and who is professor emeritus at U of Maryland's School of Public Policy. Like E.F. Schumacher, and like us, he believes that unchecked "growth at all costs" is destroying the planet and humankind. We're not becoming richer, not all of us, certainly, and not by any definition of "rich" that factors in the value of clean air and healthy parks and koalas that can get through fire season without scorched paw pads. According to the interview notes, there are several renowned economists, including two Nobel laureates, who concur with Daly's conviction that we must move toward a "steady-state economy" or find ourselves living in a world that resembles a trashed and putrid frat house the morning after the party's over. (I've born witness to a day-after frat house: rats skittering across sticky, stinky floors, toilets clogged with God knows what, sinks and counters piled high with half-eaten pizza and knocked over kegs, bongs brown with moldy water. No, thank you.)

Will he, we, get some traction, this time round? Mother Nature is clever; will melting runways in London serve to finally persuade the skeptics?

Love,
Medea

P.S. We took a hot hike this afternoon, and spotted a California Towhee, a hundred skinks and lizards, a Steller's Jay and countless Dark-eyed Juncos. The finches whistled while we walked. Summer at her finest.

*July 19, 2022 fog. Cool. Perfect sleeping temps.*

Dear Medea,
While folding table linens out of the dryer, I listened to Times Radio, London, for a taste of the conservative Brit side of things. They are consumed with finding a replacement for Boris and I despair that they will surely just find another jerk; but there was also weather news. Roads and runways melting, trains delayed, people suffering the heat. The interviewer on the train couldn't make her case though, having picked a couple of Aussie tourists to interview who were scornful of the English wimps and their heat. Half the world already suffers from these temps on a regular basis. I know this firsthand having lived at the top of the Persian Gulf where summer weather routinely hit 120°f in the shade and eggs literally could be fried on the sidewalk, or the car, and where airplanes landed and took off again in a narrow opportunity in the wee hours before dawn. Rather than playing whose heat is the highest heat, the point should be change, as in climate

change. In addition to the weather, or adjacent to it, were reports of higher than normal drownings; and it seemed necessary to the Times reporters to warn people against trying to cool off in the wild. Don't swim in mother nature's natural cooler! What is wrong with people that they don't know how to swim? I can't fathom (pun, sorry) it. And why isn't so-called "wild swimming" such a normal thing that it isn't called "wild" it's just called "swimming"? And why do we have to wait for some "influencer" to make it important or fun or delicious to follow some trend or another that should be a part of everyone's daily life? Are we already the dull, monotonous, robots of Orwell's imagination? With the repeal of Abortion rights, aren't we donning our red capes and white blinker caps and falling into line in front of the Man? How can we possible have gotten to this place without a rebellion? What is the matter? Jon Turk speaks eloquently about tribes and myth and how, from the beginning of mankind grouping together, we have created myth to expand and explain our own stories so that we have power. Power over our own world. Power over each other. Today's myths–often religious or political– are simply the latest in a long history of the stories we tell to claim power for our tribe, our family, our personal lives. Sadly, while often these identities are enriched and enlivened by the stories and linkings we make, there is an evil entitlement that grows within that same impulse. The evil that allows Russia to tell a story about Ukraine in order to justify wholesale massacre. The same evil that allowed Nazi Germany to tell a story about an entire race of people, races of peoples, in order to perpetrate genocide. This is history, but it is also present day. African tribes so full of hatred for each other that no evil is too great. Why? Is it the disparity between haves and have nots? Is it population density? And aren't both, linking here to your letter about seeking growth, aren't both of those factors to do with climate change? From deep space, aren't we the scrabbling mass willing to kill, lie, and suppress as long as we win the gold ring? If we are willing to be the evil, we are neither humane, nor able to carry empathy for any "other," be they another tribe, another race, or another creature. Growth did not bring us an elevated consciousness, did not make us luminous and generous in our wealth. Why is that?

I was going to try to be funny for once but got off on this tangent. I apologize. Maybe tomorrow will be a funny day.

Love,
Jane

*19 July 2022 68, sunny, cloudless, bare breath of breeze—and feels much like yesterday despite the temp difference.*

Dear Jane,

There's nothing funny about people dying of thirst, heat stroke, smoke inhalation, stupidity, greed. Like you, I tuned in to the British perspective on Sky News and listened to Sadiq Khan warn people in and around London to avoid swimming and barbeques. The BBQ I understand. But swimming? It appears that several young kids seeking nature's body cooler have drowned—is it because they lack swimming skills or because they passed out from the temperature differential, as Khan suggests? What about the Scandinavians? They jump from a hot sauna into a cold plunge pool. Is it a question of adaptation? My cousin who lives in England reports that today's high hit 103. In a place that rests on the same latitude line as Belle Isle, Newfoundland. In a place where a few 80-degree summer days would feel welcome and then the fog would roll in or the skies would open, or both, and the mercury settle back to its normal 69.8 degrees.

I have friends, very close friends, who may not call themselves climate change skeptics, but point out, not incorrectly, that the earth, our impermanent home, undergoes climate apocalypses regularly; this is just another one. Besides, we use so much plastic, and it takes fossil fuel to create plastic, so what are we going to do? Give up unbreakable shampoo bottles and red solo cups and car bumpers? But after this summer, it seems that more people see the world with the fairy dust knocked from their eyes. Glacial cycles that take centuries to ebb and flow are different animals than the rapid-onset warming we've created since the dawn of the Industrial Revolution, and amped up to set most corners of the planet ablaze in the past sixty years. Species adapt, yes, given a few generations. Will humans begin popping out babies with gills and/or fire-retardant skin by 2047? Doubtful.

Jon Turk's writing about myth harkens back to Marx's "opiate of the masses" remark. Or Rome deciding that women can't be priests or Yesli Vega expressing doubt that a rape victim can become pregnant as a result. The larger the lie, the louder it's yelled, the more deeply ingrained it becomes. Santa Claus, Icelandic fairies, origin stories differ, as they serve to entertain and bring communities together. They are inclusive. They are meant to comfort or add sparkle, not to pit friend against friend, neighbor against neighbor, for the sole purpose of maintaining a power structure, keeping the king/president/pope/CEO safe and wealthy in his impregnable tower.

The Seven Deadly Sins promulgated by Pope Gregory the 1st show he understood the worst traits of mankind. He wrote about these in 600AD. You'd think, with 1400 years to think about it, our species would cast off these liabilities in favor of luminosity. Instead, we are prisoners in a burning world of our own creation, stubbornly ignoring the keys that would set all creatures free.

Love,
Medea


*20 July 2022 68, sunny, cloudless, a bare flutter of breeze. Again.*

Dear Jane,
Do you know the Marc Cohen song "Walking in Memphis"? It came on Pandora when I was working in the garden today. This song touches me in a place that lays hidden except during certain vivid dreams, like the one in which someone I know in the dream but don't know in my waking life is holding me close and describes what love feels like deep in his bones. When Cohn sings the lines, "Tell me, are you a Christian, son, and I said "Ma'am, I am tonight."" I can hear the voices from a white chapel on a sun-soaked beach spilling out over the blinding white sand on Sunday morning. I hear my grandmother's church ladies telling stories over quilts they're sewing for the down-on-their-luck. My throat burns and my chest heaves and my eyes spill with tears. I feel the connection with something beyond our mortal shell, something good and beautiful and pure. Elemental. Turk describes it in his experience sticking his nose into the soil, following his dog's lead, and being swept away by the presence of life, the scent of a million organisms co-existing, most of which we fail to consciously recognize. The power of the connection between two musicians who, in the moment of offer and acceptance, raise their voice in universal praise for the unity and magnificence of the cosmos. With this knowledge, all the arbitrary, myth-made lines that separate me from you, us from them, explode into oblivion. Like shedding our ego and being fully present with the abundance of our earth, what matters is reduced to connection, to vulnerability, to love.
    Simple, right?

Love,
Medea

P.S. All of the leafy greens are safe inside the tummies of the Stephens. I caught them breaking into the net vault after they pulled up the green lawn stakes I'd so diligently pounded into the soil. I think the future of my raised beds rests with growing the far-too-spicy for squirrels habanero, jalapeno and tabasco peppers.

Dear Medea,

This is beautiful and as so often happens, your words take me in exactly the direction I needed to go—away from a prickly state of mind, frustrated, isolated, maybe even angry—music is not only the ground, but it is flight, lifting us to realms of dreams, desire, love, and yes, grief. Somehow, I need to find a way to release the wanting—it is too late for dreams in that "I could do this" kind of way. But music can envelop us, hold us while we grieve for those lost emotions, and I need that now. Merci!

As we wind this project to a close—of course we will keep watching and keep writing—but what really strikes me with both hope and sadness is that everything today is as it was last year on this day: the bunnies are hopping in their terrified scattered way into the safety of the overgrown rosemary bush, the fawns skitter across open field heading for cover in the tall grass, four ravens have learned the routine well, and I have learned to recognize their voices. So far, everyone has survived. In spite of the dread you and I feel, the very real threats all around us, threats that do not compare to life in so many places around the world such that I'm embarrassed to even call a wildfire a threat. And yet, everything is relative when you're trying to live, not just survive. I'd like to be fairy godmother to this great earth. I'd like to wave my magic wand (it would be of hawthorn and moonstone and rise from my hands with a cast of an eye) and ease the suffering of all creatures, create equity, and balance the evils done with new grace. If I invented a religion, it would require us all to stand close to water and raise our voices to declare a generosity of will never before seen. Because everything today is as it was a year ago, I should take solace in the fact that it was a gentle enough passage of time outside my windows, and perhaps it's time to find a way to make the bigger world seek grace as its motivation. It would be a mistake to simply reminisce. Jon Turk is going to find his path in the local earth of his Montana home, but that doesn't mean he will sit on his porch and think about all the adventures he's had. What it does mean is that he will envelop each day with an immediacy he has never before required of himself. Instead of planning to survive the ocean or peak or human threat, he now challenges himself to stop and whisper to the world at his doorstep.

I feel torn for myself. Part of me wants, I suppose because of my age, to tidy up the world and make it all calm the fuck down before I depart. Another part wants to put my shoes on and march for abortion rights and get "in your face" angry at everyone in my way. I feel that anger in my gut. I'm not sure any of us can truly rest at this important moment for women. It has been incredible to focus away from humans, mostly, this past year, and find the threads that bind to the wild world. It is those threads, defined and woven here, that have kept me

moving from one day to the next. What I will do with the anger, I do not yet know. We shall see, won't we?

Love,
Jane

P.S. The fog rolled back in to stay. And rightly so.


*21 July 2022 Another sunny, cloudless, almost windless day, which makes 70 feel like 80. I'm happy.*

Dear Jane,
No, we cannot rest, not for a second. In under an hour, I'll join a meeting of the Enraged and we will listen to a report from Take Back the Court. Earlier today, I wrote a letter to President Biden respectfully demanding that he declare a Climate Emergency at the urging of Bill McKibben and Third Act. Yesterday, at under the banner of the NRDC, I wrote to my legislators and the President again respectfully demanding that they avoid granting any new oil and gas leases. Did you know that current leases will allow Big Oil to extract over eleven billion barrels of oil over the next ten years? Can we just stop it, already? Thomas Edison urged a switch to renewables a century ago. His quote is one I deploy at the end of my emails, one of which wound up in the inbox of a person I respect in the financial industry. He commented upon Edison's prescience. I replied that we've known about the needs of our Mother for decades, but turning the ship is proving a Herculean task. He then, rightly, maddeningly, cited the "inertial properties of embedded economic interest" that stand squarely in the path of right actions.

Nearly one year after we began this exchange of ideas, your ravens have bloomed and grown, my tinies have proliferated and taken over. Today, three Scrub Jays *weep-ed* at me from three different trees in three different parts of the yard in a sharp chorus that drove me to my research station to discover why. Since there were no visible hawks or owls to warn about, no bunnies to munch (the little guy I saw this morning is smart enough to scuttle under the oleander after breakfast) I assume it was an announcement by one to the others to come to the feeder; with supplies low, I stocked the vertical feeder with fresh peanuts. I feed them, they feed me. Rather than a simple glance at noisy birds, engaging with you in this effort propels me to know more, not only for myself but to share with you and anyone who's interested. It's the looking outward that will save us from pulling our frazzled hair out by the roots.

Being one with the weeds, the soil, the seedlings, the Lazarus tree (rest its soul) imparts a spark of confidence in the resilience of our environment, in these geopersonae we've grown to know intimately this year. A magic spell cast from a hawthorn and moonstone wand appeals, a constructive outlet for your anger. While the economic engine of "progress" continues to churn, we will protect the homes we treasure and carry in our hearts as fiercely as we can. Let's sing songs and dance dances, shake off the false tales of frightened men that conspire to silence our voices. What a wonderful revolution this will be.

Love,
Medea


*July 22, 2022 breezy sunshine*

Dear Medea,
You go Girl! Speak for all of us. Letter writing, clearly, is our milieu, so we are required to fire off those directives as often as possible.

Today I've been thinking about what I have learned the past year. There is a lot that I think I understand, but each little bit of observation usually comes with the caveat that I can't be sure. I can't even tell Tinker from Burt unless they are standing next to each other. And speaking of that–it's extraordinary how large they are when they are on the ground as opposed to standing on the roof peak. Because I have resisted checking bird books or searching the internet for bird behavior, I have deliberately spent this year making observations here and mostly wondering aloud and to myself what is what. There are some things I know. Tinker and Burt have a loving and attentive relationship as strong as any human marriage I know. They have four children who drive them batty (apologies to the bat population) but over whom they dote, cajole, teach, and correct. As for the deer, I know the seasons of their herd cycles, when then come together and why, and how they behave within the herd. It's all so much more than I knew before, and I take pride in learning these things gradually and without the help of Google. That's what I know. What I think I know but am guessing is that ravens can count. When Tinker or Burt set up to call the family to order, it appears that they call caw, caw, a number of times equal to the number of children missing. Four times if all four young are scattered, three times if the runt is hanging on mum's tail, etc. I also know they imitate but I think I know they learned to play ball with Tweed's ball by watching us play, figuring out the game, and giving it a go. This may explain why I suddenly am down to 2 balls where only a few weeks back there were a dozen in the basket. Maybe not. I think, also, that the parent ravens and the deer mamas have been teaching the young about how to handle the dog. They haven't just got used to Tweed, they have learned how and when to be wary, and also that a little aggressive response goes a long way toward détente.

When I started watching the ravens, I knew almost nothing about them except that they are a powerful totem animal, revered by many and even known to be part of the creation story of some. Europeans fear ravens and crows as baby snatchers–whether lambs or humans–and scavengers and many farmers will pick up a rifle in response to the sight of a crow. How far we still must come before we can truly live side by side, but oh, I hope we can make progress. We have so much to overcome.

The ravens will continue to be welcome guests at my bird table, and the deer will be given all possible protection in the little forest for as long as I am here. I hope that what they have learned from Tweed and me is as interesting to them as they have been to me.

Love,
Jane


*23 July 2022 Warm and sunny, as my version of summer is meant to be.*

Dear Jane,

Despite a past history of dangerous overdoing in the garden, these past few days of heat and light have invited me to tangle with the remnant vinca that threatens to strangle the persimmon tree, and to remove some of the wandering agapanthus whose roots fan out at least six feet from the plants' bases. These last I boxed and sent home with Max, whose side yard accepts volunteers from our garden. The baby agaves that really would prefer to take over the driveway will move down the street to my friend Lisa's house. Let the circle be unbroken.

As it comes time to file final reports on the animals that have shared these pages, I feared that the Stephens had either moved, or worse. Then on Friday night, an irrigation geyser erupted and I located the new hole that one of them gnawed in the line. That repair, including encasing the horizontal part of the line in PVC and wrapping the verticals in teeth-deterring tin foil, consumed the bulk of today. We may be the only house in town wearing flashy, code-defying, disco irrigation lines. And the Stephens remain safe.

All of the tinies, a far larger population than when we began writing last July, teach me about nuance. There have been times where I've counted ten to twelve slate gray nuthatches, eight to ten capped and cloaked chickadees, two Oak Titmice and a handful of Dark-eyed Juncos at the feeders, on the tree limbs and hopping around the trunk simultaneously. I now see that the juncos are nearly twice as round as the nuthatches. The chickadees' head feathers look scruffier than those of the sleek nuthatches and juncos. When the Downy and Hairy and Nutall's Woodpeckers pop in, some wearing their bright red party hats, the tinies repair to a different feeder. The blue and gray feathers on the jays remind me of the muted light in a winter's sky; they dominate the area when they come to feed.

I read yesterday that with species diversity so severely threatened, we may soon lose the world's most flamboyant birds. To say goodbye to the peacock and parrot, birds of paradise and bower bird, unthinkable as it is, would leave us admiring the birds you and I have grown to know, appreciate and cherish this year. I don't wish for a future without resplendent birds, but I won't fear it either. We know better than to underestimate our Mother.

Love,
Medea


*July 24, 2022 overcast and cool.*

Dear Medea,
In my head I have started, deleted, erased, and started again to write this final post. Thank you for making this year a fascinating experiment in the nature of nature, but also in the nature of making friends, for reminding me that the sun is more than my enemy, that he brings all of us out of our shells and onto the broad and expansive beach that is this life. I may dwell more happily in a moonlit glow, but the sun, your sun, makes connections grow. Each of our worlds doesn't stop to mark this day. In fact, the four raven kids lined up on the garage rooftop look more like fat fluffy black chickens than sleek ravens. Puberty sucks. They seem embarrassed about their deshabille, poor things, feathers sticking out this way and that. Overnight they went from growing ravens to scruffy teens clearly distinguishable from their parents. Tinker and Burt seem satisfied, and I sense they are ready to let them go. The ground is scattered with short baby feathers and a few beautiful long ones as well. I put them on my altar for safe keeping to a future day when they will no longer come, or I will be gone.

I was searching for a next move, a way to transition from the focus that has been this project. My friend, Kristi, gave me a copy of a new biography of the poet Keats. Even a couple of pages in, I am lost in his world, and feeling the spark of poetry returning to my mind. And so, I'd like to leave with this poem. I wrote it before our project started, but it has guided me throughout, the feeling of need and connection I felt early that morning when seven ravens insisted I wake and give them my full attention.

As for you, Medea my friend, talk tomorrow?

Love,
Jane

### Seven Ravens Omen
Seven ravens in flight
a blue sky still sight
omen of abandonment.
I want them to wait
to try again:

Listen, I call.
I'll give you the trinkets,
the ones that make life worthwhile,
like the stars you pull from the sky
glittering coins of affection.

Don't leave–
I could try harder,
wake at dawn and watch,
seek out the briefest flash,
the black slickness of your cloak.

I'll bring an offering
bury it lightly–
just enough to show it's from me.
For you. Wait
please wait.

Wait while I sew a coat of black
feathers. I could join your journey,
give over the frustration
the tightening four walls bring.
I could learn.

I could bring all my gold and silver gloss:
we could make new magic together.
I would learn to listen.
Wait, oh wait, darkness comes soon,
soon we will be invisible in our weeping.

*24 July 2022 Cooler today, and the sun shines on.*

Dear Jane,

One year ago tomorrow, we embarked on this exchange. Will you please let me know via other means how Tinker, Burt, Tweed, the raven teens, the deer and the foxes fare? They've become actors on my own stage, known through your words.

What have I learned? Many of the things that you mention. Patience. Perseverance. Tolerance. Sharing my world with voracious squirrels and aerating ants and neighbors whose choices rankle. I've learned that fury and outrage are cousins of greed and hypocrisy. That winter's chill offers a chance for the natural world, and you, my friend, to pause, to rest, to luxuriate in the gloaming. That a cloud is more than water vapor and a palm tree can teach more about determination and optimism than a book full of platitudes.

Perhaps the most profound lesson is the nature of friendship. We are two writers who share a passion for birds and critters and nesting. Our husbands, both Scorpios, and our kids, all male. We're tough and fragile and tender and sometimes prickly. Our rhythms are sometimes out of sync. And yet.

I'm thrilled that you have Keats to share your coming days, to inspire you to write the poetry that feeds you. I'll be reading Ed Yong's *An Immense World* and *How to Know the Birds* by Ted Floyd. Oh, and don't forget our revolution.

Thank you for sharing "Seven Ravens Omen." Tinker and Burt live on. And thank you for sharing your wisdom, wit, insight and friendship this year. I'll never be the same.

One question remains, though, Jane: Will we, one day, toast to all we've come to know with the ocean's roar our soundtrack and the coastal fog our mantle, finally meeting face to face?

Let's talk tomorrow.

Love,
Medea

412

# Afterword

As 2022 ends, so does the work of building this book, but the furred and feathered friends we have made over the past year haven't a clue, and actually, Medea and I have continued to chronicle their comings and goings, back and forth almost daily. It seems we can't stop wondering what they are up to, and so perhaps you too, wonder how it's going. From the north coast, my backyard, many things are the same. Tweed is well. Tinker and Burt are thriving. I have a better sense of the calendar of their lives, and every day am warmed and heartened by their attention. If Tweed and I step outside, one or both of the ravens will show up almost immediately to follow me. On a sad note, the little fawn who struggled and was always smaller and less integrated into the herd, was taken by the mountain lion. It's possible we lost another juvenile the same way, or that deer is a male and has moved on. There are three females left together, two are definitely pregnant, their coats dark, their bellies growing. The third is the sibling of the one eaten by the mountain lion and may or may not be pregnant, I can't tell. Another female is on her own, sadly isolated from the small herd for a reason I cannot guess, she walks their path an outlier.

I have learned so much about the world around me these past two years. In some happy accident of email chat with Medea, we found this fascinating way to pace ourselves through the pandemic. I think I would like to close by saying, I hope you will look out into your own world with your whole being and allow the threads that surely connect us all to teach you, as they have taught us, about who we are and what we do. Turn to the primary sources, the animals and plants themselves. Resist the reference books even though we did resort to them now and then, forget Google, just absorb what comes your way and try to figure it out.

As you've seen from our letters, we had a lot to learn, and what a joy it was—the gift of a shift in focus—perhaps that's what I'd like most to give to you.

—Jane Galer, December 2022

Since we've closed the book, Jane and I have found ourselves aching to know what is happening—with the ravens, with the scrub jays, with the deer, our respective pets, the weather and each other. Thankfully, we still correspond via email. Since the end of July, the world remains chaotic, intolerably cruel, achingly beautiful. The Stephens' crazy squirrel antics still send me into fits of laughter. Three families of different varmints moved in to our crawlspace and attic: rats, field mice and skunks. While remediation is underway, I'm down to a single feeder, inaccessible to all but the birds. Odin's still jealous, Loki still wails like a newborn. Writing through the seasons, including flood and fire, we've come to a more intimate relationship with our surroundings. We've developed a keener appreciation for what it means to steward our small corners of California. We've lifted each other during times when the writing was slow to come, whether due to physical or emotional constraints. I won't speak for Jane, but I've written through to certain revelations about my own relationship with nature that only danced on the periphery of my consciousness before we wrote this book. I hope that the richness we discovered in the simple act of observing will inspire you to stop, to look, to listen. While Jane and I continue to keep each other up to date through our words, we still look forward to that eventual day when we will walk together among the Mendocino redwoods.

—Medea Isphording Bern, December 2022

# Appendix

# Bird List

Mourning Dove
Eurasian Collared Dove
Turkey
Common Redpoll
Raven (natch)
Chestnut-backed Chickadee
Nuthatch
Hairy Woodpecker
Downy Woodpecker
Nuttall's Woodpecker
Ivory Woodpecker
Pileated Woodpecker
Northern Flicker
Cattle Egret
Snowy Egret
Great Blue Heron
Boat-billed Heron
Night Heron/Black-crowned Night
  Heron
Green Heron
Flamingo
Cormorant
Seagull/Laughing Gull
Ruddy Turnstone
Pipit
Swan
Swift
Swallow
Goose/Canada Goose
Loon/Arctic Loon
Grosbeak
Crow
Wren-tit
Bushtit
Titmouse
Gnatcatcher
Hermit Thrush
House Finch
Western Kingbird
Western Bluebird
Red Robin
Quail/Bobwhite
Hummingbird/Anna's Hummingbird
Carolina Parakeet

Junco/Dark-eyed Junco
Blue Jay
Lilac-breasted Roller
Turkey Vulture
Black-capped Chickadee
Bewick's Wren
Brown-headed Cowbird
Oak Titmouse
Wilson's Warbler
Pacific Wren
Red-tailed Hawk
Red-shouldered Hawk
Sharp-shinned Hawk
Cooper's Hawk
Ruby-crowned Kinglet
Cedar Waxwing
Mockingbird
Brown Pelican
Pygmy Nuthatch
Owl/Burrowing Owl/Great Horned
  Owl
Pine Siskin
Red-winged Blackbird
House Sparrow
Osprey
Snowy Plover
Starling
Skimmer
Townsend's Warbler
California Towhee/Spotted Towhee
Sandhill Crane
Golden-crowned Sparrow
White-throated Sparrow
White-crowned Sparrow
Gray Jay
Scrub Jay CA and FL
Western Jay
Western Bluebird
Boat-tailed Grackle
Painted Bunting
Snipe
Glossy Ibis
White Ibis

# Reading List

**2021**
*Ravens in Winter*, Bernd Heinrich
*The Wind in the Willows*,
  Kenneth Grahame
*The Blue Mind*, J. Wallace Nichols, PhD
*On Walden Pond* (referenced p. 30)
  Henry David Thoreau
*The Sound of the Sea*, Cynthia Barnett
*The Radiant Lives of Animals*,
  Linda Hogan
*The Hidden Life of Trees*,
  Peter Wohllenben
*Horizon*, Barry Lopez
*How Much is Enough?* Alan Durning
*A Land Remembered*, Patrick D. Smith
*Native*, Patrick Laurie
*Waterlog*, Roger Deakin
*Fuzz: When Nature Breaks the Law*,
  Mary Roach
*Diary of a Young Naturalist*,
  Dara McAnulty
*The Summer Book*, Tove Jansson
*Bewilderment*, Richard Powers
*The Handmaid's Tale*, Margaret Atwood
*This is Happiness*, Niall Williams
*Book of Greek Myths*, D'Aulaire
*The Flame*, Leonard Cohen
*A Literate Passion* (Nin and Miller)

*Names of New York*,
  Joshua Jelly-Shapiro
*Golden Hill: A Novel of Old New York*,
  Francis Spufford
*Orwell's Roses*, Rebecca Solnit
*Animal Speak*, Ted Andrews
*Beaks, Bones & Birdsongs*,
  Roger J. Lederer
*News of the World*, Paulette Jiles

**2022**
*50 Plantes du Druide: Guide Pratique*,
  Pascal Lamour, docteur en pharmacie
*Zen and the Art of Saving the Planet*,
  Thich Nhat Hanh
*Land*, Simon Winchester
*How to Know the Birds*, Ted Floyd
*Braiding Sweetgrass*,
  Robin Wall Kimmerer
*Once a Wolf*, Brian Sykes
*At Home on an Unruly Planet*,
  Madeline Ostrander
*Tracking Lions, Myth and Wilderness in
  Samburu*, Jon Turk
*An Immense World*, Ed Yong
*Keats: A Brief Life in Nine Poems and
  One Epitaph*, Lucasta Miller

# Acknowledgments

I've been a writer all my life, but taking control of the process in a way that brought my words to paper and to a wider audience than just my adorable family required a team, a few fantastic people who brought their skills, enthusiasm, and most of all their love for me into one effort: giving me my dream. Diane Reynolds, my cousin and partner in this endeavor of publishing learned the skills of the work right alongside me and well beyond. I literally could not do this without her. My amazing cousins: Kim Englishbee for her quiet support and brilliant artwork once again gave to this project without any compensation at all, and Kathie Britton, who pushes me to work hard because that's just how life is. All three of you are the best sisters of life. To my closest friend here on the north coast, Kristi Matson Hahn, I can't begin to express my gratitude for your grace in my life. And, the other constant conversation every single day is with Barbara Saylor Rodgers, lifelong friend and the keeper of this lifetime's words. And, of course, Medea, an accidental wonderful friendship literally built in the classroom for writers. Thank you to all of you incredible women.

Finally, thank you to my husband of fifty-plus years for always supporting my work; to Chris, Michri, and Quinn for being true family; and to Tweed, patient, loyal and loved beyond words.

—Jane Galer

I would like to thank the many people who offered words of encouragement during the creation of this book. Specifically, I'd like to recognize:

Anne Zimmerman, who recognizes the diamond in the lump of coal. Diane Reynolds, whose patience and organization has enabled this book to see daylight. Jane, my writing partner and serendipitous friend, for volleying words and ideas with me through winter, spring, summer and fall.

My family: Mom, Dad and my sister, Kirsten, who remain eternally encouraging; Max and Dylan, my two most provocative teachers; Bruce, my interminable and loving husband; and Odin and Loki, my fine furred friends. I love and appreciate you more than words.

This book draws inspiration from the legions of brave and visionary environmental writers, musicians, philosophers and ordinary folks who have and continue to lay bare uncomfortable truths, and then encourage us to do better. The flora and fauna, landscapes and seascapes that share this speck of universe enrich every second of my life, and remind me to walk humbly, with reverence.

—Medea Isphording Bern

**Jane Galer** Jane Galer's background is in history, archaeology, and philosophy with a BA in philosophy, and an MA in museum studies and material culture. She is an award-winning poet and author of four books of poetry including collected works *Outskirts,* and the annotated poems *Forward & In the Dark.* She has written two non-fiction works about shamanism based on her study with the Q'ero shaman of Peru. She also authored the historical novel *The Navigator's Wife* based on the true story of a NW coast shipwreck. As a hereditary witch, it is of primary importance that all of her work be infused with the animist pagan beliefs of her Celtic ancestors. Jane lives with her husband, Gene, and dog, Tweed, on the northwest coast of California.

**Medea Isphording Bern** grew up on the beach and under the sea in Florida, collecting shells and fossilized shark teeth and exploring tide pools and coral reefs. She studied at colleges in Virginia and France, and graduated from law school at the University of Florida. Her work has appeared in print and online, and she has published two books of non-fiction. She lives in Northern California with her husband and two cats, and close to her cherished sons. She returns frequently to Florida (or any warm beach) for a tune-up.

Illustrator **Kim Englishbee** resides in Texas where she continues her love affair with creative arts and her husband Ron.

# *What the Raven Said...*

**Heart Dance**
Meet me
cloaked as Raven
and I'll teach you to dance.

Meet me
on a mountain top
never mind your broken heart.

www.ingramcontent.com/pod-product-compliance
Lightning Source LLC
Chambersburg PA
CBHW020530030426
42337CB00013B/793